VOLUME 610

MARCH 2007

D1055936

THE ANNALS

of The American Academy of Political
and Social Science

PHYLLIS KANISS, *Executive Editor*

Z50601

109052

NAFTA and Beyond:
Alternative Perspectives in the Study of Global Trade and Development

Special Editors of this Volume
PATRICIA FERNÁNDEZ-KELLY
Princeton University
JON SHEFNER
University of Tennessee

SAGE Publications
Los Angeles • London • New Delhi • Singapore

Origin and Purpose. The Academy was organized December 14, 1889, to promote the progress of political and social science, especially through publications and meetings. The Academy does not take sides in controverted questions, but seeks to gather and present reliable information to assist the public in forming an intelligent and accurate judgment.

Meetings. The Academy occasionally holds a meeting in the spring extending over two days.

Publications. THE ANNALS of The American Academy of Political and Social Science is the bimonthly publication of the Academy. Each issue contains articles on some prominent social or political problem, written at the invitation of the editors. Also, monographs are published from time to time, numbers of which are distributed to pertinent professional organizations. These volumes constitute important reference works on the topics with which they deal, and they are extensively cited by authorities throughout the United States and abroad. The papers presented at the meetings of the Academy are included in THE ANNALS.

Membership. Each member of the Academy receives THE ANNALS and may attend the meetings of the Academy. Membership is open only to individuals. Annual dues: $84.00 for the regular paperbound edition (clothbound, $121.00). Members may also purchase single issues of THE ANNALS for $17.00 each (clothbound, $26.00). Student memberships are available for $53.00.

Subscriptions. THE ANNALS of The American Academy of Political and Social Science (ISSN 0002-7162) (J295) is published six times annually—in January, March, May, July, September, and November—by Sage Publications, 2455 Teller Road, Thousand Oaks, CA 91320. Telephone: (800) 818-SAGE (7243) and (805) 499-9774; Fax/Order line: (805) 499-0871; e-mail: journals@sagepub.com. Copyright © 2007 by The American Academy of Political and Social Science. Institutions may subscribe to THE ANNALS at the annual rate: $612.00 (clothbound, $692.00). Single issues of THE ANNALS may be obtained by individuals who are not members of the Academy for $34.00 each (clothbound, $47.00). Single issues of THE ANNALS have proven to be excellent supplementary texts for classroom use. Direct inquiries regarding adoptions to THE ANNALS c/o Sage Publications (address below). Periodicals postage paid at Thousand Oaks, California, and at additional mailing offices.

All correspondence concerning membership in the Academy, dues renewals, inquiries about membership status, and/or purchase of single issues of THE ANNALS should be sent to THE ANNALS c/o Sage Publications, 2455 Teller Road, Thousand Oaks, CA 91320.Telephone: (800) 818-SAGE (7243) and (805) 499-9774; Fax/Order line: (805) 499-0871; e-mail: journals@sagepub.com. *Please note that orders under $30 must be prepaid.* Sage affiliates in London and India will assist institutional subscribers abroad with regard to orders, claims, and inquiries for both subscriptions and single issues.

Printed on acid-free paper

THE ANNALS

© 2007 by The American Academy of Political and Social Science

Editorial Office: 3814 Walnut Street, Fels Institute for Government, University of Pennsylvania, Philadelphia, PA 19104-6197.
For information about membership* (individuals only) and subscriptions (institutions), address:
Sage Publications
2455 Teller Road
Thousand Oaks, CA 91320

For Sage Publications: Joseph Riser and Esmeralda Hernandez

From India and South Asia, write to:
SAGE PUBLICATIONS INDIA Pvt Ltd
B-42 Panchsheel Enclave, P.O. Box 4109
New Delhi 110 017
INDIA

From Europe, the Middle East, and Africa, write to:
SAGE PUBLICATIONS LTD
1 Oliver's Yard, 55 City Road
London EC1Y 1SP
UNITED KINGDOM

*Please note that members of the Academy receive THE ANNALS with their membership.
International Standard Serial Number ISSN 0002-7162
International Standard Book Number ISBN 978-1-4129-5754-0 (Vol. 610, 2007 paper)
International Standard Book Number ISBN 978-1-4129-5753-3 (Vol. 610, 2007 cloth)
Manufactured in the United States of America. First printing, March 2007.

The articles appearing in *The Annals* are abstracted or indexed in Academic Abstracts, Academic Search, America: History and Life, Asia Pacific Database, Book Review Index,CABAbstracts Database, Central Asia: Abstracts &Index, Communication Abstracts, Corporate ResourceNET, Criminal Justice Abstracts, Current Citations Express, Current Contents: Social & Behavioral Sciences, Documentation in Public Administration, e-JEL, EconLit, Expanded Academic Index, Guide to Social Science & Religion in Periodical Literature, Health Business FullTEXT, HealthSTAR FullTEXT, Historical Abstracts, International Bibliography of the Social Sciences, International Political Science Abstracts, ISI Basic Social Sciences Index, Journal of Economic Literature on CD, LEXIS-NEXIS, MasterFILE FullTEXT, Middle East: Abstracts&Index, North Africa: Abstracts&Index, PAIS International, Periodical Abstracts, Political Science Abstracts, Psychological Abstracts, PsycINFO, Sage Public Administration Abstracts, Scopus, Social Science Source, Social Sciences Citation Index, Social Sciences Index Full Text, Social Services Abstracts, SocialWork Abstracts, Sociological Abstracts, Southeast Asia: Abstracts& Index, Standard Periodical Directory (SPD), TOPICsearch, Wilson OmniFileV, and Wilson Social Sciences Index/Abstracts, and are available on microfilm from ProQuest, Ann Arbor, Michigan.

Information about membership rates, institutional subscriptions, and back issue prices may be found on the facing page.

Advertising. Current rates and specifications may be obtained by writing to The Annals Advertising and Promotion Manager at the Thousand Oaks office (address above).

Claims. Claims for undelivered copies must be made no later than six months following month of publication. The publisher will supply missing copies when losses have been sustained in transit and when the reserve stock will permit.

Change of Address. Six weeks' advance notice must be given when notifying of change of address to ensure proper identification. Please specify name of journal. POSTMASTER: Send address changes to The Annals of The American Academy of Political and Social Science, c/o Sage Publications, 2455 Teller Road, Thousand Oaks, CA 91320.

THE ANNALS

OF THE AMERICAN ACADEMY OF
POLITICAL AND SOCIAL SCIENCE

Volume 610   March 2007

IN THIS ISSUE:

NAFTA and Beyond: Alternative Perspectives in the Study of Global Trade and Development

Special Editors: PATRICIA FERNÁNDEZ-KELLY
JON SHEFNER

Section Three:
Regionalization and the Foray on Primary Goods

Section Four:
Quick Read Synopsis

FORTHCOMING

The Politics of Consumption/The Consumption of Politics
Special Editors: DHAVAN V. SHAH, LEWIS FRIEDLAND,
DOUGLAS MCLEOD, and MICHELLE NELSON
Volume 611, May 2007

Religious Pluralism and Civil Society
Special Editor: WADE CLARK ROOF
Volume 612, July 2007

Social Entrepreneurship for Women and Minorities
Special Editors: JIM JOHNSON, TIM BATES, and WILLIAM JACKSON
Volume 613, September 2007

INTRODUCTION

NAFTA and Beyond: Alternative Perspectives in the Study of Global Trade and Development

By
PATRICIA
FERNÁNDEZ-KELLY

For more than three decades, rapid advances in technology, transportation, and communications have facilitated economic integration on a world scale. The North American Free Trade Agreement (NAFTA) is part of that globalizing process—one of the latest accords whose goal is to codify new arrangements of production backed by a legitimizing narrative: neoliberalism. Since its implementation in 1994, NAFTA has increased the capacity of investors to move across international borders, further fusing points in the hemisphere economically but also giving way to new patterns of migration and development. In that context, the term *free trade* bears distinct and often contradictory meanings. To account for the plurality of interpretations behind free trade and to explain the political and economic dimensions of the neoliberal project is one of the purposes of this volume. Another goal is to investigate the international context in which NAFTA emerged, that is, to reach beyond the temporal and geographic delimitations of the treaty to pinpoint the broader implications of global trade and economic change.

The articles included here were first presented at a conference held at Princeton University on December 2-3, 2005, which brought together an interdisciplinary group of distinguished scholars—economists, sociologists, political scientists, and anthropologists. Their contributions weave a comprehensive perspective interrogating the stated assumptions of conventional views

Patricia Fernández-Kelly holds a joint position in the department of sociology and Office of Population Research at Princeton University. She has written extensively on globalization, industrial recomposition, international migration, and gender. With Lorraine Gray, she coproduced the Emmy Award–winning documentary, "The Global Assembly Line." Her latest book, edited with Jon Shefner, Out of the Shadows: Political Action and Informal Economy in Latin America, *was published by Pennsylvania State University Press in 2006.*

DOI: 10.1177/0002716206297972

on the world economy, free trade, and neoliberalism. Is there such a thing as globalization? What are the social, political, and environmental repercussions of neoliberal economic policies in Latin America and elsewhere? Is the world's new economic landscape ushering in supranational institutions? What about the character of social movements, both those emerging in opposition or in compliance to globalization? These are among the questions that the articles in this volume broach.

Included in this collection are wide theoretical accounts as well as focused analyses of specific countries and regions in Asia, Latin America, and Europe. The volume is divided into three parts. The first delves into the main political and economic dimensions of free trade. The second examines neoliberalism in terms of social class, both at the national and international levels. The third section discusses the unintended effects of free trade on the extraction of primary resources and the environment. In this Introduction, I briefly sketch the evolution of liberalism to then discuss the main contributions of the articles that follow.

Liberalism Then and Now

Debates about free trade anteceded the advent of capitalism, but it was in the nineteenth century, while rapid industrialization was transforming Europe, that they took a methodical and sustained form. The outcome was neoclassical economics, a science that has undergone little change for more than a century and whose origins in the 1870s may be traced to the work of William Stanley Jevons, Carl Menger, and Leon Walras. The main objective of those authors was to account for the fundamental—and therefore universal—parameters of behaviors aimed at the production, distribution, and consumption of vital resources and, therefore, to explain markets as self-regulating mechanisms tending toward equilibrium in the interaction between supply and demand (Jevons 1866; Menger 1871/1976; Walras 1874/1984). Adam Smith, the author best known for his treatment on the subject saw the market as an *invisible hand* shaping the fate of individuals and collectivities (Smith 1776/2003). *Homo economicus*, the term coined by John Von Neumann in 1928 as part of his minimax theorem, condenses the assumptions behind the neoclassical approach: individuals compete on the basis of cost-benefit calculations to increase advantage or marginal utility. Sellers are disciplined by the capacity of buyers to withdraw support. Unimpeded choice best allow markets to function as engines in the creation and distribution of wealth (MacRae 2000). Those operations extend beyond the confines of commercial transactions to encompass every act entailing selection among various options.

In other words, from its inception, the neoclassical approach was more than science; it also entailed a series of moral prescriptions concerning individual autonomy and decision making. It does not surprise, therefore, that the modern notion of the market evolved in harmony with liberalism, a philosophical point of view derived from the Enlightenment whose main focus was on liberty as the highest political value (Hayek 1982). By the 1870s, a trust in free markets as hidden mechanisms promoting personal choice and responsibility had become identical to the aspiration for political autonomy. In that scheme, any actor or institution interfering with the ability of individuals to make decisions became highly suspect, and among all potential villains altering the natural function of the market, none was greater than the state.

The perceived opposition between the market and the state was sharp during the same period that witnessed the rise of industrial capitalism. The commercialization of arable land in countries such as England forced large numbers of peasants to seek new opportunities in cities like London and Manchester where factory work was rapidly expanding. Rural-urban migration contributed to the creation of new environments in which pauper children, prostitutes, unemployed workers, beggars, and petty criminals crowded streets and tenements vying for sheer survival. Dark squalor paralleled the rise of middle and affluent classes (Thompson 1966). From Charles Dickens to Karl Marx, the historical and literary accounts of the time portray philosophers and fledgling sociologists arguing over the causes and consequences of urban poverty. It is not a coincidence that Herbert Spencer's first popular book, *Social Statics or the Conditions Essential to Human Happiness Specified, and the First of Them Developed* (1851/1995), was a concerted argument against benevolent utilitarian perspectives such as those put forth by Jeremy Bentham (1789/1988) and John Stuart Mill (1859/2002). Where Bentham and his colleagues saw the state as a potential arbiter mediating between disempowered workers and burgeoning capitalists, Spencer, the forbear of libertarianism, argued against any form of state intervention to assuage the depredations of unfettered capitalist advance. He argued that markets, like nature, weed out inefficiency, whether it is manifested in commercial transactions or in the capacity of individuals to live and thrive. In his scheme poverty is mainly the expression of moral or physical failure.

In correspondence with those ideas, and as part of his voluminous tome, *Principles of Biology* (1861), Spencer coined the phrase wrongly imputed later to Charles Darwin, "the survival of the fittest," both as a moral dictum and as a characterization of the way competition in unfettered markets leads to efficiency and the purification of society. Still relevant, albeit chilling to modern sensibilities, is Spencer's contention that markets, like the natural order, may inflict suffering in the short term to produce a better good later. Like unfit and decrepit animals, the poor should not be given aid lest to create an idle and dependent population; instead, they should be allowed to fend for themselves and die, if necessary, to allow for the emergence of a stronger, more capable society (Spencer 1851/1995, 232). Bentham and Mill countered with images of social policy aimed at sheltering vulnerable populations from the excesses of the market. To this day, the controversy between libertarians and utilitarians continues. In the United States—its echoes reverberate in the political arguments between Republicans and Democrats, the antiwelfare rhetoric of Charles Murray (1985) and David Herrnstein and Murray (1994) and in populist media debates over small government and personal responsibility. Herbert Spencer still speaks through the voice of Rush Limbaugh.

Although it has never lost influence, the libertarian narrative receded into marginal status by the early twentieth century, largely as a result of the state's growing role in rationalizing the relationship between capital and labor (Galbraith 1988). To quell popular turmoil in response to the perceived abuses of the private sector, governments in Europe, the United States, and even Latin America increasingly passed protective legislation, including provisions meant to limit working hours; establish minimum wages; and prevent excesses among fragile populations, especially women and children. Throughout the same period, neoclassical economics grew in visibility and status. It was only in the wake of the Great American Depression of the 1930s that there was a systematic revision of its premises. Where it had been easy in the preceding period to imagine poverty and joblessness as the manifestation of individuals' incapacity to compete, the Great Depression brought attention to business cycles, that is, independent economic processes that have little to do with worker's moral stamina or independent will. Nearly 13 percent of American workers had lost their jobs by the beginning of the 1930s. In 1932, the unemployment rate rose to 23.6 percent of a predominantly white and male labor force (Krugman 1994; Watkins 1993). The same year, gross national product fell a record 13.4 percent. None of this could be attributed to workers' lack of character.

The prospect of popular uprisings and the propagation of socialist and communist ideologies prompted immediate government intervention. Franklin D. Roosevelt is remembered for his aggressive sponsorship of laws to create a safety net protecting workers and their families from the ravages of economic downturns. A society free from want, he concluded, required not just markets but also laws to harness them (Alter 2006). A legacy of that period was the Social Security Act of 1935, which almost by itself eradicated poverty among the elderly in the years that followed.

It was also in the wake of the Great Depression that John Maynard Keynes emerged as the proponent of a new approach to economic management in which the state was not condemned as a source of interference for individual choice but as an entrepreneurial actor mediating between the interests of capital and labor (J. M. Keynes 1933; see also M. Keynes 1975). In that view, government legislation acts to advance the interests of capitalists and investors but also protects the well-being of workers and their families. Aggregate demand is nurtured not only through the creation of wealth in accordance with traditional views but also by way of enlightened laws that increase workers' capacity to consume. To build aggregate demand was one of the main objectives in the Keynesian approach and fundamental to it was the promotion of welfare legislation. In the post–World War II era, Keynesianism buttressed the American Dream, understood as the capacity of working-class men with moderate levels of education but a strong commitment to work to attain middle-class standards of living. America's prosperity thus entailed a trilateral partnership between a flourishing industrial sector, the state, and the working class (Meyer 2003).

The ideas put forth by John Maynard Keynes transcended borders and spilled over into regions such as Latin America, where the inheritance of colonialism and economic dependence had produced severe risks of political destabilization in the post–World War II period. Import Substitution Industrialization (ISI)—the doctrine best systematized by the Argentinean economist Raul Prebisch as part of the Economic Commission for Latin America—was deeply influenced by the Keynesian approach. In that framework, sustained development entailed the promotion of investment in capital goods, the creation of autonomous industrial foundations at the national level, the expansion of aggregate demand, and the implementation of government policies aimed at reducing foreign competition (Comisión Económica para América Latina y el Caribe 1987).

In the post–World War II era, Keynesianism buttressed the American Dream, understood as the capacity of working-class men with moderate levels of education but a strong commitment to work to attain middle-class standards of living.

The protectionist character of ISI attracted resistance in various sectors, including those formed by international capitalists, domestic brokers, members of the *comprador* (brokering) classes, and consumers doubtful about the quality of domestic manufactures. Yet as many have shown, and contrary to the indictments of neoclassical economists, ISI paralleled sustained economic growth and the creation of respectable middle classes in countries like Brazil, Mexico, and Argentina (Crouch 1983; Evans 1995; Portes and Hoffman 2003). Mexico, for example, maintained growth rates above 3.5 percent starting in the 1960s even as aggregate demand rose in every subdivision of the consumer sector. Despite its flaws and excesses, ISI opened up the possibility of sustained national development in Latin America. By the 1970s, however, nationalistic economic policies began to give way to a new and sweeping trend: globalization. What the Peruvian sociologist Anibal Quijano once called *the opening to the exterior* entailed a renewed focus on export-led industrialization as the engine for economic growth (Quijano 1972).

In the 1970s, Mexico's *maquiladora* program—a governmental initiative aimed at attracting foreign investment in the production of exportable goods, mainly in electronics and garment assembly—soon became the most rapidly growing sector of that country's economy. Maquiladoras operate as directly owned subsidiaries or subcontractors of corporations, mostly based in the United States. To make their activities possible, the Mexican state passed incentives that suspended established norms regulating private property and investment (Fernández-Kelly 1983). For the first time in more than half a century, foreign investors were allowed 100 percent ownership of productive facilities. Taxes on temporarily imported raw materials, components, and machinery were waived as long as the finished or semifinished products resulting from their use were exported. In 1975, maquiladoras trailed only tourism and oil production as generators of revenue. By the 1980s, they constituted the world's most successful experiment in export-oriented industrialization. In retrospect, they may also be seen as the natural antecedent of the North American Free Trade Agreement implemented almost twenty years later—a burgeoning attempt at radical liberalization entailing the suppression of government regulation.

Mexico's maquiladora program was thus an exemplar of a new tendency toward economic integration on a world scale that accelerated during the second half of the twentieth century and still continues. The term *globalization* has been used haphazardly to designate various subprocesses, including faster communication at the international level, growing diffusion of cultural norms and values across borders, and escalating trade among nations in disparate regions. Underlying such phenomena, however, was a deeper event: the reconfiguration of production, especially in manufacturing, at the national and international levels (Fernández-Kelly 1983; Sassen 1999). The transfer of assembly operations from advanced to poorer regions—aptly illustrated by Mexico's maquiladora program—had simultaneous and complementary effects in developed nations. In the United States, for example, it caused ruinous waves of plant closings and a shift from manufacturing to services and high-tech (Cohen 2001; Sassen 1999). Between 1970 and 1985, millions of factory jobs were eliminated or moved to Asia, the U.S.-Mexico border, and the Caribbean Basin. At the other end of the world, South Korea, Hong Kong, Singapore, and Taiwan—the Asian Tigers of international renown—came to prominence as places whose success was predicated on the unimpeded effects of capital investment in export-manufacturing (Gereffi and Wyman 1990). More recently, China has become the planet's largest manufacturing emporium of consumer products. In light of the globalizing sweep, Keynesian approaches receded even as neoliberalism overtook the imagination of economists and policy makers.

No figure held more sway in the celebration of global trade than Milton Friedman, a main articulator of a perspective that has now inspired more than two decades of faith in free markets. Friedman, who received a Nobel Prize in Economics for his work on monetary policy, systematized and, more important, popularized the neoliberal vision. In his framework, markets are not just efficient mechanisms for the creation and propagation of wealth but also a precondition for the diffusion of democracy and the affirmation of political liberty. *Free to Choose*, Milton's documentary series produced with his wife, Rose, and broadcast on Public Television in the early 1980s, was an elaboration of ideas he had developed twenty years earlier in the book that first brought him to the attention of the world, *Capitalism and Freedom* (1962/2002). Memorable in the film is the image of Friedman himself extolling the virtues of markets and choice while standing in a Hong Kong sweatshop surrounded by diligent seamstresses, none of whom may have been expected to vote. That irony may have eluded the attention of the great economist but his eloquence and commonsense argument gained wide appeal.

No figure held more sway in the celebration of global trade than Milton Friedman, a main articulator of a perspective that has now inspired more than two decades of faith in free markets.

Although with less verve and energy other distinguished economists echoed Friedman's neoliberal views. Many attracted the attention of governments and went on to gain fortune and visibility as cabinet members and presidential advisors. Worthy of mention is Jeffery Sachs, the Columbia University professor, who made a reputation as an economist troubleshooter in countries as distant as Poland and Ecuador and whose prescriptions were always on the side of market liberalization (Sachs and Larrain 1993). Yet other scholars contested the basic assumptions of the neoliberal approach. Amartya Sen, also a Nobel Prize laureate, incisively asked whether globalization can be free—a question meant to draw attention to the disparities promoted by laissez faire economics. Sen raised doubts about the redistributive capacities of markets arguing for views reminiscent of Keynesianism in which national governments and supranational organizations act as arbiters to discipline the market's depredatory extremes through a focus on sustainable development, environmental protection, and workers' rights (Sen 2000). By the end of the twentieth century, elements of those views had become part of the mobilizing efforts of antiglobalization movements.

Given the arresting power of the neoliberal discourse, both as economic prescription and moral imperative, it is startling to realize its varying and often lackluster capacity to generate growth or foster employment (see Harvey in this volume). The application of neoliberal policies in Chile was a comparative success thanks largely and counterintuitively to the political excesses of the Augusto Pinochet regime. In that instance, market liberalization was coterminous with the installation of an authoritarian and antidemocratic regime, just the opposite of what Milton Friedman would have predicted. More typically, in Mexico and other parts of Latin America, neoliberalism produced labor displacement, the devastation of domestic industry, and the growth of social inequality (Portes and

Hoffman 2003). In some contexts, neoliberalism did not even result in sustained economic growth. Just the opposite occurred—countries like China and India rapidly developed on the basis of policies that deviated markedly from the neoliberal formula. By contrast, Argentina, the single South American country whose government bought whole cloth the neoliberal prescription saw its economy on the verge of collapse at the turn of the twenty-first century. The blow on workers and even the refined Buenos Aires middle class was so severe as to resuscitate barter and communal kitchens.

In other words, the facts emerging over the past two decades lead to two preliminary conclusions: (1) as a political doctrine, neoliberalism represents the continuation of more than a century of faith in individual freedom and a means of contestation to the authority of national states; and (2) as an economic prescription, neoliberalism has had uneven and unexpected effects, some of which are the subject of the articles contained in this volume.

Political and Economic Dimensions of Free Trade

The first four articles in this anthology give attention to the wider meaning of free trade. In "Neoliberalism as Creative Destruction," David Harvey offers a bird's-eye view of the process that led to the emergence of the new economic perspective. He gives attention to the rhetorical and substantive content of neoliberalism, arguing that such a trend was not primarily about the opening of markets but about the consolidation of a new class system operating at the international level. Put bluntly, neoliberalism was as much a political as an economic project that sharply realigned the balance of power between capital and labor. Among other things, it entailed the erosion of working-class achievements over the preceding century.

Harvey notes, for example, that the period coinciding with the application of neoliberal policies has not resulted in a better distribution of wealth within and across borders. Two-thirds of the world's population still lives in poverty. Even more revealing is the growth of income disparities that has increased not only in less developed countries but also in the United States. The period that witnessed the rise of the Washington Consensus as an initiative aimed at the liberalization of markets also saw the increase in economic inequality in the world's largest power. In 1970, the average earnings of corporate executives in the United States were twenty times larger than those of the typical American worker. Thirty years later, those earnings were more than a hundred times greater (Meyer 2003). It is not of little significance that the median wage in the United States has remained static since 1973; that is, more or less since the onslaught of industrial recomposition and the transfer of manufacturing operations to less developed areas.

During the same time span, and particularly since the beginning of the Reagan administration, American labor unions have endured devastating losses. In 1965, about one-third of workers in the United States were unionized. At present, that proportion hovers precariously above 10 percent. Furthermore, the growth of economic inequalities has not been restricted to the domestic level—globalization has also resulted in the concentration of resources in some geographical areas as a result of what Harvey calls "accumulation by dispossession." Disparities have grown both within and across nations. According to Harvey, none of this is coincidental. Rather, the assault against labor unions began by Ronald Reagan and continued throughout subsequent administrations, including the Clinton years, is symptomatic of a fierce competition that has led to the triumph of financial capital. In Harvey's view, free trade stands as a rhetorical device justifying the actions of particular segments of the dominant classes. To account for the class-related dimensions of neoliberalism is Harvey's main contributions.

In his elegant article, "Liberalism and the Good Society in the Iberian World," political sociologist Miguel A. Centeno takes the liberal point of view seriously by asking what are the conditions required for the emergence of socially responsible governments in the vast geographical region once dominated by the Spanish and Portuguese crowns. Original in conception, Centeno's article is one of a few attempts to understand the uneven performance of neoliberalism in countries with a common ancestry. Included in his analysis are Spain, the Philippines, and Portugal, as well as the rest of Latin America. Centeno demolishes cultural explanations of underdevelopment, noting, for example, the rapid progress of Spain resulting from enlightened policies on the part of its richer neighbors to promote economic advance in that country prior to its integration into the European Common Market. The idea of a unified Europe was informed not only by market liberalization but also by a consideration of workers' mobility and rights, two subjects about which the architects of NAFTA remained silent. The results are easy to see: Despite its flaws, the European Union enables individuals and their families in various countries to move freely across borders as long as they are able to earn a living. By contrast, in the case of NAFTA, imbalances created by market liberalization promoted labor displacement and out-migration. Centeno's analysis makes clear that for neoliberalism to succeed as an economic policy, liberal states, in the classic sense of the term, must impose political parameters. In agreement with the findings of economic sociologists, he shows that there are no markets without states.

In the third chapter of this volume, "Migration, Development, and Segmented Assimilation: A Conceptual Review of the Evidence," Alejandro Portes examines the relationship between international migration and national development, two subjects that have been given extensive attention since the 1960s but have almost never been investigated together. On the basis of firsthand research, Portes shows that the same routes opened up by market liberalization in Latin America are traversed in the opposite direction by workers, mostly from Mexico, in their search for opportunity. The increase in remittances sent home by those workers has paralleled the application of neoliberal policies. Cash transfers from immigrants in the United States to Latin American home towns has expanded so much over the past two decades as to be accepted as collateral by international financial institutions when awarding loans to specific countries. Portes quotes a Salvadoran scholar when noting that, in the age of globalization, remittances are a form of grassroots foreign aid bolstering the fortunes of towns and communities in Mexico and Central America.

Nevertheless, there is no reason for romanticizing the valiant efforts of immigrants who transfer resources to their places of origin. Portes notes that there are no examples showing that remittances can be used as a motor for viable development in sending countries. The opposite may be true—cash transfers accentuate inequalities at the local level between those who have relatives working abroad and those who lack such connections. Equally important is Portes's discussion of U.S. policies aimed at curtailing unauthorized immigration but that are inadvertently promoting the permanent settlement of vulnerable workers and their families, thus increasing the likelihood that some of their children will respond to hostility and limited opportunity through downward assimilation. The emergence of a Latino underclass in the United States may yet become an unintended consequence of misguided immigration policies in the age of neoliberalism.

In "Borders for Whom? The Role of NAFTA in Mexico-U.S. Migration," Patricia Fernández-Kelly and Douglas Massey continue that discussion in two parts. First, the authors retrace the steps that led to the passage and implementation of NAFTA, noting that the treaty was primarily an attempt at codifying a process of economic liberalization that had started two decades earlier. More important, NAFTA was also a mechanism meant to create stable conditions for the deployment of capital in the most advanced sectors of the economy, including finance, insurance, and real estate. That partly clarifies the reason why labor rights and mobility were not a priority—the treaty's goal was to remove barriers for capital investments not to liberalize markets. Controlled, not free, markets were NAFTA's intent.

In the second half of the article, the authors offer an analysis of the unintended consequences of restrictive U.S. immigration policies since 1986, noting the contradiction in NAFTA's attempt to open up all markets except one: labor. On the basis of data yielded by the Mexican Migration Project spearheaded by Douglas Massey and Jorge Durand, the article shows how the increased costs of reentry into the United States has reduced cyclical migration and promoted the settlement of vulnerable workers mostly from Mexico, many of whom lack proper documentation. An estimated 12 million unauthorized immigrants currently reside on American soil. Contrary to popular preconceptions, the increase of the Hispanic population in the United States is not primarily the result of increased migration from Latin America but a by-product of permanent settlement on the part of workers who previously may have engaged in cyclical migration.

In other words, NAFTA's lack of consideration to the effects of market liberalization on labor mobility, in combination with harsh anti-immigrant policies, is producing effects exactly the opposite of those made explicit by public officials. Not only have immigration curtailment efforts failed—they have also increased the likelihood of death among those trying to sneak across the U.S.-Mexico border and boosted an industry formed by identity document forgers and people smugglers.

NAFTA, Labor, and the Nation-State

In "The Strategic Role of Mexican Labor under NAFTA: Critical Perspectives on Current Economic Integration," Raúl Delgado Wise and James M. Cypher turn our attention to Mexico's export-oriented industrialization program distinguishing between actual and disguised maquiladoras. The first operate in direct response to foreign investment; the second are technically part of Mexico's domestic industrial base but largely depend on foreign inputs. The authors provide evidence suggesting that in both cases Mexico's industry is increasingly controlled by U.S.-based commercial and manufacturing interests. The extension of the principles underlying Mexico's maquiladoras has promoted the de-territorialization of Mexican labor even when Mexican workers are technically still living in their own country. The analysis in this article is doubly provocative in light of the accolades offered by Mexican politicians praising NAFTA as an engine for development.

A striking contrast to the Mexican situation is offered by Rina Agarwala in her study of Indian women informally employed in the tobacco and construction sectors, "Resistance and Compliance in the Age of Globalization: Indian Women and Labor Organizations." On the basis of more than three hundred interviews with public officials, labor leaders, union organizers and workers, Agarwala offers a first glimpse into a relatively new phenomenon: the emergence of informal unions mediating between workers and the state. In the Indian case, working women do not make demands directly upon employers for increased wages or better working conditions; instead, they appeal to government authorities for welfare benefits meant to improve family life. Agarwala shows that, ironically, it is in Indian states receptive to neoliberal reform that informal workers' unions have been most successful. This is in contrast to the limited effectiveness of informal unionization in states dominated by socialist and even communist ideologies, which make it difficult for organizers to take casual workers seriously.

Agarwala's analysis also shows that the location for organization and mobilization has dramatically shifted from the workplace to the neighborhoods where most women live and where many combine domestic and wage-earning activities. Like other authors in this volume, she points to the continued importance of national states in the age of globalization.

The relationship between indigenous movements in Latin America and national states is also the subject broached by political scientist, Deborah Yashar. In "Resistance and Identity Politics in an Age of Globalization," she sets out to investigate the effects of economic globalization on the emergence of autochthonous mobilization such as the one represented by Mexico's Ejército Zapatista de Liberación Nacional. She notes that despite the alleged affinity between neoliberal reform and contestation at the grassroots level, most indigenous movements are not a response to the global onslaught—many emerged long before that trend was in effect in reaction to the abuses of domestic, not foreign capitalists. Furthermore, it is not always in the areas where globalization has had its most visible effects that indigenous identities have emerged. Yashar underscores the continuing significance of national states as authoritative institutions targeted by autochthonous movements when making claims. Even more significant is Yashar's discussion of the preconditions necessary for the rise of indigenous identities and movements in the latter part of the twentieth century. She emphasizes as necessary elements the erosion of preexisting corporatist self-definitions, the existence of transcommunity networks, and the availability of spaces for public expression.

"Rethinking Civil Society in the Age of NAFTA: The Case of Mexico," by Jon Shefner, aptly complements the preceding chapters. It offers a thorough critique of civil society, a concept much in vogue in recent years. The weakened capacity of national states to address social needs after the implementation of neoliberal reforms contributed to the expansion of a new sector formed by not-for-profit and nongovernmental organizations whose charge was to assume some of the functions previously in the realm of governance. Enthusiasm about those organizations as representatives of a strengthened civil society was muted by their limited capacity to foster economic development and growth.

As Shefner notes, an uncritical emphasis on the capacities of civil society overlooks sharp class inequalities and contestation over scarce resources. On the basis of ethnographic research, he discusses the causes and implications of increased economic inequality in coexistence with greater political participation. In Mexico, neoliberal reform has paralleled increased democratization. The question is whether increased mobilization in the political realm can indefinitely coexist with limited economic progress and growing social inequality.

Regionalization and Primary Goods Extraction

The authors of the last four articles in this volume make a persuasive argument that a main objective of the neoliberal project may have been to dismantle barriers for the exploitation of agricultural, mining, and other primary resources. In her incisive analysis of World Bank data, "The Globalization of Capital Flows: Who Benefits?" Barbara Stallings shows the uneven effects of economic liberalization and capital volatility, observing that the countries most likely to be affected by foreign investment are those offering access to natural assets. She emphasizes small and medium-sized firms observing that capital volatility is most harmful to domestic industry while large international corporations remain immune, for the most part, to its effects. Like other authors in this volume, Stallings notes the uneven impact of neoliberal policies in various parts of the world and the tendency for many countries to fall back on the sale of agricultural resources as a means of integration into the world economy.

In "Trading Impressions: Evidence from Costa Rica," Frederick Wherry tackles an innovative subject: the role of the state in managing crafts and tourism as part of a competitive strategy in the world market. His analysis shows that public officials consciously fashion public narratives about their country's qualities as a means to highlight its commercial appeal. In the early stages of the new millennium, one of the roles assumed by governments in underdeveloped countries is to package national character and beauty as a marketing device. The Costa Rican case suggests that the promises and pitfalls of NAFTA cannot be understood adequately by solely examining structural conditions in each country. Instead, the uneven spread of benefits and liabilities will depend, in part, on how nation-states and their subnational communities are framed in the imaginations of the global marketplace.

Nothing in the global landscape should command more attention than the effects of neoliberal reform on the production of medical supplies. That is the subject of Donald Light's article, "Globalizing Restricted and Segmented Markets: Challenges to Theory and Values in Economic Sociology." He introduces the term *pernicious competition* as an alternative to the better-known concept of *market failure* to more accurately describe what happens when vital human needs are not efficiently met as a result of global competition. The extended protections of intellectual property in new free trade agreements tend to benefit large pharmaceutical companies at the expense of small agriculturalists who are unable to compete. Bio-engineering and the allocation of arable land to the production of lucrative medical products are an example of market segmentation being used to raise the prices of and reduce access to vital drugs for treating patients with lethal diseases, including Cancer and AIDS. Light's research raises new questions about the potential role of states in the maintenance of parameters aimed at propagating social wellbeing.

Last but not least is Paul Gellert's analysis of the collapse of the timber industry in Indonesia, "Renegotiating Transnational Alliances in the Production of Asian Timber: From Managed to Free(r) Markets." He shows that, although imperfect, the political alliances forged during the Suharto regime consolidated a viable plywood industry by the 1980s, bypassing Japan's dominance and enabling Indonesia to undertake an accelerated development program. The Asian crisis of 1997 to 1998 and structural adjustments imposed by the International Monetary Fund transformed Indonesia's options, diminishing its competitive capacity at the same time that China emerged as a major producer of wood-related products. The Indonesian case may well illustrate processes of market remarginalization resulting from the implementation of neoliberal policies. Gellert's study also shows that regional dynamics may be as important in determining outcomes as more general processes of globalization.

References

Alter, Jonathan. 2006. *The defining moment: FDR's hundred days and the triumph of hope.* New York: Simon & Schuster.

Bentham, Jeremy. 1789/1988. *The principles of morals and legislation.* London: Prometheus Books.

Cohen, Edward S. 2001. *The politics of globalization in the United States.* Washington, DC: Georgetown University Press.

Comisión Economíca para América Latina y el Caribe. 1987. *Raúl Prebisch: Un Aporte al Estudio de su Pensamiento: Las Cinco Etapas de su Pensamiento sobre el Desarrollo, su Ultima Intervención Pública, Bibliografía de su Obra entre 1920 y 1986.* Washington, DC: United Nations.

Crouch, Luis B. 1983. *Latin American agriculture from import substitution industrialization to neo-liberal authoritarianism.* Draft edition. Division of Agricultural Sciences, University of California.

Evans, Peter. 1995. *Embedded autonomy: States and industrial transformation*. Princeton, NJ: Princeton University Press.

Fernández-Kelly, Patricia. 1983. *For we are sold, I and my people: Women and industry in Mexico's frontier*. Albany: State University of New York Press.

Friedman, Milton. 1962/2002. *Capitalism and freedom*. Chicago: University of Chicago Press.

Gereffi, Gary, and Donald L. Wyman, eds. 1990. *Manufacturing miracles*. Princeton, NJ: Princeton University Press.

————. 1988. *Economics in perspective: A critical history*. New York: Houghton Mifflin.

Hayek, Friedrich A. 1982. *New studies in philosophy, politics, economics and the history of ideas*. London: Routledge & Keagan Paul.

Herrnstein, Richard J., and Charles Murray. 1994. *The bell curve: Intelligence and class structure in American life*. New York: Free Press.

Jevons, William Stanley. 1862. Brief account of a general mathematical theory of political economy. *Journal of the Royal Statistical Society* 29 (June 1866): 282-87.

Keynes, John Meynard. 1933. An open letter to President Roosevelt. *New York Times*.

Keynes, Milo. 1975. *Essays on John Maynard Keynes*. Cambridge: Cambridge University Press.

MacRae, Norman. 2000. *John Von Neumann: The scientific genius who pioneered the modern computer, game theory, nuclear deterrence, and much more*. Washington, DC: American Mathematical Society.

Krugman, Paul. 1994. *Peddling prosperity*. New York: Norton.

Menger, Carl. 1871/1976. *Principles of economics*. New York: New York University Press.

Meyer, David R. 2003. *The roots of American industrialization*. Baltimore: Johns Hopkins University Press.

Mill, John Stuart. 1859/2000. On liberty. In *The basic writing of John Stuart Mill*. New York: Modern Library (Random House).

Murray, Charles. 1985. *Losing ground: American social policy, 1950-1980*. New York: Basic Books.

Portes, Alejandro, and Kelly Hoffman. 2003. Latin American class structures: Their composition and change during the neo-liberal era. *Latin American Research Review* 38 (1): 41-82.

Quijano, Aníbal. 1972. *Nationalism and capitalism in Peru: A study in neo-imperialism*. New York: Monthly Review Press.

Sachs, Jeffrey, and B. Felipe Larrain. 1993. *Macroeconomics in the global economy*. New York: Prentice Hall.

Sassen, Saskia. 1999. *Globalization and its discontents: Essays on the new mobility of people and money*. New York: New Press.

Sen, Amartya. 2000. *Development as freedom*. New York: Anchor Books.

Smith, Adam. 1776/2003. *The wealth of nations*. New York: Bantam Classics.

Spencer, Herbert. 1851/1995. *Social statics or the conditions essential to human happiness specified, and the first of them developed*. London: Robert Shackelford.

Spencer, Herbert. 1861/2002. *Principals of Biology* Haddonfield, NJ: Ross and Perry.

Thompson, E. P. 1966. *The making of the English working class*. New York: Vintage.

Walras, Leon. 1874/1984. *Elements of pure economics or the theory of social wealth*. New York: Porcupine Press.

Watkins, Tom H. 1993. *The Great Depression: America in the 1930s*. New York: Little, Brown.

Political and Economic Dimensions of Free Trade

Neoliberalism as Creative Destruction

Neoliberalism has become a hegemonic discourse with pervasive effects on ways of thought and political-economic practices to the point where it is now part of the commonsense way we interpret, live in, and understand the world. How did neoliberalism achieve such an exalted status, and what does it stand for? In this article, the author contends that neoliberalism is above all a project to restore class dominance to sectors that saw their fortunes threatened by the ascent of social democratic endeavors in the aftermath of the Second World War. Although neoliberalism has had limited effectiveness as an engine for economic growth, it has succeeded in channeling wealth from subordinate classes to dominant ones and from poorer to richer countries. This process has entailed the dismantling of institutions and narratives that promoted more egalitarian distributive measures in the preceding era.

Keywords: neoliberalism; globalization; fiscalization; class dominance; subordination

By
DAVID HARVEY

Neoliberalism is a theory of political economic practices proposing that human well-being can best be advanced by the maximization of entrepreneurial freedoms within an institutional framework characterized by private property rights, individual liberty, unencumbered markets, and free trade. The role of the state is to create and preserve an institutional framework appropriate to such practices. The state has to be concerned, for example, with the quality and integrity of money. It must also set up military, defense, police, and juridical functions required to secure private property rights and to support freely functioning markets. Furthermore, if markets do not exist (in areas such as education, health care, social security, or environmental pollution), then they

David Harvey is Distinguished Professor in the Graduate Center of the City University of New York. He is author of several books, including A Brief History of Neoliberalism, The New Imperialism, Spaces of Hope, The Limits to Capital, *and* The Condition of Postmodernity.

DOI: 10.1177/0002716206296780

must be created, by state action if necessary. But beyond these tasks the state should not venture. State interventions in markets (once created) must be kept to a bare minimum because the state cannot possibly possess enough information to second-guess market signals (prices) and because powerful interests will inevitably distort and bias state interventions (particularly in democracies) for their own benefit.

For a variety of reasons, the actual practices of neoliberalism frequently diverge from this template. Nevertheless, there has everywhere been an emphatic turn, ostensibly led by the Thatcher/Reagan revolutions in Britain and the United States, in political-economic practices and thinking since the 1970s. State after state, from the new ones that emerged from the collapse of the Soviet Union to old-style social democracies and welfare states such as New Zealand and Sweden, have embraced, sometimes voluntarily and sometimes in response to coercive pressures, some version of neoliberal theory and adjusted at least some of their policies and practices accordingly. Postapartheid South Africa quickly adopted the neoliberal frame and even contemporary China appears to be headed in that direction. Furthermore, advocates of the neoliberal mindset now occupy positions of considerable influence in education (universities and many "think tanks"), in the media, in corporate board rooms and financial institutions, in key state institutions (treasury departments, central banks), and also in those international institutions such as the International Monetary Fund (IMF) and the World Trade Organization (WTO) that regulate global finance and commerce. Neoliberalism has, in short, become hegemonic as a mode of discourse and has pervasive effects on ways of thought and political-economic practices to the point where it has become incorporated into the commonsense way we interpret, live in, and understand the world.

Neoliberalization has in effect swept across the world like a vast tidal wave of institutional reform and discursive adjustment. While plenty of evidence shows its uneven geographical development, no place can claim total immunity (with the exception of a few states such as North Korea). Furthermore, the rules of engagement now established through the WTO (governing international trade) and by the IMF (governing international finance) instantiate neoliberalism as a global set of rules. All states that sign on to the WTO and the IMF (and who can afford not to?) agree to abide (albeit with a "grace period" to permit smooth adjustment) by these rules or face severe penalties.

The creation of this neoliberal system has entailed much destruction, not only of prior institutional frameworks and powers (such as the supposed prior state sovereignty over political-economic affairs) but also of divisions of labor, social relations, welfare provisions, technological mixes, ways of life, attachments to the land, habits of the heart, ways of thought, and the like. Some assessment of the positives and negatives of this neoliberal revolution is called for. In what follows, therefore, I will sketch in some preliminary arguments as to how to both understand and evaluate this transformation in the way global capitalism is working. This requires that we come to terms with the underlying forces, interests, and agents that have propelled the neoliberal revolution forward with such relentless intensity. To turn the neoliberal rhetoric against itself, we may reasonably ask, In whose particular interests is it that the state take a neoliberal stance and in what ways have those interests used neoliberalism to benefit themselves rather than, as is claimed, everyone, everywhere?

In whose particular interests is it that the state take a neoliberal stance, and in what ways have those interests used neoliberalism to benefit themselves rather than, as is claimed, everyone, everywhere?

The "Naturalization" of Neoliberalism

For any system of thought to become dominant, it requires the articulation of fundamental concepts that become so deeply embedded in commonsense understandings that they are taken for granted and beyond question. For this to occur, not any old concepts will do. A conceptual apparatus has to be constructed that appeals almost naturally to our intuitions and instincts, to our values and our desires, as well as to the possibilities that seem to inhere in the social world we inhabit. The founding figures of neoliberal thought took political ideals of individual liberty and freedom as sacrosanct—as the central values of civilization. And in so doing they chose wisely and well, for these are indeed compelling and greatly appealing concepts. Such values were threatened, they argued, not only by fascism, dictatorships, and communism, but also by all forms of state intervention that substituted collective judgments for those of individuals set free to choose. They then concluded that without "the diffused power and initiative associated with (private property and the competitive market) it is difficult to imagine a society in which freedom may be effectively preserved."[1]

Setting aside the question of whether the final part of the argument necessarily follows from the first, there can be no doubt that the concepts of individual liberty and freedom are powerful in their own right, even beyond those terrains where the liberal tradition has had a strong historical presence. Such ideals empowered the dissident movements in Eastern Europe and the Soviet Union before the end of the cold war as well as the students in Tiananmen Square. The student movement that swept the world in 1968—from Paris and Chicago to Bangkok and Mexico City—was in part animated by the quest for greater freedoms of speech and individual choice. These ideals have proven again and again to be a mighty historical force for change.

It is not surprising, therefore, that appeals to freedom and liberty surround the United States rhetorically at every turn and populate all manner of contemporary political manifestos. This has been particularly true of the United States in recent years. On the first anniversary of the attacks now known as 9/11, President Bush wrote an op-ed piece for the *New York Times* that extracted ideas from a U.S. National Defense Strategy document issued shortly thereafter. "A peaceful world of growing freedom," he wrote, even as his cabinet geared up to go to war with Iraq, "serves American long-term interests, reflects enduring American ideals and unites America's allies." "Humanity," he concluded, "holds in its hands the opportunity to offer freedom's triumph over all its age-old foes," and "the United States welcomes its responsibilities to lead in this great mission." Even more emphatically, he later proclaimed that "freedom is the Almighty's gift to every man and woman in this world" and "as the greatest power on earth [the United States has] an obligation to help the spread of freedom."[2]

So when all of the other reasons for engaging in a preemptive war against Iraq were proven fallacious or at least wanting, the Bush administration increasingly appealed to the idea that the freedom conferred upon Iraq was in and of itself an adequate justification for the war. But what sort of freedom was envisaged here, since, as the cultural critic Matthew Arnold long ago thoughtfully observed, "Freedom is a very good horse to ride, but to ride somewhere."[3] To what destination, then, were the Iraqi people expected to ride the horse of freedom so selflessly conferred to them by force of arms?

The U.S. answer was spelled out on September 19, 2003, when Paul Bremer, head of the Coalition Provisional Authority, promulgated four orders that included "the full privatization of public enterprises, full ownership rights by foreign firms of Iraqi U.S. businesses, full repatriation of foreign profits . . . the opening of Iraq's banks to foreign control, national treatment for foreign companies and . . . the elimination of nearly all trade barriers."[4] The orders were to apply to all areas of the economy, including public services, the media, manufacturing, services, transportation, finance, and construction. Only oil was exempt. A regressive tax system favored by conservatives called a flat tax was also instituted. The right to strike was outlawed and unions banned in key sectors. An Iraqi member of the Coalition Provisional Authority protested the forced imposition of "free market fundamentalism," describing it as "a flawed logic that ignores history."[5] Yet the interim Iraqi government appointed at the end of June 2004 was accorded no power to change or write new laws—it could only confirm the decrees already promulgated.

What the United States evidently sought to impose upon Iraq was a full-fledged neoliberal state apparatus whose fundamental mission was and is to facilitate conditions for profitable capital accumulation for all comers, Iraqis and foreigners alike. The Iraqis were, in short, expected to ride their horse of freedom straight into the corral of neoliberalism. According to neoliberal theory, Bremer's decrees are both necessary and sufficient for the creation of wealth and therefore for the improved well-being of the Iraqi people. They are the proper foundation for an adequate rule of law, individual liberty, and democratic governance. The insurrection that followed can in part be interpreted as Iraqi resistance to being driven into the embrace of free market fundamentalism against their own free will.

It is useful to recall, however, that the first great experiment with neoliberal state formation was Chile after Augusto Pinochet's coup almost thirty years to the day before Bremer's decrees were issued, on the "little September 11th" of 1973. The coup, against the democratically elected and leftist social democratic government of Salvador Allende, was strongly backed by the CIA and supported by U.S. Secretary of State Henry Kissinger. It violently repressed all left-of-center social movements and political organizations and dismantled all forms of popular organization, such as community health centers in poorer neighborhoods. The labor market was "freed" from regulatory or institutional restraints—trade union power, for example. But by 1973, the policies of import substitution that had formerly dominated in Latin American attempts at economic regeneration, and that had succeeded to some degree in Brazil after the military coup of 1964, had fallen into disrepute. With the world economy in the midst of a serious recession, something new was plainly called for. A group of U.S. economists known as "the Chicago boys," because of their attachment to the neoliberal theories of Milton Friedman, then teaching at the University of Chicago, were summoned to help reconstruct the Chilean economy. They did so along free-market lines, privatizing public assets, opening up natural resources to private exploitation, and facilitating foreign direct investment and free trade. The right of foreign companies to repatriate profits from their Chilean operations was guaranteed. Export-led growth was favored over import substitution. The subsequent revival of the Chilean economy in terms of growth, capital accumulation, and high rates of return on foreign investments provided evidence upon which the subsequent turn to more open neoliberal policies in both Britain (under Thatcher) and the United States (under Reagan) could be modeled. Not for the first time, a brutal experiment in creative destruction carried out in the periphery became a model for the formulation of policies in the center.[6]

The fact that two such obviously similar restructurings of the state apparatus occurred at such different times in quite different parts of the world under the coercive influence of the United States might be taken as indicative that the grim reach of U.S. imperial power might lie behind the rapid proliferation of neoliberal state forms throughout the world from the mid-1970s onward. But U.S. power and recklessness do not constitute the whole story. It was not the United States, after all, that forced Margaret Thatcher to take the neoliberal path in 1979. And during the early 1980s, Thatcher was a far more consistent advocate of neoliberalism than Reagan ever proved to be. Nor was it the United States that forced China in 1978 to follow the path that has over time brought it closer and closer to the embrace of neoliberalism. It would be hard to attribute the moves toward neoliberalism in India and Sweden in 1992 to the imperial reach of the United States. The uneven geographical development of neoliberalism on the world stage has been a very complex process entailing multiple determinations and not a little chaos and confusion. So why, then, did the neoliberal turn occur, and what were the forces compelling it onward to the point where it has now become a hegemonic system within global capitalism?

Why the Neoliberal Turn?

Toward the end of the 1960s, global capitalism was falling into disarray. A significant recession occurred in early 1973—the first since the great slump of the 1930s. The oil embargo and oil price hike that followed later that year in the wake of the Arab-Israeli war exacerbated critical problems. The embedded capitalism of the postwar period, with its heavy emphasis on an uneasy compact between capital and labor brokered by an interventionist state that paid great attention to the social (i.e., welfare programs) and individual wage, was no longer working. The Bretton Woods accord set up to regulate international trade and finance was finally abandoned in favor of floating exchange rates in 1973. That system had delivered high rates of growth in the advanced capitalist countries and generated some spillover benefits—most obviously to Japan but also unevenly across South America and to some other countries of South East Asia—during the "golden age" of capitalism in the 1950s and early 1960s. By the next decade, however, the preexisting arrangements were exhausted and a new alternative was urgently needed to restart the process of capital accumulation.[7] How and why neoliberalism emerged victorious as an answer to that quandary is a complex story. In retrospect, it may seem as if neoliberalism had been inevitable, but at the time no one really knew or understood with any certainty what kind of response would work and how.

The world stumbled toward neoliberalism through a series of gyrations and chaotic motions that eventually converged on the so-called "Washington Consensus" in the 1990s. The uneven geographical development of neoliberalism, and its partial and lopsided application from one country to another, testifies to its tentative character and the complex ways in which political forces, historical traditions, and existing institutional arrangements all shaped why and how the process actually occurred on the ground.

There is, however, one element within this transition that deserves concerted attention. The crisis of capital accumulation of the 1970s affected everyone through the combination of rising unemployment and accelerating inflation. Discontent was widespread, and the conjoining of labor and urban social movements throughout much of the advanced capitalist world augured a socialist alternative to the social compromise between capital and labor that had grounded capital accumulation so successfully in the postwar period. Communist and socialist parties were gaining ground across much of Europe, and even in the United States popular forces were agitating for widespread reforms and state interventions in everything ranging from environmental protection to occupational safety and health and consumer protection from corporate malfeasance. There was, in this, a clear *political* threat to ruling classes everywhere, both in advanced capitalist countries, like Italy and France, and in many developing countries, like Mexico and Argentina.

Beyond political changes, the *economic* threat to the position of ruling classes was now becoming palpable. One condition of the postwar settlement in almost all countries was to restrain the economic power of the upper classes and for labor to be accorded a much larger share of the economic pie. In the United States, for example, the share of the national income taken by the top 1 percent of earners fell from a prewar high of 16 percent to less than 8 percent by the end of the Second World War and stayed close to that level for nearly three decades. While growth was strong such restraints seemed not to matter, but when growth collapsed in the 1970s, even as real interest rates went negative and dividends and profits shrunk, ruling classes felt threatened. They had to move decisively if they were to protect their power from political and economic annihilation.

The coup d'état in Chile and the military takeover in Argentina, both fomented and led internally by ruling elites with U.S. support, provided one kind of solution. But the Chilean experiment with neoliberalism demonstrated that the benefits of revived capital accumulation were highly skewed. The country and its ruling elites along with foreign investors did well enough while the people in general fared poorly. This has been such a persistent effect of neoliberal policies over time as to be regarded a structural component of the whole project. Dumenil and Levy have gone so far as to argue that neoliberalism was from the very beginning an endeavor to restore class power to the richest strata in the population. They showed how from the mid-1980s onwards, the share of the top 1 percent of income earners in the United States soared rapidly to reach 15 percent by the end of the century. Other data show that the top 0.1 percent of income earners increased their share of the national income from 2 percent in 1978 to more than 6 percent by 1999. Yet another measure shows that the ratio of the median compensation of workers to the salaries of chief executive officers increased from just over thirty to one in 1970 to more than four hundred to one by 2000. Almost certainly, with the Bush administration's tax cuts now taking effect, the concentration of income and of wealth in the upper echelons of society is continuing apace.[8]

And the United States is not alone in this: the top 1 percent of income earners in Britain doubled their share of the national income from 6.5 percent to 13 percent over the past twenty years. When we look further afield, we see extraordinary concentrations of wealth and power within a small oligarchy after the application of neoliberal shock therapy in Russia and a staggering surge in income inequalities and wealth in China as it adopts neoliberal practices. While there are exceptions to this trend—several East and Southeast Asian countries have contained income inequalities within modest bounds, as have France and the Scandinavian countries—the evidence suggests that the neoliberal turn is in some way and to some degree associated with attempts to restore or reconstruct upper-class power.

We can, therefore, examine the history of neoliberalism either as a utopian project providing a theoretical template for the reorganization of international capitalism or as a political scheme aimed at reestablishing the conditions for capital accumulation and the restoration of class power. In what follows, I shall argue that the last of these objectives has dominated. Neoliberalism has not proven effective at revitalizing global capital accumulation, but it has succeeded in restoring class power. As a consequence, the theoretical utopianism of the neoliberal argument has worked more as a system of justification and legitimization. The principles of neoliberalism are quickly abandoned whenever they conflict with this class project.

Neoliberalism has not proven effective at revitalizing global capital accumulation, but it has succeeded in restoring class power.

Toward the Restoration of Class Power

If there were movements to restore class power within global capitalism, then how were they enacted and by whom? The answer to that question in countries such as Chile and Argentina was simple: a swift, brutal, and self-assured military coup backed by the upper classes and the subsequent fierce repression of all solidarities created within the labor and urban social movements that had so threatened their power. Elsewhere, as in Britain and Mexico in 1976, it took the gentle prodding of a not yet fiercely neoliberal International Monetary Fund to push countries toward practices—although by no means policy commitment—to cut back on social expenditures and welfare programs to reestablish fiscal probity. In Britain, of course, Margaret Thatcher later took up the neoliberal cudgel with a vengeance in 1979 and wielded it to great effect, even though she never fully overcame opposition within her own party and could never effectively challenge such centerpieces of the welfare state as the National Health Service. Interestingly, it was only in 2004 that the Labour Government dared to introduce a fee structure into higher education. The process of neoliberalization has been halting, geographically uneven, and heavily influenced by class structures and other social forces moving for or against its central propositions within particular state formations and even within particular sectors, for example, health or education.[9]

It is informative to look more closely at how the process unfolded in the United States, since this case was pivotal as an influence on other and more recent transformations. Various threads of power intertwined to create a transition that culminated in the mid-1990s with the takeover of Congress by the

Republican Party. That feat represented in fact a neoliberal "Contract with America" as a program for domestic action. Before that dramatic denouement, however, many steps were taken, each building upon and reinforcing the other.

To begin with, by 1970 or so, there was a growing sense among the U.S. upper classes that the antibusiness and anti-imperialist climate that had emerged toward the end of the 1960s had gone too far. In a celebrated memo, Lewis Powell (about to be elevated to the Supreme Court by Richard Nixon) urged the American Chamber of Commerce in 1971 to mount a *collective* campaign to demonstrate that what was good for business was good for America. Shortly thereafter, a shadowy but influential Business Round Table was formed that still exists and plays a significant strategic role in Republican Party politics. Corporate political action committees, legalized under the post-Watergate campaign finance laws of 1974, proliferated like wildfire. With their activities protected under the First Amendment as a form of free speech in a 1976 Supreme Court decision, the systematic capture of the Republican Party as a class instrument of *collective* (rather than particular or individual) corporate and financial power began. But the Republican Party needed a popular base, and that proved more problematic to achieve. The incorporation of leaders of the Christian right, depicted as a moral majority, together with the Business Round Table provided the solution to that problem. A large segment of a disaffected, insecure, and largely white working class was persuaded to vote consistently against its own material interests on cultural (antiliberal, antiblack, antifeminist and antigay), nationalist and religious grounds. By the mid-1990s, the Republican Party had lost almost all of its liberal elements and become a homogeneous right-wing machine connecting the financial resources of large corporate capital with a populist base, the Moral Majority, that was particularly strong in the U.S. South.[10]

The second element in the U.S. transition concerned fiscal discipline. The recession of 1973 to 1975 diminished tax revenues at all levels at a time of rising demand for social expenditures. Deficits emerged everywhere as a key problem. Something had to be done about the fiscal crisis of the state; the restoration of monetary discipline was essential. That conviction empowered financial institutions that controlled the lines of credit to government. In 1975, they refused to roll over New York's debt and forced that city to the edge of bankruptcy. A powerful cabal of bankers joined together with the state to tighten control over the city. This meant curbing the aspirations of municipal unions, layoffs in public employment, wage freezes, cutbacks in social provision (education, public health, and transport services), and the imposition of user fees (tuition was introduced in the CUNY university system for the first time). The bailout entailed the construction of new institutions that had first rights to city tax revenues in order to pay off bond holders: whatever was left went into the city budget for essential services. The final indignity was a requirement that municipal unions invest their pension funds in city bonds. This ensured that unions moderate their demands to avoid the danger of losing their pension funds through city bankruptcy.

Such actions amounted to a coup d'état by financial institutions against the democratically elected government of New York City, and they were every bit as

effective as the military overtaking that had earlier occurred in Chile. Much of
the city's social infrastructure was destroyed, and the physical foundations (e.g.,
the transit system) deteriorated markedly for lack of investment or even maintenance. The management of New York's fiscal crisis paved the way for neoliberal
practices both domestically under Ronald Reagan and internationally through
the International Monetary Fund throughout the 1980s. It established a principle that, in the event of a conflict between the integrity of financial institutions
and bondholders on one hand and the well-being of the citizens on the other, the
former would be given preference. It hammered home the view that the role of
government was to create a good business climate rather than look to the needs
and well-being of the population at large. Fiscal redistributions to benefit the
upper classes resulted in the midst of a general fiscal crisis.

Whether all the agents involved in producing this compromise in New York
understood it at the time as a tactic for the restoration of upper-class power is an
open question. The need to maintain fiscal discipline is a matter of deep concern
in its own right and does not have to lead to the restitution of class dominance. It
is unlikely, therefore, that Felix Rohatyn, the key merchant banker who brokered
the deal between the city, the state, and the financial institutions, had the rein-
statement of class power in mind. But this objective probably was very much in
the thoughts of the investment bankers. It was almost certainly the aim of
then–Secretary of the Treasury William Simon who, having watched the progress
of events in Chile with approval, refused to give aid to New York and openly
stated that he wanted that city to suffer so badly that no other city in the nation
would ever dare take on similar social obligations again.[11]

The third element in the U.S. transition entailed an ideological assault upon the
media and upon educational institutions. Independent "think tanks" financed by
wealthy individuals and corporate donors proliferated—the Heritage Foundation
in the lead—to prepare an ideological onslaught aimed at persuading the public
of the commonsense character of neoliberal propositions. A flood of policy papers
and proposals and a veritable army of well-paid hired lieutenants trained to promote neoliberal ideas coupled with the corporate acquisition of media channels
effectively transformed the discursive climate in the United States by the mid-
1980s. The project to "get government off the backs of the people" and to shrink
government to the point where it could be "drowned in a bathtub" was loudly proclaimed. With respect to this, the promoters of the new gospel found a ready audience in that wing of the 1968 movement whose goal was greater individual liberty
and freedom from state power and the manipulations of monopoly capital. The
libertarian argument for neoliberalism proved a powerful force for change. To the
degree that capitalism reorganized to both open a space for individual entrepreneurship and switch its efforts to satisfy innumerable niche markets, particularly
those defined by sexual liberation, that were spawned out of an increasingly individualized consumerism, so it could match words with deeds.

This carrot of individualized entrepreneurship and consumerism was backed
by the big stick wielded by the state and financial institutions against that other

wing of the 1968 movement whose members had sought social justice through collective negotiation and social solidarities. Reagan's destruction of the air traffic controllers (PATCO) in 1980 and Margaret Thatcher's defeat of the British miners in 1984 were crucial moments in the global turn toward neoliberalism. The assault upon institutions, such as trade unions and welfare rights organizations, that sought to protect and further working-class interests was as broad as it was deep. The savage cutbacks in social expenditures and the welfare state, and the passing of all responsibility for their well-being to individuals and their families proceeded apace. But these practices did not and could not stop at national borders. After 1980, the United States, now firmly committed to neoliberalization and clearly backed by Britain, sought, through a mix of leadership, persuasion—the economics departments of U.S. research universities played a major role in training many of the economists from around the world in neoliberal principles—and coercion to export neoliberalization far and wide. The purge of Keynesian economists and their replacement by neoliberal monetarists in the International Monetary Fund in 1982 transformed the U.S.-dominated IMF into a prime agent of neoliberalization through its structural adjustment programs visited upon any state (and there were many in the 1980s and 1990s) that required its help with debt repayments. The Washington Consensus that was forged in the 1990s and the negotiating rules set up under the World Trade Organization in 1998 confirmed the global turn toward neoliberal practices.[12]

The new international compact also depended upon the reanimation and reconfiguration of the U.S. imperial tradition. That tradition had been forged in Central America in the 1920s, as a form of domination without colonies. Independent republics could be kept under the thumb of the United States and effectively act, in the best of cases, as proxies for U.S. interests through the support of strongmen—like Somoza in Nicaragua, the Shah in Iran, and Pinochet in Chile—and a coterie of followers backed by military assistance and financial aid. Covert aid was available to promote the rise to power of such leaders, but by the 1970s it became clear that something else was needed: the opening of markets, of new spaces for investment, and clear fields where financial powers could operate securely. This entailed a much closer integration of the global economy with a well-defined financial architecture. The creation of new institutional practices, such as those set out by the IMF and the WTO, provided convenient vehicles through which financial and market power could be exercised. The model required collaboration among the top capitalist powers and the Group of Seven (G7), bringing Europe and Japan into alignment with the United States to shape the global financial and trading system in ways that effectively forced all other nations to submit. "Rogue nations," defined as those that failed to conform to these global rules, could then be dealt with by sanctions or coercive and even military force if necessary. In this way, U.S. neoliberal imperialist strategies were articulated through a global network of power relations, one effect of which was to permit the U.S. upper classes to exact financial tribute and command rents from the rest of the world as a means to augment their already hegemonic control.[13]

Neoliberalism as Creative Destruction

In what ways has neoliberalization resolved the problems of flagging capital accumulation? Its actual record in stimulating economic growth is dismal. Aggregate growth rates stood at 3.5 percent or so in the 1960s and even during the troubled 1970s fell to only 2.4 percent. The subsequent global growth rates of 1.4 percent and 1.1 percent for the 1980s and 1990s, and a rate that barely touches 1 percent since 2000, indicate that neoliberalism has broadly failed to stimulate worldwide growth.[14] Even if we exclude from this calculation the catastrophic effects of the collapse of the Russian and some Central European economies in the wake of the neoliberal shock therapy treatment of the 1990s, global economic performance from the standpoint of restoring the conditions of general capital accumulation has been weak.

Despite their rhetoric about curing sick economies, neither Britain nor the United States achieved high economic performance in the 1980s. That decade belonged to Japan, the East Asian "Tigers," and West Germany as powerhouses of the global economy. Such countries were very successful, but their radically different institutional arrangements make it difficult to pin their achievements on neoliberalism. The West German Bundesbank had taken a strong monetarist line (consistent with neoliberalism) for more than two decades, a fact suggesting that there is no necessary connection between monetarism per se and the quest to restore class power. In West Germany, the unions remained strong and wage levels stayed relatively high alongside the construction of a progressive welfare state. One of the effects of this combination was to stimulate a high rate of technological innovation that kept West Germany well ahead in the field of international competition. Export-led production moved the country forward as a global leader.

In Japan, independent unions were weak or nonexistent, but state investment in technological and organizational change and the tight relationship between corporations and financial institutions (an arrangement that also proved felicitous in West Germany) generated an astonishing export-led growth performance, very much at the expense of other capitalist economies such as the United Kingdom and the United States. Such growth as there was in the 1980s (and the aggregate rate of growth in the world was lower even than that of the troubled 1970s) did not depend, therefore, on neoliberalization. Many European states therefore resisted neoliberal reforms and increasingly found ways to preserve much of their social democratic heritage while moving, in some cases fairly successfully, toward the West German model. In Asia, the Japanese model implanted under authoritarian systems of governance in South Korea, Taiwan, and Singapore also proved viable and consistent with reasonable equality of distribution. It was only in the 1990s that neoliberalization began to pay off for both the United States and Britain. This happened in the midst of a long-drawn-out period of deflation in Japan and relative stagnation in a newly unified Germany. Up for debate is whether the Japanese recession occurred as a simple result of competitive pressures or whether it was engineered by financial agents in the United States to humble the Japanese economy.

So why, then, in the face of this patchy if not dismal record, have so many been persuaded that neoliberalization is a successful solution? Over and beyond the persistent stream of propaganda emanating from the neoliberal think tanks and suffusing the media, two material reasons stand out. First, neoliberalization has been accompanied by increasing volatility within global capitalism. That success was to materialize somewhere obscured the reality that neoliberalism was generally failing. Periodic episodes of growth interspersed with phases of creative destruction, usually registered as severe financial crises. Argentina was opened up to foreign capital and privatization in the 1990s and for several years was the darling of Wall Street, only to collapse into disaster as international capital withdrew at the end of the decade. Financial collapse and social devastation was quickly followed by a long political crisis. Financial turmoil proliferated all over the developing world, and in some instances, such as Brazil and Mexico, repeated waves of structural adjustment and austerity led to economic paralysis.

On the other hand, neoliberalism has been a huge success from the standpoint of the upper classes. It has either restored class position to ruling elites, as in the United States and Britain, or created conditions for capitalist class formation, as in China, India, Russia, and elsewhere. Even countries that have suffered extensively from neoliberalization have seen the massive reordering of class structures internally. The wave of privatization that came to Mexico with the Salinas de Gortari administration in 1992 spawned unprecedented concentrations of wealth in the hands of a few people (Carlos Slim, for example, who took over the state telephone system and became an instant billionaire).

With the media dominated by upper-class interests, the myth could be propagated that certain sectors failed because they were not competitive enough, thereby setting the stage for even more neoliberal reforms. Increased social inequality was necessary to encourage entrepreneurial risk and innovation, and these, in turn, conferred competitive advantage and stimulated growth. If conditions among the lower classes deteriorated, it was because they failed for personal and cultural reasons to enhance their own human capital through education, the acquisition of a protestant work ethic, and submission to work discipline and flexibility. In short, problems arose because of the lack of competitive strength or because of personal, cultural, and political failings. In a Spencerian world, the argument went, only the fittest should and do survive. Systemic problems were masked under a blizzard of ideological pronouncements and a plethora of localized crises.

If the main effect of neoliberalism has been redistributive rather than generative, then ways had to be found to transfer assets and channel wealth and income either from the mass of the population toward the upper classes or from vulnerable to richer countries. I have elsewhere provided an account of these processes under the rubric of *accumulation by dispossession*.[15] By this, I mean the continuation and proliferation of accretion practices that Marx had designated as "primitive" or "original" during the rise of capitalism. These include (1) the commodification and privatization of land and the forceful expulsion of peasant populations (as in Mexico and India in recent times); (2) conversion of various forms of property rights (common, collective, state, etc.) into exclusively private property rights;

(3) suppression of rights to the commons; (4) commodification of labor power and the suppression of alternative (indigenous) forms of production and consumption; (5) colonial, neocolonial, and imperial processes of appropriation of assets (including natural resources); (6) monetization of exchange and taxation, particularly of land; (7) the slave trade (which continues, particularly in the sex industry); and (8) usury, the national debt, and, most devastating of all, the use of the credit system as radical means of primitive accumulation.

The state, with its monopoly of violence and definitions of legality, plays a crucial role in backing and promoting these processes. To this list of mechanisms, we may now add a raft of additional techniques, such as the extraction of rents from patents and intellectual property rights and the diminution or erasure of various forms of communal property rights—such as state pensions, paid vacations, access to education, and health care—won through a generation or more of social democratic struggles. The proposal to privatize all state pension rights (pioneered in Chile under Augusto Pinochet's dictatorship) is, for example, one of the cherished objectives of neoliberals in the United States.

In the cases of China and Russia, it might be reasonable to refer to recent events in "primitive" and "original" terms, but the practices that restored class power to capitalist elites in the United States and elsewhere are best described as an ongoing process of accumulation by dispossession that grew rapidly under neoliberalism. In what follows, I isolate four main elements.

1. Privatization

The corporatization, commodification, and privatization of hitherto public assets have been signal features of the neoliberal project. Its primary aim has been to open up new fields for capital accumulation in domains formerly regarded off-limits to the calculus of profitability. Public utilities of all kinds (water, telecommunications, transportation), social welfare provision (public housing, education, health care, pensions), public institutions (such as universities, research laboratories, prisons), and even warfare (as illustrated by the "army" of private contractors operating alongside the armed forces in Iraq) have all been privatized to some degree throughout the capitalist world.

Intellectual property rights established through the so-called TRIPS (Trade-Related Aspects of Intellectual Property Rights) agreement within the WTO defines genetic materials, seed plasmas, and all manner of other products as private property. Rents for use can then be extracted from populations whose practices had played a crucial role in the development of such genetic materials. Bio-piracy is rampant, and the pillaging of the world's stockpile of genetic resources is well under way to the benefit of a few large pharmaceutical companies. The escalating depletion of the global environmental commons (land, air, water) and proliferating habitat degradations that preclude anything but capital-intensive modes of agricultural production have likewise resulted from the wholesale commodification of nature in all its forms. The commodification (through tourism) of cultural forms, histories, and intellectual creativity entails wholesale dispossessions (the music industry is notorious for the appropriation and exploitation of grassroots culture and creativity). As in the past, the power of the state is frequently used to force such processes through even against popular will. The rolling back of regulatory frameworks designed to protect labor and the environment from degradation has entailed the loss of rights. The reversion of common property rights won through years of hard class struggle (the right to a state pension, to welfare, to national health care) into the private domain has been one of the most egregious of all policies of dispossession pursued in the name of neoliberal orthodoxy.

The corporatization, commodification, and privatization of hitherto public assets have been signal features of the neoliberal project.

All of these processes amount to the transfer of assets from the public and popular realms to the private and class-privileged domains. Privatization, Arundhati Roy argued with respect to the Indian case, entails "the transfer of productive public assets from the state to private companies. Productive assets include natural resources: earth, forest, water, air. These are the assets that the state holds in trust for the people it represents. . . . To snatch these away and sell them as stock to private companies is a process of barbaric dispossession on a scale that has no parallel in history."[16]

2. Financialization

The strong financial wave that set in after 1980 has been marked by its speculative and predatory style. The total daily turnover of financial transactions in international markets that stood at $2.3 billion in 1983 had risen to $130 billion by 2001. This $40 trillion annual turnover in 2001 compares to the estimated $800 billion that would be required to support international trade and productive investment flows.[17] Deregulation allowed the financial system to become one of the main centers of redistributive activity through speculation, predation, fraud, and thievery. Stock promotions; Ponzi schemes; structured asset destruction through inflation; asset stripping through mergers and acquisitions; and the promotion of debt incumbency that reduced whole populations, even in the advanced capitalist countries, to debt peonage—to say nothing of corporate fraud and dispossession of assets, such as the raiding of pension funds and their decimation by stock and corporate collapses through credit and stock manipulations—are all features of the capitalist financial system.

The emphasis on stock values, which arose after bringing together the interests of owners and managers of capital through the remuneration of the latter in stock options, led, as we now know, to manipulations in the market that created immense wealth for a few at the expense of the many. The spectacular collapse of Enron was emblematic of a general process that deprived many of their livelihoods and pension rights. Beyond this, we also must look at the speculative raiding carried out by hedge funds and other major instruments of finance capital that formed the real cutting edge of accumulation by dispossession on the global stage, even as they supposedly conferred the positive benefit to the capitalist class of "spreading risks."

3. The management and manipulation of crises

Beyond the speculative and often fraudulent froth that characterizes much of neoliberal financial manipulation, there lies a deeper process that entails the springing of the debt trap as a primary means of accumulation by dispossession. Crisis creation, management, and manipulation on the world stage has evolved into the fine art of deliberative redistribution of wealth from poor countries to the rich. By suddenly raising interest rates in 1979, Paul Volcker, then chairman of the U.S. Federal Reserve, raised the proportion of foreign earnings that borrowing countries had to put to debt-interest payments. Forced into bankruptcy, countries like Mexico had to agree to structural adjustment. While proclaiming its role as a noble leader organizing bailouts to keep global capital accumulation stable and on track, the United States could also open the way to pillage the Mexican economy through deployment of its superior financial power under conditions of local crisis. This was what the U.S. Treasury/Wall Street/IMF complex became expert at doing everywhere. Volker's successor, Alan Greenspan, resorted to similar tactics several times in the 1990s. Debt crises in individual countries, uncommon in the 1960s, became frequent during the 1980s and 1990s. Hardly any developing country remained untouched and in some cases, as in Latin America, such crises were frequent enough to be considered endemic. These debt crises were orchestrated, managed, and controlled both to rationalize the system and to redistribute assets during the 1980s and 1990s. Wade and Veneroso captured the essence of this trend when they wrote of the Asian crisis—provoked initially by the operation of U.S.-based hedge funds—of 1997 and 1998:

> Financial crises have always caused transfers of ownership and power to those who keep their own assets intact and who are in a position to create credit, and the Asian crisis is no exception . . . there is no doubt that Western and Japanese corporations are the big winners. . . . The combination of massive devaluations pushed financial liberalization, and IMF-facilitated recovery may even precipitate the biggest peacetime transfer of assets from domestic to foreign owners in the past fifty years anywhere in the world, dwarfing the transfers from domestic to U.S. owners in Latin America in the 1980s or in Mexico after 1994. One recalls the statement attributed to Andrew Mellon: "In a depression assets return to their rightful owners."[18]

The analogy to the deliberate creation of unemployment to produce a pool of low-wage surplus labor convenient for further accumulation is precise. Valuable assets are thrown out of use and lose their value. They lie fallow and dormant until capitalists possessed of liquidity choose to seize upon them and breathe new life into them. The danger, however, is that crises can spin out of control and become generalized, or that revolts will arise against the system that creates them. One of the prime functions of state interventions and of international institutions is to orchestrate crises and devaluations in ways that permit accumulation by dispossession to occur without sparking a general collapse or popular revolt. The structural adjustment program administered by the Wall Street/Treasury/ IMF complex takes care of the first function. It is the job of the comprador neoliberal state apparatus (backed by military assistance from the imperial powers) to ensure that insurrections do not occur in whichever country has been raided. Yet signs of popular revolt have emerged, first with the Zapatista uprising in Mexico in 1994 and later in the generalized discontent that informed antiglobalization movements such as the one that culminated in Seattle in 1999.

4. State redistributions

The state, once transformed into a neoliberal set of institutions, becomes a prime agent of redistributive policies, reversing the flow from upper to lower classes that had been implemented during the preceding social democratic era. It does this in the first instance through privatization schemes and cutbacks in government expenditures meant to support the social wage. Even when privatization appears as beneficial to the lower classes, the long-term effects can be negative. At first blush, for example, Thatcher's program for the privatization of social housing in Britain appeared as a gift to the lower classes whose members could now convert from rental to ownership at a relatively low cost, gain control over a valuable asset, and augment their wealth. But once the transfer was accomplished, housing speculation took over particularly in prime central locations, eventually bribing or forcing low-income populations out to the periphery in cities like London and turning erstwhile working-class housing estates into centers of intense gentrification. The loss of affordable housing in central areas produced homelessness for many and extraordinarily long commutes for those who did have low-paying service jobs. The privatization of the *ejidos* (indigenous common property rights in land under the Mexican constitution) in Mexico, which became a central component of the neoliberal program set up during the 1990s, has had analogous effects on the Mexican peasantry, forcing many rural dwellers into the cities in search of employment. The Chinese state has taken a whole series of draconian measures through which assets have been conferred upon a small elite to the detriment of the masses.

The neoliberal state also seeks redistributions through a variety of other means such as revisions in the tax code to benefit returns on investment rather than incomes and wages, promotion of regressive elements in the tax code (such as sales taxes), displacement of state expenditures and free access to all by user fees (e.g., on higher education), and the provision of a vast array of subsidies and tax breaks to corporations. The welfare programs that now exist in the United States at federal, state, and local levels amount to a vast redirection of public moneys for corporate benefit (directly as in the case of subsidies to agribusiness and indirectly as in the case of the military-industrial sector), in much the same way that the mortgage interest rate tax deduction operates in the United States as a massive subsidy to upper-income home owners and the construction of industry. Heightened surveillance and policing and, in the case of the United States, the incarceration of recalcitrant elements in the population indicate a more sinister role of intense social control. In developing countries, where opposition to neoliberalism and accumulation by dispossession can be stronger, the role of the neoliberal state quickly assumes that of active repression even to the point of low-level warfare against oppositional movements (many of which can now conveniently be designated as terrorist to garner U.S. military assistance and support) such as the Zapatistas in Mexico or landless peasants in Brazil.

In effect, reported Roy, "India's rural economy, which supports seven hundred million people, is being garroted. Farmers who produce too much are in distress, farmers who produce too little are in distress, and landless agricultural laborers are out of work as big estates and farms lay off their workers. They're all flocking to the cities in search of employment."[19] In China, the estimate is that at least half a billion people will have to be absorbed by urbanization over the next ten years if rural mayhem and revolt is to be avoided. What those migrants will do in the cities remains unclear, though the vast physical infrastructural plans now in the works will go some way to absorbing the labor surpluses released by primitive accumulation.

The redistributive tactics of neoliberalism are wide-ranging, sophisticated, frequently masked by ideological gambits, but devastating for the dignity and social well-being of vulnerable populations and territories. The wave of creative destruction neoliberalization has visited across the globe is unparalleled in the history of capitalism. Understandably, it has spawned resistance and a search for viable alternatives.

Alternatives

Neoliberalism has spawned a swath of oppositional movements both within and outside of its compass, many of which are radically different from the worker-based movements that dominated before 1980. I say many but not all. Traditional worker-based movements are by no means dead even in the advanced capitalist countries where they have been much weakened by the neoliberal onslaught. In South Korea and South Africa, vigorous labor movements arose during the 1980s, and in much of Latin America working-class parties are flourishing. In Indonesia, a putative labor movement of great potential importance is struggling to be heard. The potential for labor unrest in China is immense though unpredictable.

And it is not clear either that the mass of the working class in the United States, which has over this past generation consistently voted against its own material interests for reasons of cultural nationalism, religion, and opposition to multiple social movements, will forever stay locked into such a politics by the machinations of Republicans and Democrats alike. There is no reason to rule out the resurgence of worker-based politics with a strongly antineoliberal agenda in future years.

But struggles against accumulation by dispossession are fomenting quite different lines of social and political struggle. Partly because of the distinctive conditions that give rise to such movements, their political orientation and modes of organization depart markedly from those typical in social democratic politics. The Zapatista rebellion, for example, did not seek to take over state power or accomplish a political revolution. It sought instead a more inclusive politics to work through the whole of civil society in an open and fluid search for alternatives that would consider the specific needs of different social groups and allow them to improve their lot. Organizationally, it tended to avoid avant-gardism and refused to take on the form of a political party. It preferred instead to remain a social movement within the state, attempting to form a political power bloc in which indigenous cultures would be central rather than peripheral. It sought thereby to accomplish something akin to a passive revolution within the territorial logic of state power.

The effect of such movements has been to shift the terrain of political organization away from traditional political parties and labor organizing into a less focused political dynamic of social action across the whole spectrum of civil society. But what they lost in focus they gained in relevance. They drew their strengths from embeddedness in the nitty-gritty of daily life and struggle but in so doing often found it hard to extract themselves from the local and the particular to understand the macro-politics of what neoliberal accumulation by dispossession was and is all about. The variety of such struggles was and is simply stunning. It is hard to even imagine connections between them. They were and are all part of a volatile mix of protest movements that swept the world and increasingly grabbed the headlines during and after the 1980s.[20] Those movements and revolts were sometimes crushed with ferocious violence, for the most part by state powers acting in the name of order and stability. Elsewhere they produced interethnic violence and civil wars as accumulation by dispossession produced intense social and political rivalries in a world dominated by divide and rule tactics on the part of capitalist forces. Client states supported militarily or in some instances with special forces trained by major military powers (led by the United States with Britain and France playing a minor role) took the lead in a system of repressions and liquidations to ruthlessly check activist movements challenging accumulation by dispossession.

The movements themselves have produced an abundance of ideas regarding alternatives. Some seek to de-link wholly or partially from the overwhelming powers of neoliberalism and neoconservatism. Others seek global social and environmental justice by reform or dissolution of powerful institutions such as the

IMF, the WTO, and the World Bank. Still others emphasize a reclaiming of the commons, thereby signaling deep continuities with struggles of long ago as well as with struggles waged throughout the bitter history of colonialism and imperialism. Some envisage a multitude in motion, or a movement within global civil society, to confront the dispersed and de-centered powers of the neoliberal order, while others more modestly look to local experiments with new production and consumption systems animated by different kinds of social relations and ecological practices. There are also those who put their faith in more conventional political party structures with the aim of gaining state power as one step toward global reform of the economic order. Many of these diverse currents now come together at the World Social Forum in an attempt to define their shared mission and build an organizational structure capable of confronting the many variants of neoliberalism and of neoconservatism. There is much here to admire and to inspire.[21]

Though it has been effectively disguised, we have lived through a whole generation of sophisticated class struggle on the part of the upper strata to restore or, as in China and Russia, construct class dominance.

But what sorts of conclusions can be derived from an analysis of the sort here constructed? To begin with, the whole history of the social democratic compromise and the subsequent turn to neoliberalism indicates the crucial role played by class struggle in either checking or restoring class power. Though it has been effectively disguised, we have lived through a whole generation of sophisticated class struggle on the part of the upper strata to restore or, as in China and Russia, construct class dominance. This occurred in decades when many progressives were theoretically persuaded that class was a meaningless category and when those institutions from which struggle had hitherto been waged on behalf of the working classes were under fierce assault. The first lesson we must learn, therefore, is that if it looks like class struggle and acts like class struggle, then we have to name it for what it is. The mass of the population has either to resign itself to the historical and geographical trajectory defined by this overwhelming class power or respond to it in class terms.

To put it this way is not to wax nostalgic for some lost golden age when the proletariat was in motion. Nor does it necessarily mean (if it ever should have) that we can appeal to some simple conception of the proletariat as the primary (let alone exclusive) agent of historical transformation. There is no proletarian field of utopian Marxian fantasy to which we can call. To point to the necessity and inevitability of class struggle is not to say that the way class is constituted is determined or even determinable in advance. Class movements make themselves, though not under conditions of their own choosing. And analysis shows that those conditions are currently bifurcated into movements around expanded reproduction—in which the exploitation of wage labor and conditions defining the social wage are central issues—and movements around accumulation by dispossession—in which everything from classic forms of primitive accumulation through practices destructive of cultures, histories, and environments to the depredations wrought by the contemporary forms of finance capital are the focus of resistance. Finding the organic link between these different class currents is an urgent theoretical and practical task. Analysis also shows that this has to occur in an historical-geographical trajectory of capital accumulation that is based in increasing connectivity across space and time but marked by deepening uneven geographical developments. This unevenness must be understood as something actively produced and sustained by processes of capital accumulation, no matter how important the signs may be of residuals of past configurations set up in the cultural landscape and the social world.

Analysis also points up exploitable contradictions within the neoliberal agenda. The gap between rhetoric (for the benefit of all) and realization (for the benefit of a small ruling class) increases over space and time, and social movements have done much to focus on that gap. The idea that the market is about fair competition is increasingly negated by the facts of extraordinary monopoly, centralization, and internationalization on the part of corporate and financial powers. The startling increase in class and regional inequalities both within states (such as China, Russia, India, Mexico, and in Southern Africa) as well as internationally poses a serious political problem that can no longer be swept under the rug as something transitional on the way to a perfected neoliberal world. The neoliberal emphasis upon individual rights and the increasingly authoritarian use of state power to sustain the system become a flashpoint of contentiousness. The more neoliberalism is recognized as a failed if not disingenuous and utopian project masking the restoration of class power, the more it lays the basis for a resurgence of mass movements voicing egalitarian political demands, seeking economic justice, fair trade, and greater economic security and democratization.

But it is the profoundly antidemocratic nature of neoliberalism that should surely be the main focus of political struggle. Institutions with enormous leverage, like the Federal Reserve, are outside any democratic control. Internationally, the lack of elementary accountability let alone democratic control over institutions such as the IMF, the WTO, and the World Bank, to say nothing of the great private power of financial institutions, makes a mockery of any credible concern about democratization. To bring back demands for democratic governance and for economic, political, and cultural equality and justice is not to suggest some return to a golden past since the meanings in each instance have to be reinvented to deal with contemporary conditions and potentialities. The meaning of democracy in ancient Athens has little to do with the meanings we must invest it with today in circumstances as diverse as Sao Paulo, Johannesburg, Shanghai, Manila, San Francisco, Leeds, Stockholm, and Lagos. But right across the globe, from China, Brazil, Argentina, Taiwan, and Korea to South Africa, Iran, India, and Egypt, and beyond the struggling nations of Eastern Europe into the heartlands of contemporary capitalism, groups and social movements are rallying to reforms expressive of democratic values. That is a key point of many of the struggles now emerging.

The more clearly oppositional movements recognize that their central objective must be to confront the class power that has been so effectively restored under neoliberalization, the more they will be likely to cohere. Tearing aside the neoliberal mask and exposing its seductive rhetoric, used so aptly to justify and legitimate the restoration of that power, has a significant role to play in contemporary struggles. It took neoliberals many years to set up and accomplish their march through the institutions of contemporary capitalism. We can expect no less of a struggle when pushing in the opposite direction.

Notes

1. See the Web site http://www.montpelerin.org/mpsabout.cfm.

2. G. W. Bush, "Securing Freedom's Triumph," *New York Times*, September 11, 2002, p. A33. *The National Security Strategy of the United State of America* can be found on the Web site www.whitehouse.gov nsc/nss. See also G. W. Bush, "President Addresses the Nation in Prime Time Press Conference," April 13, 2004, http://www.whitehouse.gov/news/releases/2004/0420040413-20.html.

3. Matthew Arnold is cited in Robin Williams, *Culture and Society, 1780-1850* (London: Chatto and Windus, 1958), 118.

4. Antonia Juhasz, "Ambitions of Empire: The Bush Administration Economic Plan for Iraq (and Beyond)," *Left Turn Magazine* 12 (February/March 2004): 27-32.

5. Thomas Crampton, "Iraqi Official Urges Caution on Imposing Free Market," *New York Times*, October 14, 2003, p. C5.

6. Juan Gabriel Valdez, *Pinochet's Economists: The Chicago School in Chile* (New York: Cambridge University Press, 1995).

7. Philip Armstrong, Andre Glynn, and John Harrison, *Capitalism since World War II: The Making and Breaking of the Long Boom* (Oxford, UK: Basil Blackwell, 1991).

8. Gerard Dumenil and Dominique Levy, "Neoliberal Dynamics: A New Phase?" (Manuscript, 2004), 4. See also Task Force on Inequality and American Democracy, *American Democracy in an Age of Rising Inequality* (Washington, DC: American Political Science Association, 2004), 3.

9. Daniel Yergin and Joseph Stanislaw, *The Commanding Heights: The Battle between Government and Marketplace That Is Remaking the Modern World* (New York: Simon & Schuster, 1998).

10. Thomas Byrne Edsall, *The New Politics of Inequality* (New York: Norton, 1984); Jamie Court, *Corporateering: How Corporate Power Steals Your Personal Freedom* (New York: Tarcher Putnam, 2003); and Thomas Frank, *What's the Matter with Kansas: How Conservatives Won the Heart of America* (New York, Metropolitan Books, 2004).

11. William K. Tabb, *The Long Default: New York City and the Urban Fiscal Crisis* (New York, Monthly Review Press, 1982); and Roger E. Alcaly and David Mermelstein, *The Fiscal Crisis of American Cities* (New York, Vintage, 1977).

12. Joseph Stiglitz, *Globalization and Its Discontents* (New York: Norton, 2002).

13. David Harvey, *The New Imperialism* (Oxford, Oxford University Press, 2003).

14. World Commission on the Social Dimension of Globalization, *A Fair Globalization: Creating Opportunities for All* (Geneva, Switzerland: International Labor Office, 2004).

15. Harvey, *The New Imperialism*, chap. 4.

16. Arundhati Roy, *Power Politics* (Cambridge, MA: South End Press, 2001).

17. Peter Dicken, *Global Shift: Reshaping the Global Economic Map in the 21st Century*, 4th ed. (New York: Guilford, 2003), chap. 13.

18. Robert Wade and Frank Veneroso, "The Asian Crisis: The High Debt Model versus the Wall Street-Treasury-IMF Complex," *New Left Review* 228 (1998): 3-23.

19. Roy, *Power Politics*.

20. Barry K. Gills, ed., *Globalization and the Politics of Resistance* (New York: Palgrave, 2001); Ton Mertes, ed., *A Movement of Movements* (London: Verso, 2004); Walden Bello, *Deglobalization: Ideas for a New World Economy* (London: Zed Books, 2002); Ponna Wignaraja, ed., *New Social Movements in the South: Empowering the People* (London: Zed Books, 1993); and Jeremy Brecher, Tim Costello, and Brendan Smith, *Globalization from Below: The Power of Solidarity* (Cambridge, MA: South End Press, 2000).

21. Mertes, *A Movement of Movements*; and Walden Bello, *Deglobalization: Ideas for a New World Economy* (London, Zed Books, 2002).

This article investigates the causes behind the limited success of neoliberal economic policies in the Iberian world. In addition to Latin America, the author includes Portugal, Spain, and the Philippines in the analysis. The author argues that, in the absence of strong liberal states able to enforce the rule of law, economic liberalization has failed, expanding inequalities rather than bequeathing prosperity. The article gives special attention to variations in the outcomes of liberalization that expose the limitations of cultural explanations.

Keywords: neoliberal policies; Iberian world; Latin American development; liberal state

Liberalism and the Good Society in the Iberian World

By
MIGUEL ANGEL CENTENO

Two basic questions motivate this article. The first and broadest concerns political and economic patterns of the Iberian world. Has the Iberian political economic legacy been an uninterrupted failure? If so, then the lessons for the twenty-first century are particularly important. I contend that the experiences of large parts of the Iberian world serve as a preview for outcomes in the twenty-first century. Nowhere else have the liberal ideas that dominate the current century been so assiduously (if incorrectly) applied. If liberalism has been a disappointment in what I am calling the Iberian world, then the prospects for a liberal global order are indeed bleak.

But of course, no history of such a large number of societies and people can be understood as a unilinear process, nor can we expect not to find variations over such a huge land mass. This article is also meant to address a surprisingly popular perspective on Latin America and other parts of the Iberian world that focuses on the legacy of the Black Legend.[1] According to that outlook, the supposedly universal problems

Miguel Angel Centeno is a professor of sociology and international affairs at Princeton University. He is working on two projects: Mapping Globalization *and* The Victory of the Market and the Failure of Liberalism in Latin America.

DOI: 10.1177/0002716206297173

in these countries stem from cultural traditions inherited through the Spanish Conquest. Iberian culture is seen as inimical to both market economics and electoral politics, because a combination of authoritarian centralism and what one may call the "anti-Protestant" ethic doomed those parts of the world ruled by Spain beginning in the sixteenth century. Anecdotal correlations would seem to support such theories, and the rise of the East Asian miracles (with the relevant exception of the Philippines) over the past three decades has only made it even more of the conventional wisdom. This article analyzes commonalities, as well as variations, within the Iberian world, thereby testing the validity of this form of cultural determinism.

The second subject of this article—and the larger project of which it is part—is an exploration of how classical liberalism has been applied in the Iberian world. I begin by noting the dominance of liberalism not only in Latin America but also in large parts of the world at two critical moments: the first wave of contemporary globalization in the late nineteenth century and the second wave beginning in the 1980s. Because Iberian liberalism was not an isolated instance, the cases analyzed can tell us a great deal not just about the continent, but the manner in which liberalism functioned outside of its birthplaces in Northwestern Europe and North America. As electoral democracy and market economics become more and more the only legitimate systems inside a global system, their adaptability and relevance to specific countries become particularly significant. Whether read as a cautionary tale or as a primer, this article will assist us in navigating the political economy of the new liberal world order.

The relationship between the political economic performance of the Iberian world and the application of liberalism is the theme that connects the various parts of this article and the larger project of which it is a part. Specifically I wish to explore the causal links between ideology and outcomes. To what extent did Latin America "fail" liberalism?—a common if implicit theme in much of the cultural-centric literature. To what extent was it the misguided application of an ideology that resulted in the frustrations of the continent? No simple causal order is assumed or argued; rather, I am interested in how the realities on the ground and the aspirations from above came together to produce contemporary results.

It is critical to begin with an appreciation for the historical and geographical variance we find in the political economy of the Iberian world. In the nineteenth century, observers within and outside Latin America became enamored of the "failed continent" perspective using the United States as the preferred counterfactual example. Similarly, Spain and Portugal were seen as some of the "sickest men" in Europe. In the twentieth century, similar unflattering comparisons have taken place, and now East Asia and some cases of Eastern Europe have appeared as preferred alternatives. The understandable habit of aggregating the experience of Latin America—and less so that of the Philippines and the Iberian Peninsula—has obscured potentially significant differences in how countries performed, both across time and in relation to one another. In Latin America the relative success of Chile, for instance, during both periods in question, merits attention. The failure of Argentina to live up to its early promise is another. The continuing failure of the Philippines deserves comparison with other cases in Latin America. Finally, the great success of the Spanish and Portuguese transitions to electoral democracy and market economics in the last quarter of the twentieth century is striking, especially given their position relative to Latin America in 1975.

These variations imply that the homogeneous cultural argument does not provide an adequate explanation for any empirically confirmed political and economic "underperformance" that we may establish as part of the "Iberian" legacy. Despite their continuing appeal, cultural explanations for political economic outcomes can explain neither variances within the same culture nor historical shifts in performance. The very same values that hold Mexicans "back" seem to disappear in entrepreneurial zeal in the United States; what cultural legacies do Chile or Southern Brazil enjoy that Venezuela does not? How do we explain Spain's voyage from "sickest man" in Europe to miracle?

Despite their continuing appeal, cultural explanations for political economic outcomes can explain neither variances within the same culture nor historical shifts in performance.

Much more feasible candidates for explaining the historical and geographical dispersion of performance are what we may call "institutional" legacies. Such a perspective shares with the culturalist school an appreciation for history (but not of the unchanging sort); it recognizes that the past does matter and has helped to shape the contemporary political economy of the region. But its historical view does not stop with "culture" or "worldviews." Rather, it seeks to analyze the social structures that may encourage, support, and maintain a set of behaviors. We are no longer dealing with predispositions or attitudes but rather measuring the extent to which actual human beings are behaving and the structures and institutions that encourage or prevent them from acting in particular ways. Rather than saying that someone does not wish to vote or disdains the market, we ask whether historical agents have ever seen elections matter, whether they have had opportunities to participate in the market, and whether established rules and procedures are adequate to ensure those agents will continue to behave in desirable ways.

The variations we find across countries and between historical periods are therefore nothing more complicated than the results in the sets of institutions required for the desired outcomes. Countries with more consistent economic success are assumed to have better functioning institutions that lead to these outcomes. But to simply assert this would be to engage in simplistic tautology. The question becomes why certain institutions arise in some places at some times. Using comparative methods, we can attempt to define which institutions appearing in which order are best suited for the political economic development we may wish to encourage.

My central argument is that the imposition of liberalism largely failed in the Iberian world precisely because the institutions assumed to exist by liberal dogma and that it requires for its efficient operation were not sufficiently well developed. *Specifically, the combination of high inequality and the lack of state capacity produced a social, economic, and political milieu antithetical to the assumptions of liberalism.*

Grafted onto this "different kind of wood," the structures of liberalism did not produce the desired results; instead they promoted societies both untenable and, in many cases, mired in historical inertia. The product of this combination may be most obvious in the underdevelopment in the Iberian world of the "rule of law"—the assumed universalistic and effective application of regulations. The absence of the rule of law is a constant theme in accounts of life in Latin America, from the massive travel literature of the early nineteenth century to contemporary accounts of urban life. The exceptions are few, but prominent. Chile's institutions and legal system were already recognized as exceptional in the nineteenth century. Spain and Portugal in the past thirty years have created not only much more equal societies and strong states but have also produced the political economic results expected by liberalism.

By Way of Definition

The Iberian world

What do I mean by the Iberian world? By that term I simply refer to the part of the globe that was colonized by Spain and Portugal in the sixteenth and seventeenth centuries. The empires included at least stations in every continent save Antarctica. Some have largely lost their Iberian connection (Macao, Goa), while others retain not only languages but a related set of ideological and religious symbols and values. I am interested in this broader setting as it allows us to go beyond the standard categories. Latin America is usually studied in isolation, while contemporary Portugal and Spain are more often compared to their pasts or to other Southern European societies. The Philippines is perhaps the most interesting inclusion as comparisons between it and Latin America are far too rare and may provide good avenues for comparisons to the East Asian countries. Finally, this broader set of cases will allow me to better address the question of a "cultural fit" by analyzing the variations that may exist within a single "legacy."

To explore this Iberian world and the application of liberalism, I have identified a series of cases to be analyzed by the larger project. I am dividing the "liberal era" into two waves: the first beginning immediately after nineteenth-century independence and largely disappearing after the early twentieth century, and a second wave begun in the 1970s and continuing today (see Table 1).

TABLE 1
CASES CONSIDERED

	First Wave	Second Wave
Spain	1812-1923: Critical problems include government fragility, regional divisions, and frustrated development.	1976-2005: Successful creation of welfare state supported by increasing equality, integration into international economy.
Portugal	1821-1932: Slow development and fragile government with particular costs of open trade.	1974-2005: Successful creation of democracy but continuing economic problems.
Philippines	1907-1942 and 1946-1972: Extremely limited sovereignty during first period and government fragility and corruption in second. Some economic growth.	1986-2005: Democratic but very fragile regime, some growth but little social development. Increasingly behind Asian Tigers.
Mexico	1855-1884: Some success in establishing central and democratic rule as well as some economic development, but persistent inequality.	1994-2005: Beginning with NAFTA increasing liberalization and some economic development, but problems with order and inequality remain.
Central America	Federation 1825-1838, Guatemala 1840-1885, Salvador 1871-1914, Nicaragua 1893-1909, Costa Rica 1870-1889, Honduras 1876-1914: Insertion into global economy and formal liberal ideals with massive exclusion.	Costa Rica 1948-2005, rest post-1990: Limited democratization in some cases, some economic success, still great deal of inequality and poverty.
Chile	1881-1938: Resolution of conflicts from first fifty years of independence. Increasing national integration and successful social and economic policy.	1989-2005: Arguably most successful implementation of Neoliberal reform.
Argentina	1861-1930: Successful integration into global economy and competitive democracy, but increasing social conflicts.	1983-2005: Consolidation of democratic practices, but increasing inequality and fragile economic model.
Brazil	1889-1930: Consolidation of national bourgeoisie. Regional divisions and inequality.	1985-2005: Consolidation of democratic reforms and significant growth, but continued social inequities and problems of order.

The good society

To judge the performance of a region, we need to establish some parameters. What is a good society?[2] What models of it exist that we can compare with the Iberian world? My answer to that question is anachronistically liberal because the examples I am using preceded the writings that were to form the liberal canon, but they do originate in that time and place that may represent the birth of the liberal ideal: Renaissance Italy. It is in this period that we find the virtues of ancient republicanism meeting the aspirations of contemporary liberalism: a good government will create the environment in which individuals can flourish in a secular world.

From mid-fourteenth-century Siena, we have inherited a nearly perfect allegory of what a good society might look like. Painted by Ambrogio Lorenzetti in 1338-1340, the frescoes on the "Effects of Good and Bad Government" nicely illustrate the aspirations of a liberal (or if one wishes, a liberal-republican) state. In these paintings we see that a good society must include wealth, order, and citizenship. The first is illustrated by the many representations of economic well-being found in both the city and countryside associated with virtuous government. The people are well fed, the fields are verdant, and the city is not only in respectable shape but clearly growing. Order produces peace, and both are enjoyed in such a fortunate milieu. Peasants can venture beyond the city wall without needing protection; rich and humble meet without tension on the streets. Worthy services—such as the instruction taking place in a classroom at the center of Lorenzetti's painting—are freely offered. Finally, notions of citizenship are implied in the apparent equality of those depicted in the painting. This is not a portrayal of the rich where the poor and marginal are mere background. At the center of the painting are representatives from various classes and their spacing and positions imply civil equality.

What is most interesting for our purposes is the clear mixing of the liberal ideals of a high-quality life with the republican emphasis on good government. First, while we see signs of market activity, Lorenzetti's frescoes are in the city hall of Siena—not the main market but the seat of government. They explicitly state that to have a good society, you must have moral leaders, and part of the room in which the murals are housed includes an image of upright governance in the form of an allegorical representation that includes classical virtues. We also observe an inclusive if altogether masculine parade of citizens. What is most striking is the rope that binds government to justice *through* the people and their representatives. By contrast, bad government depends on tyranny, which wraps justice in a cocoon and surrounds itself with avarice and vanity. Bad government has its consequences as well. In the corresponding fresco, the rich fields are now brown and no one is working them. The city infrastructure is fragile and falling apart, businesses are in disrepair, and, most important, violence haunts the streets.

In large parts of the Iberian world, such allegories of the good and bad government have been part of the public debate for the past two hundred years. As we will see in subsequent sections, only some societies have been able to achieve first-class governments. The question is, Why those and not others?

Liberalism

An answer to that question from a culturalist perspective brings us back to notions of virtue. According to outlooks that privilege mores and values, Iberians did not deserve the good society because their traditions were not suited to support it. More pragmatic observers have also recognized the historical limitations of the Iberian world, but asked what manner of government could best provide the desired results. The answer for most of Latin America's history and certainly for the past thirty years has been liberalism. Many contemporary observers, in fact, see the continent's and the general Iberian world's failures as stemming from the frustrated imposition of liberalism. Our next task is to provide a definition of what we mean by the liberal model.

Liberalism (or some version of it) is, in many ways, the political equivalent of a Judeo-Christian ethic in Western culture. Broad enough to encompass considerable disagreements, it still embodies the values of the "West" over the past five hundred years. We can separate the central tenets of liberalism into those having to do with behavioral assumptions and those dealing with institutional expectations.

With regards to the first, liberalism is based on the primacy of the individual and the rights thereof over and above any collective claims. When liberalism looks beyond single individuals, it is largely concerned with articulating and defending the social interactions between them, each seeking their own purposes. Liberalism does assume cognitive rationality, not necessarily in its extreme microeconomic form but as a guiding principle for social analysis. As revolutionary as its elevation of the individual is liberalism's rejection of the perfectibility of humans. The same individuals who are held to be the center of all things are also seen as potentially opportunistic. The central problem of liberalism is to secure individual freedom while also allowing social interaction in a world of possible malfeasance. How does one create order from the various desires and acts of individuals who cannot always be counted upon to be virtuous?

The solution for liberalism is mutual dependence through specialization. We interact with each other not as some expression of species, but because we want something from one another. In its most basic form, we need what each produces or has specialized access to. Property in this vision is not only an expression and extension of the self, but that which allows us to participate in basic forms of social interaction. As I cannot depend on myself for all things, I will find it necessary to deal with others. To improve my ability to do so, I will also seek to specialize in the production of some service or good that I can provide at the highest possible price or return to my investment. This process of constant specialization creates a world of mutual interdependence. The solution to the possible dangers and problems associated with this dependence is a world of contracts.

Contracts are assortments of rules by which we manage our interactions and ensure order and control. The role of the state is essentially to serve as a guarantor of these contracts through a variety of enforcement mechanisms. States serve to assure that we can engage in contracts with some certainty that opportunistic behavior will not lead us to too much harm. To ensure this role, it is critical that the state not represent only the interests of one group or another. Only by serving as an "honest broker" can the state both do its job effectively and protect its legitimacy. At the very core of a liberal state, then, is the notion of the "rule of law" as the basic glue allowing social interaction to take place.

This set of behavioral assumptions requires—implicitly and sometimes explicitly—a set of institutional arrangements. The first and most obvious is that individuals must be free to "truck and barter" to all extents possible. Not only is this a basis of individual freedom, but it allows the critical process of interaction and mutual dependence to work its social magic. Similarly, democratic participation provides some control over the state as a guarantor. Democracy at its simplest level merely applies market logic to political decisions. It not only allows for the free choice by individuals but also the sort of mutual dependence on each others' acceptance of rules that Liberalism considers the foundation of social life.

For this democratic system to function and to properly adjudicate over market interactions, it must include all relevant individuals and provide each of them with a putatively equal stake in the system. Only in this way can they be assured that their participation in it is worthwhile, and only in this way can you have an effective state ensuring the participation of all. But the most important institutional apparatus on which liberalism depends is the rule of law. Only with this assurance of fairness and universality can the hegemony of contract relations establish the felicitous combination of peace and plenty that liberalism promises.

Liberalism and the nation-state

Given the critical role through which the state underpins the institutional bases of liberalism, it is surprising to see over the past half century how much this doctrine and political power have come to be seen as antagonistic. This is especially surprising because the record shows that the advent of liberalism as a fully fledged doctrine parallels the rise of the state—both share ideological and historical paths. There is the familiar case of Hobbes and his Leviathan, but even better accepted progenitors such as Locke accept the significance of the state as a guarantor of proper market interactions. The oft-noted dichotomy between "Republicanism" and "Liberalism" obscures the reality that the state is very much to be found in the liberal canon.

It is no accident that both liberalism as a doctrine and the state as a political institution arose simultaneously. In a variety of ways they are dependent on each other and one makes the other one possible. On one hand, liberalism provides the state with a role above and beyond more contentious debates over virtues and values. Liberalism allows for the state to grow as something of an empty chalice, vacant of religious and ideological contention. In the same vein, if the contemporary state has any civic religion that unites its various parts, one could argue that it is liberalism and its notion of contract enforcement. As I have argued above, the state provides the institutional mechanism that liberalism requires for its smooth functioning. It is impossible to imagine a system of contracts in which price and value are divorced from status and where commercial relations are paramount without a system with which to assure the appropriate application of law. To paraphrase Barrington Moore: no state, no liberalism.

Liberalism also relies on the nation-state to balance the recognized economic inequalities that would result from the market with a politically based equality based on citizenship. From the very beginning, liberal authors recognized there would be a permanent social tension regarding the distribution of resources, no longer legitimated by outdated religious or feudal notions. Those authors stated

FIGURE 1
ASSUMPTIONS OF LIBERALISM I

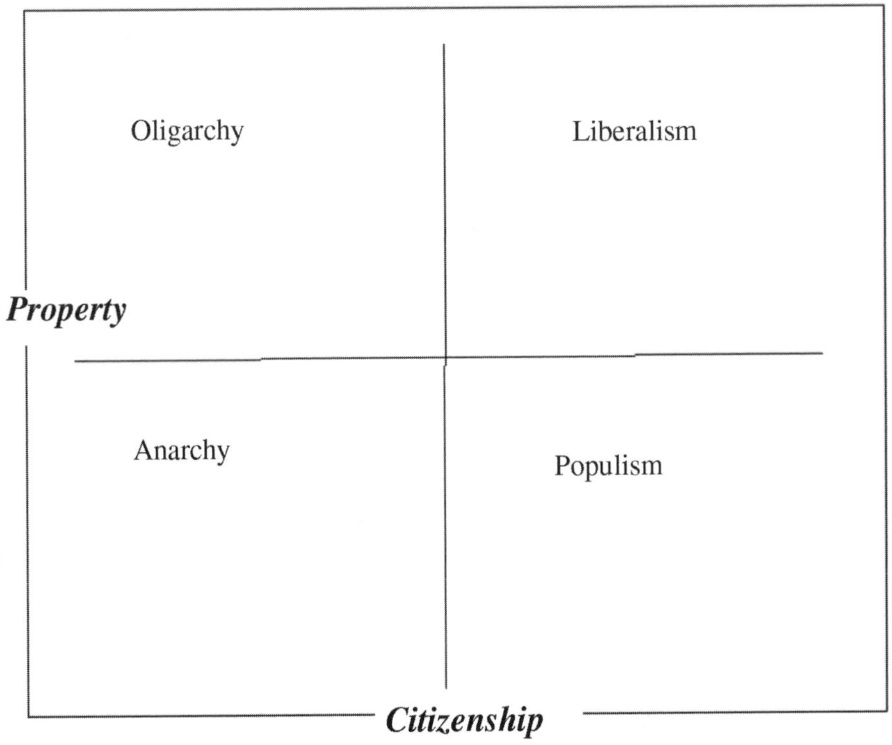

Oligarchy	Liberalism
Property	
Anarchy	Populism
	Citizenship

that the theoretical equality of citizenship and opportunity—again, dependent on and reinforcing each other—would serve to control the avarice of those with much while also serving to legitimate the system to those with little. By the last half of the nineteenth century, what we could call "national liberalism" sought to resolve the Polanyian "double movement" by allowing market forces while also channeling social responses to the market. Liberalism created mechanisms through which some social and political opposition—or better yet, safeguards—against the market could be established.

The importance of the state to the functioning of liberalism may be appreciated by noting two critical assumptions underpinning such a system. First, as noted above, liberalism assumes that the equality of citizenship will counteract and, if need be, control the inequality of resources. Liberalism can only function if there is some kind of systematic balance between representation and avarice. Consider a two-by-two space where we can define four possible combinations of property rights and citizenship rights (see Figure 1). Too much power on one or the other leads to anarchy, oligarchy, or populist demagoguery. One needs a strong state to ensure that both property and citizenship are properly respected and protected.

FIGURE 2
ASSUMPTIONS OF LIBERALISM II

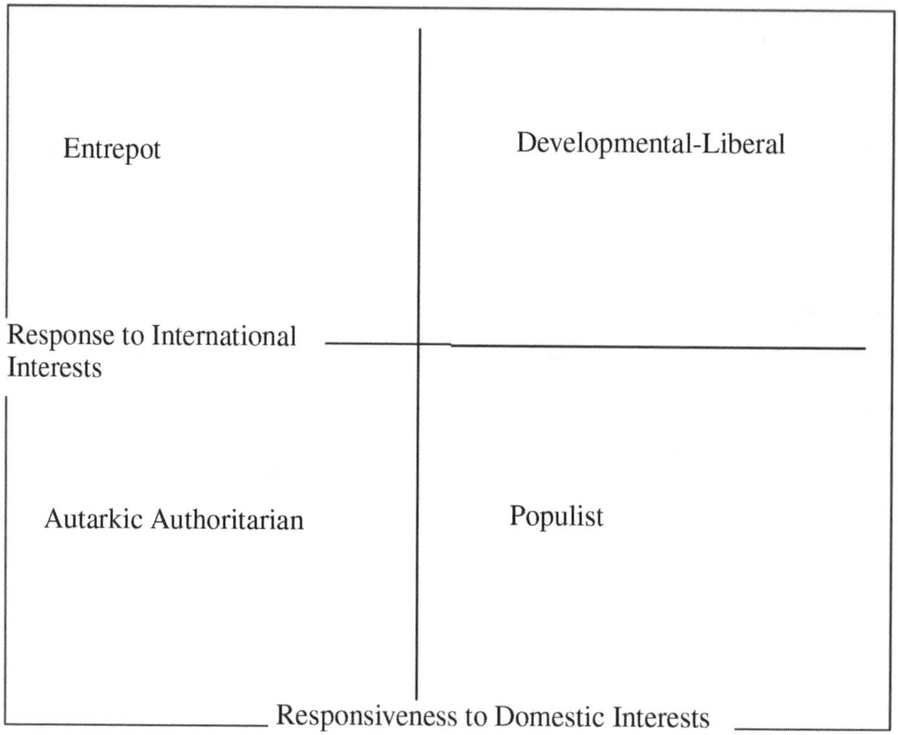

In the second example, consider the state's position within an international set-ting (Figure 2). If citizenship and property as recognized by the state are to mean anything, the state must have the capacity to secure such rights in an international arena. It not only has to protect its citizens from each other's possible opportunistic behavior but also from claims made from outside the system. At the same time, the state must also allow for the integration of those citizens and property holders into that global system. This requires a balancing of domestic and international interests.

Iberian Liberalism

Armed with a general notion of liberalism, to what extent can we say that such an outlook has been applied in Latin America and the rest of the Iberian world? Was liberalism the dominant school of thought at critical moments in the devel-opment of the contemporary Iberian world?

Not only did many prominent elites and regimes explicitly call themselves liberal for large parts of the nineteenth century, but the core ideas advocated by such groups

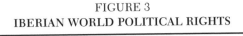

FIGURE 3
IBERIAN WORLD POLITICAL RIGHTS

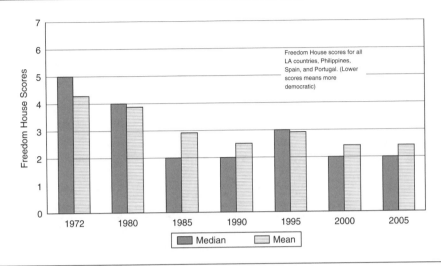

and governments reflected the basic tenets of liberalism discussed above. There are, of course, specific characteristics in the application and language used in each country, and one of the tasks of the larger project in which this article belongs is to explore the reasons for such an intellectual variation. But enough of an ideological kernel exists so that we can identify a cohesive world view in the region during this period.

The willingness of more recent adherents of the liberal worldview to call themselves by that name has been more limited. The very term "neoliberal" is usually used in a pejorative sense by those who oppose contemporary policies in Latin America. But in their beliefs about the centrality of the market, the legitimacy of elections, the significance of property, and guardedness of state power, many of these policy makers and thinkers share the goals and assumptions of their nineteenth-century predecessors. For the purposes of this article, I will concentrate on the performance of the Iberian world during the past quarter century. An analysis of the preceding stage will receive its appropriate attention in a future work.

Beginning in the 1970s the classic tenets of liberalism—politics by election and economics by markets—became increasingly accepted throughout the Iberian world. The victory of electoral democracy was clear by the 1980s and the imposition of market friendly policies became obvious after 1990 (Figures 3 and 4).

If we consider that liberalism requires the combination of market activity and political rights, a large part of the Iberian world (with the prominent outlier of Cuba) was within the "liberal" zone.[3]

Why was liberalism such a powerful intellectual force in the Iberian world? This is an important question to ask now as liberalism appears to have won the great ideological debate that raged through most of the twentieth century. Winners tend to assume that their victory was inevitable. The appeal of post facto

FIGURE 4
MARKETS AND ELECTIONS IN IBERIAN WORLD, AVERAGE, 1995-2005

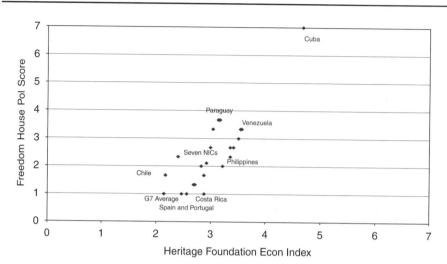

NOTE: Pol Sc = political freedom score; G7 = Group of Seven; NIC = newly industrializing countries.

functionalism is considerable, and it is understandable why those looking back may consider that history was on *their* side. Such an attitude seems to pervade among sympathizers of market economics throughout the globe, particularly in Latin America and Eastern Europe. That markets should and would win the ideological battle is often seen as a natural process.

In the case of Latin America, the appeal of liberalism needs to be judged on the basis of the "welfare return" of policies based on that outlook. There is no doubt that democratization has improved human rights. There is much less evidence, however, for the "return" of liberalism to the economic arena. Spain, Portugal, and Chile have been economic successes, but the extent to which those successes are the effect of specific policies is questionable. In other cases, there is no clear evidence that national economies are doing better thanks to liberalism. The "lumping" that we see in Figure 5 indicates that much broader and contextualized factors have important roles to play in determining outcomes. I would suggest that these forces may both advance Liberal agendas and growth and that the relationship between the latter two may well be spurious.

The repeated victory of liberalism in the Iberian world may have much to do with the validity of its ideas and concepts. It is critical to understand the precise mechanism by which ideas are channeled and imposed, no matter how good or bad they may be. In the case of liberalism, we can identify several critical strains worthy of attention.

First, there is a generation of thinkers who come to their "liberalism" through the very same processes occurring in other parts of the world. As people of their age, they adopted the leading theories bandied about in the wake of the Enlightenment

FIGURE 5
LIBERALISM AND ECONOMIC GROWTH

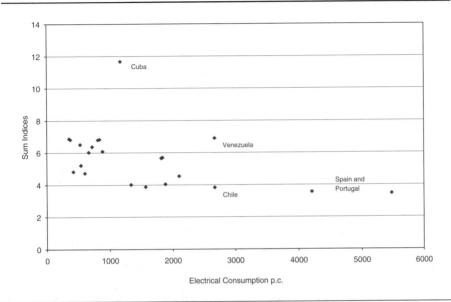

SOURCE: Freedom House, Heritage Foundation, United States Agency for International Development (USAID).

and the Age of Revolution. Partly for that generation but certainly for the one that followed, the appeal of liberalism was also fueled by the success of the United Sates and especially the perceived contrast with the fortunes of Latin America.

Nevertheless, more instrumental political and economic interests should not be neglected. In their crudest form, aspects of liberalism were imposed by a combination of domestic elites and external powers for which a property-centric ideology was not only appealing but also convenient. Liberalism was the outlook of the global markets that Iberian countries wished to entice. Here ideological isomorphism had less to do with the intellectual appeal or value of a set of ideas and more with the strategic needs to propose alternatives that would find favor with those whom one had to please.[4]

Liberalism was the outlook of the global markets that Iberian countries wished to entice.

This process of "coercive isomorphism" was particularly pronounced in the case of access to capital. Beginning in 1973, massive amounts of global lending allowed almost all countries later to have neoliberal policies to borrow beyond their wildest dreams. From Mexico to Poland and from Hungary to Indonesia, governments went on a prolonged borrowing binge. For a wide set of social, political, and economic reasons, countries needed foreign exchange. Given limited export capacity, financial institutions were their only source of "ready money." Yet such assets were unavailable unless the same countries could maintain their viability as international debtors. In part, this involved paying back some of the debt. But as amounts became astronomical, the actual payment became less important than providing banks and other relevant institutions with a reasonable case that the fulfilment of obligations would occur at an unspecified future time. Leading international banks were only too ready to play this game, which required countries to adopt the behaviors and polices of responsible international actors. As long as they were judged accountable—that is, as long as they were seen as moving toward a neoliberal alternative, they would be rewarded with more loans. The very imposition of these policies often made exit from such bargains difficult. As countries opened their markets to satisfy the conditions of their continued access to international cash, they saw previous domestic suppliers of a variety of goods and services disappear. As they were replaced by imported goods, the need for steady sources of cash with which to pay for these new imports increased. Neoliberalism not only justified itself but also appeared to make its adoption irreversible. Beginning in the 1990s, access to assets was augmented by the development of new sources of cash through portfolio investments.

Did Liberalism Forge a "Good Society" in the Iberian World?

Considering the standards described earlier for a "good society" as well as the aspirations of many Latin American thinkers, the question is whether liberalism worked in the Iberian world. What were the effects of liberal policies?

In certain countries, liberalism had more time to produce results than in others, and one cannot hold it responsible—nor give it credit—for all failures and accomplishments. The first fact drawing attention involves the large variations found within the Iberian world. We can compare two aggregate measures of well-being: the Human Development Index (HDI) and overall wealth as measured through purchasing power parity (PPP). To standardize these measures, I have expressed them in terms of an index of the OECD average (Figure 6).[5]

The variation in HDI may seem relatively small, but this measure has a very low standard deviation. Thus, the real distance between Peru (at slightly more than 80 percent of the OECD standard) and Spain (at the OECD mean) is quite large and has significant consequences for daily life. The PPP measures give us a better sense of the differences in these societies, with Spain and Portugal having practically achieved parity with the wealthiest societies in the globe while the Philippines remain among the poorest.

An even better indicator of the current state of these countries is provided by measurements of poverty. Poverty in Spain and Portugal is of a completely different

FIGURE 6
WEALTH AND WELL-BEING

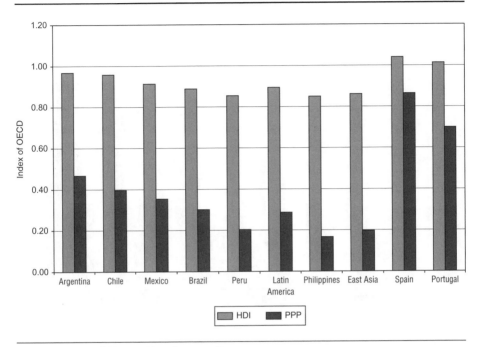

SOURCE: United Nations Development Program.
NOTE: HDI = Human Development Index; PPP = purchasing power parity.

magnitude than in the rest of the Iberian world. Among the poorer countries, we again find huge variations with Argentina and Chile on one end, the Philippines and Peru on the other, and Mexico and Brazil in the middle (Figure 7).

The same pattern may be observed if we use health or access to medical resources as a proxy for well-being (Figures 8 and 9).

The gap between Spain and Portugal and the other countries is also obvious if we use access to modern technology as a proxy (Figure 10).

One trend is clear and practically universal throughout large parts of the Iberian world: the erosion of the middle class. Given our definition of a good society, this is a damning fact. Liberalism has long been associated with the aspirations and expectations of the middle sectors. The assault on their social position does not speak well of the imposition of the doctrine in the Iberian world. During the 1980s, the second and third population quartiles saw dramatic declines in middle-class fortunes, in some cases with losses as high as 30 percent of their income.[6] Argentina is an extreme case illustrating the growth of what may be called the new poor. In 1970, only 3 percent of residents in Buenos Aires were poor; that number had increased to nearly 20 percent in 1990. In the past five years, the same process has accelerated with some sources indicating that up to half of the population of greater Buenos Aires may now be poor.

FIGURE 7
POVERTY

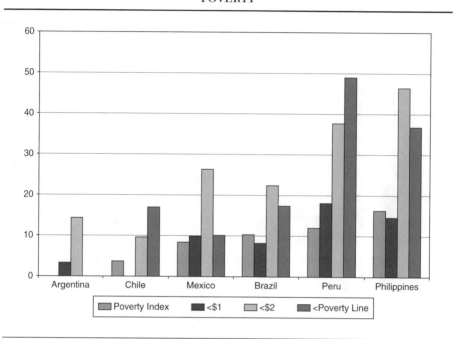

FIGURE 8
HEALTH INDICATORS

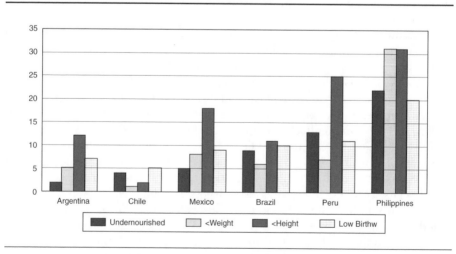

FIGURE 9
AVAILABILITY OF HEALTH PROFESSIONALS

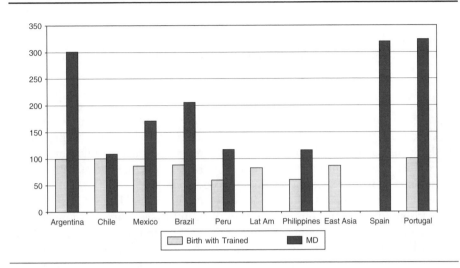

FIGURE 10
ACCESS TO MODERN TECHNOLOGY

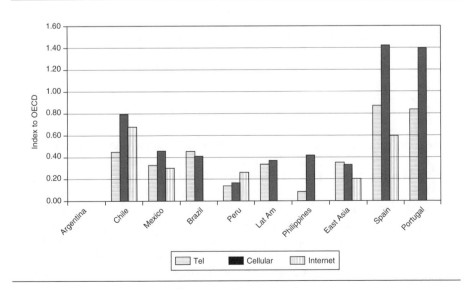

Overall, I would posit the imposition of liberal policies a qualified failure. The reason for this had nothing to do with cultural predispositions but with the contradictions between the assumptions of liberalism and the social, political, and economic reality on the ground in the Iberian world. Three critical conditions defined the Latin American experience with respect to liberalism: inequality, state incapacity, and external dependency. Below, I address each one in turn.

Inequality[7]

It has become almost a cliché to say that Latin America is the most unequal region on the planet. The Philippines exhibits comparable rates of inequality. While Spain and Portugal had until relatively recently similar profiles and resulting conflict, the past thirty years have seen a dramatic decline in disparities in the two countries. In this section I examine those variations.

Levels of inequality in Latin America defy description and belief. Cross-regional comparisons are difficult, but no other set of countries as defined by any possible criteria shares such distributional characteristics. The top 5 percent of the Latin American income ladder receives twice the comparable share of their OECD counterparts, while the bottom receives half of what they would in the same countries The past forty years have also witnessed very different dynamics of inequality in Latin America and the developing countries of East Asia. More significant for our discussion, Spain (and Portugal) have followed dissimilar patterns as well. Notice also the heterogenity within Latin America (Figures 11, 12, and 13).

The combination of poverty and inequality makes Latin America an island of a particular form of misery.

The combination of poverty and inequality makes Latin America an island of a particular form of misery. Latin Americans live worse than they need to—the correlation between the GDP and the United Nations Development Program's (UNDP's) Human Development Index declines when the Latin American countries are added to a sample, indicating that living standards are worse than the national incomes would predict. Evidence also indicates that a significant part of the deprivation for large parts of the population does not necessarily stem from poverty in and of itself, but from the consequences of radically asymmetrical distribution.

This maldistribution is not a new issue or the result of events occurring over the past few decades—although the evidence does indicate that neoliberal policies

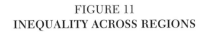

FIGURE 11
INEQUALITY ACROSS REGIONS

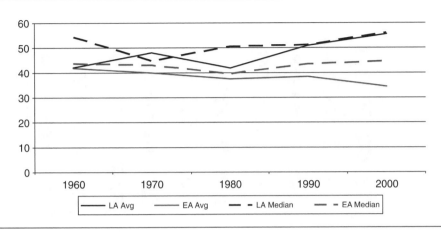

NOTE: LA = Latin America; EA = East Asia.

did contribute to the growth in disparities. Latin America historically had high rates of inequality, even during the postwar boom. From 1950 to 1970, industrialization and urbanization created some upward mobility for significant parts of the economically active population. Since the 1970s, however, every country, with the exception of Colombia in the 1980s and Mexico and Venezuela in the 1970s, experienced an increase in the concentration of income and wealth. The effects of the misdistribution were exacerbated by economic declines. For the region as a whole, per capita income dropped 10 to 11 percent during the 1980s. Figueroa spoke of a breakdown in the "distributive equilibrium" in Latin America with a subsequent disintegration of public life.[8] The data from the mid-1990s on the subject are sparse and difficult to analyze. At their most optimistic, studies indicate that the boom of the early 1990s reduced the levels of poverty in some (but not all) countries, while also producing greater inequality.

The past two decades have also seen what one analyst has called a regressive bias in policy making. Combined with a financial crunch begun with the debt crisis of 1982, these pressures have eliminated the state as a leveler of last recourse. There remains an intense debate regarding the role of neoliberal policies in the development of inequality in Latin America.

State incapacity[9]

Recent scholarship has established that it took an inordinately long time to establish a legitimate social and political order in large parts of the Iberian world. Even after the project of state building succeeded, many countries suffered through cycles

FIGURE 12
INEQUALITY WITHIN THE IBERIAN WORLD

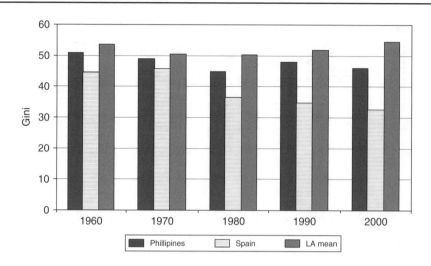

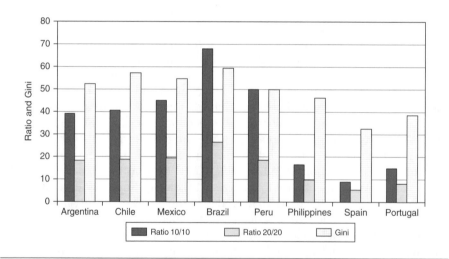

of revolt and deinstitutionalization. Over the past two hundred years, the rule of law has been consistently frustrated in Latin America and the Philippines. I argue that the absence of such a legitimate order made the balance between political and economic power mediated through the law impossible in the region.

The problems emerged at the very outset of the sovereign life of the countries included in the Iberian world. Their independence struggles shredded the legal

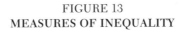

FIGURE 13
MEASURES OF INEQUALITY

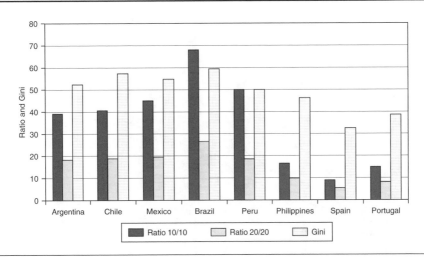

fabric of the *ancien regime* without bequeathing the means to create alternative legal structures. Liberals applied free market dogmas without inscribing an underlying juridical order capable of legitimizing public authority. The first stage of Latin American liberalism was unable to resolve the difficult contradictions between its two central tenets, an emphasis on individual liberty and the creation of state strong enough to humble any corporate groups that threatened individual liberty.

At the same time that it weakened the hold of authority on society, Republicanism discharged massive mobilization among subaltern sectors. Constitutional discord was more than a clash of ideas among revolutionary leaders to guide liberal communities into statehood; it was also the context for class, ethnic, and racial struggles over the meaning of community. Simón Bolívar complained,

> The majority of the people have been led astray by religious fanaticism and reduced by the allurements of a devouring monarchy. To the torch of liberty, which we have offered to America as the guide and object of our efforts, our enemies have applied the incendiary brand of discord, of devastation, and the strong enticement of usurped honors and fortunes for men who have been debased by the yoke of servitude and reduced to brutishness by the doctrine of superstition.[10]

Similarly, Juan Bautista Alberdi, reflecting on the failures of the 1820s, once noted that "in the first cries of triumph, (liberals) forgot a word that is less sonorous than *liberty*, but which represents a counterweight which keeps liberty afoot: *order*."[11]

FIGURE 14
RAILROADS

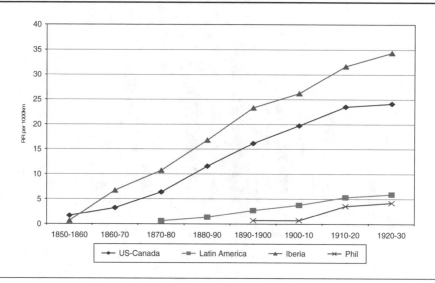

The frustrations of the early liberal state throughout the Iberian world may be observed by measures of governing capacity. One apt indicator is the ability of the state to conduct a decent national census. While the United States could hold its first population count by 1790, most of Latin America (with the exception of Chile) had to wait until quite late in the nineteenth century or even the early twentieth to obtain such basic information. The construction of infrastructure is another basic measure of state capacity. The figures that follow indicate that the Iberian World was far behind the North American republics in providing basic services. While some of the gap may be explained by differences in national wealth, the distance between the North American successes and the others is striking (Figures 14, 15, and 16).[12]

One could easily interpret the years between our two waves of liberalism as the "golden age" of the Latin American state. Although never fully institutional-ized by Weberian criteria, during the period roughly spanning the First World War and the oil crisis of 1973, the Latin American state created and fortified many of the basic institutions associated with political power. It also encroached into the economic sphere much more than its predecessors. Partly as a result of this and how these policies were perceived, an effort began in the mid-1970s to roll the state back out.

The assault on the state along with the accompanying "lost decade" of economic disaster led to a new stage of deinstitutionalization across Latin America, similar in many forms to the chaos of the postindependence years. The two archetypal cases

FIGURE 15
TELEGRAMS

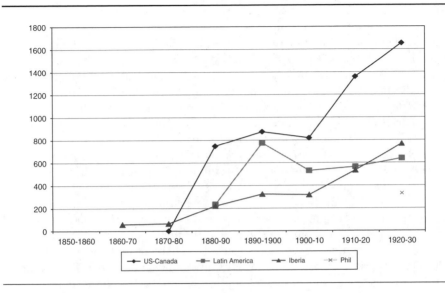

FIGURE 16
POSTAL SERVICE

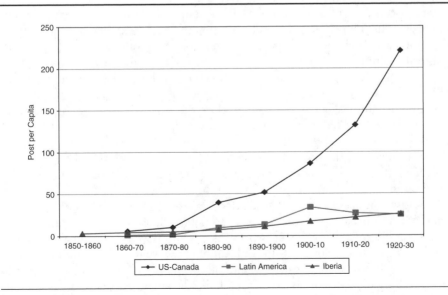

may be Colombia and Peru. In both countries, faced with a challenge to its monopoly over the means of violence, the state buckled. In Colombia it literally ceased to rule in parts of the country, while in Peru the ability of the state to provide even basic services in the capital came under assault. Argentina's collapse in 2001 and 2002 is yet another illustration of the fragility of order in the Iberian political landscape, but the trend was not just the outcome of isolated violent attacks.

Deregulation, privatization, and internationalization of domestic markets have not eradicated rent-seeking habits; nor have they put regional economies on track to sustained growth. The combination of market economics and liberal rule, far from delivering on their upbeat prophecies, has usually resulted in polarized extremes: social upheaval against market rules or praetorian brutality. In Latin America, the pattern of market allocation of resources and legal equality of political subjects was not a harmonious, self-reinforcing combination (in the idealized versions of what transpired in North America), but an explosive one.

The vast majority of Iberian states in the 1990s and in the twenty-first century shared the same problems as their predecessors. For one, they had neither the fiscal resources nor the organization to manage the challenges facing them. Overall, Latin American countries have less than half of the taxing capacity of the OECD averages (as measured by taxes as a percentage of GDP). The weakness of the state has led not only to the lack of provision of basic welfare goods but also to a skewed burden on taxes. The lack of resources helps explain the almost universal low quality of government services throughout the region. Evans and Rauch's work on comparative bureaucracy clearly indicates that Latin American countries are uniformly below the norm in their "Weberian" scale.[13]

The weakness of the state has led to a boom in the informal economy. Following Tilly's conception of the state as a protection racket,[14] the informal economy consists of transactions where the state neither provides protection nor receives a cut. The relationship between the informal economy and the state by definition is one of unending conflict. The whole point of the state is to assert its authority within a territory, but the whole point of the informal economy is not to have anything to do with formal authority. Thus, all things being equal, there is a close relationship between state strength and the development of an informal economy. An informal economy will develop when and where it can, but an economy only needs to be informal to the extent that it has to be. The relationship between the state and the informal economy is thus cyclically causal and negatively correlated to the power of the state. The weaker the state is, the greater the likelihood that many economic transactions will escape its grasp. The more ambitious the state, the more cause for escape there is.

Dysfunctions are the institutional effects of a contradiction between the state's willingness to make rules and its ability to police. Such dysfunctions arise when there is a discrepancy between two forms of state power—a despotic state can produce many regulations but it is only an effective state that can enforce them. The gap between nominal capacity and failure in implementation begets a frustrated state seeking to influence public life but lacking the resources to match its ambitions. In such cases, states have claimed primacy and an expanded scope of public interference. Yet these same states have often been unable to provide the guarantees and services required for those rights to be accepted and defended.

Over the past two decades, frustrated states have witnessed the expansion of crime in every Latin American city. Police response has been vicious and closely correlated to income: the São Paolo police killed 1,470 civilians in 1992 as compared to 25 killed by the Los Angeles Police Department. The violence of everyday life spans a wide variety of forms. In 1991, violence was the leading cause of death among adult, working-class Latin Americans. Security forces have been overwhelmed in most urban centers. In Argentina alone, the total recorded crime per 100,000 has increased nearly fifty-fold (fifty!) in the past twenty years; in Uruguay it has nearly doubled.

These phenomena indicate the failure of the rule of law. Liberal theory presupposes the existence of a legal framework capable of enforcing rights and obligations flowing from private and public entitlements. Much of Latin America's turmoil can be traced back to the incapacity of the state to enforce laws. Rather than a bedrock for markets and democracy, Latin American legality is a quicksand of rent-seeking and contestation. Reformers rushed to emancipate markets without attention to the institutional life that enable them to function. Bereft of public rules, wealth-seeking behavior often mutated into private rent-seeking; in turn, market activity aggravated social inequalities.

Global marginality and dependency

As discussed above, the notion of citizenship is critical to liberalism. Citizenship must be a valuable good, but what if a state cannot deliver? What if decisions are made or approval sought externally? The dependence of most of the Iberian nations on external forces rests on three legs: global marginality, migration, and remittances.

The first term points to the subordination of the Iberian world in the global economy and its reliance on asymmetrical relationships with one or more metroples for its financial and infrastructural needs. Mexico may be an extreme example in that it depends on a single country, the United States, for more than two-thirds of its international trade. Less obvious is the dependence of Mexico on the same country for many of its transportation and infrastructural needs. Central America is in a similar situation. Despite the increasing importance of China in its trade over the past few years, Latin American countries are tied to the United States in ways that curtail their autonomy. Venezuela is particularly interesting given Hugo Chavez's recent rhetorical attacks. While it is true that the United States depends on Venezuela for a significant portion of its oil imports, these could be replaced for higher prices in the short term. Venezuela, on the other hand, relies much more heavily on the United States for its sales. Moreover, the lower quality of Venezuelan oil would make difficult its sale and processing on a non-U.S. open market. In other words, if Venezuela and the United States were to have an international equivalent of the Fight at the OK Corral, the American gun would be much larger.

Such a dependence on external markets is even more pronounced in the financial arena. While intra-American investment is increasing, Latin America largely still depends on a global financial market skewed to the United Sates. The possibility of an investment strike organized through an American response to Latin American policies would be disastrous to the continent.

Global marginality and dependence mean that in the balance between the satisfaction of domestic and international interests—which for liberal citizenship to work must at least be neutral or favored toward domestic constituencies—is skewed toward external powers. In determining how to respond to internal challenges or demands, every Iberian state, with the possible exception of Spain and Portugal, has to consider international—and, especially, North American—responses.

For individuals, the critical significance of migration for survival and prosperity makes national citizenship less valuable as well. Consider the facts:

- Between 1980 and 1990, more than 3 million working immigrants from Latin America entered the United States. In 1990 to 2000, the numbers were larger than 6 million.
- An estimated 11 million Mexican citizens are currently residing in the United States.
- There are more than 1.5 million immigrants from Latin America in the European Union.
- More than 8 million Filipinos reside and work in other countries.

For many of these people—and maybe for the majority—the rights they may claim as citizens of their home country pale in relation to the benefits they derive from residence and employment in a different nation. The authorities that can make or break their lives are not ones for which they vote, and they, in turn, may not even recognize the claims their citizenry might make. This means that people compete in a liberal economic world with its accompanying uncertainty, but do not enjoy lives in a parallel liberal political sphere that provides protection.

The last leg of the dependency structure has to do with remittances. This is a product of migration and marginality as discussed above. Many of the relevant countries have become dependent on cash inflows sent from abroad by those who migrate abroad seeking opportunity. The numbers are staggering: according to the Inter American Development Bank, in 2005 they totaled $53.6 billion to Latin America alone, with Mexico receiving $20 billion. The Philippines received $10.7 billion that same year. In these countries, remittances have become as important a source of economic vitality as more traditional forms of foreign direct investment.

Exploring the Exceptions

To the pattern of failure sketched above, it is necessary to contrast three cases that, in the second phase of liberalism, were able to create the good society as defined earlier in this article: Chile, Spain, and Portugal. How do we account for these exceptional outcomes?

We can identify four critical elements behind the success of those countries: The first is a massive reduction in abject levels of poverty. This has been partly a product of economic growth but also of declining levels of inequality *and* the provision of some government-funded public welfare. The second critical element has been the creation of institutional capacity on the part of the state that has allowed for the establishment of a legitimate and credible rule of law. The third element is the resolution of foundational social tensions. It may not be accidental that those three societies are relatively homogeneous in racial terms and that the preexisting conflicts were along class lines—a fact thus resolvable through economic development. The final factor of critical importance in the two European cases has been external support accompanied by pressure to make the liberal hope and commitment a political reality. These themes are the subject of future work.

Conclusion: No State, No Citizens, No Market

Pulling the state out of the market, and even public activity, without putting into place a legitimate system to hold rulers and ruled accountable to the same norms, has had perverse consequences in the Iberian world. It is one thing to dismantle state intervention in Western Europe or North America where the history of liberalism has bequeathed a deeply embedded rule of law, and where deregulation and privatization do not necessarily imperil civic equalities inscribed in legal rules and procedures. Even the harsh reforms imposed by Margaret Thatcher allowed market forces to work in England without destroying its institutional base. Another thing is to free markets in environments where there was never an opportunity to strengthen liberal political structures. Liberalization on its own does not stabilize or protect property rights although it transfers ownership from the public domain and places more collective decision making in private hands. In the end, the troubles with the rule of law in Latin America beg large contextual and historical questions. Latin America suggests a need for legal and social reform, not just technocratic solutions.

In the absence of strong liberal states, we witness the failure of neoliberalism in most Iberian countries: wealth without well-being, governments without laws, markets without contracts, and citizens without rights.

Notes

1. See Howard J. Wiarda, *Politics and Social Change in Latin America: Still a Distinct Tradition?* (Boulder, CO: Westview, 1992); Claudio Véliz, *The Centralist Tradition of Latin America* (Princeton, NJ: Princeton University Press, 1980); and Lawrence E. Harrison and Samuel P. Huntington, *Culture Matters: How Values Shape Human Progress* (New York: Basic Books, 2001).

2. See Wolfgang Drechsler, *Good and Bad Government: Ambrogio Lorenzetti's Frescoes* (Budapest, Hungary: Open Society Institute, 2001).

3. Scores lower than 3 on Freedom House Political Index and Heritage Foundation economic freedom Index. For comparison, I provide the scores for the Group of Seven (G7) countries as well as seven strategic newly industrializing countries (NICs) (Czech Republic, Korea, Poland, Thailand, South Africa, India, and Turkey). See also Joseph Cohen and Miguel Centeno in "Neoliberalism and Patterns of Economic Performance, 1980-2000," *Annals of the American Academy of Political and Social Science* 606 (2006): 32-67.

4. See Miguel Centeno, "Isomorphic Liberalism and the Creation of Inevitability," in *Globalization and Uncertainty in Latin America*, ed. Diane Johnson and Fernando López-Alves (New York: Palgrave, forthcoming).

5. Unless otherwise specified, sources for charts are the United Nations Development Program (UNDP) and the United States Agency for International Development (USAID).

6. Alberto Minujin, "Squeezed: The Middleclass in Latin America," *Environment and Urbanization* 7, no. 2 (1995): 153-66.

7. See Miguel Centeno and Kelly Hoffman, "Inequality in Latin America," *Annual Review of Sociology* 29 (2003).

8. Adolfo Figueroa, "The Distributive Issue in Latin America," *International Social Science Journal* 148 (June 1996): 231-44.

9. For an initial discussion, see Miguel Centeno and Jeremy Adelman, "Between Liberalism and Neo-liberalism: Law's Dilemma in Latin America," in *Global Prescriptions: The Production, Exportation, and Importation of a New Legal Orthodoxy*, ed. Bryant Garth and Yves Dezalay (Ann Arbor: University of Michigan Press, 2002).

10. Simón Bolívar, "Manifesto to the People of Venezuela, September 7, 1814," in *Selected Writings of Bolivar*, ed. Harold A. Bierck Jr. (New York: Colonial Press, 1951), 63.

11. Juan Bautista Alberdi, "La republica Argentina," in *Obras completas* (Buenos Aires, Argentina: Imprenta de la Tribuna, 1886).

12. For these I used B. R. Mitchell, *International Historical Statistics: The Americas, 1750-1993* (London: Macmillan Reference; New York: Stockton Press, 1998).

13. Meter B. Evans and James Rauch, "Bureaucratic Structure and Bureaucratic Performance in Less Developed Countries," *Journal of Public Economics* 75 (January 2000): 49-71.

14. Charles Tilly, "War Making and State Making as Organizational Crime," in *Bringing the State Back In*, ed. Peter Evans, Dietrich Rueschemeyer, and Theda Skocpol (Cambridge: Cambridge University Press, 1985).

Migration, Development, and Segmented Assimilation: A Conceptual Review of the Evidence

ALEJANDRO PORTES

This article first gives attention to the ongoing debate about the role of remittances on development. The author presents evidence showing that monetary transfers can induce economic vitality but also expand inequalities in countries of origin. Second, the author examines a phenomenon given little attention until now: the extent to which policies aimed at curtailing unauthorized immigration to the United States are promoting instead the permanent immigration and settlement of vulnerable workers and their families, thus increasing the likelihood that some of their children will respond to hostility and limited opportunity through downward assimilation. When deported, those youngsters transfer deviant styles of life learned abroad to their home communities. International migration has thus become a key element in the study of development.

Keywords: migration; downward mobility; segmented assimilation; remittances

The development model adopted in the immense majority of labor-exporting American countries has not generated opportunities for growth nor economic or social development. On the contrary, it has meant the emergence of regressive dynamics: unemployment and job precarization; greater social inequalities; loss of qualified workers; productive disarticulation and stagnation; inflation and greater economic dependency. As a consequence, we experience a convergence between depopulation and the abandonment of productive activities in areas of high emigration.

Declaracion de Cuernavaca, May 2005

One important reason for the pessimism that characterizes most community studies is the lack

Alejandro Portes is a professor of sociology and director of the Center for Migration and Development at Princeton University. He has written extensively on international development and international migration. His most recent books are Immigrant America: A Portrait, *3rd ed. (with R. G. Rumbaut; University of California Press, 2006) and* Repensando Las Migraciones *(Spanish) (with Josh DeWind; Porrua Editores, 2006).*

DOI: 10.1177/0002716206296779

of a good theoretical yardstick to measure the effects of migration on economic growth. Village studies universally confuse consumption with the non-productive use of remittances, ignoring the extensive and potentially large economic linkages that remittances create in local economies. They also tend to confound remittances use with the effect of remittances on family expenditures; and many studies employ a rather limited definition of "productive investments," restricting them to investments in equipment while ignoring productive spending on livestock, schooling, housing, and land.

Massey et al. (1998, 262)

Migration and remittances are the true economic adjustment programs of the poor in our country.

Carlos Guillermo Ramos, Salvadoran sociologist (2002)

How do we reconcile these seemingly contradictory statements? The study of international migration and development has been wracked by the controversy between perspectives that see the outflow of people not only as a symptom of underdevelopment but also as a cause of its perpetuation, and those that regard migration both as a short-term safety valve and as a potential long-term instrument for sustained growth. The disjuncture also has disciplinary overtones, with sociologists and anthropologists most often found in the pessimistic camp, and economists, especially neoclassical ones and those guided by the "new economics" of migration, supporting a much more optimistic assessment.

To seek a possible reconciliation between these contrary positions, we may consider, first of all, certain assumptions and conclusions about the consequences of migration that seem to be agreed upon by proponents of all perspectives:

- The move abroad is economically beneficial for most migrants and their families. Otherwise, they would not undertake the journey.
- The flow is welcomed and often demanded by employers in the receiving countries who need and may come to depend on migrant labor.
- The philanthropic contributions made by transnational migrant organizations help local communities and commonly provide them with services and infrastructure that otherwise they would not have.
- At the national level, remittances from major labor-exporting countries acquire "structural" importance as a key source of foreign exchange.

On the other hand,

- There is no known instance of remittances economically "developing" by themselves a labor-exporting country.
- Migrant investments in direct productive activities in their home countries have, at best, a modest effect on national economic growth.

NOTE: This article was first presented at the conference of "Migration and Development: Perspectives from the South," Bellagio Study and Conference Center, Italy, July 10-13, 2006. It was sponsored by the Rockefeller Foundation and the International Network on Migration and Development. The editors acknowledge and thank the INMD for its permission to publish this article.

- While the indirect multiplier effects of migrant remittances can be considerable, they are countermanded by the cumulative character of migration leading to depopulation of sending communities and regions.
- Migration may decelerate active efforts by sending country governments to promote autonomous national development, insofar as it provides a short-term solution to domestic unemployment and fiscal bottlenecks.

Less universally recognized, but backed by considerable empirical evidence are the following assertions:

- When migrants bring their families with them, the process of depopulation accelerates, as return migration becomes less probable.
- When labor migrants bring their families with them, they foster the growth in receiving countries of a second generation growing up in conditions of singular disadvantage.
- The downward assimilation experienced by second-generation youth reinforces negative stereotypes about the migrant population in receiving countries raising the probability of its conversion into an impoverished caste-like minority.

There are key factors leading to alternative outcomes of international migration. These have to do with the behavior of migrants themselves, the behavior of governments in sending and receiving nations, and the passage of time. The migrant population must be differentiated between the flow of manual low-skill labor and the movement of highly trained professionals and technical personnel. For brevity, the first flow will be referred to as labor migrants and the second as professional migrants. The behavior and conduct of both flows over time are different, although, as we shall see, their potential for national or local development depends on the same set of factors. I consider each of them in turn and conclude with an assessment of second-generation adaptation effects on both sending and receiving nations.

Labor Migrants, Networks, and Remittances

The origins of labor migration as well as the place of theories designed to explain them is by now well established. Neoclassical economic theory receives support from the universal wage differentials between labor-exporting and labor-receiving countries which, in the case of the Mexico-U.S. migratory system, is at present seven to one for unskilled labor. The limitations of this individualistic theory have also been made evident by the fact that this wage differential operates unevenly, leading to wide disparities in the timing and the size of labor migrant flows within the same country and even within the same region. In effect, the theory neglects the social context in which such individual calculations are made. This context accounts for the varying awareness of wage gaps in potential regions of out-migration, the meaning that these differentials have, and the availability of means to act upon them. Absent these elements, wage differentials, no matter how large, do not translate into sustained labor flows.

The most optimistic prognosis about the developmental effects of labor flows comes from the "new economics of migration," pioneered by Oded Stark and endorsed by, among others, Douglas S. Massey and J. Edward Taylor. This theory places emphasis on the concept of "relative deprivation" said to affect non-migrant families when they compare their situation with those that have migrants abroad. It also singles out the nonexistence or imperfection of credit, insurance, and futures markets in rural areas of sending countries. Migration is said to represent a form of self-insurance by rural families who use it as one of several strategies for economic survival.

The positive effects of migration come from its ability to compensate for market imperfections, enabling families to engage in productive activities. Even when remittances are spent in direct consumption, they are said to generate indirect multiplier effects because they create new demand for locally produced goods and services. Thus, according to Massey et al. (1998, 249), every additional "migradollar" sent to Mexico generates a $2.90 contribution to the country's gross national product.

While superior to the unrealistic neoclassical approach, the "new economics" perspective leaves open the question of how the early migrants who induce "relative deprivation" among their neighbors started their journey in the first place. Second, its optimistic assessment of the economic effects of migration is questionable when depopulation of the countryside makes it impossible to put migrants' remittances to productive use. In this sense, the "new economics" may be seen as a realistic but limited-range approach applicable under certain macroeconomic conditions, but not others.

At a higher level of abstraction, we find world systems and other neo-Marxist theories that view labor migration as a natural response to the penetration of weaker societies by the economic and political institutions of the developed world. The concept of "structural imbalancing" (Portes and Walton 1981) was introduced to highlight this process that takes multiple forms—from direct recruitment of workers to the diffusion of consumption expectations bearing little relation to local lifestyles and economic means.

Although it has been seldom noted, direct recruitment of peasants for work in ranches and farms of the American Southwest lies at the core of mass migration from Mexico to the United States (Barrera 1980). Once the flow was initiated by the actions of paid recruiters in the interior of Mexico in the nineteenth and early twentieth centuries, it became self-sustaining through the operation of the forces outlined by the new economics of migration model. Sentiments of relative deprivation were reinforced by the increasing capitalist penetration of the Mexican countryside that diffused new wants and consumption expectations among the mass of the population. As Delgado-Wise and Covarrubias (2006) noted, the process of structural imbalancing reached its culmination with the signing of the North American Free Trade Agreement (NAFTA), which, in effect, greatly reduced the autonomy of the Mexican state to implement national economic initiatives or protect domestic enterprise, turning the country instead into a giant labor reservoir for U.S. industry and agriculture.

As a historical concept, structural imbalancing in the center-periphery global system does not seek to account for the dynamics of migration from a particular locality or region but to provide the necessary framework to understand the broad forces that initiated and sustain the movement over time. It is within a context of extensive social and economic penetration of peripheral societies by the institutions of advanced capitalism that individual cost-benefit calculations or the emergence of relative deprivation as a motivator for out-migration make sense. In essence, migration resolves the inescapable contradiction between the undermining of local autonomy and the increasing diffusion of new consumption expectations in weaker nations without the parallel diffusion of the economic resources to attain them (Alba 1978; Sassen 1988).

Regardless of the various perspectives on the origins of labor migration, all contemporary scholarship converges on the concept of social networks as a key factor sustaining it over time (Portes and Bach 1985; Massey, Durand, and Malone 2002). Social networks not only link migrants with their kin and communities in sending countries; they also connect employers in receiving areas to migrants. These ties underlie the emergence of such phenomena as chain migration, long-distance referral systems to fill job vacancies, and the organization of a dependable flow of remittances back to sending communities. At later stages, they are also the key factor in the consolidation of transnational organizations that endow migrant populations with increasing voice in the affairs of their localities and even countries of origin (Guarnizo, Portes, and Haller 2003; Goldring 2002). Figure 1 presents, in schematic form, the dynamics of immigrant transnationalism as portrayed by recent empirical scholarship.

Social networks operate as a double-edged sword on the effects of migration on community and national development. They underlie the optimistic prognosis by researchers such as Stark and Massey concerning the resolution of local market deficiencies and other production bottlenecks as well as the onset of indirect multiplier effects of remittances. On the other hand, the progressive lowering of the costs of migration that networks make possible can lead, in the absence of countervailing forces, to severe depopulation of sending towns and regions. In the end, there would be few people to send remittances to and no productive apparatus to be reenergized by migrant investments or increased local demands. The cumulative effects of networks over time would lead, in these circumstances, to the desolate extremes portrayed by some ethnographic studies—ghost towns and "tinsel towns" adorned only for the return of migrants for the annual patronal festivities but populated otherwise only by the old and infirm (Reichert 1981; Grasmuck and Pessar 1991; Smith 2005). Already one-third of Mexican municipalities have experienced population loss, in varying measures, during the last intercensal period.

The operation of social networks over time hence lies at the core of contradictory accounts of the effects of labor migration on development. The next logical question is what kinds of networks lead to one outcome instead of the other or, alternatively, under what conditions they encourage sustained growth in places of origin versus demographic implosion. The answer to this question

FIGURE 1
THE PROCESS OF IMMIGRANT TRANSNATIONALISM

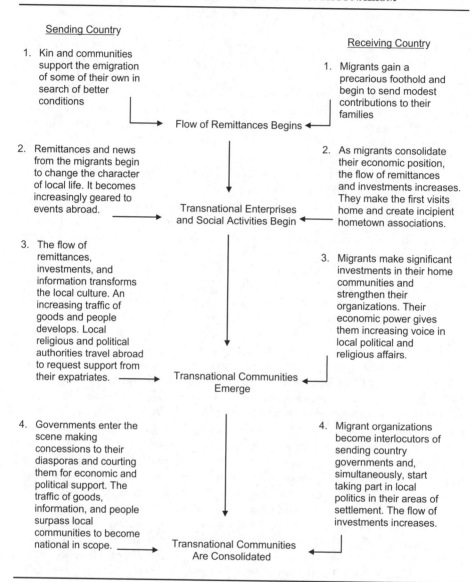

appears to hinge on two key factors: governmental intervention and the character of migration itself.

Effective governmental programs in the form of public works, subsidies and support for productive activities, and the direct launching of employment-creating enterprises can make a great deal of difference. By motivating productive-age adults to stay and work, they create the necessary sociodemographic infrastructure for migrant remittances and investments to be productively used. Even when some families choose to live off remittances, the demand for goods and services that they generate can be met by other working adults in the community—merchants, farmers, construction crews—thus generating the predicted spin-off effects.

More important still is the character of migration itself. When it is composed of young adults who travel abroad for temporary periods and return home after accumulating enough savings, the direct and indirect positive effects described previously have every chance to materialize. On the other hand, when it is formed by entire families, the cumulative depopulating effects of migration are much more likely. Entire families seldom return, and migrant workers have fewer incentives to send large remittances or make sizable investments in places of origin when their spouses and children no longer live there.

Entire families seldom return, and migrant workers have fewer incentives to send large remittances or make sizable investments in places of origin when their spouses and children no longer live there.

In a nutshell, *cyclical* labor migration can have positive developmental effects, especially at the community level. Permanent family migration does not, leading instead to the emptying of sending places. This is, according to all evidence, what has been happening in Mexico. The story of how progressive border enforcement by the United States did not stop the Mexican labor flow, but stopped its cyclical character, has been told in detail by Massey and his associates (Massey, Durand, and Malone 2002). The parallel story of how NAFTA hollowed out Mexican industry and severely weakened peasant farming through cheap food imports and capital-intensive mechanized agriculture has been told in similar detail by Delgado Wise and his associates (Delgado-Wise and Covarrubias 2006). The end of employment in a number of sectors of the Mexican economy and the severe reduction of opportunities for productive investment in the countryside have stimulated permanent family migration to the north, reinforcing the effects of a militarized border.

The Paris-based International Federation for Human Rights has recently produced a report on NAFTA that poignantly highlights the same issues:

> [As] a result of open borders, national manufacturing production capacity has been dismantled and the agricultural industry destroyed. The main beneficiaries of NAFTA are the big transnational companies, while the effects on employment and wages have been deeply detrimental to Mexican workers. The destruction of the agricultural industry has driven Mexican families to the urban areas where they now live on conditions of extreme poverty (*Latin America Weekly Report* 2006, 13).

One may add that the same conditions lead families to migrate north braving the desert and death if necessary. Once established on the other side of the border, there is little for these families to return to and, hence, the alleged positive effects of migration on development dissipate.

Under these difficult conditions, the only bright spot is the rise of transnational organizations created by migrants abroad. Existing research has shown that participation in these cross-border civic and philanthropic initiatives does not decline but actually grows with time because it is the better-established and more economically secure immigrants who have the means and the motivation to do something for their hometowns (Guarnizo, Portes, and Haller 2003; Portes 2003; Portes, Escobar, and Walton forthcoming).

In the case of Mexico, hundreds of *clubes de oriundos* (hometown committees) and dozens of federations of such committees organized according to the state of origin have emerged in recent years. They have acquired such power and visibility as to become interlocutors of Mexican state and federal authorities and to acquire a frequently decisive significance in the development prospects of their hometowns. Mexican governmental initiatives such as the creation of the Institute for Mexicans Abroad (IME is the Spanish acronym) and the launching of the *tres-por-uno* program where each dollar contributed by migrant organizations to philanthropic causes is matched by the Mexican federal, state, and municipal governments, emerged in response to the spontaneous organizational initiatives of migrant communities abroad (Gonzalez Gutierrez 1999; Instituto de los Mexicanos en el Exterior 2004).

Migrants' transnationalism can thus be understood as a form of grassroots response to the inequities and the economic difficulties that motivated their migration in the first place. It is a form of "globalization from below" that countermands, at least in a partial way, the inequality-deepening "globalization from above" promoted by the interests of corporate capitalism. It is in this context that one fully understands the implications of Carlos Ramos's (2002) remark, cited at the start of this article, that migration and remittances are the true economic adjustment program of the poor.

Professional Migration:
The Brain Drain and the Brain Gain

Demand for migrant labor in the developed world is not limited to labor-intensive industries and sectors. In the United States, in particular, sustained economic growth has led to a rising demand at the other end of the spectrum, that is, for professionals and technicians of high caliber. Technological booms like those giving rise to the Silicon Valley in California, Route 128 around Boston, and the Research Triangle Park in North Carolina have produced sustained demand for well-trained engineers and gifted programmers (Saxenian 1999, 2002; Alarcon 1999). In more traditional sectors, a perennial scarcity of nurses, general medical practitioners, and scientists in certain fields has been met by foreign-trained professionals (Portes 1976; Espenshade and Rodriguez 1997).

The U.S. Congress, recognizing this rising demand, created in 1990 the H-1B visa program under which highly skilled professionals could be hired for temporary work in the United States. The visa and work permits are issued for a maximum of three years, renewable for another three. In practice, many "H-1B workers" eventually shift their status to legal permanent residents. In 1990, the authorized ceiling for this program was 65,000. The American Competitiveness and Work Force Improvement Act of 1998 (ACWIA) increased that number to 115,000, and in 2002, it was further increased to 195,000. In 2003, 360,498 H-1B permits were issued to temporary workers with college degrees, of which approximately half were renewals. Principal specialty areas included computer science, engineering, and information technologies. The main national sources of this professional inflow in the same year were India (75,964), Canada (20,947), Mexico (16,290), China (12,501), and Colombia (10,268) (Office of Immigration Statistics 2004).

While occupational preferences continue to be a mainstay of the permanent immigration system of the United States and while thousands of foreign professionals come through this channel every year, there is little doubt that the H-1B program has become the primary source of "flexible" labor supply for the high-tech, highly skilled sectors of the U.S. economy. Table 1 presents additional information about the sources, education, and remuneration of H1-B migrant workers in recent years.

Dubbed "brain drain" in the sending countries, the determinants of these flows have been analyzed in terms similar to manual labor migration, and with the same theoretical lenses. The individualistic cost-benefit framework of neoclassical economics finds support in the fact that professional migration commonly originates in poor countries where the expected remunerations for professionals are but a fraction of what they can receive in the United States and other developed countries. The theory is contradicted, however, by the fact that it is midincome, not the poorest nations that are the major sources of professional migration and that, within these countries, there are great variations in the motivations and probability of migration. Regardless of home country conditions, most professionals do not leave.

A perspective akin to the "new economics of migration" emphasizes the relative deprivation of would-be migrant professionals in relation to two reference groups: well-situated professionals at home and similarly trained professionals abroad (Portes 1976). The first group has acquired the wherewithal to practice their careers in relatively good conditions and to lead a middle-class existence in their own country. The inability to meet this standard is a powerful motivator for

TABLE 1
PROFILE OF H-1B TEMPORARY IMMIGRANTS, 2002

Industry	Number	Percentage of Total	Median Income ($)	Percentage with Master's Degree or Higher	Leading Country of Birth (%)
All	197,537	100	55,000	48	India (34)
Top six industries					
Computer systems design	50,776	25.7	60,000	36	India (68)
Colleges and universities	18,401	9.3	37,000	93	China (26)
Architecture and engineering	8,963	4.5	48,000	44	India (21)
Scientific and technical consulting and management	7,458	3.8	55,000	43	India (39)
Scientific research and development	6,695	3.4	54,000	43	China (24)
Telecommunications	4,357	2.2	70,000	48	India (38)

SOURCE: U.S. Department of Homeland Security, 2002 *Yearbook of Immigration Statistics* (Washington, DC: Government Printing Office), Table L.

departure. In other words, it is not the invidious comparison of salaries with those paid in the developed world but the inability to access remunerations that make possible a decent lifestyle *in their own countries* that becomes a key determinant of brain drain.

In relation to professionals abroad, the central source of relative deprivation is not salary differentials, but work conditions and opportunities for self-development. At this point, the theory of structural imbalancing of peripheral societies becomes relevant as it highlights how diffusion of scientific innovations and modern professional practices from the global centers commonly lead to forms of training that bear little relationship to conditions in peripheral countries (Portes and Walton 1981, chap. 2). Engineers and physicians are thus trained in the latest and most scientific ways of practicing their profession, when the equipment and conditions to put these skills into practice in their own countries are scarce and, at times, entirely absent. In this fashion, less developed nations end up spending scarce resources in educating personnel whose future potential for career development is situated abroad. This is the dynamics underlying the syndrome labeled in past empirical studies "modernization for emigration" (Portes and Ross 1976). Figure 2 graphically summarizes the forces at play.

The classical literature on the brain drain described it as an unmitigated disaster for peripheral countries, whose scarce pools of professional and scientific personnel were constantly siphoned off by the richer nations, and whose painful efforts to create and expand cadres of domestic talent came to naught (Oteiza 1971;

FIGURE 2
DETERMINANTS OF THE BRAIN DRAIN

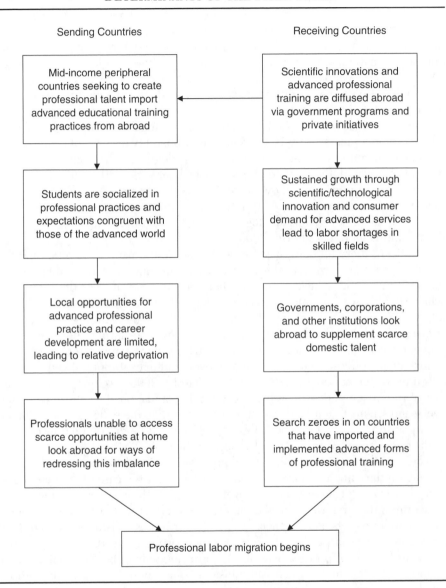

Sending Countries   Receiving Countries

Mid-income peripheral countries seeking to create professional talent import advanced educational training practices from abroad

Scientific innovations and advanced professional training are diffused abroad via government programs and private initiatives

Students are socialized in professional practices and expectations congruent with those of the advanced world

Sustained growth through scientific/technological innovation and consumer demand for advanced services lead to labor shortages in skilled fields

Local opportunities for advanced professional practice and career development are limited, leading to relative deprivation

Governments, corporations, and other institutions look abroad to supplement scarce domestic talent

Professionals unable to access scarce opportunities at home look abroad for ways of redressing this imbalance

Search zeroes in on countries that have imported and implemented advanced forms of professional training

Professional labor migration begins

Diaz-Briquets and Weintraub 1991). In recent years, however, new evidence, along with the advent of the transnational perspective on immigration, have partially modified these conclusions.

In an increasingly globalized system, ever-growing innovations in transportation and communications technologies have greatly facilitated contact across international borders. If this is the case among labor migrants, how much more so among professionals whose economic resources and levels of information are significantly greater. The same empirical literature on determinants of participation in transnational organizations, cited earlier, uncovered the fact that higher education and occupational status had positive and significant effects on the probability of engaging in different forms of transnational activism—economic, political, and sociocultural.

These findings, summarized in Table 2, indicate, for example, that a high school diploma increases by 172 percent the probability of migrants engaging in transnational political activism and that a college degree further increases it by 38 percent. Along with the positive effects of social networks and length of U.S. residence, these results clearly show that it is the better educated, more comfortably established, more secure, and better connected migrants who are most likely to participate in organizations linking them to their home countries (Guarnizo, Portes, and Haller 2003; Portes 2003).

Intuitively, these findings make sense. In addition to national loyalties and the weight of nostalgia, migrant professionals commonly have a sense of obligation to the institutions that educated them. When, on the basis of this education, they achieve wealth, security, and status abroad, it is only natural that they seek to repay the debt. Some do so through philanthropic activities; others through transferring information and technology; still others through sponsoring the training of younger colleagues. Professionals who have become successful entrepreneurs may go further and endow their alma maters or even found institutions of higher learning and research at home (Vertovec 2004; Guarnizo 2003; Saxenian 1999). As the case of India exemplifies, the growth of a sizable population of professionals, engineers, and scientists abroad does not necessarily lead to the hollowing out of home country institutions, but may actually energize them through a dense transnational traffic of personnel, resources, and ideas (Saxenian 2002).

The positive or negative effects of professional emigration on development depend on the same two factors already examined for the case of manual migration: the actions of home country governments and the character of migration. Concerning the first, the official creation of centers of higher learning, support for research projects, and financial incentives for the establishment of high-tech private industry can provide the necessary infrastructure to receive and absorb the contributions of professionals abroad. For migrants to be able to make economic, scientific, and technological transfers home, there have to be institutions capable of receiving and benefiting from such contributions. Otherwise, migrant good intentions can at best fund charity projects that do not further the scientific or technological development of their countries.

India exemplifies again the ways that a country can benefit from large-scale professional migration. While the country continues to export thousands of engineers and computer scientists, the institutions that trained them continue to exist

TABLE 2
DETERMINANTS OF TRANSNATIONALISM AMONG
LATIN AMERICAN IMMIGRANTS IN THE UNITED STATES, 1998

Predictor[a]	Economic (Transnational Entrepreneurs)[b]		Political (Strict Definition)[c]		Sociocultural[d]
	Coefficient	p[e]	Coefficient	Percentage Change[f]	Coefficient
Demographic					
Age	0.013	—	0.101°°	10.6	−0.008
Age-squared	—	—	−0.001°°	−0.1	—
Sex (Male)	1.035°°°	.08	1.209°	235.3	0.697°°
Marital status	0.440°	.03	0.118°°°	12.6	—
Number of children	−0.049	—	—	—	0.120°°
Human capital					
Education (years)	0.114°°°	.01	—	—	0.402°°
High school graduate	—	—	1.003°°°	172.7	—
College graduate	—	—	0.324°°	38.3	—
Professional/executive background	1.191°°°	.10	—	—	0.375
Assimilation					
Years of U.S. residence	0.036°	.003	0.034°°°	3.5	0.018
U.S. citizenship	—	—	−0.041	—	0.141
Experienced discrimination in United States	0.308	—	—	—	0.287°
Downward mobility[g]	0.402°°	−.03	−0.058	—	—

a. Predictors not included in each regression are indicated by a dash in the column marked "coefficient." Some predictors of the regression of sociocultural transnationalism are omitted.
b. Logistic regression of the log-odds of transnational entrepreneurship. Source: Portes, Haller, and Guarnizo (2002).
c. Negative binomial regression of the number of political activities, electoral and civic, in which respondents are involved on a *regular* basis. Source: Guarnizo, Portes, and Haller (2003).
d. Ordered logit regression of an additive index of occasional or regular participation in a set of sociocultural activities. Source: Itzigsohn and Saucedo (2002).
e. Increase/decrease in the net probability of economic transnationalism associated with a unit increase in each predictor. Nonsignificant effects are omitted.
f. Increase/decrease in the percentage of regular transnational political activities in which respondents engage associated with a unit increase in each predictor. Nonsignificant effects are omitted.
g. Ratio of last country occupation to first occupation in the United States, both coded along a 5-point hierarchical scale.
°$p \leq .05.$ °°$p \leq .01.$ °°°$p \leq .001.$

and flourish with strong government support. Protected national industry also generates technological development and creates new employment opportunities for returnees. Dense institutional networks give scientists and engineers on temporary visas abroad something to go back to. It also lays the groundwork for the transnational activities of those permanently settled in North America, Europe, or Australia who wish to contribute to India's scientific development or even to establish new enterprises there. The maturing of these transnational networks has much to do with the dynamism acquired by Indian industry and the country's scientific/technological establishment in recent years (Saxenian 2002; *The Economist* 2006).

Mexico too has a well-developed network of universities and scientific institutions and, hence, the capacity to benefit from its own sizable population of professionals in the United States. However, the evisceration of domestic industry caused by NAFTA has reduced significantly the capacity for autonomous technological innovation and hence the attractiveness of the country to would-be professional returnees. Unlike India or China, Mexico succumbed to external pressures to unconditionally open its borders, thus placing the prospects of economic development in the hands of foreign investors and greatly reducing its capacity for high-tech innovation. In the process, it seriously weakened the institutional network upon which a transnational community of Mexican professionals and scientists could develop (Alarcon 1999; Pozas 2002).

The character of migration also bears on the development potential of professional outflows. When the movement is cyclical, with temporary journeys abroad followed by return to permanent positions at home, the technology transfer potential of migration is augmented. Returned professionals and scientists can immediately put to use what they have learned abroad. In this sense, the U.S. H1-B program represents a welcome development. Although there is no doubt that it was implemented to increase the flexibility of the high-tech labor supply to American industry, the program also has had the consequence of promoting the cyclical character of the foreign labor flow, as migrant professionals are legally required to return after a maximum of six years.

Unlike permanent labor migration, permanent professional migration does not necessarily have negative consequences for the sending country. First, the departure of professionals does not depopulate the countryside, as it comes from cities and it is scarcely a massive outflow. Second, although professionals abroad may be permanent residents and may even become citizens of the receiving country, they can *make the process cyclical* by using their economic resources and know-how for regular transfers to their home country and for sizable investments or programmatic activities there. Unlike labor migrants whose cross-border contributions yield at best philanthropic projects and hometown public infrastructure, professional transnationalism has the potential to alter significantly the level of scientific expertise and technological know-know in the home countries.

Whether temporary professional migrants in fact return (as opposed to making every effort to remain abroad) and whether established professional migrants invest seriously in transnational activities for scientific/technological development depends, ultimately, on the first condition stipulated previously. There must be something to return to. As the remittances and investments of labor migrants lack any development potential when their hometowns become bereft of productive infrastructure and people, the contributions that professional communities abroad can make evaporate when there is no institutional structure, no network of national high-tech industries to receive them and put them to use.

Segmented Assimilation and Development

As is well known, most labor migration to the United States today comes clandestinely. The same is true of a significant proportion of labor flows to Western Europe. From a theoretical standpoint, enough empirical information exists to arrive at a general understanding of the determinants of these unauthorized flows. They emerge out of the clash between attempts to enforce borders by receiving states and the mutually supportive forces of migrant motivations, their networks, and employer demand for low-wage labor in host societies. The networks constructed by migrants across national borders and the migration industry of travel agents, lawyers, people smugglers, document forgers, and the like have proven extraordinarily resilient over time. The lengths to which people are willing to go to reach the developed world have been demonstrated repeatedly, both at the U.S. border and in the Mediterranean straits separating Europe from North Africa (Zolberg 1989; Castles 1986, 2004).

Simultaneously, stagnant or declining populations, growing economies, and an increasing reluctance by educated workers to engage in menial, low-wage labor creates a structural demand in the labor market of wealthy nations that migrants are more than happy to fill. Common depictions of alien invasions in the popular literature conveniently overlook the fact that labor migrants in general, and unauthorized ones in particular, come not only because they want to but because they are wanted. While the general population may oppose their presence, firms and employers in a number of sectors need and rely heavily on this labor supply (Portes and Rumbaut 1996, chap. 3; Massey, Durand, and Malone 2002).

Faced with the combined forces of migrant networks, the migration industry, and structural labor demand, receiving states have not been able to consistently and effectively control their borders. As we have seen above, a series of unexpected consequences emerge instead out of this clash. One of the most important and least noticed is the link between unauthorized migration and the fate of the second generation. The issue of illegality is generally studied as a first-generation phenomenon, in terms of the migrants' origins, their ways of overcoming legal barriers, and their impact on host labor markets. Forgotten is the reality that illegals, like other migrants, can spawn a second generation that grows up under conditions of unique disadvantage.

The concept of *segmented assimilation* was coined to highlight the point that, under present circumstances, children of immigrants growing up in the United

States confront a series of challenges to their successful adaptation that will define the long-term position in American society of the ethnic groups that contemporary immigration spawns. Facing barriers of widespread racism, a bifurcated labor market, the ready presence of countercultural models in street gangs, and the drug culture, immigrants' success depends on the economic and social resources that they, their families, and their communities can muster (Portes and Zhou 1993; Rumbaut 1994). Immigrant professionals and entrepreneurs commonly possess the necessary human capital and economic means to protect their children. They can face the challenges posed by the host society with a measure of equanimity.

Forgotten is the reality that illegals, like other migrants, can spawn a second generation that grows up under conditions of unique disadvantage.

On the other hand, poorly educated migrants who come to fill menial positions at the bottom of the labor market and who lack legal status have greater difficulty supporting their youth. Because of poverty, these migrants often move into central-city areas where their children are served by poor schools and are daily exposed to gangs and deviant lifestyles.

The trajectory followed by a number of children of immigrants trapped in this situation has been labeled *downward assimilation*. The term means that, in their case, acculturation to the norms and values of the host society is not a ticket to material success and status advancement, but exactly the opposite. Dropping out of school, adolescent pregnancies, incidents of arrest and incarceration, injuries or death in gang fights, and increasing conflict and estrangement from parents are all consequences and indicators of downward assimilation. Because of their condition of vulnerability, children of unauthorized immigrants are among the most likely to confront the challenges posed by the host society unaided and, hence, to see their fortunes decline (Fernandez-Kelly and Curran 2001; Lopez and Stanton-Salazar 2001).

In the past, it made sense to study unauthorized immigration as a one-generation phenomenon because the flow was made up of young adults who came to the United States for cyclical work periods, such as those marked by agricultural harvests, and then returned home. More recently, vigorous border enforcement has

FIGURE 3
IMMIGRATION BORDER CONTROL AND ITS UNEXPECTED CONSEQUENCES

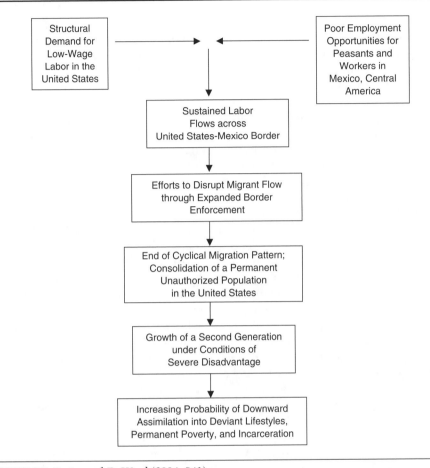

SOURCE: Portes and DeWind (2004, 841).

encouraged unauthorized migrants and others in a tenuous legal position to bring their families along because cyclical returns home have become too costly or dangerous. A settled unauthorized population establishes the demographic basis for the emergence of a handicapped second generation and, therefore, for the theoretical link between determinants of these labor flows and the process of segmented assimilation in the second generation. Figure 3 graphically portrays the process, as it has taken place in the United States.

In Mexico, in particular, massive family migration brought about by deteriorating labor market conditions in the post-NAFTA period, along with the militarization of the border, has been analyzed in terms of depopulation of the Mexican countryside and the consolidation of a vast unauthorized and impoverished population in the United States. The literature on migration and development seldom extends to consider what happens to families once they are on the other side of the border, except for the volume of remittances that they continue sending home. Raising children under the difficult conditions that unauthorized immigrants endure in the developed world and, in particular, in American society, has a series of other important consequences for the sending nation.

First, Mexican immigrant children and children of immigrants may not only be lost to Mexico in the sense that immigrant families are unlikely to return. They may be lost altogether when the difficult conditions under which they grow up lead to downward assimilation. Second, the school abandonment, premature pregnancies, and deviant behavior that are part of this process consolidate the position of Mexicans at the bottom of American society and reinforce racial/ethnic stereotypes among the native white population. Such stereotypes increase hostility and opposition to subsequent waves of labor migrants and reduce their chances for successful adaptation.

Third, when young immigrants who have become socialized in deviant lifestyles return to Mexico or are deported there, they bring along these behaviors and often recruit local youngsters into similar activities. Several authors have noted that the *maras* or youthful gangs that have become a public security problem in Mexico and Central America were, in their origins, an import from Los Angeles, Houston, and other U.S. cities. Deportees from these cities, thoroughly enmeshed in American countercultural orientations, can have a negative influence among the younger population of the areas to which they return. The outcome of this socializing process is that youth gangs suddenly emerge where none existed before, compounding the public security problem of poor nations (Vigil 2002; Smith 2005). Citizen victimization and insecurity have emerged in recent years as a major social problem in such countries, a situation to which the rise of the *maras* has directly contributed (Portes and Hoffman 2003; Perez-Sainz and Andrade-Eekhoff 2003).

This new twist in the history of Mexican and Central American labor migration to the north can be fruitfully compared with what happens to children of professional immigrants in the United States. For the most part, those youth move upward, achieving high-status positions on the basis of advanced education. Their success reflects back on their ethnic communities, reducing negative stereotypes and even creating positive ones as model minorities. In addition, successful second-generation professionals and entrepreneurs can continue making contributions, material and intellectual, to the countries where their parents came from (Zhou and Bankston 1998; Zhou 2004; Min 1987).

Not all children of labor immigrants, not even the unauthorized, undergo downward assimilation in the United States. Nevertheless, a substantial minority is at risk of doing so, and as noted earlier, the negative behaviors and lifestyles in which they become socialized can play back on the countries of origin, compounding the problems that they already confront. While money remittances have captured the bulk of attention among scholars and government officials, highlighting the benefits of migration, the costs of *social* remittances, including the return of disaffected youth and their local influence, have only recently started to come into focus.

While money remittances have . . .
highlight[ed] the benefits of migration, the
costs of social *remittances, including the return*
of disaffected youth and their local influence,
have only recently started to come into focus.

Empirical evidence of segmented assimilation in the second generation is already at hand. Data from the 2000 U.S. Census on school abandonment, male rates of incarceration, and female rates of adolescent and early youth childbearing are presented in Table 3. As indicators of downward assimilation, premature childbearing is far more common among females, while incarceration for a crime is much more prevalent among males. Males are also more likely to drop out of high school. The table presents data for U.S.-born youth of Mexican and Central American origin; for comparative purposes, it also presents figures for native whites and blacks, as well as for second-generation Chinese, Koreans, Indians, and Filipinos. These are the Asian groups whose first generation includes a high proportion of professionals and entrepreneurs.

As shown in the table, close to one-fourth of U.S.-born Mexicans and Central Americans drop out of high school, a figure that more than doubles the corresponding proportion among native whites and quadruples the figure among all second-generation Asian groups. Among males (whether U.S.-born or foreign-born), the proportion of those without a high school education is much higher, the figure approaching half of all young Mexican Americans and surpassing half of Central Americans. This last figure quintuples the rate for native whites.

Figures on childbearing for U.S.-born adolescent and young women tell a similar story. Among second-generation Mexican American female teenagers, the rate is 5 percent as compared with 0.4 percent for Chinese Americans and just 0.2 percent for Korean Americans. The pattern repeats itself among young women aged twenty to twenty-four, with 16 percent of second-generation Salvadorans and Guatemalans and 25 percent of Mexicans with children. These figures are comparable to those among native African Americans but are much

TABLE 3
INDICATORS OF DOWNWARD ASSIMILATION AMONG SECOND-GENERATION AND NATIVE PARENTAGE YOUTH, 2000 (IN PERCENTAGES)

Group	Education		Early Childbearing		Incarcerated for a Crime	
	School Dropouts, Age Twenty-Five to Thirty-Nine	School Dropouts, Males, Twenty-Five to Thirty-Nine[a]	Females, Fifteen to Nineteen	Females, Twenty to Twenty-Four	Males, Eighteen to Thirty-Nine	Male Dropouts, Eighteen to Thirty-Nine
U.S.-born of foreign parentage						
Mexican	24.1	43.0	5.0	25.2	5.8	10.0
Guatemalan, Salvadoran	22.3	52.8	3.0	16.5	3.0	4.8
Chinese	3.6	8.3	0.4	0.9	0.6	4.7
Indian	5.9	6.7	0.6	1.6	1.0	6.7
Korean	3.2	3.3	0.2	2.8	0.9	2.1
Filipino	5.9	7.1	1.6	7.3	1.2	4.8
U.S.-born of native parentage						
Non-Hispanic whites	9.1	10.5	1.9	15.6	1.7	4.8
Non-Hispanic blacks	19.3	21.8	4.5	22.5	11.6	22.2

SOURCE: Rumbaut (2005), based on figures from the U.S. 2000 Census, 5 percent Public Use Microdata Sample.
a. Figures include foreign-born males of all groups.

TABLE 4
INDICATORS OF DOWNWARD ASSIMILATION AMONG
SECOND-GENERATION YOUTH IN SOUTHERN CALIFORNIA
(IN PERCENTAGES)

Group	Inactive in High School, Mean Age Seventeen[a]	Had a Child, Females, Mean Age Twenty-Four	Incarcerated for a Crime, Males, Mean Age Twenty-Four
Mexico	26.7	47.5	20.2
Other Latin America[b]	31.5	16.1	18.8
China, Taiwan	3.9	0.0	0.0
Philippines	17.6	24.5	6.8
Vietnam	18.2	5.2	14.6
Other Asia	23.2	16.7	9.5
Totals	20.8	28.7	11.9

SOURCE: Rumbaut (2005), based on data from the Children of Immigrants Longitudinal Study (CILS).
a. Data provided by the San Diego Unified School District for full CILS-I sample.
b. Mostly second-generation Salvadorans and Guatemalans.

higher than those among Asian American young women, less than 3 percent of whom have become mothers.

According to the U.S. Census, the rate of incarceration among native white males aged eighteen to thirty-nine is less than 2 percent, and among second-generation Asian Americans, it is less than 1 percent. The figure climbs to 3 percent among Central Americans and 5 percent among Mexican Americans. To show the interaction between school abandonment and incidents of arrest and incarceration, the table includes rates of imprisonment among U.S.-born males without a high school degree. The rates increase significantly for all groups, reaching almost 5 percent among native whites and 10 percent among Mexican Americans. Only native African Americans exhibit worse rates.

The Children of Immigrants Longitudinal Study (CILS) is the largest long-term study of second-generation youths in the United States (Portes and Rumbaut 2005). CILS includes a large sample of second-generation Mexicans, Filipinos, and other Asians interviewed in schools in the San Diego metropolitan area when they were in the eighth and ninth grades (average age fourteen) and then followed over time. The sample was reinterviewed at average age seventeen, by the time of high school graduation, and then at average age twenty-four, when entering young adulthood. Table 4 presents data from this sample on three variables: rates of school inactivity, premature childbearing, and rates of incarceration.[1]

School inactivity is a proxy for school abandonment prior to high school graduation. The pattern of results is similar to that observed in census data, with very low rates among second-generation Chinese, climbing to the teens among Filipinos and Vietnamese, and surpassing one-fourth of Mexican Americans. The same trend is observable in the other indicators of downward assimilation, except that differences among second-generation nationalities are wider than in census data. Thus, while rates of female premature childbearing or young male imprisonment are exactly 0 among Chinese Americans, they reach 47 percent of Mexican American females (premature mothers) and 20 percent of males (incarcerated).

These compelling differences go on to reinforce stereotypes about the presumed cultural differences of immigrant groups, some of which are depicted as innately inferior, while others are promoted to the status of model minorities. Those post hoc explanations ignore historical processes that have given rise to contemporary realities. Differences in human capital among first-generation labor and professional immigrants, in addition to differences in their contexts of reception—legal and protected for professionals but often unauthorized and persecuted for laborers—are the structural features that account for the long-term evolution and varying outcomes in the fates of ethnic communities. Depending on these structural factors, children and young people of similar potential may be propelled forward to careers of achievement and success or downward to lives of poverty and marginality in the receiving country. They will become part of high-status model groups poised to be integrated promptly into the American mainstream or into caste-like, impoverished minorities. As we have seen, the communities and the countries that their parents left behind can also be significantly affected by the process of segmented assimilation in the second generation.

Conclusion

Theories of national development in Latin America and elsewhere have seldom paid much attention to international migration. At best, these flows have been treated as a marginal phenomenon—a reflection of the problems of underdevelopment. That position is no longer sustainable. The size of expatriate communities and the volume of the remittances that they send home have prompted a reorientation of theoretical models in which the massive resources put into motion by immigrants take center stage (Guarnizo 2003). For some authors, remittances can play a key role in resolving past financial bottlenecks and furnishing the necessary resources for long-term development.

I argue that such rosy predictions are exaggerated. There is no precedent that any country has taken the road toward sustained development on the basis of the remittances sent by its expatriates. More important, the positive effects of these contributions are contingent on other factors. Depending on them, migration can lead to vastly different consequences—economic stagnation, the emptying out of sending places, and the massive loss of talent versus the energizing of local economies, new productive activities, and significant contributions for scientific and technological development.

For labor migration, the key consideration is whether the cyclical character of the flow can be preserved. While migration inevitably produces a settlement process in the host country, the extent to which the normative pattern returns after temporary stays abroad governs the potential of the movement for strengthening local economies and preventing depopulation. Cyclical migrations work best for both sending and receiving societies. Returnees are much more likely to save and make productive investments at home; they leave families behind to which sizable remittances are sent. More important, temporary migrants do not compromise the future of the next generation by placing their children in danger of downward assimilation abroad. To the extent that sending country governments provide the necessary educational resources, these children can grow up healthy in their own countries, benefiting from the experiences and the investments of their parents. The nightmare of young deportees carrying with them the crime culture learned abroad can thus be effectively avoided.

Professional migration need not be formally cyclical to become so in practice. For reasons explained previously, migrant professionals commonly have the necessary motivation and resources to engage in transnational activities in favor of their home country institutions. As the cases of India, Taiwan, and other major sources of professional migrants attest, these activities can often make major contributions to scientific and technological development in sending nations.

In this area, as in all others pertaining to national development, the role of the state is decisive. The positive relationship between migration and development is not automatic. Market forces alone will not establish the connection. The proactive intervention of the state to create productive infrastructure in rural areas and scientific/technological institutions capable of innovation are necessary conditions for the developmental potential of migration flows to materialize. Countries that simply open their borders, hoping that the "magic" of the market will do the rest, will not reap these benefits. The contrasting experiences of countries that have followed this path versus those that have taken a proactive stance toward their expatriate communities and their economic/scientific potential provide a clear lesson for the future.

Note

1. Rates have been adjusted for sample mortality in the third Children of Immigrants Longitudinal Study (CILS) survey, which retrieved approximately 70 percent of the original respondents. School inactivity rates were computed on the full CILS-I sample.

References

Alarcon, Rafael. 1999. Recruitment processes among foreign-born engineers and scientists in Silicon Valley. *American Behavioral Scientist* 42:1381-97.

Alba, Francisco. 1978. Mexico's international migration as a manifestation of its development pattern. *International Migration Review* 12:502-51.

Barrera, Mario. 1980. *Race and class in the Southwest: A theory of racial inequality*. South Bend, IN: Notre Dame University Press.

Castles, Stephen. 1986. The guest-worker in Western Europe: An obituary. *International Migration Review* 20:761-78.

———. 2004. The factors that make and unmake migration policies. *International Migration Review* 38:852-84.

Delgado-Wise, Raul, and Humberto Marquez Covarrubias. 2006. *The reshaping of Mexican labor exports under NAFTA: Paradoxes and challenges*. Zacatecas, Mexico: University of Zacatecas, Red Internacional de Migración y Desarrollo.

Diaz-Briquets, Sergio, and Sidney Weintraub. 1991. *Migration, remittances, and small business development, Mexico and Caribbean Basin countries.* Boulder, CO: Westview.

The Economist. 2006. A survey of business in India. Special report. June 3.

Espenshade, Thomas J., and German Rodriguez. 1997. Completing the Ph.D.: Comparative performance of U.S. and foreign students. *Social Science Quarterly* 78:593-605.

Fernandez-Kelly, Patricia, and Sara Curran. 2001. Nicaraguans: Voices lost, voices found. In *Ethnicities: Children of immigrants in America,* ed. R. G. Rumbaut and A. Portes. Berkeley, CA: University of California Press and Russell Sage Foundation.

Goldring, Luin. 2002. The Mexican state and transmigrant organizations: Negotiating the boundaries of membership and participation. *Latin American Research Review* 37:55-99.

Gonzalez Gutierrez, Carlos. 1999. Fostering identities: Mexico's relations with its diaspora. *Journal of American History* 86:545-67.

Grasmuck, Sherri, and Patricia Pessar. 1991. *Between two islands: Dominican international migration.* Berkeley: University of California Press.

Guarnizo, Luis E. 2003. The economics of transnational living. *International Migration Review* 37:666-99.

Guarnizo, Luis E., Alejandro Portes, and William J. Haller. 2003. Assimilation and transnationalism: Determinants of transnational political action among contemporary immigrants. *American Journal of Sociology* 108:1211-48.

Instituto de los Mexicanos en el Exterior. 2004. *Bi-annual report of activities,* 2003-04. Mexico, D.F.: Secretariat of Foreign Relations, Government of Mexico.

Itzigsohn, Jose, and Silvia G. Saucedo. 2002. Immigrant incorporation and sociocultural transnationalism. *International Migration Review* 36:766-98.

Latin America Weekly Report. 2006. Mexico: NAFTA's impact on rights criticized. WR-06-19. May 16, p. 13.

Lopez, David, and Ricardo D. Stanton-Salazar. 2001. Mexican-Americans: A second generation at risk. In *Ethnicities: Children of immigrants in America,* ed. R. G. Rumbaut and A. Portes, 57-90. Berkeley, CA: University of California Press and Russell Sage Foundation.

Massey, Douglas S., Joaquin Arango, Graeme Hugo, Ali Kouaouci, Adela Pellegrino, and J. Edward Taylor. 1998. *Worlds in motion: Understanding international migration at the end of the millennium.* Oxford, UK: Clarendon.

Massey, Douglas S., Jorge Durand, and Nolan J. Malone. 2002. *Beyond smoke and mirrors: Mexican immigration in an era of economic integration.* New York: Russell Sage Foundation.

Min, Pyong Gap. 1987. Factors contributing to ethnic business. *International Journal of Comparative Sociology* 28:173-93.

Office of Immigration Statistics. 2004. *2003 yearbook of immigration statistics.* Washington, DC: Department of Homeland Security.

Oteiza, Enrique. 1971. La Migracion de Profesionales, Techicos y Obreros Calificados Argentinos a los Estados Unidos. *Desarrollo Economico* 10:429-54.

Perez-Sainz, Juan Pablo, and Katharine Andrade-Eekhoff. 2003. *Communities in globalization.* Lanham, MD: Rowman & Littlefield.

Portes, Alejandro. 1976. Determinants of the brain drain. *International Migration Review* 10:489-508.

———. 2003. Theoretical convergencies and empirical evidence in the study of immigrant transnationalism. *International Migration Review* 37:874-92.

Portes, Alejandro, and Robert L. Bach. 1985. *Latin journey: Cuban and Mexican immigrants in the United States.* Berkeley: University of California Press.

Portes, Alejandro, and Josh DeWind. 2004. A cross-Atlantic dialogue: The progress of research and theory in the study of international migration. *International Migration Review* 38:828-51.

Portes, Alejandro, Cristina Escobar, and Alexandria Walton. Forthcoming. Immigrant transnational organizations and development: A comparative study. *International Migration Review.*

Portes, Alejandro, William Haller, and Luis E. Guarnizo. 2002. Transnational entrepreneurs: An alternative form of immigrant adaptation. *American Sociological Review* 67:278-98.

Portes, Alejandro, and Kelly Hoffman. 2003. Latin American class structures: Their composition and change during the neoliberal era. *Latin American Research Review* 38 (1): 41-82.

Portes, Alejandro, and Adreain R. Ross. 1976. Modernization for emigration: The medical brain drain from Argentina. *Journal of Interamerican Studies and World Affairs* 13:395-422.

Portes, Alejandro, and Rubén G. Rumbaut. 1996. *Immigrant America: A portrait*. Berkeley: University of California Press.

Portes, Alejandro, and Rubén G. Rumbaut. 2005. The second generation and the Children of Immigrants Longitudinal Study. *Ethnic and Racial Studies* 28:983-99.

Portes, Alejandro, and John Walton. 1981. *Labor, class, and the international system*. New York: Academic Press.

Portes, Alejandro, and Min Zhou. 1993. The new second generation: Segmented assimilation and its variants among post-1965 immigrant youth. *Annals of the American Academy of Political and Social Sciences* 530:74-96.

Pozas, Maria de los Angeles. 2002. *Estrategia de la Gran Empresa Mexicana en la Decada de los Noventa*. Mexico, D.F.: El Colegio de Mexico.

Ramos, Carlos Guillermo. 2002. Rapporteurs' comments. Delivered at the Conference on Immigrant Transnationalism and Its Impact on Sending Nations. Sponsored by the Center for Migration and Development, Princeton University and Latin American School of Social Science (FLACSO), Santo Domingo, D.R., January.

Reichert, Joshua S. 1981. The migrant syndrome: Seasonal U.S. wage labor and rural development in Central Mexico. *Human Organization* 40:59-66.

Rumbaut, Rubén G. 1994. The crucible within: Ethnic identity, self-esteem, and segmented assimilation among children of immigrants. *International Migration Review* 28:748-94.

———. 2005. Turning points in the transition to adulthood: Determinants of educational attainment, incarceration, and early childbearing among children of immigrants. *Ethnic and Racial Studies* 28:1041-86.

Sassen, Saskia. 1988. *The mobility of labor and capital: A study in international investment and labor flow*. New York: Cambridge University Press.

Saxenian, Anna Lee. 1999. *Silicon Valley's new immigrant entrepreneurs*. San Francisco: Public Policy Institute of California.

———. 2002. *Local and global networks of immigrant professionals in Silicon Valley*. San Francisco: Public Policy Institute of California.

Smith, Robert C. 2005. *Mexican New York: Transnational worlds of new immigrants*. Berkeley: University of California Press.

Vertovec, Steven. 2004. Migrant transnationalism and modes of transformation. *International Migration Review* 38:970-1001.

Vigil, Jaime Diego. 2002. *A rainbow of gangs: Street cultures in the mega-city*. Austin: University of Texas Press.

Zhou, Min. 2004. Revisiting ethnic entrepreneurship: Convergencies, controversies, and conceptual advancements. *International Migration Review* 38:1040-74.

Zhou, Min, and Carl Bankston. 1998. *Growing up American: How Vietnamese immigrants adapt to life in the United States*. New York: Russell Sage Foundation.

Zolberg, Aristide. 1989. The next waves: Migration theory for a changing world. *International Migration Review* 23:403-30.

Borders for Whom? The Role of NAFTA in Mexico-U.S. Migration

In this article, the authors first give attention to main factors that resulted in the passage of NAFTA and subsequently investigate Mexican migration to the United States during roughly the same period that the bilateral treaty has been in effect. At the center of the relationship between economic liberalization and immigration is the paradox of increasing capital mobility and attempts at controlling more tightly the movement of immigrant workers. Although immigration from Mexico has remained flat over the past ten years, the Mexican population in the United States has grown rapidly, partly as a result of the unanticipated effects of harsh immigration policies since 1986. Prior to that date, Mexicans engaged in cyclical movements, but as security measures became harsher, especially in the 9/11 period, more immigrants and their families settled in the United States hoping to avert the dangers of exit and reentry. This analysis shows the slanted function of borders that have become permeable for capital but increasingly restrictive for immigrants.

Keywords: Mexican Migration Project; NAFTA; Immigration Reform and Control Act; undocumented migrants

By
PATRICIA
FERNÁNDEZ-KELLY
and
DOUGLAS S. MASSEY

Borders are neither natural nor fixed phenomena; they come and go in response to political and economic transformations. Most national boundaries were established less than two centuries ago. In 1985, the world's total number of sovereign states was roughly 180; but over the next decade, following the collapse of the Soviet Union, that number grew to 202. Africa is filled with borders imposed as part of colonial domination or redrawn after wars of independence, which often run through populations with shared traditions and history. The North American Free Trade Agreement (NAFTA) represents the latest attempt to tear down barriers to capital mobility, even as territorial demarcations were tightened for workers.

Whether tangible or not, the drawing of borders always exposes hierarchies of power and authority. In this article we analyze the enforcement of boundaries under NAFTA. We argue

DOI: 10.1177/0002716206297449

ANNALS, *AAPSS*, 610, March 2007

that neoliberal economic policies were applied throughout Latin America to solve financial problems precipitated by the external debt crisis of the 1980s. During the 1970s, North American banks were awash in petrodollars. Desperate to find profitable investments, they made what were perceived to be secure loans to Latin American governments to finance development projects under import substitution industrialization (ISI). Ultimately, however, many countries were unable to repay these loans, and U.S. banks and federal officials turned to NAFTA as a means of transforming risk into opportunity.

Thus, the purpose of NAFTA was not merely to facilitate trade and open markets, but to expand opportunities for capital investment. The treaty paid little attention to worker mobility, in striking contrast to the European Union, which made labor central to the broader process of market integration. The consolidation of European markets was effected by multilateral policies designed to harmonize social policies, equalize economic infrastructures, and guarantee worker rights and mobility within the trade zone. In contrast, NAFTA omitted these provisions, and its U.S. backers instead insisted on the unilateral right to prevent Mexican workers from migrating through restrictive border policies.

The result of this contradiction was a lopsided process of development in North America, in which rising capital mobility and growing U.S. investment south of the border coincided with repressive efforts to limit the cross-border movement of Mexicans, although the number of workers seeking opportunities in the United States had increased as a result of NAFTA. The privatization of Mexico's collective farms under neoliberalism and the elimination of agricultural subsidies under NAFTA also increased the number of displaced peasants seeking economic opportunities elsewhere. The combination of continued pressures for emigration and increasingly restrictive border policies had a profound effect on patterns and processes of Mexico-U.S. migration. Although migrants continued to arrive at the border and cross into the United States, they did not return to Mexico in the same numbers as before. Instead, unauthorized migrants reduced cyclical movements to spare themselves the greater costs and risks of reentry after 1986. The reduction in return migration led, in turn, to unprecedented accretions to the Mexican population living north of the border. We conclude by offering concrete recommendations to rationalize U.S. immigration policy in the context of the economic integration that is occurring under NAFTA.

Patricia Fernández-Kelly holds a joint position in the department of sociology and Office of Population Research at Princeton University. She has written extensively on globalization, industrial recomposition, international migration, and gender. With Lorraine Gray, she coproduced the Emmy Award–winning documentary, "The Global Assembly Line." Her latest book, edited with Jon Shefner, Out of the Shadows: Political Action and Informal Economy in Latin America, *was published by Pennsylvania State University Press in 2006.*

Douglas S. Massey is the Henry G. Bryant Professor of Sociology and Public Affairs at Princeton University and president of the American Academy of Political and Social Science. With Jorge Durand (University of Guadalajara), he directs the Mexican Migration Project, the largest and preeminent database on the subject. His most recent book, Categorically Unequal: The American Stratification System, *was published in 2007 by Russell Sage Foundation.*

NAFTA and the American Financial Dilemma

Almost forgotten in current debates over NAFTA is the fear that was voiced with shrill alarm in the 1980s that the U.S. banking system would collapse because major Latin American countries would not be able to pay off their foreign debts (Gan 2004; Trebat 1991). The roots of this drama extend back a decade to when Brazil, Mexico, and Argentina sought to achieve economic independence under the philosophy of import substitution industrialization (Middlebrook 2004). To fund what some critics call "pharaonic" projects—such as hydroelectric dams, expanded metallurgy industries, boosted oil production, nuclear plants—these countries turned to U.S. banks, which were then eager to make loans as a means of expanding profits (Evans 1995).

The fervor with which financial institutions in the United States courted borrowers from south of the border reflected momentous transformations in the global economy. Starting in the late 1960s, American firms began to relocate manufacturing operations to Asia, northern Mexico, and the Caribbean in an effort to circumvent high taxes and union pressures for improved wages and benefits. Advances in transportation and communications technology enabled companies to locate lucrative stages of production (administration, inventory control, research and development, marketing) at home while transferring labor-intensive assembly to areas of the world where wages constituted a small fraction of those paid in the United States (Fernández-Kelly 1993).

The 1970s and 1980s witnessed a radical reconfiguration of the U.S. economy, with waves of plant closings and millions of manufacturing jobs exported or eliminated. From the point of view of industry, globalization was not just a search for better conditions of production but also a realignment of power between workers and investors. With declining investment opportunities in the United States, financial institutions explored new alternatives. The U.S. Federal Reserve raised interest rates several times during the 1970s and, under the leadership of Paul A. Volcker, pushed them above 20 percent during the 1980s, ushering in the deepest recession since the 1930s. Although ultimately such policies did solve the American conundrum of stagflation, they also tightened the noose around the neck of Latin American economies (Dávalos 2006).

Of special concern was Mexico. High oil prices in the second half of the 1970s improved that country's international credit and fueled massive increases in government spending, which, in turn, led to trade imbalances; a growing budget deficit; and, once oil prices began to decline, ballooning inflation (Gereffi, Spener, and Bair 2002). Investors responded by reducing inputs and converting their Mexican bank deposits to dollars, leading to a sharp devaluation of the peso in February of 1982. By August of that year, President Miguel López Portillo was forced to admit that Mexico could not meet its short-term, dollar-denominated obligations (Quentin and López 2006). Brazil and Argentina faced a similar predicament, and after the collapse of oil prices they could not even pay the interest on their crippling debts. Along with Mexico, they owed $435 billion to Western creditor nations, $54 billion of it to commercial banks.

The magnitude of the debt created a very real potential for financial catastrophe. At this juncture, other actors came into play. Scarcely had the 1982 debt crisis begun when U.S. financial institutions sought new arrangements through the International Monetary Fund (IMF) to advance their interests. The IMF had helplessly presided over the collapse of the Bretton Woods agreement in 1971, when the Nixon administration suspended convertibility of the dollar to gold. Yet only a decade later, international lenders found the IMF to be a very useful instrument for imposing structural adjustments throughout Latin America (Babb 2003).

The IMF's refurbished role as an agent of economic change signaled the beginning of a new stage of preeminence for financial capital in the western hemisphere. Latin America's foreign debt facilitated a political transformation in which a new narrative centered on free trade enabled the recovery of large financial institutions and promoted the activities of transnational corporations (Herzenberg 1991). It is in this context that NAFTA was negotiated.

The Dual Identity of NAFTA

Critics of NAFTA tend to portray it as a tool of American economic domination, ignoring the fact that the initiative for the treaty first came from Mexico, not the United States. For this reason, both American and Mexican interests must be taken into consideration in any assessment of why and how the accord was implemented. From the viewpoint of U.S. business interests, NAFTA is a concerted attempt to achieve financial hegemony throughout the hemisphere. From the Mexican perspective, it represents an attempt to integrate into the global economy through trade liberalization and a reconfiguration of Mexico's authoritarian state (Herzenberg 1991; Gereffi, Spener, and Bair 2002). In the first instance, free trade offered an opportunity to reshuffle capitalist forces by defining new and more favorable conditions for the profitable deployment of assets overseas. In the second instance, free trade allowed policy-making elites to break away from earlier models of development based on import-substitution industrialization (Centeno 2004).

In both countries, therefore, NAFTA continued earlier attempts to find a solution to the debt crisis of the 1980s. What began as a search for a way to turn losses into gains for U.S. financial and industrial interests gradually translated into a trade agreement that would not only guarantee a return on investments but also the institutionalization of conditions under which those gains could be permanently realized (Fernández-Kelly 1993; Shaiken 2001, 2004a). In this sense, NAFTA's architects are found on both sides of the U.S.-Mexican border.

The American Side

In the United States, the intellectual power behind NAFTA came from a tightly woven network of bankers, politicians, lobbyists, and corporate representatives brought together during the 1970s by the Trilateral Commission, the

Council of Foreign Relations, the American Bankers Association, the U.S. Business Round Table, and the National Association of Manufacturers. Some of the names in that group are familiar: Kay Whitmore, Chair of Eastman-Kodak; former U.S. Secretary of State Henry Kissinger; Donald V. Fites, CEO of Caterpillar, Inc.; Paul Volcker, Chairman of the U.S. Federal Reserve; and the former head of Chase Manhattan Bank, David Rockefeller. In an address delivered in 1987, Rockefeller (1987) captured a concept of critical import for the understanding of the new treaty:

> [The] real question of concern to lenders is the ability of borrowers to service their debt, not whether they can pay it off. Debt is a fundamental component of creative investment and growth, and rare is the nation or private enterprise that can function effectively without it.

That declaration, emblematic of the times, reclassified and normalized a situation perceived less than a decade earlier as potentially disastrous. It also reveals that a main objective of NAFTA was to ensure that Mexico—and later, through similar treaties, other Latin American countries—would have the funds to increase the extension of credit substantially. In Rockefeller's (1992) words, "[This] route is the most efficient and least expensive vehicle we have to protect our own self-interest in maintaining the creditworthiness of Latin America."

[A] main objective of NAFTA was to ensure that Mexico—and later, through similar treaties, other Latin American countries— would have the funds to increase their extension of credit substantially.

In the previous sentence, the term "self-interest" refers to that of the United States as a whole; but it is significant that the group most directly responsible for the design of NAFTA did not include labor unions, public interest organizations, or small business associations (B. Campbell et al. 1999; Shaiken 2004b; Stanford 1993). It does not take a great deal of imagination to suspect that this exclusion was deliberate, and certainly not without historical precedent. Since the 1930s the National Association of Manufacturers, a principal mover behind NAFTA, had engaged in systematic attempts to discredit unions by portraying them as antidemocratic cells in the heart of a free America (Griffin, Wallace, and Rubin 1986). Like Charles Wilson, chairman of General Motors, who famously stated in

1953 that "what's good for General Motors is good for America," the architects of NAFTA tacitly assumed that what is good for America's banks is good for all Americans. In one stroke it codified a twenty-year-long process of economic liberalization during which manufacturers had relocated much of their production to Asia and the U.S.-Mexico border.

In addition to providing factory owners with unhindered access to cheap Mexican labor, NAFTA had a second purpose—eliminating barriers to capital mobility in the most advanced sectors of the economy by issuing new rules for expanded investment in telecommunications, banking, insurance, biogenetics, and computers. The interests of capital are reflected in the considerable emphasis NAFTA puts on intellectual property rights, patents and copyrights, and the rights and privileges of ownership compared with its curious silence on issues related to labor and the environment. From the American point of view, the twin purposes of NAFTA were thus to provide manufacturers free access to Mexican workers, thereby enabling a new international division of labor, while at the same time giving investors unhindered access to Mexican property and financial assets.

The Mexican Side

In Mexico, the proponents of free trade belonged to two interrelated circles. One included large commercial interests that were increasingly receptive to and permeated by foreign capital, including telecommunications firms such as Televisa and Telmex, banking organizations such as Banamex, and industrialists associated with the powerful Grupo Monterrey (Camp 2002). The other clique included young public officials with links to an older political structure—an energetic new generation whose members had been educated in elite U.S. colleges and universities and were firm believers in free enterprise (Babb 2001). They were swept into government in the emergency created by Mexico's external debt. Carlos Salinas de Gortari was the most prominent among them, taking over Mexico's presidency in 1988 under seething allegations of electoral fraud.

Almost from the beginning, Salinas identified NAFTA as a top priority (Centeno 2004). His earnestness was puzzling because U.S. investments already controlled two-thirds of the Mexican economy. The country's *maquiladora* program, set into motion in 1968, and Mexico's admission into the Generalized Agreement on Tariffs and Trade (GATT) in 1986 had further opened new avenues for the removal of barriers to business activity. Maquiladoras, in particular, operated under strict neoliberal principles and experienced their most rapid expansion after Mexico's peso devaluation in the 1980s, thus guaranteeing the primacy of export-oriented industrialization as a new approach to development.

At the same time, Salinas favored privatization to an extent that would have impressed even the most fervent believer in the Chicago School of Economics. All this occurred in the absence of a treaty. Why then his commitment to formalize the process? The answer to that question requires attention to specific economic and political interests within Mexico. The most distinctive trait of the

Salinas administration was not its genuflection to technocracy, as critics believed, but a willingness to shape new alliances to revitalize the troubled Mexican economy and improve the standing of the Partido Revolucionario Institucional (PRI), the political machine that had governed Mexico since 1929. Since then, the Mexican state adhered to a populist rhetoric while presiding over an increasingly open economy. Salinas exchanged nationalist bravado for a pragmatic discourse favoring integration into the global economy (Evans 1995; Middlebrook 2004). His bold reforms, unimaginable in the preceding era, were a response to popular mistrust and the PRI's loss of legitimacy following the national debt imbroglio.

Elevated to power in shaky conditions, the new president first sought to regain credibility by inaugurating the Programa Nacional de Solidaridad (PRONASOL), whose purpose was to shift power and resources away from the state to smaller units such as neighborhoods and community organizations, which were granted greater autonomy (T. Campbell and Freedheim 1994). Then, in response to pressures from international development organizations such as the World Bank and the IMF, Salinas implemented neoliberal reforms that included privatizing the banking system, selling government firms, deregulating markets, and making fundamental modifications to Mexican property law, the most dramatic of which was the repeal of Article 27 of the Mexican Constitution, which had created the *ejido* system. Ejidos were parcels of land given in trust by the Mexican government to peasants involved in subsistence agriculture. Although it had been a cornerstone of Mexico's political system for six decades, the constitutional change authorized private ownership of ejido land.

Finally, Salinas pursued new trading arrangements with other countries in Latin America. From Mexico's perspective, NAFTA was part of a larger plan to open the border to repatriated and foreign investment (Middlebrook 2004). In this sense, the objectives of the Mexican government coincided with those of U.S. investors. Nevertheless, the divergences were equally important. While the goals of financial capitalists were narrow—the realization of profits—Mexico's commitment to neoliberalism and free trade was part of a larger vision for national development. The Salinas administration held several precedents in mind, including the economic success of the so-called Asian Tigers (Taiwan, Hong Kong, Singapore, and South Korea), the emergence of the European Common Market—especially the rapid development of Spain—and the growth of Mexico's own maquiladora program. By opening markets, cutting public spending, and withdrawing state intervention from the economy, the Mexican government hoped to bring about national prosperity. The goal was to "Taiwanize" Mexico.

In light of developments over the past decade, these hopes seem tragically naive. The Mexican government failed to observe that the ascent of the Asian Tigers depended not on the weakening of the state, the radical implementation of laissez faire economics, and the triumph of unhampered markets, but exactly the opposite (Gereffi and Wyman 1990). Their success was predicated on robust entrepreneurial actions taken by government itself; the maintenance of strict controls on capital flows; and, in the case of South Korea, a combination of export-oriented industrialization with domestic investments in capital goods to boost internal markets (Deyo 1987, 1989; Evans 1995; Gereffi, Spener, and Bair 2002).

At the same time, NAFTA's architects on both sides of the border ignored key elements that made the European Union integrate so successfully. Years before the approval of the Maastricht Treaty in 1992, richer European countries channeled investments and resources into weaker links of the continental chain: Spain, Portugal, and to some extent Greece. The intent was to level the field and prevent the subsequent rush of impoverished workers from poor to rich nations. The European Union created among other things a common market, a shared customs, a single currency—the euro managed by the European Central Bank and adopted by twelve of the twenty-five member states—and shared agricultural and trade policies (Nelsen and Stubb 2005). In 1985, the Schengen Agreement further abolished passport controls for some member states. Customs checks were eliminated at many internal borders, creating to some extent a single space of mobility for people to live, travel, work, and invest. The European Union thus became a supranational category in which citizens were relatively free to cross borders as long as they could support themselves (Nelsen and Stubb 2005; Centeno 2007 [this volume]).

By contrast, NAFTA utterly ignored international labor mobility and took no steps to equalize different levels of economic development among the participating countries (Gereffi, Spener, and Bair 2002; Hufbauer and Schott 1992; Moody and McGinn 1992). NAFTA represented an attempt at economic integration without political integration (see also Brady, Beckfield, and Seeleib-Kaiser 2005). This last point is especially poignant given President Salinas de Gortari's assertion that "the whole point of NAFTA for Mexico is to be able to export goods and not people. That means creating jobs in Mexico" (Zarsky and Gallagher 2004).

By contrast, NAFTA utterly ignored international labor mobility and took no steps to equalize different levels of economic development among the participating countries.

Such a laudable end did not materialize, however, for greater economic integration did not reduce the pool of displaced Mexican workers. The deregulation of agriculture; the selling of land to foreigners; the withdrawal of farm subsidies; and the opening of Mexico's food, seed, and feed markets to competition from Canada and the United States led to the migration of many peasants who found themselves unable to compete with mechanized grain exports once Mexican agricultural protection was broken down (Andreas 1998; Gereffi, Spener, and Bair 2002; Light 2007 [this volume]; Martin 2003; Singer and Massey 1998).

In sum, the narrow interests of financial, industrial, and policy elites on both sides of the border did less for workers in either country than for the consolidation of a new and powerful binational class of professionals, investors, managers, and politicians. The stated objectives of NAFTA—economic development in Mexico and balanced growth throughout North America—were from the outset opposite those actually implemented, which served narrow economic and political interests rather than the welfare of ordinary Mexicans or Americans. In the next section, we consider the accidental and cumulative consequences of this policy mismatch.

U.S. Immigration Policy Then and Now

Throughout their history, Mexico and the United States have been linked by political, economic, and geographical ties. In 1848, almost half of Mexico's territory passed to its northern neighbor as a result of armed conflict. An entire population of Mexicans suddenly changed national status while maintaining kinship and friendship bonds in their country of origin. The early part of the twentieth century witnessed recurring hostility toward Mexican immigrants and ongoing discrimination against their descendants (Massey 2007). In search of a low-cost and pliant labor force, agricultural firms turned southward to bring in workers through private and government-assisted recruitment (Durand and Arias 2000). During the 1920s, immigration from Mexico reached such massive levels that historians labeled it a "flood tide" (Cardoso 1980).

The advent of the Great Depression, however, brought about a new round of xenophobia and anti-Mexican hysteria that led to the deportation or voluntary repatriation of half a million Mexicans (Hoffman 1974). During the 1930s, the flood tide of the 1920s was reduced to a trickle. With U.S. entry into the Second World War, however, labor shortages recurred in the American Southwest, and in 1942, the two countries signed the Bracero Accord, a bilateral agreement that arranged for the temporary entry of Mexican workers for agricultural labor (Calavita 1992). Although originally envisioned as a temporary wartime measure, the Bracero Program was extended after 1945 and dramatically expanded in the mid-1950s before finally being terminated in 1964 as a feature of President Lyndon Johnson's broader civil rights initiative (Galarza 1964). During the program's twenty-two years, more than 4.5 million Mexican workers circulated in and out of the United States as *braceros*.

After 1964, the de facto immigration policy of the United States devolved to a loose-fitting combination of limited legality and expansive tolerance (Massey, Durand, and Malone 2002). Amendments to the Immigration and National Act passed in 1965 and later restricted the avenues for legal migration from Mexico, first by applying numerical limits to immigration from the Western Hemisphere, then by applying a numerical quota to Mexico itself, and finally by forcing Mexicans to compete for scarce visas with immigrants from the entire world (Massey 2007). With the termination of the Bracero Program and the progressive limitation of legal immigration, a growing fraction of Mexicans entered in unauthorized status, in which they simultaneously experience abuses but also expanding labor market opportunities in America's farming, manufacturing, and service sectors.

In essence, after 1965 the United States shifted from a de jure guest worker program based on the circulation of braceros to a de facto guest worker program based on the circulation of undocumented labor. All in all, U.S. immigration policies and practices adapted themselves to the realities of economic interdependence and the expanded demand for Mexican labor and immigration to the United States became a common experience for young Mexican workers. By the end of the twentieth century, two-thirds of all Mexicans knew someone who had been to the United States and almost 60 percent were socially connected to someone living on American soil (Massey, Durand, and Malone 2002).

Despite the historical realities of U.S.-Mexico interdependence, and for reasons having more to do with cold war politics than economic exigencies, immigration policies started to tighten in 1986, coincidentally the same year that Mexico entered GATT under pressure from the U.S. Treasury. While commercial liberalization took a step forward, measures to liberalize the free flow of labor took a step backward (Massey 2005). Even as U.S. officials deliberated with Mexican authorities to integrate markets for goods, capital, information, raw materials, and services, they acted to prevent the integration of Mexican and American labor markets (Bean et al. 1994).

The passage in 1986 of the Immigration Reform and Control Act (IRCA) marks a turning point, as U.S. immigration and border policies shifted from tolerance to repression. This act simultaneously criminalized the hiring of unauthorized workers by U.S. employers and massively increased funding for the U.S. Border Patrol to begin a marked expansion of enforcement that would build over two decades. The 1990 Immigration Act added new numerical limitations to the immigration of family members, further reducing the avenues for legal entry and then in 1993, when the imminent passage of NAFTA was making headlines, the U.S. Border Patrol launched Operation Blockade in the El Paso–Ciudad Juarez sector and followed that with a similar intervention, Operation Gatekeeper, in San Diego–Tijuana during the following year. These two ventures deployed massive resources to intercept Mexican migrants at the two busiest crossing points along the Mexico-U.S. border (Nevins 2002).

Paralleling the huge increase in enforcement resources deployed along the border was a massive increase in trade between Mexico and the United States over the same period. From 1986 to 2003, commercial transactions between the two countries grew by a factor of eight, reaching $235 billion (U.S. Department of Commerce 2003). The number of Mexicans entering the United States on business visas more than tripled, from 128,000 to 438,000 annually, while the number of intracompany transferred personnel rose even more rapidly, from 4,300 to 16,000. There were only 73 Mexican treaty investors—that is, operations managers and investors in companies located within the United States—in 1986; by 2003, almost 5,000 Mexicans boasted that designation (U.S. Department of Homeland Security 2006).

The spectacular growth in commercial and business migration mimicked other cross-border movements. Mexican tourists entering the United States increased six-fold to 3.6 million between 1986 and 2003, while the number of individuals arriving as students doubled to 22,500, and that of educational and cultural exchange visitors more than doubled, from about 3,000 to 6,600 (U.S. Department of Homeland Security 2006). Similarly, the total number of single border crossings by car, bus, train, and on foot also grew rapidly from 114 million in 1986 to more than 290 million in 2000. After the 9/11 catastrophe, transit across the border fell, but it still was almost twice as high as it was in 1986 (Massey 2005).

In sum, over the past two decades the United States has pursued an increasingly contradictory set of policies with respect to Mexico, moving toward greater integration in markets for capital, goods, services, commodities, and information while insisting on separation in labor markets. Under NAFTA, the United States has moved forcefully to fuse all markets save one—that for labor—and the contradiction only became more acute after the 9/11 attacks on New York and Washington. In addition to continuing the expansion of the Border Patrol, the newly established Department of Homeland Security increased internal enforcement, using officers from Immigration and Customs Enforcement (ICE) to conduct sweeping raids looking for immigrants under deportation orders or otherwise out of status. On the legislative front, anti-immigrant fervor reached a climax when, on December 16, 2005, the U.S. House of Representatives passed HR 4437, the Sensenbrenner Bill, that sought to label as felonies not just unauthorized crossings of the border but also the hiring of and provision of services and humanitarian aid to undocumented immigrants. Although it has not become the law of the land, that bill hangs like the sword of Damocles over the fate of immigrants.

Perhaps even more important has been the shift in outlook to position immigration a matter of national security rather than labor regulation. The dismantling of the Immigration and Naturalization Service (INS) and the transfer of its powers to the Office of Homeland Security led to a reframing of immigrants as risks to the integrity of the United States, regardless of their provenance. Homeland Security was established with a clear mandate to protect the nation from terrorist threats, but its principal effect has been to terrorize immigrant workers from Mexico and Central America, many of whom were displaced by NAFTA and its more recent counterpart, the Central American Free Trade Agreement (CAFTA).

Especially untoward has been the treatment of Guatemalans, many of whom first entered the United States as refugees in search of asylum after fleeing a twelve-year-long civil war abetted covertly by the United States. When their appeals were denied by the American government, they became among the first to suffer the consequences of measures originally intended to deport potential terrorists. There is little public awareness about such matters. Instead, the past five years have witnessed a strong undercurrent of anti-immigrant feeling spurred by opportunistic politicians, the popular media, and some members of the academic community.

Other Effects of an Inconsistent Policy

Few in Washington have stopped to consider the contradiction involved in the growing militarization of a border separating the United States from a country that poses no strategic threat and is, in fact, an ally and major trading partner (Andreas 1998; Bean et al. 1994; Dunn 1996; Massey 2005). Although politicians in both nations viewed NAFTA as a way for Mexico to export goods and not people, many elements in the treaty accelerated the cross-movement of persons, including workers. The expanding binational web of transportation and communication links, which facilitate commercial transactions, also make the movement of individuals easier and cheaper. Interactions between Mexicans and Americans in the course of daily business create new friendship and kinship networks that transcend formal boundaries (Dunn 1996; Orme 1996; Singer and Massey 1998).

Few in Washington have stopped to consider the contradiction involved in the growing militarization of a border separating the United States from a country that poses no strategic threat and is, in fact, an ally and major trading partner.

That voluminous stock of social links between Mexicans and Americans, combined with heightened economic integration, presents a formidable obstacle for U.S. attempts to seal the border selectively. That such policies are failing cannot surprise anyone who understands the functioning of markets. What many do not realize, however, is that restrictive border policies are not only ineffective; they are counterproductive. Instead of deterring Mexicans from moving to the neighboring country, they have promoted a more rapid growth in the size of the undocumented population (Massey 2005) because of a simple cost-benefit calculation on the part of potential migrants—the greater the risks involved in reentry, the more they have tended to stay in the United States rather than returning home;

and the longer they remain north of the border, the more likely they are to bring in their spouses and dependents to live with them. U.S. policies have thus been instrumental in transforming a circular flow of male workers into a settled population of families.

In a similar vein, erecting a wall of enforcement resources selectively in a few sectors of the U.S.-Mexico border has proved ineffective because there are always other, less protected—albeit more dangerous—points of passage along an international demarcation line that spans nearly two thousand miles and is one of the longest in the world. Harsh enforcement in El Paso and San Diego in the late 1980s diverted flows to the Arizona desert causing authorities to launch new containment operations in that area. Those actions did not succeed either, but they did usher in a new and gruesome phase in the history of Mexican immigration. Before 1986, the number of people dying as they attempted to enter the United States was negligible; at present, nearly five hundred people die every year in their determination to find new opportunities in America (Eschbach, Hagan, and Rodriguez 1999). However, while migrants are more likely to perish while attempting entry in remote sectors, they are also less likely to be caught and the probability of apprehension during an undocumented border crossing has actually fallen as border enforcement has risen (Massey 2005).

Since 1982, the Mexican Migration Project (MMP), codirected by Douglas S. Massey at Princeton University and Jorge Durand at the University of Guadalajara, has regularly undertaken representative surveys of Mexican immigrants in their home communities and in U.S. destination areas to create an exhaustive database of binational migrant communities that yields information on some seventeen thousand households. Each head of household with migratory experience in the United States was interviewed to obtain a full history of border crossings, both attempted and completed, and these enable accurate estimation of the odds of apprehension as well as the place and circumstances of border crossing.

Figure 1 uses MMP data to show changes in the location of border crossing and the probability of apprehension among unauthorized Mexican migrants between 1980 and 2002, the latest year for which reliable estimates are available. The dashed line shows the proportion of migrants crossing at a nontraditional crossing point, which is defined as anyplace except Tijuana–San Diego or Ciudad Juarez–El Paso. As can be seen, from 1980 to 1987 the proportion of immigrants crossing through one of these two sectors steadily increased, until by 1988 more than 70 percent of all border crossings occurred at these two traditional points of entry. Harsher enforcement begun with the passage of the 1986 IRCA focused on those two high-volume passageways, a trend that was exacerbated with the targeted enforcement operations launched in 1993 and 1994. As a result, after 1988 the proportion of migrants passing through nontraditional areas rose steadily from 29 to 64 percent in 2002.

The figure also shows that through the 1970s and early 1980s, the probability of apprehension along the U.S.-Mexico border held relatively steady, averaging about 33 percent. Thereafter, it fell into the 20 to 30 percent range. Following the implementation of Operations Blockade and Gatekeeper in 1993 and 1994,

FIGURE 1
TRENDS IN THE USE OF NONTRADITIONAL CROSSING POINTS
AND THE PROBABILITY OF APPREHENSION, 1980-2002

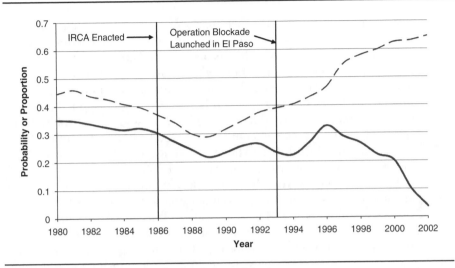

NOTE: IRCA = Immigration Reform and Control Act.

the likelihood of capture increased temporarily but then plummeted as migrants shifted to new crossing points guarded by fewer Border Patrol officers. By 2002, the odds of arrest had reached an all-time low of 5 percent.

Although the unilateral militarization of the U.S.-Mexican border has not been successful in reducing the inflow of undocumented migrants, it has achieved one outcome—it has dramatically increased the costs and risks of border crossing. By channeling undocumented flows to remote and more hazardous regions, blockades have tripled the rate of death along the border (Massey, Durand, and Malone 2002); and rather than giving up and staying in Mexico, immigrants have rationally invested more resources to minimize risks and maximize the odds of a successful border crossing. As the United States deployed more personnel and materiel at key points along the border, smugglers on the Mexican side upgraded their services. In the preceding era, they led small parties of would-be immigrants on foot across the well-trod pathways from Tijuana to San Diego and delivered them to anonymous urban settings. Now they transport people to remote areas, guide them across hostile physical environments, and make arrangements for others to meet them at the end of the journey. In other words, the net effect of U.S. policies has been to increase the quality, quantity, and cost of border-smuggling services (Spener 1999, 2001).

The extent of those increases is suggested by estimates of the average disbursements made by undocumented immigrants to cover the expenses of relocation. From 1980 to 1992 the cost of hiring a coyote or *pollero* was relatively flat, averaging approximately $400 per crossing. After 1993, however, the price of a smuggler's assistance rose steadily, leveling off at about $1,200 in 1999 (Massey 2005). In the post-9/11 furor over national security, those costs rose again. Unauthorized immigrants from Mexico currently pay up to $2,800 for the privilege of entering the United States. In other words, one of the accidental consequences of recent U.S. immigration policy has been to stimulate a robust industry comprising people smugglers and counterfeit-document manufacturers whose ingenuity in the production of visas, drivers licenses, and other official certificates has increased in scale and refinement over the last few years (Spener 2001).

Despite the increased costs and risks of unauthorized border crossing, the relative number of Mexicans arriving at the border seeking to enter the United States has not changed. The solid line in Figure 2 shows the probability that a Mexican undertakes a first undocumented trip to the United States from 1980 to 2002, computed from MMP data. This curve shows that the rate of undocumented migration has hardly changed in two decades, fluctuating narrowly in the range of 1 to 2 percent per year. Reliable data thus indicate that the inflow of undocumented migrants from Mexico continues more or less unabated.

Perhaps the most important but unexpected effect of current immigration policies was to decrease the likelihood that unauthorized workers will return home. If the first priority after any relocation trip is to recover the cost of travel and settlement, then holding constant the rate of remuneration and hours worked per week, the stay abroad would have to be three times as long by comparison to what it was a decade earlier. Beefing up the Border Patrol may not have reduced the inflow of unauthorized immigrants but it has substantially increased the probability that they will stay longer in areas of destination. Another way of viewing the increase in trip lengths is in terms of the decline in the probability of return migration: fewer migrants go back within one year of their original entry.

Perhaps the most important but unexpected effect of current immigration policies was to decrease the likelihood that unauthorized workers will return home.

The dashed line in Figure 2 uses MMP data to compute the probability of return to Mexico within twelve months of entry into the United States. As may be seen, before the passage of IRCA in 1986, the annual likelihood of return migration fluctuated between 40 and 50 percent with no clear trend. After 1986,

FIGURE 2
PROBABILITY OF LEAVING AND RETURNING FROM
A FIRST UNDOCUMENTED TRIP TO THE UNITED STATES

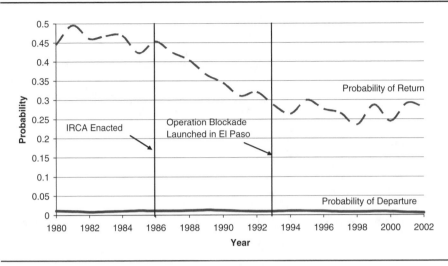

NOTE: IRCA = Immigration Reform and Control Act.

however, there was a steady and sustained decline in the likelihood of return migration, which bottomed out at 24 percent in 1996 and then began to oscillate. Roughly speaking, the average probability of return migration went from around 45 percent before the passage of IRCA to around 25 percent today. Thus, although undocumented migration from Mexico has not increased in relative terms, the size of the Mexican population in the United States has expanded. What has declined dramatically is the rate of return migration, which increased net undocumented population growth.

The growth of the Mexican population living in the United States as recorded by the U.S. Bureau of the Census is presented in Figure 3. From 1980 through the mid-1990s, that population grew at a steady rate, roughly tripling in the period between 1980 and 1995. After 1990, the trend accelerated, going from 7 million in 1997 to around 10 million in 2002, an increase of 43 percent in just five years. By 2002, Hispanics had surpassed African Americans as the largest minority group in this country, with 32.8 million representing 12 percent of the total population. Sixty percent of Hispanics are of Mexican origin. In addition, an estimated 12 million unauthorized immigrants now live on American soil. About a million of them are persons brought into this country as children. A significant proportion of the undocumented population comprises families who have opted out of return to their home country for fear of detention upon reentry to the United States. They and their children are increasingly at risk of forming a new underclass formed by people with few rights and avenues for successful integration into the larger American society (Portes 2007 [this volume]).

FIGURE 3
NUMBER OF MEXICANS IN THE UNITED STATES, 1980-2002

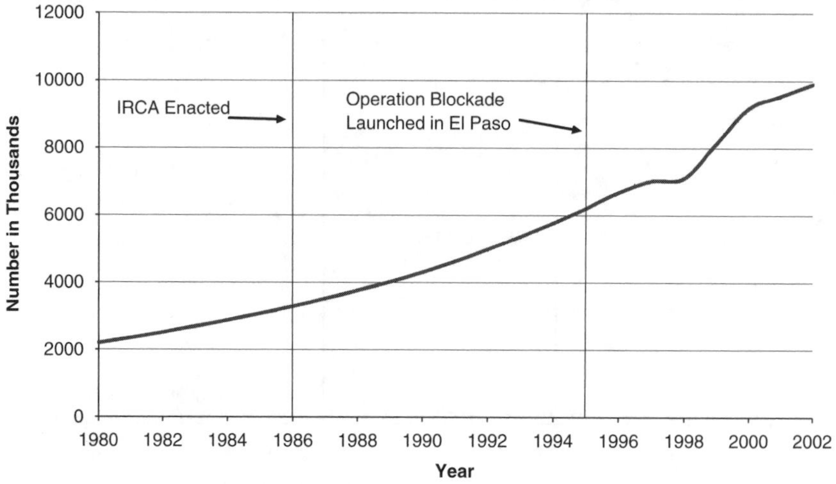

NOTE: IRCA = Immigration Reform and Control Act.

Bringing Reason Back In

The futility of recent immigration policies and their devastating effects upon the well-being of individuals and families need not continue. Elsewhere, Massey (2005; Massey and Durand 2002) has proposed specific measures that would reconcile U.S. immigration policy with the realities of growing economic integration brought about under NAFTA. Most important among those recommendations is to bring current flows of Mexican labor into the open through the creation of a temporary visa program that would permit individuals to enter, live, work, and be accounted for in the United States. Those new visas would be available to residents of Canada and Mexico, the two countries joined to the United States by territorial proximity but also by NAFTA. If 300,000 two-year visas were issued annually, there would be 600,000 temporary workers in the United States at any time, a small share of the U.S. labor force but a large fraction of the undocumented population.

A rational and consistent immigration policy would also require potential immigrants to pay substantial fees—but not as large as those now paid to smugglers and counterfeit documents manufacturers—for visas and work permits issued by the U.S. government. The funds amassed from such measures could be put to good use by supporting educational and employment opportunities in U.S. communities. Those resources could also be directed to the enforcement of measures aimed at keeping dangerous individuals and potential terrorists away from the United States.

Finally, it is imperative to increase the number of permanent resident visas available to Mexicans to one hundred thousand. Mexico is a country of 105 million people with a one-trillion-dollar economy that shares a two-thousand-mile border with the United States, to which it is linked by a free trade agreement that has increasingly integrated the North American economy to make Mexico and the United States one another's largest trading partners. Yet despite these intimate linkages, Mexico has the same immigration quota as Nepal or Botswana. Maintaining a quota of twenty thousand visas per year for a nation to which the United States is so closely bound by history, geography, and free trade is unrealistically low, bringing about waiting periods that surpass ten years, creating frustration among qualified applicants, and making it all but certain that illegal migration will continue.

Conclusions

In this article, we have developed a synoptic account of the historical events leading to the passage of NAFTA, a treaty ostensibly intended to reduce barriers to investment, open markets, and fuel economic development on both sides of the border. We have argued, however, that a major objective behind NAFTA was not simply the liberalization of trade but the creation of suitable conditions for the realization of profits by U.S. financial institutions and manufacturers through carefully regulated investment in Mexico. In that sense, NAFTA is more about controlled than free trade.

Our historical account of the events leading to the implementation of NAFTA revealed critical alliances on both sides of the U.S.-Mexico border. The financial crisis of the 1980s in Latin America, and consequently in the United States, brought about a new coalition that included U.S. banking interests and their representatives in Washington, Mexican public officials, and large business interests in both countries. In essence, the Latin American debt crisis of the 1980s acted as an agent for economic reconfiguration and the assumption of new state functions on both sides of the border.

NAFTA's silence with respect to labor rights and worker mobility is comprehensible in the observation that, contrary to the basic precepts of the European Union and its project of political and economic integration, the overarching goal of the treaty was to advance the economic interests of a new binational class of investors, not the fortunes of citizens in general. In that respect, NAFTA may be seen as part of a class project (Harvey 2007 [this volume]). Although the treaty may have had mixed effects on workers in Mexico and the United States, its effects in terms of profits and capital accumulation are clear—never before have large firms experienced such an economic bonanza. At the same time, the period coinciding with NAFTA's implementation has witnessed significant growths in class inequality in the two countries.

Unique in the international landscape is the contradiction of attempting to liberalize trade while at the same time trying to force workers to remain fixed in space. The refusal on the part of the architects of NAFTA to consider labor flows as part of the neoliberal project has given rise to several unintended consequences. First, the reduction of public spending in Mexico, the removal of subsidies to subsistence agriculture, the opening of feed and seed markets, and the commercialization of communal lands have had a displacing effect, leading peasants to seek economic opportunities in the neighboring country.

Second, the continuation of migration flows have been met in the United States with growing attempts at curtailment. Since 1986, and especially in the 9/11 aftermath, U.S. immigration policy has become increasingly repressive and equally ineffective. Border blockades have led would-be immigrants to more remote and hazardous points of entry, boosting the number of deaths but reducing the probability that they will be detained. Paradoxically, greater repression has not reduced the likelihood of undocumented migration.

Third, tighter migration policies have also fomented the growth of a finely tuned machine of smugglers and false document manufacturers, all of whom are paid sizeable sums to aid immigrants. That vibrant economic sector increasingly includes drug traders and sex traffickers whose resources are now needed to oil the wheels of undocumented migration.

Fourth, and perhaps most important, the harsher character of U.S. immigration policy is leading to the expansion of the undocumented Mexican population in the United States. Immigrants are behaving just as economists would predict by engaging in cost-benefit calculations that lead them to stay in areas of destination for longer periods of time to avoid the risks of exit and reentry. The presence of an expanded undocumented population on American soil does not bode well for individuals or families. Without avenues for integration, in the face of public hostility, and with few opportunities to improve their educational and occupational standing, many of those immigrants may yet become part of a new Latino underclass.

This dire forecast is not only counter to the image of a country defined by democracy, fair play, and opportunity but is also in conflict with the stated objectives of a treaty that has demolished barriers for capital with unprecedented success. Time is running out, but perhaps it is still possible to reconcile facts with theory. Borders for whom? The present situation indicates that borders stand mainly to contain the most vulnerable sectors of society while they become more and more permeable for those in positions of power.

References

Andreas, Peter. 1998. The escalation of U.S. immigration control in the post-NAFTA era. *Political Science Quarterly* 113:591-601.

Babb, Sarah L. 2001. *Managing Mexico: Economists from nationalism to neoliberalism.* Princeton, NJ: Princeton University Press.

———. 2003. The IMF in sociological perspective: A tale of organizational slippage. *Studies in Comparative International Development* 38:3—27.

Bean, Frank, Roland Chanove, Robert G. Cushing, Rodolfo de la Garza, Gary Freeman, Charles W. Haynes, and David Spener. 1994. *Illegal Mexican migration and the United States border: The effects of Operation Hold-the-Line in El Paso/Juarez*. Austin: University of Texas at Austin, Population Research Center.

Brady, David, Jason Beckfield, and Martin Seeleib-Kaiser. 2005. Economic globalization and the welfare state in affluent democracies, 1975-1998. *American Sociological Review* 70:921-48.

Calavita, Kitty. 1992. *Inside the state: The Bracero Program, immigration, and the I.N.S.* New York: Routledge.

Camp, Roderick A. 2002. *Mexico's mandarins: Crafting a power elite for the twenty-first century*. Berkeley: University of California Press.

Campbell, Bruce, Andrew Jackson, Mehrene Larudel, and Teresa Gutierrez Haces. 1999. *Labour market effects under CUFTA/NAFTA*. Geneva, Switzerland: International Labor Organization, Employment and Training Department.

Campbell, Tim, and Sara Freedheim. 1994. *PRONASOL in principle: Basic features and significance of Mexico's Solidarity Program*. Report 016. Washington, DC: World Bank, Latin America and the Caribbean Region Department.

Cardoso, Lawrence. 1980. *Mexican emigration to the United States 1897-1931*. Tucson: University of Arizona Press.

Centeno, Miguel. 2004. *Democracy within reason: Technocratic revolution in Mexico*. University Park: Pennsylvania State University Press.

———. 2007. Liberalism and the good society in the Iberian world. *Annals of the American Academy of Political and Social Science* 610: 45-72.

Dávalos, Pablo. 2006. *The geopolitics of Latin American foreign debt*. ZNET, http://www.zmag.org/content/showarticle.cfm?ItemID=10936.

Deyo, Frederick C. 1987. *The political economy of the new Asian industrialism*. Ithaca, NY: Cornell University Press.

———. 1989. *Beneath the miracle: Labor subordination in the new Asian industrialism*. Berkeley: University of California Press.

Dunn, Timothy J. 1996. *The militarization of the Mexico-U.S. border 1978-1992*. Austin: University of Texas Press.

Durand, Jorge, and Paricia Arias. 2000. *La Experiencia Migrante: Iconografía de la Migración México-Estados Unidos*. México, D.F.: Altexto.

Eschbach, Karl, Jacqueline Hagan, and Nestor Rodriguez. 1999. Death at the border. *International Migration Review* 33:430-54.

Evans, Peter. 1995. *Embedded autonomy: States and industrial transformation*. Princeton, NJ: Princeton University Press.

Fernández-Kelly, Patricia. 1993. Labor force recomposition in electronics: Implications for free trade. *Hofstra Labor Law Journal* 10 (2): 623-717.

Galarza, Ernest. 1964. *Merchants of labor: The Mexican bracero story*. Santa Barbara, CA: NcNally and Loftin.

Gan, Jie. 2004. Banking market structure and financial stability: Evidence from the Texas real estate crisis in the 1980s. *Journal of Financial Economics* 73 (3) 567-601.

Gereffi, Gary, David Spener, and Jennifer Bair. 2002. *Free trade and uneven development: The North American apparel industry after NAFTA*. Philadelphia: Temple University Press.

Gereffi, Gary, and Donald L. Wyman, eds. 1990. *Manufacturing miracles: Paths of industrialization in Latin America and East Asia*. Princeton, NJ: Princeton University Press.

Griffin, Larry J., Michael E. Wallace, and Beth A. Rubin. 1986. Capitalist resistance to the organization of labor before the New Deal: Why? How? Success? *American Sociological Review* 51:147-67.

Harvey, David. 2007. Neoliberalism as creative destruction. *Annals of the American Academy of Political and Social Science* 610: 22-44.

Herzenberg, Stephen A. 1991. *The North American free auto industry at the onset of continental free trade negotiations*. Economic Discussion Paper no. 38. Washington, DC: U.S. Department of Labor.

Hoffman, Abraham. 1974. *Unwanted Mexican Americans in the Great Depression: Repatriation Pressures 1929-1939*. Tucson: University of Arizona Press.

Hufbauer, Gary C., and Jeffrey J. Schott. 1992. *North American Free Trade: Issues and recommendations*. Washington, DC: Institute for International Economics.

Light, Donald W. 2007. Globalizing restricted and segmented markets: Challenges to theory and values in economic sociology. *Annals of the American Academy of Political and Social Science* 610:232-45.

Martin, Philip. 2003. *Economic integration and migration: The Mexico-U.S. case*. Discussion Paper no. 2003/35. Annankatu, Helsinki, Finland: World Institute for Development Economics Research (WIDER).

Massey, Douglas S. 2005. Backfire at the border: Why enforcement without legalization cannot stop illegal immigration. *Cato Institute Trade Policy Analysis* 29 (June 13): 1-14.

———. 2007. *Categorically unequal: The American stratification system*. New York: Russell Sage Foundation.

Massey, Douglas S., and Jorge Durand. 2002. *Beyond smoke and mirrors: Mexican immigration in an age of economic integration*. New York: Russell Sage Foundation.

Massey, Douglas S., Jorge Durand, and Nolan J. Malone. 2002. *Beyond smoke and mirrors: Mexican immigration in an era of economic integration*. New York: Russell Sage Foundation.

Middlebrook, Kevin J. 2004. *Dilemmas of political change in Mexico*. La Jolla, CA: Institute of Latin American Studies, Center for U.S.-Mexico Studies, University of California, San Diego.

Moody, Kim, and Mary McGinn. 1992. Unions and free trade: Solidarity vs competition. In *Labor notes*. San Francisco: Institute for Food and Development Policy.

Nelsen, Brent F., and Alexander Stubb, eds. 2005. *The European Union: Readings on the theory and practice of European integration*. Boulder, CO: Lynne Rienner.

Nevins, Joseph. 2002. *Operation Gatekeeper: The rise of the illegal alien and the making of the U.S.-Mexico boundary*. New York: Routledge.

Orme, William A. 1996. *Understanding NAFTA: Mexico free trade and the new North America*. Austin: University of Texas Press.

Portes, Alejandro. 2007. Migration, development, and segmented assimiliation: A conceptual review of the evidence. *Annals of the American Academy of Political and Social Science* 610:73-97.

Quentin, Erwan, and José Joaquín López. 2006. Mexico's financial vulnerability: Then and now. *Economic Letter—Insights from the Federal Reserve Bank of Dallas* 1 (6, June). http://www.dallasfed.org/research/eclett/2006/el0606.html.

Rockefeller, David. 1987. Let's not write off Latin America. *New York Times*, July 5, p. E15.

———. 1992. Remarks to Forum of the Americas Conference Luncheon. Sheraton Washington Hotel, April 23.

Shaiken, Harley. 2001. The new global economy: Trade and production under NAFTA. *Journal Fur Entwicklungspolitik* 17 (4): 241-54.

———. 2004a. Crossing borders: Trade policy and transnational labour education. *Labour, Capital and Society* 35 (2): 342-68.

———. 2004b. *The high road to a competitive economy: A labor law strategy*. Washington, DC: The Center for American Progress.

Shefner, Jon. 2007. Rethinking civil society in the age of NAFTA: The case of Mexico. *Annals of the American Academy of Political and Social Science* 610:182-200.

Singer, Audrey, and Douglas S. Massey. 1998. The social process of undocumented border crossing. *International Migration Review* 32:561-92.

Spener, David. 1999. This coyote's life. *NACLA Report on the Americas* 33 (3): 22-23.

———. 2001. El Contrabando de Migrantes en la Frontera de Texas con el Nordeste de México: Un mecanismo para la Integración del Mercado Laboral de América del Norte. *Espiral: Estudios sobre Estado y Sociedad* 7 (21): 201-47.

Stanford, James. 1993. Continental economic integration: Modeling the impact on labor. *Annals of the American Academy of Political and Social Science* 526:92-110.

Trebat, Thomas J. 1991. The banking system crisis in Latin America. *Contemporary Economic Policy* 9:54-66.

U.S. Department of Commerce. 2003. *U.S. international trade in goods and services: Annual revision for 2003*. www.census.gov/foreign-trade/Press-Release/2003pr/final_revisions.

U.S. Department of Homeland Security. 2006. *The 2004 yearbook of immigration statistics*. Washington, DC: Government Printing Office.

Zarsky, Lyuba, and Keving Gallagher. 2004. *NAFTA, foreign direct investment, and sustainable industrial development in Mexico*. Silver City, NM: American Program Policy Brief, International Relations Center.

SECTION TWO

NAFTA, Labor, and the National State

The Strategic Role of Mexican Labor under NAFTA: Critical Perspectives on Current Economic Integration

By
RAÚL DELGADO WISE
and
JAMES M. CYPHER

This article aims to reveal the precise meaning of Mexico's export platform by focusing on maquiladoras and the disguised maquila industry. In both sectors, imported components account for 75 to 90 percent of export value. As a result, benefits for the Mexican economy are basically restricted to wages, that is, the value of the labor incorporated into the exports. The authors argue that what is actually taking place is the disembodied exportation of labor or, alternatively, that the workforce is being exported without requiring Mexican workers to leave the country. The authors thus demystify the purported orientation of Mexican exports toward high-value-added manufactured goods and reveal the regressive movement of the export platform.

Keywords: NAFTA; maquiladora industry; disguised maquila; export-led industrialization; transnational corporations; Mexican conglomerates

In this article, we present a new theoretical formulation of the Mexican economy under the North American Free Trade Agreement (NAFTA)—the cheap-labor export-led model. We maintain that, in one guise or another, Mexico's new role consists of exporting its cheap labor, not in achieving new high-value-added forms of production through enhanced specialization.

This model stands in stark contrast to a vision projected by those who gave shape to NAFTA; advocates portrayed that treaty as a win-win proposition for Mexico and the United States and as an avenue for reducing asymmetries between those two countries and Canada. Furthermore, NAFTA was presented as an antidote to emigration. In spite of the widespread presumption that the NAFTA model is merely a trade-enhancing process, we maintain that its underlying objective—its inner rationality—is the export of cheap, largely poorly trained labor through three interrelated mechanism: (1) the maquila industry (the processing of imported materials by low-skilled, low-paid Mexican workers, which are then reexported, overwhelmingly

DOI: 10.1177/0002716206297527

to the United States), (2) the *disguised* maquila sector, and (3) the emigration of Mexican labor to the United States. The first two processes constitute the disembodied export of cheap labor, with this labor actually embodied in the exported products. Emigration, on the other hand, is the direct export of labor, but in all three instances Mexico is not really exporting goods because, with minor exceptions, the only Mexican-made value/input in this complex transnational process is cheap labor. We use NAFTA to designate a series of agreements, informal accords, and economic policy changes largely initiated by the United States to confront the new structural forces arising from the present era of intense international economic rivalry among the Northern (first tier) nations. We further argue that the new labor-export model constitutes a fundamental element in the process of industrial restructuring of the U.S. economy that began in the 1980s and continues in the new millennium.

We present data that show the emergence of a disarticulated economy in Mexico, one where a significant division is to be found between the two maquila sectors and the remainder of the economy. The net result is a lack of economic continuity, autonomy, and dynamism where the productive apparatus has been dismantled and reassembled to fit the structural requirements of the United States, leaving Mexico in control of certain low-value-added resource-based activities, and a range of other rentier pursuits in tourism, finance, and real-estate. Instead of advancing its productive capacity, Mexico is falling farther behind in relative terms because, in essence, the labor export-led model is structurally designed to transfer Mexico's economic surplus away from its potential domestic usage. This process of subordinated integration fails to advance the productive apparatus of the economy through investments in expanded research, development, and technological applications and through public sector infrastructural investments designed to rapidly improve Mexico's quality of education, public health, and autonomous industrial base. Mexican elites coexist symbiotically with and facilitate the restructuring process as delimited by U.S. economic interests. In this process, certain benefits befall the elite, while its members carefully maintain their option of engaging in devastating capital flight—or deploying the threat of capital flight—to preserve their benefits.

Our analysis is divided into six sections. First, we examine NAFTA both in terms of how the Mexican government has portrayed its effects and in terms of its actual impact when using less selective data. Second, we focus on maquiladoras and the indirect export of cheap labor as embodied in products from that sector.

Raúl Delgado Wise is director of the Doctoral Program in Development Studies at the Universidad Autónoma de Zacatecas (Mexico), and executive secretary of the International Network on Migration and Development. He has published eight books and is the editor of Migración y Desarrollo *and the book series "Latin America and the New World Order."*

James M. Cypher is a professor in the Doctoral Program in Development Studies at the Universidad Autónoma de Zacatecas (Mexico). He is the author of State and Capital in Mexico *(Westview, 1990); the coauthor of* The Process of Economic Development *(Routledge, 2004); and the author of more than one hundred scholarly publications, several of which deal with NAFTA-related themes.*

Third, we analyze the disguised maquila sector and the ways in which it corresponds to and can be differentiated from the maquiladora industry. Fourth, we briefly review some of the more salient characteristics of the Mexican emigration process as they pertain to our model. Next, we explain processes pertaining to the cheap-labor export-led model that have served to facilitate a restructuring of the U.S. production system. In the sixth section, we turn to the impact that all of the above processes have imposed upon Mexico and the reasons why—despite those adverse affects—the Mexican political class and the business elite have been stalwart advocates of Mexico's neoliberal restructuring. We show why the positive effects anticipated by neoclassical economic theorists have failed to appear. Last, we offer conclusions derived from the research undertaken.

Situating the Problem: The Apologetic Vision of NAFTA

Throughout the world there is a perception—carefully nurtured by the Mexican government—that Mexico's economic restructuring based on the growth of foreign transactions (exports + direct foreign investment) in accordance with the NAFTA accord has yielded tremendous results. Public officials point out that (1) between 1991 and 2000 exports grew at an annual average rate of 16.3 percent, forming the leading sector of the economy; (2) maquiladora exports were the most dynamic of all, growing at an annual average rate of 19.6 percent; (3) manufactured exports rose from less than 25 percent of total exports in 1982 to more than 90 percent in the late 1990s; and (4) Mexico has become Latin America's top exporter while rising to seventh place in terms of foreign trade (exports + imports) (Leon González and Dussel Peters 2001, 653). Overall, in this new model the export/GDP ratio rose from less than 10 percent in 1988 to more than 25 percent in the late 1990s, with more than 90 percent of these exports flowing into the United States.

We, on the other hand, find that NAFTA has exhibited the following effects: (1) it has been a losing proposition for workers, small and medium-sized businesses and, particularly, peasants; (2) in the United States, for the working class and portions of the middle class, and for some sectors of business, the impact of NAFTA has been negative (Cypher 2001; Delgado Wise 2006). At the same time, NAFTA has directly benefited a small set of interests on both sides of the border, especially U.S.-based transnational corporations (TNCs) and Mexico's largest conglomerates (or *grupos*). The sweeping changes in policy have correlated with massive waves of emigration. This injection of cheap labor has served to indirectly lower reproduction costs and, therefore, the wages of U.S. workers. Such results may be surprising to neoliberal policy makers but are consistent with the objectives of specific sectors—for separate but complementary reasons both Mexican conglomerates and some of the largest U.S. manufacturing interests converged on the idea of a subordinated integration of the two distinct national production systems in the late 1980s.

The widely disseminated vision portraying Mexico's restructuring as a resounding success stands in sharp contrast to the continued growth of emigration, to the degree that Mexico has now become the principal country of emigrants in the world. Ironically, neoliberal restructuring was conceived as the very antidote to emigration, with proponents asserting that the workings of the free trade arrangement would lead Mexico to specialize in labor-intensive activities. These, in turn would absorb most of the idle and underused labor force. Instead, few jobs in the formal sector, and even fewer decent jobs of a nonprecarious nature, have been created, forcing as many as 89 percent of the annual new entrants into a free-to-choose scenario where the options are (1) to work in the informal sector as house servants, street vendors or suchlike or (2) to migrate to the United States.[1] It is generally conceded that Mexico needs to create 1.2 million net new jobs per year to keep the unemployment rate constant and accommodate new entrants to the workforce. Yet under President Vicente Fox's administration, only 40,000 permanent jobs were created per year. That means an annual jobs deficit of more than 1.1 million that forces the new entrants into *temporary* formal jobs—640,000 such slots were created in six years—the informal sector or emigration for the roughly 6.5 million who remained (Cadena 2006a, 21). Of that total, nearly 3 million emigrated in the latest *sexenio* (six-year presidential term). Indeed, emigration has become such a powerful current that 31 percent of the municipalities in Mexico are now suffering from depopulation. Emigration is at the center of our interpretation of the complex economic processes unleashed by the neoliberal restructuring program.

Mexico has now become the principal country of emigrants in the world. Ironically, neoliberal restructuring was conceived as the very antidote to emigration.

Over the six years that Vicente Fox was president, Mexico's gross domestic product (GDP) grew at an estimated annual real rate of 2 percent. Taking the three sexenios during which Mexico embraced the free trade policies that culminated in NAFTA and beyond (1988-2006), the average annual real rate of GDP growth was 3 percent, roughly one-half that achieved in the import-substitution era between 1940 and 1982 (Gutiérrez 2006, 3A; Cypher 1990). Manufacturing growth for the 2000 to 2006 period was roughly 0.6 percent per year, with employment in that sector falling 15 percent between 2000 and 2005 (Dussel Peters

2006a, 74). Despite its image as Latin America's most successful case of transformation toward an export-led economy based in manufacturing, the constraints imposed on the internal market have been such—given the exploding importation of manufactured products and the limits set by weak aggregate demand, itself the result of low and falling wages—that Mexico is actually de-industrializing. The average level of manufacturing expressed as a percentage of the GDP under the administration of President Ernesto Zedillo was nearly 20 percent, whereas under Fox that figure fell to 18 percent, and the ratio dropped from 20 percent in 2000 to 17 percent in 2005 (Becerril 2006b, 18, Dussel Peters 2006a, 69). According to the World Economic Forum's method of calculating competitiveness for 104 nations, Mexico's manufacturing sector fell from 31st place in 2000 to 59th place in 2005 (Becerril 2006b, 18). Most commentators associate this spectacular drop to Mexico's determined stance in opposition to investments in research and development and the virtual absence of anything that could be termed a national innovation system.[2] Meanwhile, throughout the Fox administration (and before), overall manufacturing exports proved insufficient to pay for overall imports—Mexico encountered an estimated trade deficit of $20.4 billion for 2005 (Zúñiga and Rodríguez 2005, 24). Thus, even while Mexico's economy enjoyed a modest two and a half year expansion (2003 to mid-2006), the manufacturing sector remained stagnant, and its failure to cover the cost of overall imports means that, in essence, manufacturing performance is serving to *reduce* Mexico's standard of living and GDP, not the opposite.

Consider, for example, the case of wages in the manufacturing sector: mid-2005 levels were on average 24 percent lower than real wages received in December 2000 (Bendensky 2005, 25) but real average wages overall in *2000* were only 73 percent of the 1982 level (Unger 2002, 3). *If* the maquila sector (or more broadly the export sector) had the effect that its proponents contend—positing manufacturing export-led development as a viable strategy for Mexico—one should anticipate that real wages would have some positive correlation with the rate of growth of exports and the rise in the export/GDP ratio over the 1982 to 2005 period. Yet that correlation has been negative, and it has persisted long enough to belie the perception that it is a temporary anomaly. Instead, the negative correlation in question is an expression of the cheap-labor export-led model—Mexico's static comparative advantage rests in the exportation of labor, either (1) embodied in the products of the maquiladoras; or (2) embedded in the disguised maquila sector involving large corporations that export through the use of inputs from the maquiladoras (often depending on products exported by them and then reimported), or directly importing untaxed inputs into their production system); or (3) via migration. Thus, this model cannot, and does not, offer development in the most basic sense *because it cannot. All* the benefits of economic growth are either being exported via transfer prices, repatriation of profits, lavish salaries and benefits paid to high-level transnational firm employees, payments of interest on foreign debts; *and/or* high incomes, ample profits, rents and interest transfers received by Mexico's technocrats, its political class, and the owners of the giant Mexican conglomerates.

FIGURE 1
MEXICO: COEFFICIENT OF NATIONAL INTEGRATION
(IN PERCENTAGE TERMS)

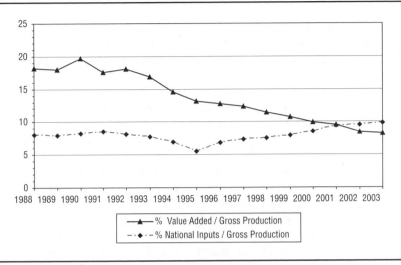

SOURCE: Instituto Nacional de Estadística (INEGI; 2004b).

The Embodied Labor Export Process: Part I

The maquila sector constitutes the starting point in the examination in our analysis because it has by definition been associated with manufacturing exports, and in many formulations it has been linked to the concept of cheap, unprotected, and nonunionized labor.[3] In the three-thousand-plus maquiladora firms that cluster along the U.S.–Mexican border are employed more than 1.2 million workers who generated 55 percent of Mexico's manufactured exports in 2004 (Banco Nacional de Comercio Exterior 2005).[4] For the most part, maquiladoras import inputs—components, parts, design, engineering, and so on overwhelmingly from the United States, combine those various inputs with cheap assembly (pay per day in 2005 ranged from $4 to $10) and a slight element of technical labor, assemble the finished products and reexport the finished products back to the United States.

Figure 1 shows that the value added in the maquila sector constitutes a declining share of the total value of gross production (sales) in that sector. Thus, notwithstanding the overall growth in maquila employment in the NAFTA era, and despite the rise in the total value of Mexico's maquila exports, Mexico retains a smaller and smaller relative share of benefits derived from those activities even as the costs in terms of aggregate physical effort rise—the ratio dropped from 18 percent in 1988 to only 8 percent in 2003—a decline of 55 percent. In terms of opportunity costs, Mexico also gives up more relatively every year—which is to say that if Mexico had a viable developmental strategy it could either extract a larger share of the benefits from the maquila industry or engage in a national upgrading process that would eventually lead to a viable development project based in other forms of manufacturing.

Also worth noting in Figure 1 is the essentially static level of integration of the maquila sector as indicated by the corresponding coefficient (national inputs/gross production). The data presented in Figure 1, however, exaggerate the degree of national linkage between the maquila industry and the national production system: roughly 60 percent of the national inputs in 2003, for example, derived from the service sector in terms of cleaning, accounting, packaging and shipping, and similar activities. Only 3 percent of total production value are component/manufacturing inputs.

Although the quantitative data repeatedly demonstrate the futility and negative impact of the maquila industry, a significant number of Mexican researchers continue to furnish qualitative studies of so-called second- and third-generation maquila firms that, according to that body of research, hold the potential for the many externalities posited by new growth theory (Cypher 2004; Dutrénit and Vera-Cruz 2005; Lara, Arellano, and García 2005; Villavicencio and Casalet 2005).[5] None of those studies, however, has ever presented convincing quantitative data suggesting that *in the aggregate* the maquila sector is anything more than a cheap-labor assembly operation with virtually no backward or forward linkages to Mexico's economy. Nor, in spite of many efforts to do so, have these studies ever established a significant dynamic trend sufficiently large to change the fundamental character (cheap dispensable labor) of the maquila industry.

[T]he maquila project was never a national development strategy, and is even less so today.

Once thought to be a serious generator of employment (as well as a source of skill-upgrading), the maquila sector has ceased to create new jobs, with employment, in August 2005, 16 percent below levels achieved in August 2000. When the maquila sector was growing, in employment terms, between 1994 and 2000, jobs created paid 52 percent less than nonmaquila manufacturing, while living costs for maquila workers clustered along the U.S.-Mexican border were considerably higher than in other states (Cypher 2004, 362). In short, and despite the rosy predictions of an indefatigable cadre of Mexican researchers, the maquila project was never a national development strategy and is even less so today. Above all, it should be emphasized that by its nature the maquila industry does not represent the exportation of Mexican manufactured products—instead it represents the export of Mexican labor power embodied in the final assembled and exported products.[6]

The Embodied Labor Export Process: Part II

There is a twofold division of Mexico's manufacturing sector, which normally accounts for roughly 85 percent of all exports—maquila manufacturing and non-maquila manufacturing.[7] Yet within the second sector 38 percent of all export output in recent years was undertaken via temporary import incentive schemes (such as Pitex and Altex) that largely grant the same subsidies and fiscal exemptions to firms engaging in exports under "temporary import programs" as those that are designated as maquiladora plants (Capdevielle 2005, 564-65; Dussel Peters 2006a, 83-85).[8] Thus, a significant and rapidly growing volume of production is generated by the maquila firms or other supplier firms that are exempt from certain taxes if they produce inputs for the Pitex or Altex firms.[9] The disguised maquila—most of them large transnationals (TNCs), overwhelmingly U.S.-based—are located throughout the interior of Mexico. They incorporate maquila-made parts and components, or parts/components from the designated Mexican supplier web, and generated finished manufacturing products—often of a sophisticated nature, such as autos—which are then exported, primarily into the U.S. market (see Figure 2). In addition, *a larger process* consists of temporarily importing parts and components which are then reexported after they have been processed or assembled in the disguised maquila plants. A third aspect of this *triangulation* structure is to export maquila products and then, perhaps with further processing, to reimport products as inputs into the disguised maquila sector—wherein they are then processed and again exported. In 2006 a total of 3,339 firms were involved in the disguised maquila sector, excluding the supplier base—160 more than were operating in the well-known maquila sector. Together the disguised maquila and maquila firms accounted for 70 percent of all exports in 2005—in the entire NAFTA period the two maquila sectors accounted for an average of 78 percent of all exports (Becerril 2006a, 18, Dussel Peters 2006a, 75).

Frequently, this movement of inputs from the maquila firms to the larger TNCs constitutes intrafirm transactions since through joint-ventures or direct ownership the large TNCs control many maquila supplier firms. U.S. intrafirm transactions for imports in the auto and electronics sectors—the two largest export sectors for Mexico—stood at 76 percent and 68 percent, respectively, in 2002 (Dúran Lima and Ventura-Dias 2003, 59). Such disguised maquila activities employ at minimum 500,000 workers, representing approximately 37 percent of all nonmaquila manufacturing workers that are normally assumed to be working in the *national* manufacturing sector[10] (Capdevielle 2005, 568). Workers employed in the indirect labor export or disguised maquila sector have somewhat higher skill levels, better representation of their rights via their unions, and

FIGURE 2
MEXICO: MANUFACTURED EXPORTS BY TYPE

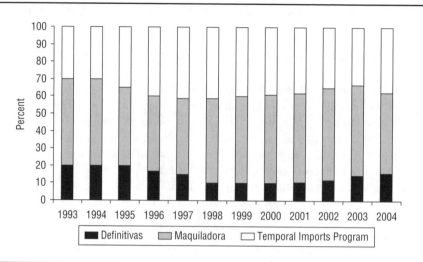

SOURCE: Banco Nacional de Comercio Exterior (2005).
NOTE: Definite exports refer to those that are not reexport platforms. Here we can locate scarcely refined commodities such as glass, steel, cement, and beer where technological inten-sive products and processes are not a defining characteristic of the production process, and where ownership is largely controlled by the Mexican conglomerates (*grupos*).

are generally paid at least 50 percent more than direct maquila workers because their productivity levels are higher given their union representation, a legacy from the Import Substitution Industrialization Policies (ISI) era, and also given that the major TNCs tend to accept a policy of industrial relations in accordance to which payment of subsistence wages is not a priority (Cypher 2004, 363). Nonetheless, workers receive meager compensation although their productivity often approximates levels found in the (Northern) industrial nations—fre-quently the South/North wage differential (Mexico/United States) will be in the range of 1:7 in the indirect maquila sector, and nearly double that ratio in the maquila sector. Thus, the International Labor Organization (ILO) has found that for Mexican manufacturing workers *overall* (maquila + nonmaquila) in rela-tion to U.S. manufacturing sector workers in 2003, the ratio was 1:11.39 (Howard 2005, 2). Throughout the NAFTA period, wages in the disguised maquila sector have fallen by more than 12 percent, while in the maquila sector, despite some rising productivity, they have increased only 3 percent or less—3 percent of the lowest paid maquila workers' daily wage was 12 U.S. cents in 2004 (Cypher 2004, 363).

In the disguised maquila sector, nationally produced inputs/components have fallen from 32 percent in 1993 to 22.6 percent in 2004 (Cadena 2005, 13). In essence, export firms outside of the maquila sector are progressively *de-industrializing*, leaving only the value of Mexican labor as the determining component of value-added as 77 percent of the inputs into the production process are imported. Once again, we emphasize that in the final analysis for Mexico the net result in this sector is almost completely reducible to the disembodied export of the Mexican labor force as embodied in the exported products. Furthermore, when Mexican-made inputs are reduced the impact is not limited to destroying supplier firms and jobs, but also the complex set of socioeconomic relationships and skills that have accumulated over decades. Once this web of relationships has been swept away only long-term, systematic industrial policy can reverse the deindustrialization/ deskilling effects. As the giant firms emphasize greater subcontracting, they also demand large levels of output with higher quality and performance standards and production processes that demand greater levels of capital-intensity, thereby eliminating thousands of Mexican firms while often turning to other TNCs as suppliers. One study estimates that of the six to eight hundred first-tier suppliers in the auto sector and the ten thousand second-tier suppliers in 2001, only twenty-five to one hundred first-tier suppliers and two to four thousand second-tier suppliers would remain in 2010 (Mortimore and Baron 2005, 10). Increasingly, it is U.S. first-tier suppliers—subsidiaries of U.S. transnationals— that are dominating the auto parts industry (Mortimore and Baron 2005, 19). Enhancing outsourcing has collateral benefits in that the U.S. transnational firms can sidestep or fragment unions by shifting significant portions of inputs production to captive suppliers—this has been well documented at the giant Volkswagen plant in Puebla that primarily exports finished autos to the United States (Juárez and Babson 1999).[11]

As these effects continue, the significance of the informal sector (workers without benefits or standard on-the-job forms of protection) increases. In 2000, according to government data, 24.9 percent of the labor force was relegated to the informal sector—in mid-2005 the percentage had risen to 28.3. That means that an additional 2.21 million workers had descended into informality (Fernández-Vega 2005, 28). Those underemployed, unemployed, and in the informal sector account for nearly 40 percent of all Mexicans of working age who would normally be counted as part of the labor force in an industrial nation. If anything, these estimates seem to be conservative—the OECD maintains that at least 40 percent of the workforce subsists in the informal sector (Cadena 2006a, 12).

Direct Exportation of the Mexican Labor Force

Because inputs into the maquila and disguised maquila sectors (other than labor) are primarily imported or limited to small additions of value-added in the service sector, employment multiplier effects via forward and backward linkages have been minimal. Instead, the institutional policies that sustain the export-led

FIGURE 3
MEXICO: MANUFACTURING PRODUCTIVITY AND REAL
WAGES (INDEX 1993 = 100)

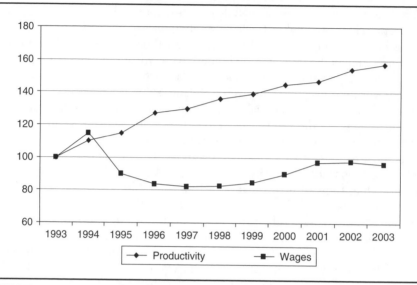

SOURCE: Instituto Nacional de Estadística (INEGI; 2004a).
NOTE: Productivity and wage data cover both production and nonproduction workers.

model—neoliberal market fundamentalism, a tax regime that favors the temporary importation of inputs, subsidies of various types—all tend to narrow the market demands for Mexican labor. This combination of policies has given rise to a
near stagnant economy when viewed from the perspective of the rate of growth
of per capita income: between 1980 and 2003, per capita income increased only
0.5 percent per year. Between 1988 and 2005, the level was an unimpressive 1.4
percent per year—far below the nearly 3 percent rate achieved from 1940 to
1980 under a policy of state-led development (Cypher 1990; Dussel Peters
2006b, 77). Further exacerbating the situation, the growth in productivity in the
nonmaquila manufacturing area (which includes the disguised maquilas, the
source of major dynamism in this area) has failed to lift wages, as Figure 3 shows.

   This effect, in turn, has undermined whatever possibility might exist for growing wage payments to serve as a catalytic factor in terms of the growth of the
internal market.[12] Furthermore, viewing the matter from the supply side, the
wide range of growing imports in intermediate inputs and capital goods, which
largely could have been produced within Mexico, also undermines the possibility
of a growing internal market deriving from wage and other forms of income
linked to domestic production. This vicious circle can be broken, but only when
Mexico marshals the social forces to adopt vigorous industrial policies similar to
those employed by the developing nations of Asia.

FIGURE 4
POPULATION OF MEXICAN ORIGIN IN THE UNITED STATES

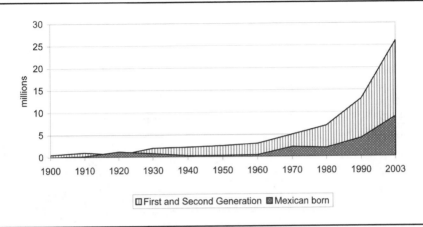

SOURCE: Consejo Nacional de Población (CONAPO; 2004).

The preceding analysis serves to show that the export-led model employed in Mexico is characterized through its low capacity to create national employment, the counterpart of which is the blooming of the informal sector, which has accounted for roughly 50 percent of the *growth* in employment in recent years.[13] As a direct result of the failure of the model, between 1984 and 2004, the number of households registering at either the poverty level or the extreme poverty level rose from 12,970,000 to 15,915,000 (Cypher 2005; Dussel Peters 2006b, 87). Furthermore, this situation has been the nurturing ground for the explosive international migration process that currently characterizes Mexico.

Under this model, as can be clearly seen in Figure 4, migration from Mexico to the United States has grown rapidly over the past two decades. This growth was accentuated with the implementation of NAFTA, whereby Mexico became the main source of immigrants for the United States.

In 2004 the population of Mexican origin residing in the United States was estimated at 26.6 million, including immigrants (both documented and undocumented) born in Mexico (10.2 million) and U.S. citizens of Mexican descent. This is the world's largest Diaspora to have settled in a single country. According to 2006 UN estimates, between 2000 and 2005 Mexico was the country with the highest number of people annually establishing their place of residence in a foreign country (400,000, compared to 390,000 for China and 280,000 for India). In line with this dynamic, the country experienced an escalating growth in its receipts of remittances, making it the third largest receiving country in the world (World Bank 2005). In 2005, total remittances accruing to Mexico amounted to US$20 billion (Banco de México 2005). As Figure 5 shows, remittances now have parity with oil exports and value-added by the maquila firms.

FIGURE 5
MEXICO: THE CONVERGENCE PROCESS

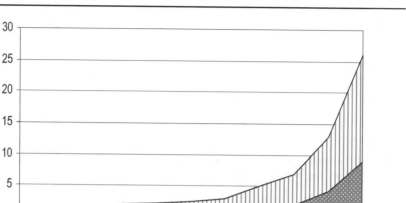

SOURCE: Banco de México (2005) and Instituto Nacional de Estadística (INEGI; 2004b).

Practically the entire Mexican territory reports international migration: in 2000, 96 percent of the country's municipalities reported some form of association with the phenomenon. This territorial expansion fueled the emergence of new migratory circuits (historic, indigenous-traditional, emerging, etc.) with contrasting dynamics and sets of problems (Zúñiga and Leite 2004). Parallel to this, the population of Mexican origin—although remaining concentrated in a handful of states—has expanded in recent years in most of the American territory. It should be noted, inter alia, that the migratory circuits are currently spilling over into the eastern and north-central states (Zúñiga and Hernández-León 2005) where some of the most dynamic industrial restructuring centers are located (Champlin and Hake 2006).

In terms of schooling, 39 percent of the population aged fifteen years and older born in Mexico and residing in the United States have attained a level higher than a high school diploma. This figure rises to 52 percent if the full spectrum of the population of Mexican origin in the United States is taken into consideration. By contrast, the average figure for Mexico is 28 percent, which means that in general, and in contrast to what is commonly believed, more qualified workers are leaving than remaining in the country. In other words, there is a clear selective trend, in line with the underlying rationale behind international migrations. It should also be noted, however, that in comparison to other immigrant groups in the United States, the Mexican contingent is the one with the lowest average levels of schooling.

> *[I]n general, and in contrast to what is commonly believed, more qualified workers are leaving than remaining in [Mexico].*

One high-profile form of migration that does not fall in with the stereotypes involves Mexican residents in the United States who have university degrees or postgraduate qualifications. This population includes slightly more than 385,000 individuals born in Mexico. Of those, 86,000 have postgraduate studies, and 10,000 have doctorates (Current Population Survey, http://www.census.gov/cps). This indicates that "brain drain" is beginning to emerge as a major problem.

All of these changes have paralleled a *transformation within migration patterns*: from a predominantly circular migration, it is evolving into one in which *established migrants* dominate, including variants such as greater participation by women and entire families (Delgado Wise, Márquez, and Rodríguez 2004). This trend, which is associated to the abandonment of productive activities in Mexico, is leading in some cases to a growing and worrisome *depopulation*: between 2000 and 2005, of the country's 2,435 municipalities, 832 (one out of every three) reported a negative rate growth (Instituto Nacional de Estadística Geografía e Información [INEGI] 2006).

The Cheap-Labor Export-Led Model and the U.S. Production System

NAFTA and the general neoliberal restructuring of the Mexican economy that began in the 1980s have had a profound impact on the U.S. production system. Notable in this process has been the shifting of U.S. investment into Mexico. Without the neoliberal restructuring process in Mexico, such investments would have been directed—in most instances—to the United States, creating jobs, raising the skill level, enhancing productivity, and producing spread effects via forward and backward linkages, along with stimulating aggregate demand through the consumer spending of workers.[14] Increasing capital mobility has undermined the rate of capital formation in the United States. A countertendency was created through the increasing portion of the Mexican economic surplus that was displaced to the United States as profits rose from the Mexican operations of U.S. transnationals. This countertendency was reinforced as Mexican immigrants flowed into the United States and into industrial sectors, lowering production costs and raising profits. Thus, the impact of capital shifting to Mexico fell on the U.S. labor force, particularly organized labor, while the U.S. restructuring process created two significant avenues to increased profits, with these benefits flowing to a small percentage of owners and managers and stockholders located in manufacturing and finance.

At the same time, the U.S. economy receives a certain type of stimulus from Mexican emigration to the degree that new investments occur—derivative of substantially different consumption patterns arising from the 7 million Mexican emigrant workers and their dependents. This is to be noted in the so-called migration industry (Guarnizo 2003).

Shifting capital to Mexico destroyed jobs in the United States, as did the sizeable trade deficit the United States developed with Mexico once the NAFTA agreement had been consummated. Bringing more of Mexico's economic surplus back to the United States stimulated the economy, and the influx of millions of Mexican emigrants helped push down labors' share of national income. The net effect was to create a new social structure of accumulation; a leaner and meaner social environment for all workers, emigrant or not; and a corpulent, more contented, business elite in the United States now better positioned to meet foreign competitors either by locating production in the United States or in Mexico, as profit maximization strategies indicated.

The resulting macroeconomic relationships, however, did not determine the repositioning of U.S. capital in Mexico. Viewing the matter from the standpoint of the restructuring of the U.S. production system, a separate logic—driven by the desire to maximize profits and out-perform the competition—prevailed. Under this logic, shifting capital to Mexico could enable U.S. firms to purchase labor processes at as low as 9 percent of the cost in the United States while accepting that productivity per hour might not be as high as that in the United States.[15] At the microeconomic level of the firm—assuming the stability of final demand for products exported from Mexico to the United States—shifting capital to Mexico to achieve labor efficiencies was a logical step in many instances. In highly oligopolized industries, such as autos, the available research indicates that the cost-saving production processes adopted in Mexico were taken as profits (Cypher 2001). In less capital-intensive industries, such as apparel, where brand identity is strong, similar profit-enhancing results should be anticipated.

Shifting production to Mexico made credible the threat of further production transfers, thereby weakening all U.S. labor and particularly organized labor. The stagnation in U.S. production workers' pay is broadly consistent with the increasing tendency of U.S. corporations to move their production operations to Mexico. Thus, in the process of restructuring the U.S. production system—a perceived necessity during the course of the 1980s—a complex, mutually reinforcing, triple movement began: (1) significant elements of U.S. capital shifted to Mexico, thereby lowering costs of production; (2) while capital often threatened to move to Mexico, thereby strengthening its bargaining power over labor, either reducing wage increases or lowering wages; and (3) growing numbers of workers were displaced by the production movement to Mexico thereby reducing the portion of the labor force in unions and thus reducing the impact of unionized labor that tends to push up wages for all (but near minimum-wage) workers.

By 2003, 1.2 million Mexican emigrants were working in the manufacturing sector (U.S. Census Bureau 2003). Since 1995, through October 2005, the U.S. labor force employed in manufacturing has declined by 17 percent—from 17.1 million to 14.2 million (Norris 2005; U.S. Bureau of Labor Statistics 2005). In the manufacturing sector, emigrants in great numbers are to be found in basic wage goods industries such as meatpacking, where paltry compensation serves to cut production costs, and that, in turn, serves to lower the reproduction costs of workers in general who are able to purchase basic wage goods at a lower cost. Emigrants are also well represented in the production of goods used as inputs of production processes in steel, aluminum, and heavy machinery and equipment, as well as in consumer durables such as autos and home appliances.

The role of Mexican labor in U.S. manufacturing, however, is actually much higher than the sketch above would suggest. If we include under the heading of U.S. manufacturing not only that which is physically based in the U.S., but also what is based in Mexico in either the disguised maquila or maquiladora sectors, we find a total of 1.2 million Mexican manufacturing workers in the United States, an estimated 0.5 million in disguised maquila production and 1.2 million in the maquiladoras as of August 2005—2.9 million in all. Adding the Mexican-based workers into the base number of manufacturing workers (14.2 + 1.7 million) generates a total of 15.9 million manufacturing workers in the amplified (or globally integrated) U.S.-Mexico production system, of which an estimated 18 percent are derived from Mexico's cheap-labor export-led model.

Mexico: Subordinated Integration under NAFTA

The vast restructuring of the Mexican economy via NAFTA could not, and did not, occur without the consent and active participation of Mexico's political class and its industrial elite. The business class supported the indiscriminate opening of the economy not because they necessarily were convinced of David Ricardo's theory of comparative advantage or the applications of the new growth theory to international economics. Rather, the large conglomerates or *grupos*, particularly those based in Monterrey, had always held a neoliberal/antistate view. Economic stagnation in the 1980s had forced many of them to seek growing markets in the international economy and closest and cheapest was to export to the vast U.S. market. In the 1980s, many of the grupos faced legal difficulties as they were accused and convicted of dumping by U.S. trade authorities. In other instances they faced nontariff trade barriers or other hurdles that the U.S. adroitly placed in the way of would-be foreign competitors. In their struggle to find ways to expand production, the largest conglomerates eventually became convinced that a new bilateral trade agreement (NAFTA) could circumvent the legal hurdles complicating access to the vast U.S. market. These conglomerates, however, were specialized in the production of one or a few key potential exports, all with a common denominator: low-value-added products such as cement, minerals, beverages, and undifferentiated intermediate-goods industrial products, such as steel or plastics, were their specialties. Expanding the output of these products has benefited the grupos, but not Mexico. The expected spin-offs of learning and technological deepening have never occurred. Instead, the grupos modernized as they expanded their sales by importing new, cutting-edge machinery and equipment. If there were any learning or technological spin-offs from this process, they occurred in Europe, the United States, and Japan, where the new technologies were created.

According to neoliberal and neoclassical economic theory, the spread effects of learning and technological know-how would penetrate to small and medium-sized suppliers as the giant firms were compelled to share their knowledge, while forcing supplier firms to adopt high-quality control standards, just-in-time delivery procedures, and so on. This, however, never occurred in Mexico, partly because producers there have relatively low levels of technical expertise and are not prone to diverting their profits into long-term (and often unfruitful) research. Primarily, however, it is the secretive vertically integrated nature of the conglomerates that has nullified the naïve scenarios of the neoliberal economists: the grupos do not spin off their know-how to suppliers. They tend to create their own tightly controlled suppliers. They also tend to import inputs of higher technology, or buy other inputs from other large national grupos. When they do resort to a supplier network, these small and medium-sized companies tend to be part of the web of international production at the lowest possible level—labor-intensive requiring low-quality control and assembly standards. No learning is transmitted, no modern forms of production are needed and no spread effects occur. In a study of one of the major conglomerates' supplier relationships, María de los Ángeles Pozas (2002, 226-27) found that 60 percent of the value of industrial inputs came from subsidiaries within the vast complex of the grupo itself, 35 percent of the inputs were either supplied by other grupos—or, in the case where inputs had a high degree of technological sophistication, by TNCs—leaving a mere 5 percent of inputs—the least complex and the lowest value added products—to be supplied by small and medium firms.

Implications for Mexico

- In its essence, the labor export-led model gives rise to a process of disaccumulation as the economic surplus is transferred abroad, depriving Mexico of potential multiplier and spread effects through forward and backward linkages. Surplus transference has taken many forms, including net reallocation of profits, interest income, licensing fees, and disguised profits through transfer pricing and intrafirm transactions in the maquiladora and disguised maquila firms.

- Net transference also entails the derived benefits from education, health care, and the nurturance of children to maturity. An impressively large fund of social capital created in Mexico is then reassigned to the United States as emigrants produce there while the costs of their training are paid in Mexico. Substantial levels of spending by the Mexican State on education and health care are essentially subsidized inputs into the U.S. transnational production system.
- To the above transfers should be added the subsidies and lost tax revenues that the Mexican government has permitted to continue up to the present. Firms operating in the maquila and disguised maquila sector pay no tariff charges, are exempt from the value added tax, and pay no income tax. For the maquila sector in 2000, the value of subsidies received exceeded taxes paid to the degree that these firms had a net profit tax rate of −7.2 percent (Dussel Peters 2003, 334; Schatan 2002).
- Inside Mexico, the labor export-led model has involved collateral costs in terms of deindustrialization and rising unemployment, along with deskilling as industrial workers are forced to shift to the informal sector or to underemployment—in effect dismantling much of the productive apparatus of Mexico. Making matters worse, neoliberal policy makers have imposed very restrictive monetary policies in their single-minded effort to contain inflationary pressures. The result has been a long-term overvaluation of the peso—estimated to be 30 percent—which has undercut the export market for Mexican producers, particularly medium-sized producers who might otherwise be able to generate employment through the export of Mexican-made products. For these Mexican producers, a second impact is that imported inputs are essentially subsidized, making it extremely difficult for these firms to play the role of domestic suppliers to either the transnational or the Mexican conglomerates (Dussel Peters 2006a).[16] Furthermore, these firms, as well as numerous small firms, have every incentive to buy imported inputs, further strengthening the vicious circle.

All this points to a process of asymmetric and subordinated integration in Mexico—a process to a great degree accelerated by NAFTA and the neoliberal policies that created the framework for the NAFTA accord. At the same time, the process captures the passivity and emptiness of state policy making in Mexico—the adoption of a neoliberal horizontal stance where there will be no intervention to attempt to direct production by way of the creation of new forms of dynamic competitive advantage, or to forestall processes that are clearly undermining Mexico's production base. Instead, the Mexican state has adopted a posture wherein it is assumed that the dynamic external effects of new forms of production directed toward the foreign market will bring automatically—through the forces of the market—a positive restructuring of Mexico's economy. State policy has been limited to a series of opportunistic maneuvers: seeking more maquilas, pursuing more foreign direct investment, using the boom in oil prices to cover the public sectors' debt and boost the economy through government spending that generally will not build vital skills or infrastructure, and relying upon massive inflows of foreign remittances from emigrants to create an informal social welfare system.

Conclusions

The theoretical and empirical analysis presented above comprises a complex set of elements. Among them, certain components stand out in terms of their sharp contrast with the widely-disseminated image of Mexico under NAFTA.

First, the actual model deployed by Mexico is not a triumphant example of outward-oriented industrialization; instead it represents a basic form of *primarization*. Many Latin American nations—most notably, Argentina—have taken a step backward into specializing in low-value-added exports of commodities or undifferentiated resource-based industrial products. Mexico has taken two steps backward, reverting even further, offering up as its absolute advantage cheap and unskilled labor in an institutional setting wherein such labor can be deployed with few constraints either in terms of unions, benefits, labor rights, legal recourse to adverse health effects, or severance protections.

Second, Mexico is undergoing a process of *precarization and disaccumulation*— the labor force employed is offered subsistence wages under working conditions that frequently lead to job-related injuries and overwhelming economic insecurity coupled with the failure of the model to create an economic surplus for Mexicans to use. Instead, the surplus is transferred to the United States, where it serves to expand the production base and assist in the restructuring of the economy. The imagined or anticipated external effects of the subordinated integration process— in the form of backward and forward linkages, process upgrading, technological learning, and so on, fail to arrive. In their place emerges a nefarious form of profit transfer centering on the disembodied export of cheap labor, giving rise *to the total export of revenues derived from the productive process other than wages that constitute an incidental cost*. This is a process that reaches far beyond the vitiating relationships described by the dependency writers of the 1960s and 1970s.

Third, we have demonstrated that the NAFTA process was not in any fundamental sense a trade-based policy, leading to a benign and mutually beneficial exchange of economic specializations through economic competition on both sides of the border, as portrayed in textbook models. Rather than trade, let alone "free" or competition-based trade, the neoliberal program was constructed to serve the end of oligopoly power—the control of markets—by displacing significant portions of the U.S. production system to Mexico. In short, NAFTA was not a trade accord; it was an investment/production and restructuring agreement enabling U.S. firms to shift production to Mexico and benefit from cheap migrant—mainly undocumented—labor. U.S. firms were allowed to expand their production without domestic content legislation, or export quotas or restrictions on the repatriation of profits, technology sharing agreements, or any other constraints on the use of capital. For the United States, the potential dynamic impacts of the labor export-led model are the following: lowering production costs in Mexico and/or the United States through the insertion of cheap labor into the production process which, on a transnational basis, will increase profits. Those gains can then

1. fund greater research and development spending, which, conceivably, leads to greater innovation levels—with these innovations potentially spreading across much of the U.S. industrial system; and
2. fund investment in the modernization of machinery and/or equipment and/or labor/managerial organizational restructuring programs and/or labor training programs.

Additionally, if the lowering of production costs in Mexico and/or the United States is partially passed on to U.S. consumers via lower prices, then the labor export-led model serves to cheapen the reproduction costs of U.S. labor, enabling U.S. corporations and businesses to operate with lower wages than otherwise would be necessary. This too enhances the competitiveness of the U.S. production system, while raising profit margins.

Fourth, economic integration under NAFTA, rather than promoting convergence in the development levels of Mexico and the United States, has deepened the asymmetries that exist between the two countries: whereas in 1994, per capita GDP in the United States was 2.6 times that of Mexico, by 2004 the ratio had increased to 2.9. Similarly, average manufacturing wages in dollars per man-hour in the United States were 5.7 times higher than those reported in Mexico in 1994, and 6.8 higher in 2004 (Delgado Wise and Márquez 2006, 32).

In Mexico, however, this new form of asymmetric integration has clearly not been associated with new possibilities for economic development. Stagnating or dropping wages, rising unemployment and informal activities have constituted the environment that has led to increasing emigration. The lack of linkage effects in the Mexican economy has negated the potential dynamic spillover effects that, according to the new growth theory, would spread across much of the production system due to enhance foreign investment under NAFTA. On one hand, this has meant that Mexico has become increasingly dependent upon remittances to stabilize the macro-economy and society at large—to the point where remittances, net export earnings from oil (even during a boom in prices), and the net export earnings of the maquila sector have all converged, for the first time. On the other hand, the uncontrolled leap in emigration has called into question the sustainability of the cheap-labor export-led model—particularly in terms of the depopulation effects in many parts of Mexico. With increasing marginalization and poverty, the pressures to emigrate escalate, and this could very well collide with U.S. policy given the desire of the U.S. citizenry to heighten security in the post-9/11 period.

Hence, given the labor export-led model's incapacity to make dynamic the Mexican economy, increase salaries, create employment positions, encourage advancements in technological know-how, and incorporate national supplier firms into the matrix of production relationships, we conclude that the model is ineffective as an instrument for development. Vast and fundamental changes will be needed to turn the tide. The implications here center on and arise from the way in which economic integration has thus far been conceived and orchestrated.

In the final analysis, socioeconomic development has never been achieved by a nation as a result of exogenous forces. The history of economic development shows that the responsibility for initiating and maintaining a process of economic development depends on endogenous social forces, particularly on the ability of the state to mount and sustain a national project of accumulation rather than searching out and adopting policies that are generators of asymmetric accumulation processes such as NAFTA.

Notes

1. A moderate and declining percentage of the new labor force entrants find an outlet through incorporation into formal, family-owned businesses. The rapid shrinkage of the peasantry due to NAFTA, however, has closed off much of this option.

2. In 2005, the share of GDP devoted to all forms of research and development was a mere 0.44 percent—Japan's share was more than seven times greater. Furthermore, according to the OECD, nearly two-thirds of Japan's outlays were in development processes (where the private sector searches for innovations), whereas in Mexico 56.5 percent of research and development (R&D) outlays was basically theoretical science, largely undertaken at government sponsored universities (Guadarrama 2006, 16).

3. For details on many qualitative points regarding the maquilas, see Cypher (2004).

4. Maquila firms are also present, to a much lesser degree of concentration, in many of the interior states—78 percent of output occurs in the border region.

5. The new growth theory of the 1980s posited impressive dynamic effects from greater trade and foreign investment, particularly positive externalities due to learning effects, technological diffusion and the applications of new forms of production and administrative organization.

6. In 1996, Carlos Tello (1996) maintained that Mexico's manufacturing export boom consisted of no more than the export of cheap labor power, but subsequently the implications of his comment were not formally pursued.

7. Record prices for oil and minerals, along with a 26 percent increase in mining production in 2004 and 2005, have lowered this ratio to 80 percent in the 2006 period.

8. Pitex and Altex firms conform to specific income tax legislation that can vary somewhat from exemptions extended to maquila firms. Firms under these designations are exempt from the IVA (value-added tax) and import duties, they are allowed accelerated depreciation on investments, and the Altex firms have access to below market rate credits from Bancomext—the foreign trade development bank.

9. In 2000, according to the Secretariat of the Economy, there were thirty-six hundred firms that produced inputs exempt from the value-added tax when they provided inputs to either the maquilas or the *disguised* maquila firms.

10. We are referring to formally registered workers as defined by coverage under the social security system as tabulated by the secretary of labor. All maquila workers are included in the formal manufacturing labor force.

11. Fragmenting unions is also a transnational tactic employed by the U.S. auto producers who, in the face of an unprecedented crisis of overproduction in 2006, have decided to decimate the United Auto Workers—letting go 113,000 workers via buyouts at GM-Delphi and 75,000 workers at Ford. Most of these jobs will be going to Mexico, where wages are $3.50 per hour versus $27 per hour in the United States. GM recently announced a large "greenfield" plant to be located in San Luis Potosi, employing 1,800 workers, while Ford is planning to open a new plant in Mexico while expanding its two existing plants and its engine plant. DaimlerChrysler will inject $1 billion into its operations in Mexico. Further U.S. investments will flow to the auto parts sector where already 430,000 are employed (Malkin 2006, C1, C4). The major portion of the new investments ($4 billion from 2005 to mid-2006) will flow into the disguised maquila sector.

12. In actuality the situation is even more restrictive, given that 77 percent of maquila activity remains along the U.S. frontier, where a considerable portion of workers consumption is diverted into the U.S. economy, further undermining whatever potential multiplier effects might be anticipated through rising wage payments.

13. The "jobs deficit" in Mexico (jobs created − [jobs needed to employ school dropouts + high school graduates + university graduates]) stated on an annual basis has been estimated at −500,000 per year, on average, from 1988 to 2003 (Dussel Peters 2006b, 75).

14. We are aware of, but not convinced by, neoclassical economists' assertion that NAFTA created no special stimulus for capital to exit from the U.S. In their vision, had direct foreign investment not flown to Mexico, it would have gone in equal amounts elsewhere in the "developing" world.

15. Difference in productivity levels are much narrower than the variation in wages. In the auto sector, it is common to find statements that productivity levels are 60 to 80 percent of those in the United States, in some instances productivity is *higher* than in U.S. plants (Mortimore and Barron 2005, 18).

16. Since the transnationals often do the bulk of their transactions in dollars and/or work with their subsidiaries or their strategic partners or within their own globally integrated production system, they have generally found means to circumvent foreign exchange transactions. For the *grupos*/conglomerates, peso overvaluation is not an issue that their peak business organizations have addressed, perhaps because of the advantage it serves in terms of acquiring capital goods, technology, and other inputs at a subsidized rate, or because they have some price-setting power as oligopoly corporations. Financial considerations could play a role wherein heavily indebted firms borrow in dollars, make earnings in overvalued pesos, and service their debt in undervalued dollars. Most of the grupos/conglomerates are highly leveraged and well-schooled in the arts of foreign currency financing.

References

Banco de México. 2005. *Remesas familiares*. http://www.banxico.org.mx (accessed March 3, 2005).

Banco Nacional de Comercio Exterior. 2005. *Atlas de Comercio Exterior*. http://www.bancomext.com/ Bancomext (accessed March 3, 2005).

Becerril, Isabel. 2006a. Marco regulatorio del comerico exterior, un obstáculo. *El Financiero*, September 4, p. 18.

———. 2006b. México, reprobado en competitividad. *El Financiero*, September 1, p. 18.

Bendensky, León. 2005. La Inflación. *La Jornada*, August 15, p. 25.

Cadena, Guadalupe. 2005. Manufactura, en la ruta de la "desindustrialización." *El Financiero*, August 16, p. 13.

———. 2006a. En la economía informal, 40% de la PEA en México. *El Financiero*, June 14, p. 12.

———. 2006b. Incierto, el panorama laboral mexicano. *El Financiero*, September 1, p. 21.

Capdevielle, Mario. 2005. Procesos de producción global: ¿alternativa para el desarrollo mexicano? *Comercio Exterior* 55 (7): 561-73.

Champlin, D., and E. Hake. 2006. Immigration as industrial strategy in American meatpacking. *Review of Political Economy* 18 (1): 49-70

Consejo Nacional de Población (CONAPO). 2004. *Migración internacional*. http://www.conapo.gob.mx (accessed January 7, 2005).

Cypher, James. 1990. *State and capital in Mexico: Development policy since 1940*. Boulder, CO: Westview.

———. 2001. Nafta's lessons: From economic mythology to current realities. *Labor Studies Journal* 26 (1): 5-21.

———. 2004. Development diverted: Socioeconomic characteristics and impacts of mature Maquilization. In *The social costs of industrial growth in Northern Mexico*, ed. Kathryn Kopinak, 343-82. San Diego: Center for U.S.-Mexico Studies, University of California, San Diego.

———. 2005. Poverty (Mexico). In *Encyclopedia of social welfare history in North America*, ed. John M. Herrick and Paul H. Stuart, 281-83. London: Sage.

Delgado Wise, Raúl. 2006. Migration and imperialism: Mexican labor under NAFTA. *Latin American Perspectives* 33 (2): 33-45.

Delgado Wise, Raúl, and Humberto Márquez. 2006. The Mexico-United States migratory system: Dilemmas of regional integration, development, and emigration. In *Conference Proceedings: Migration and Development: Perspectives from the South, Bellagio, Italy (July 10-13)*, 25-45. Zacatecas, Mexico: Doctorado en Estudios del Desarrollo, Universidad Autónoma de Zacatecas.

Delgado Wise, Raúl, Humberto Márquez, and Humberto Rodríguez. 2004. Organizaciones transnacionales de migrantes y desarrollo regional en Zacatecas. *Migraciones Internacionales* 2 (4): 159-81

Durán Lima, José, and Vivianne Ventura-Dias. 2003. *Comercio intrafirma: concepto alcance y magnitude*. Comercio Internacional 44. Santiago, Chile: CEPAL.

Dutrénit, Gabriela, and Alexandre O. Vera-Cruz. 2005. Acumulación de capacidades tecnológicas en la industria maquiladora. *Comercio Exterior* 55 (7): 574-86.

Dussel Peters, Enrique. 2003. Ser maquila o no ser maquila, ¿Es esa la pregunta? *Comerico Exterior* 54 (4): 328-36.

———. 2006a. Hacia una política de competitividad en Mexico. *Economía UNAM* 39:65-82.

———. 2006b. Liberalización comercial en México. In *México en Transición*, ed. Gerardo Otero, 69-105. Mexico, D.F.: Miguel Ángel Porrúa.

Fernández-Vega, Carlos. 2005. El gobierno de "cambio" sigue empecinado en seguir la fiesta. *La Jornada*, August 15, p. 28.

Guadarrama, José. 2006. En pañales, el desarrollo tecnológico en México. *El Financiero*, June 9, p. 16.

Guarnizo, Luis. 2003. The economics of transnacional living. *International Migration Review* 37 (3): 666-99.

Gutiérrez, Elvia. 2006. Bajo crecimiento económico y desempleo. *El Financiero*, September 1, p. 3.

Howard, Gorgina. 2005. El papel del Trabajo: México, Empleos, Pocos y Malos. *La Jornada*, November 11, p. 2. www.jornada.unam.mx/2004/08/09/004n1sec.html.

Instituto Nacional de Estadística Geografía e Información (INEGI). 2000. *Censo General de Población y Vivienda*. Mexico, D.F.: INEGI. http://www.inegi.gob.mx (accessed July 9, 2005).

———. 2004a. *Encuesta Industrial Mensual*. http://www.inegi.gob.mx (accessed July 9, 2005).

———. 2004b. *Estadísticas Económicas*. http://www.inegi.gob.mx (accessed July 9, 2005).

Juárez, Huberto, and Steve Babson, coordinators. 1999. *Enfrentando el cambio—Confronting Change*. Puebla, Mexico: Universidad Autónoma de Puebla.

Lara, Arturo, Jaim Arellano, and Alejandro García. 2005. Coevolución tecnológica entre maquiladoras de autopartes y talleres de maquinado. *Comercio Exterior* 55 (7): 586-600.

Leon González, Alejandra, and Enrique Dussel Peters. 2001. El comerico intraindustrial en Mexico, 1990-1999. *Comercio Exterior* 51 (7): 652-64.

Malkin, Elisabeth. 2006. Detroit, far south. *New York Times*, July 21, pp. C1, C4.

Mortimore, Michael, and Faustino Barron. 2005. *Informe sobre la industria automotriz mexicana*. Serie Desarrollo Productivo no. 162, pp. 1-50. Santiago, Chile: CEPAL (agosto).

Norris, Floyd. 2005. OFF THE CHARTS; proof, near and far, that it's not 1950 anymore. *New York Times*, October 15. http://select.nytimes.com/search/restricted/article?res=F40B13FD3F (accessed November 12, 2005).

Pozas, María de los Ángeles. 2002. *Estrategia internacional de la gran empresa mexicana en la década de los noventa*. Mexico, D.F.: El Colegio de México.

Schatan, R. 2002. Regimen tributario de la industria maquiladra. *Comercio Exterior* 52 (10): 916-26.

Tello, Carlos. 1996. La economía mexicana: Hacia el tercer milenio. *Nexos* 19 (223): 47-55.

Unger, Kart. 2002. *Determinantes de la exportaciones manufactureras Mexicanas*. Mexico, D.F.: CIDE.

U.S. Bureau of Labor Statistics. 2005. *Current employment statistics (manufacturing)*. www.bls.gov/iag/manufacturing.htm (accessed November 6, 2005).

U.S. Census Bureau. 2003. *Current population survey*. March. Washington, DC: Government Printing Office.

Villavicencio, Daniel, and Mónica Casalet. 2005. La construcción de un entorno institucional de apoyo a la industria maquiladora. *Comercio Exterior* 55 (7): 600-611.

World Bank. 2005. *Global economic prospects 2006 OVERVIEW: Economic implications of migration and remittances*. Washington, DC: World Bank.

Zúñiga, V., and R. Hernández-León, eds. 2005. *New destinations: Mexican immigration in the United States*. New York: Russell Sage Foundation.

Zúñiga, E., and P. Leite. 2004. Los procesos contemporáneos de la migración México-Estados Unidos: una perspectiva regional y municipal. Presented in the seminar "Migración México-Estados Unidos: Implicaciones y retos para ambos países." Mexico: Conapo.

Zúñiga, Juan Antonio, and Israel Rodríguez. 2005. El crudo mexicano, en su máximo histórico. *La Jornada*, August 12, p. 24.

Resistance and Compliance in the Age of Globalization: Indian Women and Labor Organizations

By
RINA AGARWALA

This article summarizes findings obtained through ethnographic research conducted in three states in India between 2002 and 2004. On the basis of interviews with more than three hundred labor leaders, government officials, and working women, the author reports on the efforts of informal workers in construction and tobacco manufacturing to organize and improve their conditions of life. Contrary to mobilizations in the formal sector, those workers do not make direct demands on their employers. Instead they appeal to the state to obtain welfare benefits. The study shows that neoliberal reform has surprisingly opened up new channels for informal workers to constitute themselves as a class. This represents an amendment to earlier analyses that focused exclusively on the mobilizing capacity of workers in the formal sector. The author concludes by highlighting the importance of this work for the study of social movements and labor's relationship with the state.

Keywords: India; neoliberal reform; informal economy; labor-state relations

Although the geographic focus of my research is far from Latin America, the questions that motivate it and the findings that arise from it resonate all too well with the other articles in this volume. My study examines the changing relationship between the state and labor as countries throughout the world liberalize their economies and integrate with one another and the percentage of people living in perpetual insecurity—that is, informal workers, who by

Rina Agarwala is an assistant professor in the Department of Sociology at Johns Hopkins University. Her research interests include labor, gender, globalization, international development, and migration. She holds a Ph.D. in sociology and demography from Princeton University, a master's in public policy in political and economic development from Harvard University, and a BA in economics and government from Cornell University. She has worked at the United Nations Development Program (UNDP) in China, the Self-Employed Women's Association (SEWA) in India, and Women's World Banking (WWB) in New York. She may be contacted via e-mail at agarwala@jhu.edu.

DOI: 10.1177/0002716206297520

definition receive no guaranteed benefits from either an employer or a state—increases.

For decades, rich and poor countries have organized around a model that held the state responsible for ensuring workers' security and basic needs. In return, workers provided their labor without strife. Although states varied in the degree of protection promised and ultimately provided, the basic contract remained consistent across nations. Since the 1980s, however, a new economic and political model has emerged and begun to proliferate. States and firms are increasingly seeking economic expansion through competition in a global marketplace. To survive the competition, firms face (or at least claim to face) mounting pressures to reduce labor costs by hiring informal workers who, by definition, are *not* protected by state law. States support companies in their decision to use unprotected labor by (among other efforts) initiating incentive programs that encourage formally protected workers to leave their jobs, creating free trade zones where firms are not held to labor laws, and contracting public sector services to private sector firms that can hire informally. As opportunities in the formal sector diminish, a growing proportion of household members are forced to engage in informal employment. These trends have altered normative roles of both workers and the state, thereby changing the relationship between the two. State governments portray informal workers as the ideal worker, although they operate outside state regulation; multilateral institutions and the public media tag states that retreat from their welfare functions toward workers as modern and efficient.

A burgeoning literature about globalization and labor has begun to analyze this new relationship between the state and workers. Many scholars argue that economic reforms that encourage free trade, increased capital and labor mobility, and heightened global competition (often combined under the common rubric of "neoliberalism") have pushed labor movements into a crisis characterized by declining union density and a diminishing ability of workers to influence the state (Castells 1997; Tilly 1995, Western 1995). Although scholars have extensively written about the important role organized workers have played in shaping transformative events, modern societies, and institutions (Collier and Collier 1991; Heller 1999; Moore 1966; Rueschemeyer, Stephens, and Stephens 1992; Thompson 1966; Tilly 1978), recent media coverage has celebrated the supposed crisis by showing a growing skepticism about the intentions and the ability of workers' movements to improve people's living conditions. In response to the massive international outpouring of resistance to economic reforms by organized workers in France, Germany, Austria, Britain, India, and the United States during the spring of 2003, for example, *The Economist* magazine warned, "Do not be fooled by events in Europe this week. . . . Unions everywhere are in decline, and to a large extent they deserve to be" ("Adapt or Die" 2003, 13).

Some scholars claim that as a result of these trends, workers are no longer organizing as a class to improve their situation, and state governments are increasingly abandoning their responsibility for ensuring the welfare of labor. Based on these claims, a consensus is beginning to emerge in academic theory that class analytics may be losing its significance as a tool with which to explain the differentiation of life chances among interdependent economic actors, as well as the political dynamics that follow from such inequities.

If scholars of the recent globalization and labor literature are correct, what strategies are people using (if not class struggle) to improve their livelihoods when they are increasingly unattached to a single employer and are operating outside the state's jurisdiction? What role is the state playing in managing its conflicting constituencies as its primary economic goal enables increased capitalist exploitation through the isolation of workers from employers and government legislation? Given the empirical evidence across time, geography, and industry showing that workers organize to protect their livelihoods during economic busts and booms, is it reasonable to assume that alterations in structures of production can undermine all struggles motivated by economic relations?

[R]ecent media coverage has celebrated the supposed crisis by showing a growing skepticism about the intentions and the ability of workers' movements to improve people's living conditions.

To address these questions, I conducted 340 in-depth interviews with informal workers, government officials, and union leaders to examine how workers in India are responding to their changing circumstances. After building a relatively closed, state-planned economy for four decades, India began liberalizing for the first time in 1991. Reforms were conducted against the backdrop of India's formal democratic system, which ensures equal rights under constitutional law and has existed for nearly sixty years.[1] Although some have argued that democracy has not yet reached all Indian citizens at the deepest level, the nation's large and vibrant civic and political life is undeniable. India has long been recognized by scholars and activists for bearing a strong workers' movement, as well as holding the longest-running, democratically elected Communist Party in power (at the state government level). Today, however, 93 percent of the country's labor force (82 percent of its nonagricultural workers) is employed in the informal sector; by most accounts, this percentage is growing as a result of the 1991 reforms (National Sample Survey Organisation [NSSO] 2001).

By contrast to the skepticism shown in recent scholarship and press toward the power of workers' movements, my study revives scholars' earlier understanding of their importance. Based on my interviews, I analyze (1) how the informal nature of employment shapes workers' collective action strategies in India and (2) the conditions under which informal workers' organizations succeed or fail in attaining material benefits for their members. Specifically, this study attempts to better understand the role of workers in shaping the current phase of economic and political transitions by taking an in-depth look at informal workers' organizing strategies and their interactions with the state.

An Overlooked Field:The Informal Sector

The informal sector consists of economic units that produce legal goods and services but in operations that are not registered or regulated by fiscal, labor, health, and tax laws.[2] Thus, the primary difference between informal and formal workers is that the latter are protected and held accountable by state legislation while the former are not (Portes, Castells, and Benton 1989). Informal workers include the self-employed (such as street vendors or trash pickers), employees in informal enterprises, and casual labor or contractors who work for formal enterprises through subcontractors. Self-employed workers include those who hire or do not hire employees. Informal workers may labor at home, on an employer's location, or in a third site, such as a subcontractor's workshop.

Few scholars have examined informal workers' organizing strategies in much depth. Students of class politics have often argued that informal workers cannot organize along class lines due to the nature of their employment. Informality disperses production through home-based work, complicates employer-employee relationships through multiple subcontracting arrangements, and atomizes labor relationships by eliminating the daily shop floor gathering of workers. Implicit in these arguments is that informal workers are an expression of what Karl Marx (1906) called "the reserve army of labor"—that is, those who perform odd jobs while waiting to be formally employed. In other words, only once informal workers are formally employed, so the argument goes, will they become an integral part of the workforce and join the labor struggle (Bairoch 1973; Geertz 1963; Harris and Todaro 1970; Lewis 1954; Marx 1906).

This view of the informal sector has marked the labor literature since the early 1900s, thereby limiting most studies to urban formal sector workers and, in some cases, rural peasants (Herring and Hart 1977). Even the relatively recent surge in studies on labor movements has tended to ignore the informal sector, despite the increasing informalization of production structures (Burawoy 1984; Chibber 2003; Collier and Collier 1991; Deyo 1989; Fernandes 1997). The growing literature on social movements has de-emphasized movements where work status, rather than a social issue or an adscriptive characteristic, provides the primary organizing axis (Katzenstein, Kothari, and Mehta 2001; Omvedt 1993). Here again, informal workers' organizations are not acknowledged.

The dearth of literature on informal workers and the state is particularly surprising, because the very definition of the informal sector, as economic activities that operate outside legal protection and regulation, intricately ties its workers with the government bureaucracies in a way that is starkly different from formal workers. Thus, informal workers pose an important challenge to the existing literature on the state and labor, which largely draws from the periods when workers were first beginning to organize (Badie and Birnbaum 1983; Chakrabarty 2000; Chandavarkar 1994; Rudolph and Rudolph 1987).

Part of the lack of focus on informality is explained by the minimal amount of information available. Since the term "informal sector" was first coined in the early 1970s by Keith Hart (1973), social scientists have debated its meaning and the reasons for its existence.[3] Studies of informal economic activities in India focus on definition and measurement.[4] Some projects have examined the social and political lives of informal workers (Beneria and Roldan 1987; Cross 1998; Grasmuck and Espinal 2000; Gugler 1991; Macharia 1997). These case studies, which tend to focus on Latin America and Africa, show that, contrary to the claims of the class and social movement literature, the growing numbers of informal workers are indeed organizing to improve their conditions. Nevertheless, more such studies in varying regional settings are essential to understanding the global context. The few that examine the social and political lives of informal workers in India are consistent with research showing that coordinating activities among informal workers improves their circumstances (Carr, Chen, and Jhabvala 1996; Chowdhury 2003; Sanyal 1991; Sharma and Antony 2001). Still little is known about informal workers' specific organizing strategies, and even less about the conditions needed for success in attaining state-supported benefits. Finally, almost none of the studies have connected informal workers' experiences to the theoretical literature on class politics and the state. It is along those lines that my work makes a contribution.

Summary of Findings

To explore how the informal nature of employment shapes workers' collective action strategies in India, I examined informal workers' organizations across three Indian states with varying political and economic histories. In each state, I studied movements in two industries—construction and tobacco (or *bidi*)—whose conditions of work vary enormously. The findings from this portion of the study illustrate that informal workers, like formal workers, organize along class lines to improve their livelihoods. Nevertheless, while state-sanctioned alterations in structures of production may have undermined formal workers' movements, the same alterations have forced informal workers to seek new and different collective action strategies.

Since the mid-1980s, Indian informal workers in both construction and bidi have launched a labor movement that, on one hand, accommodates unprotected, flexible production structures and, on the other hand, fights for new sources of protection for the working poor. Rather than making work-related demands, such as minimum wages and job security, on employers (as formal sector workers have done in the past), informal workers have focused on making welfare demands on the state. Their actions have led to the industry-specific welfare boards for informal workers. Employers, governments, and workers fund the boards, and in return for membership, workers are supposed to receive benefits such as education scholarships for their children, housing allowances, health care, pensions, and marriage grants. Regional state governments are responsible for implementing such boards, and informal workers' unions are actively involved in holding the government accountable. In addition, informal workers are forcing the state to acknowledge their status as legitimate workers, even when employers will not. The state's acknowledgement of worker status has been instituted through the provision of a state-certified identity card to informal workers. Interviewees across the three states and two industries emphasized that the identity card enabled them to be viewed as legitimate and worthy citizens when they made demands in their children's schools, municipal offices, and even against police harassment. Finally, by definition, informal workers frequently change employers. Therefore, informal workers organize around the neighborhood, rather than the shop floor. In return for state-provided welfare benefits and identity cards, they enter an implicit contract by providing low cost, flexible labor to employers on an unregulated, insecure basis.

[B]y definition, informal workers frequently change employers. Therefore, informal workers organize around the neighborhood, rather than the shop floor.

By incorporating these findings into existing models of how workers in a particular class location (as a class-in-themselves) mobilize to pursue their interests (as a class-for-themselves), I offer support for a reformulated labor movement model. Unlike the traditional labor movement models that focused primarily on the relationship between employers and the minority of workers who have already won formal rights from the state, the revised model aims to help scholars understand forms of class-based exploitation and resistance in the swelling informal sector, where workers are denied the right to make any official claims on employers. The reformulated model acknowledges that informal workers occupy their own position in the class structure (as a class-in-itself). Capitalist accumulation in the modern economy relies on the labor of informal workers. Nevertheless, their relationship to employers remains tenuous; employers are not obligated to pay minimum wages, and they can hire and fire according to market needs. The amended model also acknowledges that informal workers' unique class location has led to unique interests around which they can and do mobilize (as a class-for-itself). To attain state attention in their demands for welfare goods, an identity card, and neighborhood provisions, they use the currency of votes and their flexible, cheap labor. While some informal workers' unions are simultaneously fighting for minimum wages, the structures of production have undermined their bargaining power vis-à-vis employers. Therefore, they expend more resources and energy on, and have encountered more successes in fighting for welfare benefits from the state. Figures 1 and 2 present a condensation and comparison of the traditional and revised models under consideration.

Informal workers' collective action strategies are cementing new forms of political ties between labor and the state by shifting the movement focus away from workers' rights to citizen rights. In turn, organized informal workers have created a new class identity that distinguishes informal from formal workers. Unlike formal employees who identify themselves as antitheses to capital, informal workers identify themselves as connected to the state through their social consumption needs.

Drawing from both the literature on states in developing economies and my reformulated labor movement model—where informal workers are pulling the state into playing an even more central role than it did in formal workers' movements—I developed a theoretical framework to answer my second question regarding the conditions under which informal workers' organizations succeed or fail in their efforts to secure material benefits for their members. This framework was designed to predict how economic policies (i.e., those that support vs. resist liberalization) and ruling party ideologies (i.e., those that are populist vs. programmatic) interact with one another, and with informal workers' organizations, to ultimately determine organizational aptitude. Despite differences in the conditions of work and current growth patterns in the construction and tobacco industries, I found no evidence for industry-specific variation in the effectiveness of informal workers' movements. Rather, the variation in strategy and success in attaining state-supported benefits is largely determined by regional state characteristics.

To test my framework, I examined the interaction between governments and informal workers' movements in three regional states of India. Each case represented a different combination of political ideologies and economic policies that was supported by an in-depth historical analysis of each state's political patterns. The theoretical framework predicted that the most effective organizations would be in Tamil Nadu, where populist leadership supports liberalization policies. The least effective organizations would be in West Bengal, where there is a programmatic leadership that resists liberalization policies. Organizations in Maharashtra, where

FIGURE 1
CONVENTIONAL MODEL—THE STATE, FORMAL
AND INFORMAL WORKERS

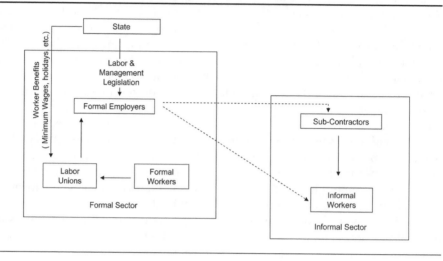

FIGURE 2
REFORMULATED MODEL—THE STATE, FORMAL
AND INFORMAL WORKERS

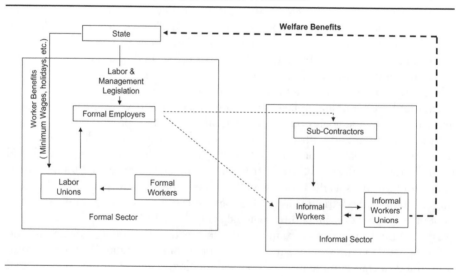

a programmatic leadership supports liberalization policies, were expected to have midlevels of success.

The findings from my three state case studies show full support for my theoretical framework in Tamil Nadu and West Bengal and mixed support in

Maharashtra. Indeed organizations in Tamil Nadu have been most successful in attaining state protection for informal workers. The state's workers enjoy higher wages than in either West Bengal or Maharashtra. In addition, the state government has extended more welfare benefits to informal workers than in any other state. The number of state-administered benefits achieved by Tamil Nadu's informal workers relies on (1) the interests of incumbent political parties in mobilizing votes and (2) the ability of an organization to mobilize their members as a large vote bank for local politicians. In addition, workers' ability to attain the state's attention in Tamil Nadu ironically relies on the state's commitment to a liberalization agenda. As the state's commitment increases, so does informal workers' bargaining power because their flexible, cheap labor is a vital peg in the state's economic project.

On the flip side, organizations in West Bengal have failed to attain state protection for informal workers. At first glance, Indian scholars will be surprised by this finding, especially given that the state has been ruled by the Communist Party of India-Marxists (CPM) for more than three decades. Nevertheless, my findings show that CPM's programmatic style, along with its disinterest in liberalizing, have made it difficult for unions to frame informal workers' demands in terms that would appeal to the CPM's top priority, staying in power. First, CPM has retained preeminence by implementing a reformist ideology and focusing almost exclusively on rural interests. This has constrained urban workers' struggles. Second, CPM's entrenched, nearly unthreatened, political rule has restricted informal workers' ability to make new demands by appealing to the state's interest in attaining more votes. Finally, CPM's rhetorical criticism of liberalization policies has undermined informal workers' ability to convince the authorities to privilege informal workers as a vital part of the new economy.

Finally, the case of Maharashtra lends mixed support for my framework, which predicted medium levels of success in that region. On one hand, as predicted, the level of benefit provision or state commitment in Maharashtra is less than that found in Tamil Nadu. On the other hand, informal workers in Maharashtra have attained some minimal levels of welfare benefits from the state, and the state government expresses some commitment to protecting informal workers. At the same time, the levels of success achieved in Maharashtra were not as far above that of West Bengal as might be expected by the Maharashtrian government's pursuit of liberalization. The state's entrenched programmatic leadership, which has traditionally been led and driven by intermediate and elite interests, has undermined informal workers' ability to make demands on the state in return for political support. Then again, the state government's deep commitment to liberalization and rapid, private sector industrialization has increased its interest in unregulated, informal labor. These factors have forced informal workers' organizations in Maharashtra to pursue a cooperative strategy with the state, where they frame themselves as an essential *partner* in the economic agenda. By not fighting as hard for a minimum wage and job security, informal workers in Maharashtra assure state officials that they will not resist the informal nature of their work. In return, the state must address their welfare needs, such as housing, health care, and education.

Despite a decline in the popularity of welfare spending during the promarket, neoliberal era, these three case studies show that informal workers' new strategies have led to state concessions that vary according to economic policy and political ideology. These findings do not aim to make a normative argument that the new form of unionism by informal workers is better than the traditional form. In part, the new movement may even be viewed as inferior to the traditional one since it does not make the structural changes necessary to eradicate social injustices. Moreover, welfare demands are not a perfect substitute for worker demands (such as minimum wages and job security). Rather, worker and welfare demands would ideally be met *in conjunction with* one another. At the moment, however, India's informal workers are attaining more success by mobilizing members and attaining state attention based on their welfare demands than on traditional workers' rights demands. This new form of workers' organization is expanding, and students of democratic participation should be interested in how informal workers are shaping the current phase of economic and political transition. Informal workers' movements provide key insights into the strategies that marginalized groups use to express their political voice, even as state policies erode their material circumstances. These new forms of unionism must not be discounted.

Given growing attention to the decline of labor mobilization (Western 1995), together with more evidence of states' decreasing capacity to protect their citizens due to their loss of control over capital flows (Castells 1997; Tilly 1995), my findings are surprising. They show that neoliberalism has uneven effects on working-class people and their options for attaining better conditions of life. They also yield insights into the strategies that marginalized groups use to express their political voice even as state and economic policies erode their material well-being.

---

*[My findings] show that neoliberalism
has uneven effects on working-class people
and their options for attaining
better conditions of life.*

Implications

Several important implications follow from my argument. First, informal workers' organizational strategies provide important clues about how they can mobilize in a system with little regulation and blurred employer-employee relations. For decades, industrialized workers have fought to formalize their identity and work status through legislation designed to protect them against employer exploitation. Their efforts, while laudable, have affected only a minority of the world's workers.[5] Now, due to the industrial restructuring of the 1980s and 1990s, even the small global share of formally protected workers is diminishing. These changes have brought the scholarship of labor movements to a critical juncture by questioning traditional mobilization strategies that rely on formal protections.

My analysis of collective action strategies among a growing population of informal workers in India lends key insights into how workers adjust to the changing structures around them. Although economic reforms are increasing Indian workers' vulnerability, I find that the poorest workers are holding the one actor that cannot escape (i.e., the state) responsible for their welfare. Informal workers are forcing government authorities to acknowledge that they simply cannot live on the below-subsistence wages and unstable employment into which they are currently being forced. This finding alone makes it urgent for scholars to rethink the pessimism dominating the recent race-to-the-bottom literature. Labor movements may indeed be facing new challenges due to globalization. But it does not necessarily follow that workers are compliant in the face of these challenges.

Second, my findings call for a qualification of the prevailing definition of the informal sector. In particular, characterizations of the informal sector should specify that the lack of state regulation and protection of informal workers is limited to the conditions of their work and their employers and does not necessarily apply to their welfare at home or in their family. Informal workers in India continue to be unprotected in their work or by their employer. Yet they have managed to attain some welfare protections/benefits from the state, and they are actively fighting for more. Although these benefits are implemented with varying degrees of success, they are now required and regulated under law. Notably, the provision of these welfare benefits does not extend to the general public but is limited by law to informal workers.

Third, this study reasserts class as an important analytical tool with which to examine differences in life chances and resistance against exploitation. Class relationships, especially those in developing countries undergoing neoliberal reorganization, are being transformed as economic reforms alter structures of production. Despite other claims to the contrary, this study illustrates that class remains an important organizing vector allowing marginalized populations to identify, articulate, and demand a shared set of unique interests (based on their access to resources and relationship with other classes). These interests, and the strategies used to attain them, however, evolve over time. In recent years, Indian informal workers have put mounting pressure on the state, rather than the employer, to "de-commodify" their labor power. Karl Marx (1906) famously argued that a key trait of a capitalist market economy is that human labor is treated as a commodity. If there is no demand for labor power, there is no return to the living bearer of labor power and, in the end, no claim on subsistence. Capitalists are no longer being held responsible for that dilemma. Therefore, informal workers in India are trying to hold the state responsible for meeting their basic, social consumption

needs—*regardless* of their informal labor status—by demanding welfare benefits. If the state will not ensure a living wage sufficient to meet the costs of labors'
reproduction, then the state must directly compensate for the deficiency and
ensure that reproduction is possible. Acknowledging and understanding the
development of informal workers' unique interests (ensuring basic subsistence at
home and for the family, despite their low, insecure wages) is vital to ensuring an
adequate response from policy makers and scholars.

Fourth, these findings warrant rethinking state-society relations in the modern
era. Neoliberal strategies may have succeeded in taking the state out of the
detailed planning and control of the economy. Ironically, however, these same
strategies have pulled the state deeper into directly managing and providing for
people's daily lives. In India, informal workers are forcing the state to participate
in decisions involving their children's education, health care, marriages, and even
personal identity. These findings raise important questions on what impact class
structures and class politics in the neoliberal context may have on state autonomy.

On one hand, the theoretical framework tested in this study shows that informal workers are most successful in states that have a populist leadership, especially one that supports liberalization policies. That workers in states merely
pursuing liberalization policies (and without a populist leadership) were not as
successful as initially predicted, lends further support for the significance of populism in the new workers' movement. In India, informal workers have attained
state protection by identifying ways to capitalize on populist leaders' interest in
retaining or attaining power.

This raises important questions as to the sustainability and the economic efficiency of informal workers' movements in the neoliberal era; populist leaders are
not particularly known for either trait. At the same time, neoliberalism may be
providing an ideal breeding ground for increased populism, especially if leaders
become the only hope mass workers have for survival and security.

On the other hand, traditional left-oriented political parties that strive to meet
workers' needs, such as the CPM, were found to be least helpful to informal
workers. Left-oriented parties are resistant to changing their traditional labor
movement strategies. Yet class structures, conditions of work, and structures of
production are rapidly changing for all laborers. If left-oriented parties do not
soon start appealing to the growing informal workforce, they may soon lose their
claim as leaders of class struggle and representatives of workers' interests. If left-
oriented parties can instead extend their ideological commitments to social justice toward supporting informal workers' movements, the vast majority of the
world's workers may greatly benefit.

Fifth, this study sheds new insights into the role women play in linking the
public and private spheres in contemporary labor movements. To date, labor
movements have separated the workplace from the home environment. Most
labor benefits tend to directly affect the worker in the workplace. Formal sector
labor leaders and fellow union members rarely enter the privacy of workers' homes.
Organization and solidarity has traditionally been built on the shop floor. As the
structures of production become increasingly flexible and the relationships

between employer and employees blur, however, so do the distinctions between the public and private spheres. In India, the home has become the site of production, as in the case of bidi; the site of production has become the home, as in the case of construction. In either case, family issues, such as childrearing, education, health care, marriage, and home ownership are intertwined with the conditions of work. In India's informal workers' movement, therefore, women have played a key role in pushing for welfare benefits, because such benefits aid in spheres for which women are held responsible.

Finally, this study makes important contributions to the growing literature on global cities. According to the United Nations, between 2000 and 2030, the world's urban population will grow by 2.12 billion; only 28 million of this increase will come from developed countries. By 2030, 60 percent of the world's population will be living in cities; the vast majority will be in poor cities in developing nations (UN-HABITAT 2004). The social and political consequences of these changes are sure to be profound. With increased social vulnerabilities as well as job insecurities, absolute poverty and inequality are expected to rise to unprecedented levels. It is vital we understand the mechanisms poor, urban workers are using to attain a political voice. This study begins to address that issue.

Areas for Further Research

This study also raises several questions for further research. First, how prevalent are these trends in the non-Indian context? These findings from India should be compared in a cross-national perspective to other informal workers' movements around the world. Some recent studies have shown evidence of similar findings in other countries, including Peru, Brazil, South Africa, and the United States. Janice Fine's (2006) recent study on workers' centers in the United States found that immigrant workers are fighting for welfare rights, rather than worker rights, and they are organizing around neighborhoods and community, rather than workplace. Dan Clawson's (2003) study on social movements among minority workers in the United States, Gay Seidman's (1994) study of workers in South Africa and Brazil, and Kim Moody's (1997) study of workers in France and Canada have also found that workers are instigating a new form of mass politics that simultaneously straddles worker and citizen identities. These movements, dubbed "social movement unionism," use union democracy as a source of power and social vision to connect the masses with the state, and their findings resonate with my Indian case study. More such studies focusing on informal workers throughout the world are needed to assert whether a modern blend of class politics may now be finding a new echo in the informal sector.

Second, how do informal workers' movements vary by sector and industry? Studies across more sectors will provide further insight into how pervasive informal workers' movements are and how they may differ according to conditions of work. This study examines casual labor in manufacturing (specifically in the construction and bidi industries). Future research should examine movements among casual labor in the service industry, which is rapidly growing in both developing and developed countries. In India, domestic servants have recently organized to initiate a welfare board that is similar to that of construction and bidi workers.

In addition, future studies should examine workers' movements among the self-employed. Indian self-employed workers occupy a slightly larger share of the informal sector than casual workers. Moreover, self-employment is being encouraged by states and multilateral institutions throughout the world. In India, street vendors (who are self-employed) are currently organized into large, politically influential unions, and they too are negotiating for welfare boards. In the United States, home care workers and family day care workers have waged similar campaigns where they organized to elect a representative, who in turn won them an increase in the rate of pay and benefits. Further study is required to examine the varying strategies used in these movements and the varying conditions for their success.

Finally, future research should investigate how formal sector labor movements are reacting to informal workers' movements. Formal sector trade union membership is declining the world over, and they may be open to new strategies for the sake of survival. Indian formal sector trade unions are indeed turning to informal workers' movements for new ideas and strategies on how to handle a future of blurred employer-employee relationships. At the 2005 annual meeting for CITU, one of the largest and oldest union federations in India, union leaders made understanding and coordinating informal workers their top priority agenda item for the year. On the other hand, informal workers' movements may be viewed by formal sector unions as a threat to traditional class-based mobilizations (that focused on guaranteeing workers benefits from employers). During the 1880s in the United States, the Knights of Labor presented an alternative organizing model based on residential communities. Nevertheless, their efforts were undermined by a direct attack from the established trade unions and indirect sabotage by political parties. Both saw the Knights as competitors. Further research on how political parties and formal unions react to informal workers' movements throughout the world can lend greater insights into the sustainability of informal workers' movements.

This study has shown that informal workers are playing a vital role in shaping a new relationship between the state and labor in the current era of liberalization and globalization. Further studies should expand on the findings from India to examine how this movement grows and whether it generates spillover. The informal workers' movement is at a critical juncture in terms of its future growth. On one hand, it could grow to shape the state's role in workers' lives across all sectors of the economy. On the other hand, the movement could fall backward into a scenario where the state continues to extend its responsibilities to its workers, but in an ad hoc manner that eventually mirrors traditional patron-client relations. Further research into informal workers' movements in a liberalization context is essential to understanding the myriad of problems arising in the implementation of state benefits for workers.

The findings in this study reflect a global trend toward what some scholars have termed "social-movement unionism," in which traditional union movements are converging with newer social forms to create a new mass politics that straddles people's worker and citizen identities. These movements use union democracy as a source of power and social vision to connect the masses with the state. As Gay Seidman (1994, 2-3) wrote,

> Marx suggested that levels of reproduction of labor power, on which wages and living standards are based, are historically determined, through struggles between classes. Social-movement unionism consists of precisely such struggles over wages and working conditions, and also other living conditions in working-class areas.

Social movement unionism has been documented in Brazil; South Africa; and even France, Canada, and the United States (Clawson 2003; Moody 1997; Seidman 1994). This study contributes to this literature by adding further evidence from the world's most populous democracy. But more important, this study shows that India's social movement unionism is being spearheaded by the informal sector. It is intriguing that a modern blend of class politics may now be finding a new echo in, of all places, the informal sector.

Notes

1. The only exception was the National State of Emergency, declared by then–Prime Minister Indira Gandhi from 1975 to 1977.

2. Although there are several debates on the exact definition of the informal sector, this definition has been largely accepted in much of the literature (see Cross 1998; De Soto 1989; Portes 1994). To operationalize this definition, I utilize the worker-based definition of informal work that was endorsed by the 17th International Conference of Labor Statisticians (ICLS) in 2003 and utilized by the National Sample Survey of Employment and Unemployment (NSS) in India in 1999.

3. For a concise summary of this debate, see Rakowski (1994).

4. See Kundu and Sharma (2001); and Oberai and Chadha (2001).

5. This is a narrow claim, specific to worker protection. Collective action by industrialized workers has, of course, made substantial contributions to the mass population in other arenas, such as suffrage and citizenship. (See Collier and Mahoney 1997; Rueschemeyer, Stephens, and Stephens 1992).

References

Adapt or die: Unions must start providing services their members need. 2003. *The Economist*, June, p. 13.

Badie, Bertrand, and Pierre Birnbaum. 1983. *The sociology of the state*. Chicago: University of Chicago Press.

Bairoch, Paul. 1973. *Urban unemployment in developing countries: The nature of the problem and proposals for its solution*. Geneva, Switzerland: International Labor Organization.

Beneria, Lourdes, and Martha Roldan. 1987. *The crossroads of class & gender: Industrial homework, subcontracting, and household dynamics in Mexico City*. Chicago: University of Chicago Press.

Burawoy, Michael. 1984. Karl Marx and the satanic mills: Factory politics under early capitalism in England, the United States, and Russia. *American Journal of Sociology* 90:247-82.

Carr, M., M. Chen, and R. Jhabvala, eds. 1996. *Speaking out*. New Delhi, India: Vistaar.

Castells, Manuel. 1997. *The information age*. Vol. 2, *The power of identity*. Oxford, UK: Blackwell.

Chakrabarty, Dipesh. 2000. *Rethinking working-class history*. Princeton, NJ: Princeton University Press.

Chandavarkar, Rajnarayan. 1994. *The origins of industrial capitalism in India: Business strategies and the working classes in Bombay, 1900-40*. Cambridge: Cambridge University Press.

Chibber, Vivek. 2003. *Locked in place: State-building and late industrialization in India*. Princeton, NJ: Princeton University Press.

Chowdhury, Supriya Roy. 2003. Old classes and new spaces: Urban poverty, unorganised labour and new unions. *Economic and Political Weekly*, December 13, p. 38.

Clawson, Dan. 2003. *The next upsurge: Labor and the new social movements*. Ithaca, NY: Cornell University Press.

Collier, Ruth Berins, and David Collier. 1991. *Shaping the political arena: Critical junctures, the labor movement, and regime dynamics in Latin America*. Princeton, NJ: Princeton University Press.

Collier, Ruth Berins, and James Mahoney. 1997. Adding collective actors to collective outcomes: Labor and recent democratization in South America and Southern Europe. *Comparative Politics* 29:285-303

Cross, John. 1998. *Informal politics: Street vendors and the state in Mexico City*. Stanford, CA: Stanford University Press.

De Soto, Hernando. 1989. *The other path: The informal revolution*. New York: Harper & Row.

Deyo, Frederic. 1989. *Beneath the miracle: Labor subordination in the New Asian industrialism*. Berkeley: University of California Press.

Fernandes, Leela. 1997. *Producing workers: The politics of gender, class, and culture in the Calcutta jute mills*. Philadelphia: University of Pennsylvania Press.

Fine, Janice. 2006. *Worker centers: Organizing communities at the edge of the dream*. Ithaca, NY: ILR Press/Cornell University Press.

Geertz, Clifford. 1963. *Peddlers and princes: Social change and economic modernization in two Indonesian towns*. Chicago: University of Chicago Press.

Grasmuck, S., and R. Espinal. 2000. Market success or female autonomy? Income, ideology, and empowerment among microentrepreneurs in the Dominican Republic. *Gender & Society* 14:231-55.

Gugler, Josef. 1991. Employment in the city. In *Cities, poverty, and development: Urbanization in the third world*, ed. Alan Gilbert and Josef Gugler. Oxford: Oxford University Press.

Harris, J., and M. Todaro. 1970. Migration, unemployment and development: A two sector analysis. *American Economic Review* 40:126-42.

Hart, Keith. 1973. Informal income opportunities and urban employment in Ghana. *Journal of Modern African Studies* 11:61-89.

Heller, Patrick. 1999. *The labor of development: Workers and the transformation of capitalism in Kerala, India*. Ithaca, NY: Cornell University Press.

Herring, Ronald, and Henry C. Hart. 1977. *Land tenure and peasant in South Asia*. Edited by Robert E. Frykenberg. New Delhi, India: Orient Longman.

Katzenstein, Mary, Smitu Kothari, and Uday Mehta. 2001. Social movement politics in India: Institutions, interests, and identities. In *The success of India's democracy*, ed. Atul Kohli. Cambridge: Cambridge University Press.

Kundu, Amitabh, and Alakh N. Sharma, eds. 2001. *Informal sector in India: Perspectives and policies*. New Delhi, India: Institute for Human Development and Institute of Applied Manpower Research.

Lewis, W. A. 1954. *Economic development with unlimited supplies of labour*. Pp. 139-91. Manchester, UK: Manchester School 22.

Macharia, Kinuthia. 1997. *Social and political dynamics of the informal economy in African cities: Nairobi and Harare*. Oxford: University Press of America.

Marx, Karl. 1906. *Capital: A critique of political economy*. Chicago: C.H. Kerr & Company.

Moody, Kim. 1997. *Workers in a lean world: Unions in the international economy*. London: Verso.

Moore, Barrington. 1966. *Social origins of dictatorship and democracy: Lord and peasant in the making of the modern world*. Boston: Beacon.

National Sample Survey Oganisation (NSSO). 2001. Employment and unemployment situation in India, 1999-2000. Calcutta: NSSO, Government of India.

Oberai, A. S., and G. K. Chadha, eds. 2001. *Job creation in urban informal sector in India: Issues and policy options*. New Delhi, India: International Labor Organization.

Omvedt, Gail. 1993. *Reinventing revolution: New social movements and the socialist tradition in India*. Armonk, NY: M. E. Sharpe.

Portes, A. 1994. The informal economy and its paradoxes. In *Handbook of economic sociology*, ed. Neil J. Smelser and Richard Swedberg, 426-49. Princeton, NJ: Princeton University Press.

Portes, Alejandro, Manuel Castells, and Lauren A. Benton. 1989. *The informal economy: Studies in advanced and less developed countries*. Baltimore: Johns Hopkins University Press.

Rakowski, Cathy A. 1994. *Contrapunto: The informal sector debate in Latin America*. Albany: State University of New York Press.

Rudolph, Lloyd I., and Susanne Hoeber Rudolph. 1987. *In pursuit of Lakshmi: The political economy of the Indian state*. Chicago: University of Chicago Press.

Rueschemeyer, Dietrich, Evelyne H. Stephens, and John D. Stephens. 1992. *Capitalist development and democracy*. Chicago: University of Chicago Press.

Sanyal, Bishwapriya. 1991. Organizing the self-employed: The politics of the urban informal sector. *International Labour Review* 130:39-56.

Seidman, Gay W. 1994. *Manufacturing militance: Workers' movements in Brazil and South Africa, 1970-1985*. Berkeley: University of California Press.

Sharma, Alakh N., and Piush Antony. 2001. *Women workers in the unorganised sector: The more the merrier?* New Delhi, India: Institute for Human Development.

Silver, Beverly J. 2003. *Forces of labor: Workers' movements and globalization since 1870*. Cambridge: Cambridge University Press.

Thompson, E. P. 1966. *The making of the English working class*. New York: Vintage Books.

Tilly, Charles. 1978. *From mobilization to revolution*. Reading, MA: Addison-Wesley.

———. 1995. Globalisation threatens labor's rights. *International Labor and Working-Class History* 47:1-23.

UN-HABITAT. 2004. *State of the world's cities: Globalization and urban culture*. New York: UN-HABITAT.

Western, Bruce. 1995. A comparative study of working-class disorganization: Union decline in eighteen advanced capitalist countries. *American Sociological Review* 60:179-201.

Resistance and Identity Politics in an Age of Globalization

By
DEBORAH J. YASHAR

This article questions the widely held view that indigenous movements in Latin America during the last decades of the twentieth century were caused by globalization. The author reviews several bodies of literature and concludes that, although globalization may be a fit descriptor for some of the actions and narratives of indigenous movements, it cannot be understood as a causal determinant. Many indigenous movements emerged long before the neoliberal current started, others coincide with it, and yet others lag significantly. The author proposes an alternative framework that gives primary significance to state–society relations. Contrary to the idea that national states may have lost prominence in the age of globalization I contend the opposite, suggesting also that indigenous movements have emerged where there are (1) challenges to preexisting corporate identities, (2) transcommunity networks to provide the resources for mobilization, and (3) associational spaces to facilitate collective expression.

Keywords: globalization; indigenous movements; transcommunity networks; national states and neoliberalism

On January 1, 1994, the North American Free Trade Agreement (NAFTA) went into effect and the Ejército Zapatista de Liberación Nacional (EZLN/Zapatistas) took over several towns in the state of Chiapas. Both events captured international attention. The former represented the first step toward an equally celebrated and maligned Trade Agreement for the Americas. The latter was embraced and repressed for trying to deepen Mexican democracy by advancing new kinds of citizenship claims. Much ink has been spilled debating the costs and benefits of both NAFTA and the EZLN. But most analysts would find common ground in arguing that both NAFTA and the EZLN are intimately tied to globalization. While NAFTA represents an effort to institutionalize greater integration of international markets (not including the labor market), the EZLN was initially portrayed as a fundamental challenge and critique of globalization writ large.

DOI: 10.1177/0002716206297960

With the EZLN, other recent indigenous movements throughout the Americas have been described as reactions against neoliberalism and globalization. The Zapatistas certainly helped project this image—timing their rebellion to coincide with the beginning of NAFTA and hosting conferences that denounced neoliberalism, including the 1995 intercontinental conference for humanity and against neoliberalism (a conference that was later dubbed the *intergalactic* conference for humanity and against neoliberalism). At this latter conference, thousands of activists and public intellectuals came to Chiapas to make common cause with the Zapatistas and to strategize about ways to challenge the new global era.[1]

---

*[T]his article is a cautionary tale about the
scope of globalization arguments.*

Throughout the Americas, indigenous movements have emerged and deployed discourses opposing neoliberalism, condemning privatization, the sale of public lands to private interests (oil, logging, cattle, etc.), and the decline in social services. Alison Brysk (2000) has analyzed the ways in which indigenous movements have reacted against and taken advantage of a range of global forces and institutions. Brysk significantly advanced our understanding of strategies, alliances, and framing to demonstrate how indigenous movements successfully allied with international actors and deployed strategies to effect change. In light of this journal volume's focus on globalization, and given my opening remarks, it would be logical to assume that I am going to extend this type of argument, highlighting how globalization has shaped the patterns of identity politics found in the Americas. Nevertheless, I do not plan to embark on that task, which Brysk has already undertaken with great success. Instead, this article is a cautionary tale about the scope of globalization arguments.

I argue that, despite the contemporary cache of globalization arguments among activists and scholars alike, globalization is perhaps better suited to describe contemporary campaigns and frames than to explain the *origins* of movements and

---

Deborah J. Yashar is an associate professor of politics and international affairs and director of the Program in Latin American Studies (PLAS) at Princeton University. Alongside many articles and chapters, she is the author of two books: Demanding Democracy: Reform and Reaction in Costa Rica and Guatemala 1870s-1950s *(Stanford University Press, 1997) and* Contesting Citizenship in Latin America: The Rise of Indigenous Movements and the Postliberal Challenge *(Cambridge University Press, 2005), which received the 2006 Best Book Prize awarded by the New England Council on Latin American Studies and the 2006 Mattei Dogan Honorable Mention from the Society for Comparative Research. She is currently writing a book on violence and citizenship security in postauthoritarian Latin America.*

collective action more broadly. I make this contention with specific reference to the contemporary indigenous movement in the Americas. The rest of this article focuses on four types of globalization narratives. I will end by briefly sketching out an alternative perspective that focuses squarely on changing *state-society* relations (citizenship regimes) and efforts to defend local autonomy. In this sense, identity politics should first be anchored in studies of the *state* rather than taking the global arena as the point of departure.

Globalization and Social Movements[2]

It is commonly asserted that globalization has catalyzed social movement activity, particularly around ethnic identity. The burgeoning globalization literature has underscored significant changes in recent years—a greater interpenetration of economic markets, technological changes that increase the speed and density of global communications, a growth of international organizations and networks, and the emergence of new norms that span borders. The literature as a whole skates between those components.[3] Yet there has been little effort to disentangle how the term has been used; to discuss whether and how the various types of globalization relate to one another; and to analyze systematically the impact, if any, on social movements in various regions. It is therefore not surprising that popular perceptions and some scholarship would marshal globalization arguments to account for indigenous movements. This section takes up four types of arguments and highlights their limited ability to *explain* the emergence of Latin America's indigenous mobilization.[4]

Economic globalization

"Globalization" as a concept was first introduced by a diverse group of scholars to capture fundamental changes in the world economy—the rising mobility of international capital, the reconfiguration of production, and the development of communications and computer technology.[5] Such trends, it is commonly argued, have tightly bound economies together and forecast an era of ever more interdependent socioeconomic orders. While some scholars praise the impact of globalization on macroeconomic growth, others question its effects on state sovereignty, social security, democratic accountability, and the rights and responsibilities of citizens.

Examples of such arguments can be found throughout the social sciences. Sassen, a critic of globalization, argued that it increases the power of international capital at the expense of democracy, citizen accountability, and governance.[6] Loker contended that globalization has undermined the authority of the state in key socioeconomic fields and increased inequality, thereby generating local pockets of resistance.[7] Rodrik, a qualified proponent of globalization, argued that it does not inexorably lead to the breakdown of the welfare state[8] but can generate social tensions that in turn pressure politicians to sidetrack or even undermine globalization policies. Because globalization threatens to disadvantage unskilled workers in advanced industrial countries, many labor unions find reason to mobilize against it. Strikes in France and Germany, in particular, have pointed to organized social opposition to economic globalization at the expense of state protection for workers. Moody has argued that the rise in mass strikes between 1994 and 1997 is in large part a response of the working class to "the pressures of lean production, neo-liberal austerity, and international competition."[9] The less dramatic labor and environmentalist protests in the United States against NAFTA, the World Bank, and other world trade negotiations are also part of this pattern. Discussing an earlier period in Latin American history, Dornbusch and Edwards have noted a similar process by which organized unions in Latin America created the imperative for politicians to implement what they consider ill-advised populist policies of protectionism against free trade and a more global or open economy.[10] In other words, for all of these scholars, globalization can create the very social pressures that undermine it. From this perspective, economic globalization can provoke its own antithetical social movements and protest.

One might hypothesize, therefore, that this new stage of globalization (or at the very least the drive to create more open markets) has catalyzed the rise in indigenous movements in Latin America. With the signing of international trade agreements, the opening of domestic markets, the dismantling of state protection programs, and the like, we might expect a rise in new forms of protest in Latin America.[11] At first blush, some of the emerging indigenous movements would seem to support this argument. Mexico's Zapatistas proclaimed that they were mobilizing, in part, against NAFTA. We also find that indigenous movements in the Amazon have denounced the boom in foreign oil exploration that followed the liberalization of foreign investment, ownership, and patrimony clauses. Indigenous groups have organized impressive marches against foreign oil exploration and even kidnapped foreign oil company workers in Ecuador; they have threatened massive suicide in Colombia. The liberalization of markets has also facilitated the entry of other foreign enterprises, each confronting some form of indigenous protest (i.e., gold miners in Brazil and Venezuela, loggers in Brazil and Bolivia, and cattle grazers in Bolivia).[12]

Globalization therefore is an important part of the story insofar as Latin American states have opened up their economies since the 1980s and 1990s to foreign companies and rescinded restrictive clauses regulating foreign ownership and exploration. In many of these cases, foreign exploration has threatened the territorial integrity and sustainability of areas in which indigenous communities have resided. In this context, we do find indigenous mobilization opposing global pressures.

But this type of globalization argument, on its own, is inadequate for studies of indigenous mobilization for several reasons. First, there is no consensus that the current economic era marks a significant *departure* from earlier periods. Indeed, a series of scholars have argued persuasively that globalization has been an ongoing process and that, in point of fact, the turn from the nineteenth to the twentieth century exhibited greater degrees of economic interdependence than the current phase.[13] For globalization arguments to hold, we would expect to find indigenous movements responding to each peak or at least wave of globalization. This does not occur. Sustained regional and national indigenous movements emerge in the latter part of the twentieth century, not before. Consequently, we cannot attribute (primary or sole) causality to economic globalization, writ large, which has a much longer historical trajectory than the indigenous movements that have emerged only recently.

Second, even if we limit our analyses to the contemporary wave of economic globalization, a problem of timing remains. While some of Latin America's indigenous movements have formed to struggle against and/or negotiate with international companies that have taken advantage of more open Latin American property and investment regimes, this is not so for all or even most of the region's indigenous movements. Latin America's first indigenous movements emerged *prior* to the contemporary wave of economic globalization in Ecuador and Bolivia. In the Amazon, indigenous movements started to form beginning in the 1960s and in response to the penetration of domestic cattle grazers and development agencies. In the Andes, most movements have their origins in the 1960s and 1970s, again responding to domestic developments rather than international pressures. It is only in the late 1980s and 1990s that campaigns against foreign penetration of native lands began, and in that context some, but not all, indigenous movements emerged. Even in Mexico, where the globalization argument seemed most credible, the timing is off. While the EZLN announced its goals on the day that NAFTA took effect, the movement and its constitutive organizations had a history that preceded NAFTA negotiations for many years.[14]

Latin America's first indigenous movements emerged prior to the contemporary wave of economic globalization in Ecuador and Bolivia.

Moreover, anti-NAFTA movements did not occur in all indigenous communities. This raises questions about the causal role of NAFTA. So too, in Central America (Nicaragua and Guatemala, in particular), globalization resonates little or not at all with the emergence of indigenous mobilization. What this suggests is that globalization is perhaps more helpful as a descriptor of some cases rather than a causal argument to explain the emergence of ethnic and indigenous movements throughout the region.

Third, were economic globalization to provide the master argument for indigenous social movements, one would expect them to emerge similarly throughout the region. But this has not happened. Indigenous movements remain weak in Peru, moderately strong in Guatemala and Mexico, and strong in Bolivia and Ecuador—all of the Latin American countries experienced economic liberalization through the 1980s and 1990s, yet the strength of autochthonous mobilization varies, with Peru as the real outlier.

Finally, the economic globalization argument cannot explain why *ethnic* as opposed to any other identities have become politically salient at this particular juncture. In fact, scholars of economic globalization (who have primarily worked on Europe) had predicted the reaction of *class*-based groups—class-based both because of the economic consequences of globalization for workers and because of the prior existence of labor federations with defined constituencies and entrenched interests. Yet contemporary protest in Latin America is not solely about class. Latin America has witnessed the emasculation of many unions—rural as well as urban—that have lost their capacity to organize workers and peasants as such. Unions' strikes and protests have decreased in number, and unsurprisingly, unions in many countries are in an even weaker bargaining position to negotiate with the state.[15]

Yet while older unions have lost the power to mobilize and shape policy, new forms of identity politics to contest foreign exploitation have emerged. Rather than protesting foreign companies using a language of class, as predicted by some scholars of globalization, in Latin America movements have most forcefully emerged around ethnic identities.[16] Moreover, they have articulated an agenda that includes but is not limited to material demands. They are also calling for recognition of ethnic rights and a reconfiguration of what it means to be a citizen. Globalization arguments (as currently stated) about more open markets cannot explain such phenomena. To address this problem, we need to look at how more open markets reshape rural property relations and rural cleavages in ways that politicize ethnic identities.

In short, economic globalization provides a handle neither on the timing nor the identity claims of indigenous movements. This is so even while it describes many of the campaigns of greatest international renown. It perhaps proves more useful as a description of the target of some protests rather than the primary explanation of why and where indigenous movements have emerged in the region.

Globalization of resources and networks

A second take on globalization has focused on the formation and growth of a global civil society or what Falk labeled globalization from above, Melucci called a planetary society, and Wapner designated as world civic politics.[17] Scholars have been impressed by the rise in international organizations and advocacy networks that support social movements and pressure for policy change. Keck and Sikkink, in particular, have argued that transnational advocacy networks can provide the material and information resources that enable movements to act effectively for change. They have highlighted how social movements confronted with severe political obstacles at home can and do turn to the international arena to lobby for change and try to effect social transformation. Keck and Sikkink called this the "boomerang effect." Brysk, Fox and Brown, and Edelman have also analyzed transnational alliances.[18] The domestically bounded social movements literature might expect that where domestic options are foreclosed, movements will not emerge. Nevertheless, scholars highlight the resourcefulness of actors to take advantage of and create new political opportunities at the international level; they do not see this process as overdetermined but as open to the possibilities of change at home:

> The international system we present is made up not only of states engaged in self-help or even rule-governed behavior, but of dense webs of interaction and interrelations among citizens of different states which both reflect and help sustain shared values, beliefs, and projects. . . . The globalization process we observe is not an inevitable steam-roller but a specific set of interactions among purposeful individuals. Although in the aggregate these interactions may seem earthshaking, they can also be dissected and mapped in a way that reveals greater indeterminacy at most points of the process. There is nothing inevitable about this story: it is the composite of thousands of decision which could have been decided otherwise.[19]

There no doubt has been a significant rise in international networks and resources for Latin America's indigenous movements. Alison Brysk, for example, has detailed the various ways in which movements have appealed to international organizations (including the United Nations, solidarity groups, legal centers, and the like) to draft United Nations documents and to pressure for change at home.[20] Certainly, international funding has risen for indigenous organizations (i.e., Oxfam, Ford, etc.) and international solidarity organizations (i.e., the Amazon Coalition, The Legal Defense Fund, Cultural Survival, Rainforest Action, among many others) that promote their causes.[21] And it is impossible to think about the Zapatistas in Chiapas without commenting on their brilliant use of solidarity organizations, global resources, and international forums.

Moreover, indigenous organizations have reached across national borders—first witnessed on a large scale in the years leading up to the Quincentennial in 1992. Significant indigenous forums that have emerged include Coordinadora de Organizaciones Indígenas de la Cuenca Amazónica (Coordinating Body for Indigenous Organizations of the Amazonian Basin; COICA) for the Amazon and The South and Meso American Indian Rights Center (SAIIC) for indigenous peoples of the Americas, among others. They represent significant advances at the international level. Their power of mobilization remains weak, however.

The descriptive evidence might seem overwhelmingly to favor an argument about the globalization of networks and resources. Certainly there is a descriptive fit. But how powerful is the causal argument? As prior scholars have noted, here we need further work to analyze the mechanisms by which successful change does and does not occur. As Fox (2002, 2005) noted, we cannot and should not presume that international statements of endorsement translate into support on the ground, nor can we assume that all outside involvement serves to advance social movement causes. Moreover, we need to be careful not to equate contemporary discourse and alliances with movement origins—since discourse and alliances can change over time. Clifford Bob's work (2005) makes abundantly clear, moreover, that the very international networks and discourse that increase international visibility and clout might in turn serve to weaken organizational and ideological ties to local constituencies. In short, these international campaigns are important but not determinative of either movement origins or success.

It would be irresponsible to disregard the role and impact of international organizations (which in some cases has been quite significant), but we cannot assume that they were necessary or sufficient factors. When we look at the range of cases in Latin America, we find that while some notable organizations received funding from Ford and Oxfam in their early years,[22] others emerged with no international funding. Moreover, on-the-ground studies have demonstrated that international intervention can both support and undermine the emergence and endurance of movements. It has not infrequently divided them, particularly where communities confront more than one organization working within the same location or with the same population. Outside funding and intervention can lead to a greater divide between the leaders who travel in international circles and the communities that they claim to represent. In short, the globalization of networks and resources is not unambiguously positive for movement emergence and formation. These arguments are off on the timing and unclear about the conditions under which global resources are beneficial, problematic and/or inconsequential to movement formation and policy change.[23]

Once formed, indigenous movements in Latin America took on multiple forms, in some cases leveraging the international community (reacting against it, mobilizing with it) to act in favor of a much broader set of campaigns. It is this leveraging that has made movements more modular, more visible—sometimes both more successful in their campaigns while more fragile in their organizational structure (Tarrow 2005; Bob 2005). This indeterminate relationship is what needs to be teased out, not by asserting that globalization matters but by analyzing, comparing, and assessing which factors matter most.

Globalization of norms

A third argument has highlighted the globalization of norms.[24] This body of literature focuses on changes in international rules, as evidenced by conventions and declarations by international organizations such as the United Nations, the World Bank, and the International Labor Organization (ILO). The argument is made that such norms provide both the parameters for constituting national interests and legislation as well as ideational resources for social movement claim-making.

Soysal (1994), for example, has argued that human rights norms articulated at the transnational level have affected national discourses, movement strategies, and membership rights in Europe. She outlined how European states have historically developed different models of political incorporation that were generally tied to beliefs about national membership and citizenship. In the postwar period, however, these different states have started to extend to migrants the civil and social rights associated with citizenship, even when migrants do not enjoy the political rights of suffrage. So too we find migrants demanding these rights in one form or another. Soysal explained both of these postwar trends (the extension of membership rights and the mobilization for those rights) with reference to a new set of transnational norms about citizenship and personhood.

Finnemore (1996) also emphasized the causal importance of international norms. Drawing on three case studies, she argued that international norms increasingly shape values and constitute state interest and actions. She suggested that emerging international norms in UNESCO, the Red Cross, and the World Bank reshaped state values regarding the importance of state science bureaucracies, the Geneva Convention, and development. She concluded by underscoring three foundational normative elements (bureaucracy, markets, and human equality) that came to organize international social life by the end of the twentieth century (p. 131).

These suggestive arguments compel us to consider the role of international norms and how they might (re)define political interests, values, and actions, both for states and social movements. In the Latin American context of indigenous organizing, this argument might seem quite credible. It could be said that, with the legislation of the ILO's Convention 169 on Indigenous and Tribal Peoples in Independent Countries, states and indigenous populations have greater agreement about the rights of indigenous and tribal peoples. In fact, Latin American states with less than impressive human rights records toward native groups have increasingly signed on to the Convention in recent years.[25] So too, with the wave of democratization that has swept across Latin America, we find a greater support for norms on international human rights. Moreover, indigenous movements do use ILO and human rights discourse in much of their work.

Yet these norm arguments seem strangely isolated from the push and pull of politics, including, power relations, coercion, diplomacy, economic constraints, coalition building, pressure groups, bargaining, and so on. To make this argument stick, we need to demonstrate when, why, and how norms matter. This is a particular challenge in Latin America, where it is difficult to take the global norms arguments at face value. States in that region have rarely implemented international norms at home, even when they support them in international forums. Authoritarian rule and human rights abuses against nationals were widespread in the 1970s and 1980s, just as human rights regulations were presumably accepted in international arenas. A serious chasm grew between public discourse and political practice—human rights, for example, were not even extended to national citizens, never mind persons of other national origins. Perhaps for this reason, efforts by indigenous activists to hook up their demands with a human rights agenda were generally less than successful. Indeed, some indigenous activists found environmental discourses and allies more useful, as Brysk's work highlights.[26] It remains an open question as to whether states will abide by Convention 169. While Bolivia has made some important advances, other states have experienced many more setbacks as they fail to implement what they signed or, as in Guatemala, populations at times reject referenda designed to ratify some of the items therein. Consequently, we are forced to ask: Under what conditions do states abide by international norms? Which norms, if any, have had an impact and to what degree? At present international norms have had nothing more than contingent support in Latin America, and only a partial impact on citizenship within states. This is surely a question of political bargains and pressure rather than a direct adoption of international norms.[27]

Under what conditions do states abide by international norms? Which norms, if any, have had an impact and to what degree?

Second, and related, it is difficult to argue that international norms have changed state values and beliefs (as most boldly asserted by Finnemore [1996, 129]) when Latin American states have demonstrated only a secondary and contingent concern for citizenship rights, universal personhood, and human equality (the international norms highlighted by Soysal [1994] and Finnemore [1996]). In the current wave of democratization, regimes have extended political and civil rights once again, although in a rather uneven fashion. Yet the social rights that T. H. Marshall (1963) and Soysal (1994) discussed have been under attack in contemporary Latin America as governments prioritize fiscal balance over social policy. Countless social policies have been dismantled or severely weakened in the face of the 1980s and 1990s economic crisis in the region. Indeed, the current round of economic globalization (itself a response to the debt crises and the economic crises that ensued) generated, as Rodrik (1997, 1998) suggested earlier, the drive to dismantle social programs. This resulted in a striking reduction in social programs. In other words, contrary to what Soysal has found in Europe (where social rights have been extended to all members), in Latin America economic globalization in the 1990s trumped global norms about social citizenship.

Third, I have found that indigenous movements (as with the migrants to Europe) sometimes do appeal to international discourse and norms (and increasingly so). Yet we need to be careful not to mistake discourse for motives and international audiences for social movement constituencies. On the one hand, international discourse was rarely used or cited at the founding and formation of most indigenous movements. As elaborated below, indigenous movements largely emerged in response to domestic changes, quite independently of international norms about human and indigenous rights. Once founded, indigenous movements have increasingly appealed to international norms as they have reframed their work to capture broader national and international support. In every case we need to be vigilant to avoid using contemporary discourse to explain why movements emerged at a prior moment.

In short, the important use of international norms—be they about human rights, democracy, the environment, or native peoples—followed rather than catalyzed the movements in question. Globalization can and does affect discourse for international consumption but not necessarily domestic practices. Proclamations about international norms by movement leaders do not necessarily resonate with concerns, discourse, and agendas at the local levels—the very level at which we need to explain indigenous movement emergence and mobilization. Internationally directed and derived discourse does not always reflect community beliefs (which are not homogeneous to begin with); nor does it necessarily filter back down to the local level. Temporality and mechanisms must be evaluated before we can assert the causal impact of globalization. This task requires us to focus more squarely on domestic politics and power.

Political globalization

Finally, a fourth possible take on globalization and collective action flows from arguments about the end of the cold war and its impact both on the global balance of power and on left politics.[28] In both versions of this narrative, the collapse of a global and domestic left alternative presumably allows other identity politics to flourish. Huntington argued, for example, that the cold war privileged central identities and conflicts and suppressed or at least dampened others. With the end of the cold war, there has been greater political and economic interaction between and among states. While it was once easy for states to frame other states within the cold war paradigm, this is no longer the case. Fukuyama has argued that the end of the cold war engendered the end of history, but Huntington has argued quite the contrary.[29] Without a defining paradigm to type allies and enemies, but in a context of greater interactions, Huntington argued that civilizational (very loosely defined as primordial ethnic, cultural, religious, and/or national) identities and differences become more salient. "The end of ideologically defined states in Eastern Europe and the former Soviet Union permits traditional ethnic identities and animosities to come to the fore."[30] In his controversial article and then book, Huntington has argued that this greater prominence of civilizational identities will erupt between the West and the non-West as well as among those within the non-West as they compete for more land, more political power, and more economic resources.[31] In short, civilizational conflicts that were latent have become manifest with the end of the cold war. One would presume therefore that movements would emerge along these same lines.

Certainly the cold war and its end have had an impact on social movements and state responses in Latin America. For example, states in that region during the 1970s and 1980s engaged in some of the most widespread and brutal political repression. Fearful of the "communist" threat from within, states perpetrated human rights abuses against people suspected of communist sympathies. The state helped to frame antiauthoritarian or propoor movements as communist conspiracies that had to be contained if not eliminated. Indigenous peoples who mobilized in places like Guatemala and Peru were inevitably seen by state officials as part and parcel of communist movements, even when they were independent organizations. Those two countries, in particular, witnessed the worst of the repression in the countryside as civil wars left communities and families destroyed and scattered. Anonymous activists (indigenous and otherwise) in both countries have highlighted in interviews how difficult it was to organize in the context of war. For regardless of whether they supported Marxist revolutionaries, the state assumed that they did. Their voice was not heard and their actions were met with state repression.[32]

Against this backdrop, it is possible to argue that the end of the cold war provided this greater space for ethnic identities and organizations to emerge. In important ways, the end of the cold war did expand political opportunities, particularly in Guatemala, although much less so in the other cases studied here. Yet this argument overlooks an important fact: movements, where they emerged in Guatemala, began in the mid-1980s, with the process of democratization, not the end of the cold war. Moreover, the framework under consideration does not account for why similar movements emerged prior to the cold war throughout Latin America or why, despite the end of the cold war, they have not emerged in any significant and sustained way in the contemporary Peruvian context.

The assumptions behind civilizational identities are even more problematic. On one hand, it is not clear what a civilization is. It is difficult to assume, as Huntington (1993) did, that these, or any, identities are static and primordial. Huntington used a loose definition that is grafted onto "civilizations" with no clear prior reasoning. For example, he referred to a Latin American civilization, but it is not clear what that means either descriptively or conceptually and why Latin America has been singled out as a single civilization as opposed to many or any. On the other hand, it is not clear why civilizations would necessarily engage in conflict with one another. Why should we assume that global conflict will emerge? And how do we explain conflicts from within—both among those that presumably form part of the civilization and those that challenge it?

Admittedly, Huntington (1993) was not particularly concerned about internal conflicts as much as global ones, but his fixed understanding of primordial identities belies the ways in which self-definitions have been forged and reforged. Just as Arab states did not have a natural affinity for one another, neither did indigenous communities in Latin America easily forge their panethnic image. The identity and organizations of these movements depended on political action. Huntington's thesis cannot easily travel to explain the conditions under which ethnic movements will emerge within and among states to protest current policies and to demand greater inclusion.

An alternative end of cold war argument focuses on the ensuing collapse of the Left. In its most colloquial form, this argument suggests that with the collapse of the Left, there was a new space and imperative for other forms of identity politics. The Left was no longer able to organize with the same conviction and capacity. With this free terrain, new self definitions found greater space for organization and expression, including the emergence of indigenous movements.[33] This argument is not without merit; some Left organizations remade themselves as Indian movements in the 1990s. Nevertheless, most indigenous movements in the region predate the end of the cold war by years, if not decades.

The Importance of States and Citizenship Regimes

Each of the aforementioned globalization approaches is at first blush compelling and aptly describes movements that have gained substantial press, including the EZLN's protest against NAFTA, indigenous protests against international oil exploration, indigenous participation in United Nations working groups and professional conferences, and the passing of the ILO's Convention 169. In other words, there appears to be a descriptive fit between certain aspects of globalization and the campaigns launched by some social movements.

My review has highlighted, nonetheless, that globalization approaches remain blunt instruments to address the regionwide politicization of ethnic cleavages in general and indigenous movements in Latin America in particular. This is so for several reasons. Conceptually, the term remains imprecise. What does it (not) cover? When did it begin? The competing and vague concepts used do not entirely answer this question and, consequently, make it hard to ascertain if and how globalization does or does not matter. For how can one discern the causal mechanisms when the timing and sequencing of globalization are in fact in question? First, in some cases, the movements to be explained emerge prior to the onset of key moments in economic, political, and normative globalization. Second, even if one grants a common and bounded definition, the globalization arguments themselves beg the question as to why such a process catalyzes collective action in some places and not others and why ethnicity (or any political identity) becomes the primary basis for mobilization in some locations and yet not in others. When we pitch our arguments in terms of globalization, without greater attention paid to why, how, and where domestic actors can and do engage in collective action, we lose sight of the variation that exists among cases. For collective action is not universal; it remains an outcome that requires us to explain variation across and within cases. It is this variation that we need to explain and it this variation that becomes a tool for discerning and substantiating arguments about when and where movements emerge and when and where they do so along ethnic lines. Radcliffe (2001) drew similar conclusions: "the transnational engagement of global organizations, states and subjects are not decided *a priori*, and leave room for agency and dynamics processes of change" (p. 20), adding,

> In light of recent research on transnational networks' influence on policy formulation, it is clear that transnationalism matters in politics and development. The mapping out of such transnational networks however relies upon a detailed *empirical* understanding of the actors involved, their means of communication and the power relationships between them. (p. 27)

In short, the globalization literature thus far largely suffers from an ahistorical and often universalizing understanding of where, if, and how this phenomenon matters for identity politics and collective action. So too this literature often suffers from the assumption, rather than demonstration, that the state is of declining relevance in contemporary politics. As a rich literature on social movements has noted, however, contemporary social movements are often fundamental responses to the state.[34]

In short, the globalization literature thus far largely suffers from an ahistorical and often universalizing understanding of where, if, and how this phenomenon matters for identity politics and collective action.

Tarrow cautioned us against drawing overeager conclusions about globalization.[35] Empirically, rather than theoretically speaking, the international arena has not displaced the (nation) state as the target of political change nor has a global civil society displaced domestically rooted social movements. To the contrary, some (but not all) social movements have appealed to the international arena to bolster preexisting *domestic* currents and struggles. For while borders are more porous, states still maintain the final right of arbitration, legislation, and regulation within the territories and over the population that they govern.[36] They have the final power to determine who has access to membership and under what terms. In this sense, states (still) remain the targets of political protest, much as Tilly (1978) observed years back. Tarrow took this one step further by pointing to the *mechanisms* by which transnational, global, and cosmopolitan actors maneuver to effect change. His findings lead us to research the domestic and international interactions rather than to presume their relationship.

My own research has led to a set of alternative arguments about the emergence of ethnic politics in Latin America. When analyzing indigenous movements against the landscape of the twentieth century, I see indigenous movements as fundamentally claiming and demanding a series of *state-based reforms* to reconfigure citizenship; they seek formal *national* recognition, *local* autonomy, legal pluralism, additional land reforms, and bicultural education, among other changes. As a whole, these demands form part of a "postliberal challenge" (Yashar 1999, 2005) since indigenous people demand both respect and incorporation as individual citizens (the liberal promise) and legal recognition as collectively autonomous units (the postliberal challenge). To pursue these goals, indigenous movements have voiced their demands through social movement politics. They have organized unprecedented marches from the Amazon to the Andes (particularly in Bolivia and Ecuador), staged highway disruptions, occupied government buildings, and organized street protests against various political and economic reforms. As of late, they have also turned to electoral politics to introduce their demands into formal politics.[37] While the movements and their claims as a whole are quite varied, the point to emphasize here is that indigenous people are organizing and articulating ethnic-based agendas that contest the definition and terms of *national* citizenship, both insisting on greater inclusion in the national state *and* greater autonomy from it. Such claims are state-centric. It is this contemporary mobilization of indigenous people in response to changing national conditions that calls out for explanation.

To elucidate these new patterns of claim making, I have argued that contemporary indigenous movements in the Americas emerged in the last third of the twentieth century when three factors were at play: (1) a challenge to local autonomy that resulted from *changing citizenship regimes* (first the erosion of a corporatist regime and then its replacement by a neoliberal one),[38] (2) *transcommunity networks*, and (3) *political associational space* (Yashar 1998, 2005). To make this argument, I compared indigenous movements over time and across cases to explain why the erosion of corporatist citizenship regimes provided the *motive* (by threatening to disrupt local property regimes in ways that challenged indigenous autonomy); why transcommunity networks (built by churches, unions, and NGOs) provided the organizational capacity enabling indigenous leaders to mobilize across disparate communities, including those separated by geographic distance and language; and when political associational space provided the opportunity. Only where these three factors were present did indigenous people have not only the motive but also the capacity and opportunity to forge regional and national movements (as in Ecuador, Bolivia, Guatemala, and Mexico). Where these factors did not *all* come together, movement organizing confronted significant obstacles (as in Peru, where the civil war destroyed networks *and* foreclosed political associational space despite the nominal existence of electoral democracy).

By the mid-1990s, significant indigenous movements existed throughout North, Central, and South America, with the strongest organizations in Ecuador and Bolivia. In Ecuador, the most important group is the Confederación de Nacionalidades Indígenas del Ecuador (CONAIE, or Confederation of Indigenous Nationalities of Ecuador). Bolivia has several important groups: the Confederación Sindical

Unica de Trabajadores Campesinos de Bolivia (CSUTCB, or Unified Peasant Workers Trade Union Confederation of Bolivia); the Confederación Indígena del Oriente, Chaco, y Amazonía de Bolivia (CIDOB, or Indigenous Confederation of the East, Chaco, and the Amazon); and more recently, the *cocalero*, or coca growers movement headed by now-President Evo Morales. Moreover, there are prominent organizations in Mexico, Colombia, and Guatemala. On a regionwide scale, the weakest organizational indigenous movements still exist in Peru—although the gap appears to be closing now that transcommunity networks are being rebuilt and political associational space has been extended.

Whether one buys this argument or some alternative is less the issue of this article than to say that we should not presume that globalization matters without assessing causes and consequences against the cases—paying close attention to concepts, mechanisms, and temporality. In other words, we need to research these questions rather than presume their answers.

Conclusion

This volume addresses the significance of globalization and certainly the changing international environment is something to behold as we witness an ever more integrated world economy, transnational networks, international norms, and global hegemony. Such characteristics push us to think about the ways in which international factors shape collective action in general and indigenous social movements in particular. They compel us to think about the limits on state sovereignty and the ways in which globalization engenders collective action. It is important to acknowledge the ways in which state borders have changed and new actors have emerged. States have modified their restrictions on free markets, reforged international political alliances, confronted new actors that pressure states to reform their relations with citizens, and come up against a new set of (de)legitimating discourses to which they are expected to respond. In short, globalization arguments portray striking developments that are occurring at the expense of state sovereignty over domestic affairs. Those changes affecting state sovereignty have catalyzed both a defensive form of collective action (against economic globalization) and new kinds of claims making that are shaped by and take advantage of the opportunities offered by the international environment (international networks and norms).

Nevertheless, in this article I struck a cautionary note. For once we look comparatively at collective action, it is apparent that the international arena does not simply shape social movements. Nor does globalization help to explain the timing or intensity of movements that emerge, with some prior to the heyday of globalization (Latin America's indigenous movements), others following on the heels of globalization conjunctures (such as the WTO protests), and yet others emerging several years later (as in human rights movements that adopted United Nations language after it was proclaimed). Finally, globalization does not provide a handle on which identities become the salient basis for collective action. To the contrary, a great deal of diversity exists across cases at any given point in time, as illustrated by the resurgence of labor protest in Europe, indigenous protests in the Americas, environmental movements in the West, and fundamentalist movements in the Middle East.

Given these outstanding questions, globalization is no panacea for studies of collective action (Yashar 2002). Even though changes are taking place in the international economy, networks, and norms, one should not be too quick to assume that these descriptive developments have causal significance. For it is neither clear why, when, and where these changes do or do not generate collective action nor which form collective action is likely to take. Globalization's impact on collective action appears to be highly indeterminate. It is the exploration of this indeterminacy that seems so vital—a task that Tarrow (2005) has taken up.

The theoretical task for studies of collective action then is to articulate better the structured and contingent relations among international processes, states, nongovernmental organizations, and actors. In doing so, they will have to take particular care to pay attention to temporality and mechanisms—to *demonstrate* causality rather than to impute it and to explain *which* identities become salient and why. Globalization arguments alone cannot explain this important diversity in timing, location, and identity. While apparently omnipresent, globalization is not omnicausal.

Notes

1. In many ways, the themes addressed in this conference echoed the kinds of themes debated at subsequent World Social Forum meetings in Brazil, India, and Venezuela.

2. This section parallels Yashar (2002).

3. For reviews of globalization, see Held (1998); Tarrow (1998, chap. 11, 1999, 2005).

4. Here I introduce (briefly though the case may be) a set of related but different globalization arguments to tease out if and how they might help to explain the emergence of indigenous movements in Latin America. I do not introduce arguments about parallel demonstration across borders or international borrowing. Nor do I discuss the role of modularity, as movements adopt and adapt things from others. Anderson (1991), Tarrow (1998), and others have insightfully highlighted how repertoires of contention move within and across borders. This is for several reasons. First, while repertoires cross borders, they are crossing state boundaries rather than borrowing from a global set of norms, institutions, and or practices. In this sense, there is a fluidity of borders but not globalization per se. Moreover, it is hard to argue that this form of cross-border sharing is a new phenomenon; we have seen the ways in which political frames travel with the revolutions of 1848 and the student protests of 1968. In short, this pattern is not globalization but "cross-bordering/crossing of borders." Finally, these arguments do not explain the *emergence* of movements, even if they are helpful in describing the strategies that are adopted.

5. The economic globalization literature is vast and growing and has focused on several important issues—including trade, capital flows, labor markets, and investment climates. I discuss this literature only insofar as it introduces arguments that address and/or have implications for the question of collective action.

6. Sassen (1996).

7. Loker (1999).

8. See Rodrik (1997, 1998) and Garrett (1998).

9. Moody (1997, 55).

10. Dornbusch and Edwards (1991).

11. For arguments that neoliberalism (economic globalization) is largely responsible for a new growth in civil society, see Alvarez, Dagnino, and Escobar (1998, 21-23); and Yúdice (1998).

12. In a partial twist of this story, we find coca growers in Bolivia effectively protesting the uneven practice of globalization. While the Bolivian state has tried to privatize state industries and open up the economy to the international market, they have regulated the production of coca—working with the U.S. government to eradicate the crop. Coca growers, both Quechua and Aymara, have protested the state's violent efforts to do so—particularly given the economic profits to be had on the international market.

13. See Rodrik (1997), Adelman (1998), Wade (1996), and Weiss (1997, 1998).

14. Harvey (1996, 1998).

15. Labor protest has varied considerably across the region, a variation that is explained by factors other than (or in addition to) globalization. See Murillo (2001).

16. I do not mean to suggest here that material/socioeconomic conditions are unimportant or that these are postmaterial movements. Clearly, indigenous peoples in the Americas are largely impoverished. One of their fundamental demands is for land. However, I am suggesting that we cannot identify and explain these movements as a whole as primarily a class issue. Certainly we cannot explain why they identify in many cases primarily as Indians rather than as peasants in response to such material changes—for after all, this is what distinguishes these movements from prior modes of rural organizing. The movements discussed here do not label themselves as "peasant-based movements" but as "indigenous movements"—some of which are peasant based, other which are not. While struggling for land is a central demand, they privilege their ethnic identity and make claims to the land that stem from their rights and beliefs as Indians.

17. Falk (1993), Melucci (1998), and Wapner (1995).

18. Keck and Sikkink (1998a, 1998b, 217-18), Brysk (1994, 1996, 2000), Fox and Brown (1998); Edelman (1988).

19. Keck and Sikkink (1998a, 213).

20. Brysk (1994, 1996, 2000).

21. See Warren (1998) and Brysk (1994, 1996). Warren, for example, highlighted how Guatemalan Pan-Mayan activists have appealed (ambivalently at times) to the international arena and international agencies to promote their cause. "In sum, Pan-Mayanists have internationalized and hybridized Mayan culture to intensify and re-politicize the cultural differences between indigenous and Ladino communities at home" (p. 179).

22. Chase Smith (1984).

23. Network-based arguments, in general, cannot yet answer some of these criticisms that I have leveled against the global networks arguments—in particular the conditions under which networks enable versus divide communities. For this reason, network arguments cannot explain movement formation in isolation from other factors.

24. Soysal (1994), Finnemore (1996), and Aziz (1999). Aziz presented an alternative perspective on the hegemony of human rights discourse as part of the process of globalization from above (by Western countries or global financial institutions) or from below (by social movements).

25. The International Labor Organization's (ILO's) Convention 169 outlines the rights of indigenous peoples and the responsibilities of multiethnic states toward them. To date, the following Latin American states have ratified ILO 169: Mexico (1990), Bolivia (1991), Colombia (1991), Costa Rica (1993), Peru (1994), Paraguay (1993), Honduras (1995), Guatemala (1996), Ecuador (1998), Argentina (2000), Brazil (2002), and Venezuela (2002). Most of these Latin American states have yet to live up to the terms of the Convention. Mexico (1992) and Bolivia (1994), however, passed constitutional amendments that recognize the multiethnic and pluricultural makeup of each country. A 1999 referendum on this issue took place in Guatemala and was rejected by the population; turnout, however, ran at almost 18.4 percent of registered voters. *CNN Interactive*, May 17, 1999; and *Prensa Libre*, May 17, 1999.

26. Keck (1995), Keck and Sikkink (1998a), and Brysk (2000).

27. Keck and Sikkink (1998a, 210-11) raised a similar objection to world polity theorists. It is important to note that Soysal argued that national *institutional* contexts are different and differentially filter and institutionalize international norms. However, she did not seem to question that those norms will be implemented in some fashion.

28. It is debatable whether the end of the cold war can be called a form of globalization politics or a change in global politics. I tend to think that it is the second. Huntington (1993), whose work is primarily

discussed here, did not label his argument as a globalization argument. However, his argument rested on the idea that global changes have precipitated a set of global responses that manifest themselves as the clash of civilizations. For this reason, and given the impact of this argument on policy makers, it seems necessary to at least mention it and discuss it, however briefly.

29. Fukuyama (1992).

30. Huntington (1993, 29).

31. Huntington's thesis has been duly criticized in the pages of *Foreign Affairs* and elsewhere for its imperialist and orientalist assumptions. I do not rehearse these critiques here—first, because they have already been stated and, second, because my intention is not to argue for or against the internal logic/coherence of these positions but to see what purchase they do and do not have for explaining Latin America's diverse but growing indigenous movements.

32. Yashar (1997). Statement draws on fieldwork conducted in Guatemala (March 1989 to February 1990, December 1992, and February 1996) and in Peru (August 1997). Also see Stern (1998).

33. For examples, see Canel (1992) and Cardoso (1992).

34. See Tilly (1984); Bright and Harding (1978/1984), Tarrow (1996, 1998), Foweraker (1995), Nagel (1986), and Brass (1985).

35. Tarrow (1998, 1999, 2005).

36. The breakdown of states in Africa and the countries of the former Soviet Union are notable exceptions—although the weakness of their states has little to do with globalization.

37. See Van Cott (2003, 2005), Rice and Van Cott (2006), and Madrid (2005a, 2005b).

38. I borrow the phrase "citizenship regime" from Jane Jenson and Susan Phillips (1996). They used the term to refer to the varying bundles of rights and responsibilities that citizenship can confer. I use the term in a more expansive sense to refer to (1) who has citizenship, (2) what are the terms of interest intermediation (i.e., corporatist versus pluralist), and (3) what bundle of rights are extended (i.e., T. H. Marshall's [1963] trilogy of civil, political and/or social). Corporatist citizenship regimes advanced corporatist modes of interest intermediation and social and civil rights (only sometimes also extending political ones); in practice corporatist citizenship regimes nominally granted indigenous people some civil rights (previously denied them through debt peonage); some collective land that was inalienable and indivisible (hence sustaining the land base for sustaining existing indigenous *communities*), and the promise of some social services to sustain their communities. Corporatist citizenship regimes therefore eased ethnic cleavages by promising both indigenous incorporation and unwittingly granting indigenous autonomy. As corporatist citizenship regimes eroded, however, the informal basis of indigenous local autonomy was challenged as well. And once neoliberal citizenship regimes started dismantling social rights (including the property regimes that had secured the geographic space within which indigenous communities had survived), the integrity and stability of indigenous communities was effectively threatened. Under these circumstances, I argue, ethnic cleavages were politicized in much of contemporary Latin America. In the Amazon, we see a modified version of this process, in large part because Latin American states have always been weak in this region and citizenship regimes have therefore been less visible; however, in a parallel process, ethnic cleavages in the Amazon were politicized where the state promoted corporatist and neoliberal development policies (colonization and land development) that threatened indigenous autonomy.

References

Adelman, Jeremy. 1998. Latin America and globalization. *LASA Forum* 29 (1): 10-12.

Alvarez, Sonia E., Evelina Dagnino, and Arturo Escobar. 1998. Introduction: The cultural and the political in Latin American social movements. In *Cultures of politics, politics of culture: Re-visioning Latin American social movements*, ed. Sonia E. Alvarez, Evelina Dagnino, and Arturo Escobar. Boulder, CO: Westview.

Anderson, Benedict. 1991. *Imagined communities: Reflections on the origin and spread of nationalism.* London: Verso.

Aziz, Nikhil. 1999. The human rights debate in an era of globalization: Hegemony or discourse. In *Debating human rights*, ed. Peter Van Ness. New York: Routledge.

Bob, Clifford. 2005. *The marketing of rebellion: Insurgents, media, and international activism.* Cambridge: Cambridge University Press.

Brass, Paul R. 1985. Ethnic groups and the state. In *Ethnic groups and the state*, ed. Paul R. Brass. London: Croom Helm.

Bright, Charles, and Susan Harding, eds. 1978/1984. *Statemaking and social movements: Essays in history and theory*. Ann Arbor: University of Michigan Press.

Brysk, Alyson. 1994. Acting globally: Indian rights and international politics in Latin America. In *Indigenous peoples and democracy in Latin America*, ed. Donna Lee Van Cott. New York: St. Martin's.

———. 1996. Turning weakness into strength. *Latin American Perspectives* 23 (2): 38-57.

———. 2000. *From tribal village to global village: Indian rights and international relations in Latin America*. Stanford, CA: Stanford University Press.

Canel, Eduardo. 1992. Democratization and the decline of urban social movements in Uruguay: A political-institutional account. In *The making of social movements in Latin America: Identity, strategy, and democracy*, ed. Arturo Escobar and Sonia Alvarez. Boulder, CO: Westview.

Cardoso, Ruth Correa Leite. 1992. Popular movements in the context of the consolidation of democracy in Brazil. In *The making of social movements in Latin America: Identity, strategy, and democracy*, ed. Arturo Escobar and Sonia Alvarez. Boulder, CO: Westview.

Chase Smith, Richard. 1984. A search for unity within diversity: Peasant unions, ethnic federations, and Indianist movements in the Andean republics. *Cultural Survival Quarterly* 4 (December): 6-13.

Dornbusch, Rudiger, and Sebastian Edwards, eds. 1991. *The macroeconomics of populism in Latin America*. Chicago: University of Chicago Press.

Edelman, Marc. 1988. Transnational peasant politics in Central America, *Latin American Research Review* 33 (3): 49-86.

Falk, Richard. 1993. The making of global citizenship. In *Global visions*, ed. Jeremy Brecher. Boston: South End Press.

Finnemore, Martha. 1996. *National interests in international society*. Ithaca, NY: Cornell University Press.

Foweraker, Joe. 1995. *Theorizing social movements*. London: Pluto Press.

Fox, Jonathan. 2002. Lessons from Mexico-US civil society coalitions. In *Cross-border dialogues: US-Mexico social movement networking*, ed. David Brooks and Jonathan Fox. La Jolla: University of California, San Diego, Center for US-Mexican Studies.

———. 2005. Unpacking transnational citizenship. *Annual Review of Political Science* 8: 171-201.

Fox, Jonathan A., and David L. Brown, eds. 1998. *The struggle for accountability: The World Bank, NGOs, and grassroots movements*. Cambridge, MA: MIT Press.

Fukuyama, Francis. 1992. *The end of history and the last man*. New York: Free Press.

Garrett, Geoffrey. 1998. *Partisan politics in the global economy*. Cambridge: Cambridge University Press.

Harvey, Neil. 1996. Impact of reforms to Article 27 on Chiapas: Peasant resistance in the neoliberal sphere. In *Reforming Mexico's agrarian reform*, ed. Laura Randall. Armonk, NY: M.E. Sharpe.

———. 1998. *The Chiapas rebellion: The struggle for land and democracy*. Durham, NC: Duke University Press.

Held, David. 1998. Democracy and globalization. In *Re-imagining political community: Studies in cosmopolitan democracy*, ed. Daniele Archigugi, David Held, and Martin Kohler. Stanford, CA: Stanford University Press.

Huntington, Samuel P. 1993. The clash of civilizations? *Foreign Affairs* 72 (3): 22-49.

Jenson, Jane, and Susan D. Phillips. 1996. Regime shift: New citizenship practices in Canada. *International Journal of Canadian Studies* 14 (Fall).

Keck, Margaret. 1995. Social equity and environmental politics in Brazil: Lessons from the rubber tappers of Acre. *Comparative Politics* 27:409-24.

Keck, Margaret E., and Kathryn Sikkink. 1998a. *Activists beyond borders: Advocacy networks in international politics*. Ithaca, NY: Cornell University Press.

———. 1998b. Transnational advocacy networks in the movement society. In *The social movement society: Contentious politics for a new century*, ed. David S. Meyer and Sidney Tarrow. Lanham, MD: Rowman & Littlefield.

Loker, William F. 1999. Grit in the prosperity machine: Globalization and the rural poor in Latin America. In *Globalization and the rural poor in Latin America*, ed. William F. Loker. Boulder, CO: Lynne Reinner.

Madrid, Raúl. 2005a. Ethnic cleavages and electoral volatility in Latin America. *Comparative Politics* 38 (1): 1-20.

———. 2005b. Indigenous parties and democracy in Latin America. *Latin American Politics and Society* 47 (4): 161-79.

Marshall, T. H. 1963. *Citizenship and social class. Class, citizenship, and social development*. Garden City, NY: Doubleday.

Melucci, Alberto. 1998. Third world or planetary conflicts. In *Cultures of politics, politics of culture: Re-visioning Latin American social movements*, ed. Sonia Alvarez, Evelina Dagnino, and Arturo Escobar. Boulder, CO: Westview.

Moody, Kim. 1997. Towards an international social-movement unionism. *New Left Review*, September-October, pp. 52-72.

Murillo, María Victoria. 2001. *Labor unions, partisan coalitions, and market reforms in Latin America*. Cambridge: Cambridge University Press.

Nagel, Joanne. 1986. The political construction of ethnicity. In *Competitive ethnic relations*, ed. Susan Olzak and Jane Nagel. Orlando, FL: Academic Press.

Radcliffe, Sarah A. 2001. Development, the state, and transnational political connections: State and subject formations in Latin America. *Global Networks* 1:19-36.

Rice, Roberta, and Donna Lee Van Cott. 2006. The emergence and performance of indigenous peoples' parties in South America. A subnational statistical analysis. *Comparative Political Studies* 39 (6): 709-32.

Rodrik, Dani. 1997. *Has globalization gone too far?* Washington, DC: Institute for International Economics.

———. 1998. Why do more open economies have bigger governments? *Journal of Political Economy* 106 (5): 997-1032.

Sassen, Saskia. 1996. *Losing control? Sovereignty in an age of globalization*. New York: Columbia University Press.

Soysal, Yasemin Nuhoglu. 1994. *Limits of citizenship: Migrants and postnational membership in Europe*. Chicago: University of Chicago Press.

Stern, Steve J., ed. 1998. *Shining and other paths*. Durham, DC: Duke University Press.

Tarrow, Sidney. 1996. Social movements and the state: The political structuring of social movements. In *Comparative perspectives on social movements: Political opportunities, mobilizing structures, and cultural framings*, ed. Doug McAdam, John D. McCarthy, Mayer N. Zald, 41-61. Cambridge: Cambridge University Press.

———. 1998. *Power in movement: Social movements, collective action, and politics*. Cambridge: Cambridge University Press.

———. 1999. International institutions and contentious politics: Does internationalization make agents freer—or weaker? Paper presented at 1999 American Sociological Association annual meeting, Chicago.

———. 2005. *The new transnational activism*. Cambridge: Cambridge University Press.

Van Cott, Donna Lee. 2003. Institutional change and ethnic parties in South America. *Latin American Politics and Society* 45 (2): 1-39.

———. 2005. *From movements to parties in Latin America: The evolution of ethnic politics*. Cambridge: Cambridge University Press.

Tilly, Charles. 1978. *From mobilization to revolution*. Reading, MA: Addison-Wesley.

Tilly, Charles. 1984. Social movements and national politics. In *Statemaking and social movements*, ed. Charles Bright and Susan Harding, 297-317. Ann Arbor: University of Michigan Press.

Wade, Robert. 1996. Globalization and its limits: Reports of the death of the national economy are greatly exaggerated. In *National diversity and global capitalism*, ed. Suzanne Berger and Ronald Dore, 60-88. Ithaca, NY: Cornell University Press.

Wapner, Paul. 1995. Politics beyond the state: Environmental activism and world civic politics. *World Politics* 47 (3): 311-40.

Warren, Kay B. 1998. Indigenous movements as a challenge to the unified social movement paradigm for Guatemala. In *Cultures of politics, politics of culture: Re-visioning Latin American social movements*, ed. Sonia E. Alvarez, Evelina Dagnino, and Arturo Escobar. Boulder, CO: Westview.

Weiss, Linda. 1997. Globalization and the myth of the powerless state. *New Left Review* 225 (September-October): 3-27.

————. 1998. *The myth of the powerless state*. Ithaca, NY: Cornell University Press.

Yashar, Deborah J. 1997. The Quetzal is red: Military states, popular movements, and political violence in Guatemala. In *The new politics of inequality in Latin America: Rethinking participation and representation*, ed. Douglas A. Chalmers, Carlos Vilas, Katherine Roberts-Hite, Scott B. Martin, Kerianne Piester, and Monique Segarra, 239-60. Oxford: Oxford University Press.

————. 1998. Contesting citizenship: Indigenous movements and democracy in Latin America. *Comparative Politics* 31 (1): 23-42.

————. 1999. Democracy, indigenous movements, and the postliberal challenge in Latin America. *World Politics* 52 (October): 76-104.

————. 2002. Globalization and collective action. *World Politics* 34 (3): 355-75.

————. 2005. *Contesting citizenship in Latin America: The rise of indigenous movements and the postliberal challenge*. Cambridge: Cambridge University Press.

Yúdice, George. 1998. The globalization of culture and the new civil society. In *Cultures of politics, politics of culture: Re-visioning Latin American social movements*, ed. Sonia E. Alvarez, Evelina Dagnino, and Arturo Escobar. Boulder, CO: Westview.

Rethinking Civil Society in the Age of NAFTA: The Case of Mexico

By
JON SHEFNER

This article offers an analysis and critique of the concept of civil society and its relationship to neoliberalism as an economic and political project. The author argues that the high level of imprecision in the usage of civil society has enabled both opponents and advocates of neoliberal policies to claim it. We forget that civil society must be understood as a stratified body whose members occupy specific class positions and, therefore, contend for control of vital resources. The author's critique is largely based on the ignoring of class among those who study the intersection of neoliberalism and civil society. In the second part of this article, the author offers an illustration by focusing on Mexico's recent history of democratization in tandem with the application of neoliberal policies.

Keywords: NAFTA; civil society; neoliberalism; class; nongovernmental organizations

The concept of civil society has been with us since political theorists recognized that political action and social change emerge from social sectors other than the state. In the past twenty years, that concept has become ubiquitous, especially in discussions of globalization, neoliberalism, and democratization. Why has that notion carried such heavy weight in its application to the most important macroeconomic and macropolitical issues of the current phase of globalization? This article seeks, first, to explain why analysts have so embraced the idea of civil society. Second, I discuss the variety of usages to which it has been put, especially in regard to popular action in Latin America. I will next suggest that the idea's analytic utility has been damaged by its overuse and describe

Jon Shefner is an associate professor of sociology and director of the Interdisciplinary Program in Global Studies at the University of Tennessee. His work examines the relationship of economic deprivation and democratization in Mexico within a comparative study of IMF austerity policies, protest, and regime change. He is the coeditor, with Patricia Fernandez-Kelly, of Out of the Shadows, *a volume that examines the intersection of the informal economy and grassroots political action.*

DOI: 10.1177/0002716206296797

a case that argues for a more careful application of the concept. Finally, I argue that specific analysis of social sectors will prove both more rigorous and revealing for genuinely useful theorizing and empirical application.

Rehabilitation of a Concept

Beginning in the 1980s, accelerating in the 1990s, and with no halt in sight, social scientists and others have increasingly focused on the participation of civil society in social change efforts across the globe. Depending on who the analyst is, civil society has emerged, reemerged, is resurgent, has reconstituted, is weak or strong.[1] The search for civil society has focused on various locations, ranging from the urban landscape, to the vagaries of nongovernmental organizations, to international forums, to U.S. bowling alleys.

Reasons for such enthusiasm and analytical focus are many. First, historical changes have driven the interest in civil society. Organized social groups that are neither part of governments, nor aligned with established political parties, participated in important struggles in countries from Latin America to the ex–Soviet bloc. Many researchers have documented social transformations brought about in large part through social movements, labor, faith-based groups, nongovernmental organizations, and other such organizations.

Second, this trend appeared at a time that governments have been de-legitimized and are becoming less likely to be perceived as actors able to resolve social problems as diverse as poverty and representation. Processes of de-legitimization have had several roots. New social movements emerging in the 1980s confronted prevailing orders, often advocating for cultural change rather than the capturing of state power. The failure of governments to address such challenges led many movement leaders and their chroniclers to denounce the capacity of states and political parties to address social ills.[2]

Third, the collapse of the Soviet bloc caused a crisis among analysts who had advocated state intervention as the biggest hammer in the social policy toolbox. The fall of governments with some resemblance to socialism had collateral costs: the horizon of possible state intervention, especially providing social welfare, narrowed. As White (1996, 179) wrote, the civil society concept became increasingly popularized in response to the crisis of authoritarian states and "became embroiled in a demonology of the state, often serving as an idealized counter-image, an embodiment of social virtue confronting political vice." Oppressive right-wing governments also fell during the 1980s and 1990s. Similar to the fall of the Soviet bloc, these governments were challenged and toppled by coalitions of what increasingly became called civil society. As a result, the lionization of the groups responsible for such feats increased.

Fourth, the failure of revolutionary options similarly brought state-centered solutions into question. The hopes raised by revolutionary governments in Nicaragua and by revolutionary alternatives in El Salvador, Guatemala, and (for some) Peru and Colombia had been dashed by the 1990s. The fortunes of those struggles ranged from wars of attrition, to conversion into political parties, to the crushing of a state. The failure to take over and hold on to state power seemed to further convince many analysts that government bureaucracies cannot pursue progressive political action. Almost by default, that function fell to civil society.

Fifth, perhaps the most significant root of state de-legitimation is the hegemonic influence of neoliberalism. Neoliberal reforms target states' abilities to provide for the social development and social welfare of citizens (Harris and Seid 2000; D. Harvey 2005; Portes and Hoffman 2003). Governments across the globe have cut expenditures on housing, health, transportation, and education, with results ranging from declining wages to increased unemployment to diminished caloric intake.

Assaults on the welfare state also led to popular action in two related areas: (1) organized groups protested changed state policies (Walton and Ragin 1990; Walton and Seddon 1994; Shefner, Pasdirtz, and Blad 2006); and (2) many organizations stepped up to fill the social vacuum left by state inaction, taking on tasks of social development, and resolving other basic survival needs.

The 1980s and 1990s brought about a confluence of new empirical and analytical models that highlighted collective action.[3] As states became the carriers of deprivation, or failed to resolve the needs of a differentiated social base, civil society sectors increased their activities aiming to supply what states could not. Academic and political analysts increasingly focused on such popular actions. Scholars of Latin America appeared especially captivated by civil society analysis, perhaps because these nations were so dramatically subjected to the crimes of repressive governments, failures of progressive contenders, and the early and long lasting damage incurred during the neoliberal turn.

Defining Civil Society

Despite the popularity of the concept, there has been little agreement as to what it means. Civil society has been used to designate social movements of every kind, any respondents to a survey, and a multiplicity of political organizations not directed at or dependent on governments. There has been little effort to standardize the use of the concept despite its level of penetration throughout academia, journalistic circles, social change foundations, and even formal politics. The discussion seems in no danger of abating; a recent Google search revealed 99,100,000 hits related to civil society. Below, I give further attention to the multiple uses of civil society as a concept. I focus, in particular, on the activities of groups assigned that label in response to neoliberalism and its relationship to democratization in Latin America.

The Activities of Civil Society

In the 1970s, neoliberal theory attained great influence when it was touted as providing the cure to the ills of failed industrial policies in the Global North, poverty and debt in the Global South, and expanding state activity and growing inflation in both hemispheres. Surging debt forced Latin American policy makers to submit to the dictates of neoliberals in international financial institutions who characterized state regulation as the source of poverty and inefficiency and of national economies' failure to modernize. As collective action confronted the ravages of neoliberal policy, analysts increasingly focused on the activity of civil society.

According to researchers, civil society plays a variety of roles, some of them contradictory, in response to neoliberalism. That contradictory roles are posited for civil society should not surprise us, given the use of the concept in strongly diverging theoretical frameworks. One consistent agreement, however, is the assumption of a zero-sum space of political action, in which the only counterpart is the state or, more widely envisioned, political organizations. This model implies that if one actor expands its power, the space available for another will contract. The zero-sum game is alluded to in analyses that describe "increased participation" by civil society (Gomá et al. 2003; see also Alvarez, Dagnino, and Escobar 1998). Rucht (1999, 215) also referred to the zero-sum space, describing how "the modern nation-state, with its monopoly of formal power and its tendency to assume more and more responsibilities, was widely perceived as a potential threat to civil society. Strengthening civil society thus became synonymous with reducing the role of the state." Jelin's (1997, 79) comment can be read similarly: in her view, new movements in Latin America (consistently listed as civil society actors) emerged largely due to "the closing of institutionalized channels of participation." As political space closes, civil space opens.

Civil society poses varying responses to neoliberalism, depending on the analyst's political perspective. Many see civil society providing important sources of resistance to neoliberal policies. These actors offer protest and representation, even advocating alternative social interventions in the face of austerity measures. Although some authors suggest that neoliberalism has provided a spur to civil society (Yúdice 1998), others comment on its demobilizing influence. Roxborough (1997), for example, noted that civil society declines as neoliberal reforms deepen. Although the neoliberal project renews some social movements as they take defensive postures, others go through a process of de-articulation. Zermeño (1997) agreed, writing that global integration has meant the "radical dismantling of these collective actors of civil society" in Mexico, including many "institutions and intermediaries that have traditionally inhabited the space between social actors and the state" (p. 124).

Neoliberal policy making and civil society have been linked in inconsistent ways to political democratization. For some, democratization opens markets controlled by authoritarian states. For others, it is civil society's resistance to neoliberalism that makes it such an important actor in the democratization process. Dagnino (1998, 39) offered comments typical among those who view civil society as crucial in transitions to democratization. He maintained that "the strengthening of civil society [is] paramount to the building of democracy." His research showed that political actors perceive civil society and its organizations as "crucial terrains and agents of democratization" (p. 55).

Similarly, others have argued that an autonomous civil society representing multiple constituencies is a requisite for democratic participation (Keane 2003). Blair (1977, 28), for example, maintained that "a strong civil society directly supports democracy by widening participation in several ways" including "educating and mobilizing citizens generally to exercise their right to participate: . . . encouraging previously marginalized groups into the political arena to participate, and building a complex net of groups . . . and by deepening policy accountability to its citizens." Civil society can also "alter the balance of power between state and society in favor of the latter," pushing the state to obey standards of accountability, influencing how states and patrons interact with citizens, and "redefining the rules of the political game along democratic lines" (White 1996, 185-87).

Yet another author, Hedman (1997), echoed de Tocqueville and more recently Putnam (2000) by interpreting a strong associational life as indicative of and crucial to democracy. Hollifield and Jillson (2000) agreed that civil society is important during transitions to democracy because "not only must a society be strong enough to weather the transition without a complete breakdown of political order, it must also be capable of providing alternative sources of rule and leadership" (p. 10).

In contrast, others find these same organizations of citizens facilitating global and national elites to institutionalize state-civil society relations in ways that polyarchic democracy triumphs over popular democracy (Robinson 1996). Civil society organizations may in fact ease the implementation of neoliberal policies by providing safety nets to populations made increasingly vulnerable by the withdrawal of social welfare efforts. Far from being institutional symptoms of democracy, then, civil society may provide cover for states based on economic exclusion.

One reason the concept of civil society has proven so attractive is that its lack of precision allows it to be used by greatly varying theoretical perspectives. On one hand, civil society poses a critique to neoliberalism's project of "thinning" the state. On the other hand, the diminishing of the state is part of civil society's contribution to democratization (Diamond et al. 1999). Lucian Pye (2000, 30), for example, found that democracies require "a substantial body of autonomous, nongovernmental institutions and power centers that are strong enough to stand up to the state and serve as a counterbalance to the authority of the government." Pye's vision is simultaneously pluralist and antistate, as he found civil society supplying a level of representation "so that the people cannot be easily intimidated by government. . . . In the modern world the strength of a country depends not on the power of its government but on the vitality of its civil society" (p. 31). Pye's position is echoed by others who bolster the neoliberal project of diminishing state power and advocate "a pluralistic, autonomously organized civil society to check the power of the state and give expression democratically to popular interests" (Diamond et al. 1999, 54).

On the other hand, critics have noted how the concept has been applied, rather than focused on the concept itself. Alvarez, Dagnino, and Escobar (1998, 17) identified civil society as a "terrain of struggle mined by sometimes undemocratic power relations and the enduring problems of racism, hetero/sexism, environmental destruction, and other forms of exclusion." Levine and Crisp (2000, 372) found that "not all groups labeled as 'civil society' are small in scale and egalitarian in character: traditional actors including political parties, trade unions, and business associations also constitute civil society."

Such a variety of interpretations suggests a multiplicity of relationships between civil society sectors and the state and raises questions about how specific social actors defined as part of civil society interact with other actors or institutions. Yet such critiques offer little sustained analysis on the varying implications of the concept of civil society itself.

One reason the concept of civil society has proven so attractive is that its lack of precision allows it to be used by greatly varying theoretical perspectives.

Robinson (1996) provided a more trenchant critique, relying on a Gramscian perspective that recognizes at least dual possibilities for civil society. He urged us to remember that civil society does not possess an exclusively liberationist character, but can be part of the organizational life that maintains systemic hegemony. In this view, "The hegemony of a ruling class or fraction is exercised in civil society, as distinct from its coercive power deployed through the state. Civil society is the arena of those social relationships which are based on consent—political parties, trade unions, civic associations, the family, and so forth" (p. 23). Far from challenging the inequity of a system of domination, Robinson suggested that civil society may indeed be part of the legitimizing apparatus of that system, as part of Gramsci's "extended state." He also acknowledged the potential for civil society to act as bedrock for the creation of popular democracy, the challenge to hegemonic domination. Elites and popular sectors contend for hegemony in civil society, and seek to use various institutions to further divergent aims.

Robinson's (1996) work notwithstanding, few note that civil society analysis requires understanding the activity of differentiated groups that have disparate political interests, oftentimes in conflict. Because of such varying political interests, different civil society actors will have singular relationships to states.

Civil Society and the Ignoring of Class

The de-emphasizing of class in most studies of civil society is a mistake for many reasons. Different social sectors have varied relationships to neoliberalism:

social assistance groups, for example, facilitate neoliberalism by providing, minimally, for the welfare of vulnerable populations left even more vulnerable after the withdrawal of the state from traditional welfare roles. Some of these civil society groups are held in favor by the state, as their work facilitates state thinning, on one hand, and provides rationale for the commercialization—or marketization— of social welfare on the other. In contrast are some of the human rights or civic nongovernmental organizations (NGOs) that often challenge state prerogatives. In further contrast are still other NGOS, which may first challenge the state to become more formally democratic and later work with the state in their acceptance of neoliberal politics that limit the role of the state. The relationships NGOs have with the state vary by the class location of their members, and with respect to the class position of those for whom they advocate. The level of challenge these organizations pose to the state is also likely to be linked to their class character. If class and state relationship differ so greatly within nongovernmental organizations as just one broad exemplar of civil society, these relationships will vary even more across the wide spectrum of groups to which the concept refers.

The de-emphasizing of class is especially problematic in analyzing how civil society influences, and is influenced by, neoliberalism and democratization processes. Neoliberalism is inherently a class project.[4] Centeno (1997), and Babb (2001) demonstrated how neoliberalism provides ideological and policy cover for class fragments and institutions, which have justified the thinning of the state, especially those programs that previously provided poor and working people with a margin of survival, or allowed the middle class to progress. The result, as Portes and Hoffman (2003) documented, is that neoliberalism has exacerbated class divisions in Latin America.

The economic policies of the class project are furthered, according to Robinson (1996), by a political project of democratization that allows greater participation, but only within a very limited spectrum of political possibilities. Democratization has been a strategic choice made by disparate actors seeking unity in the postcolonial and neoliberal era. Democratization, however, provides a goal that resolves the problems of civil society actors in very different ways. Analytic overemphasis on civil society, especially in democratization struggles, helps us ignore the class roots of neoliberal policy. I illustrate this argument in the following case study.

From Quiescence to Action

Mexico's twentieth-century political history reveals patterns of quiescence and action among popular sectors that have become analyzed as civil society. This section reviews how state power was established and maintained, then how the ruling party was destabilized, and finally how it suffered electoral defeat. Throughout this history, different social sectors enjoyed varying levels of state favor until the neoliberal policies of the ruling party undercut its ability to maintain loyalty.

The Partido Revolucionario Institucional (Institutionalized Revolutionary Party, or PRI) emerged out of Mexico's revolutionary chaos to rule Mexico for the next seven decades. Beginning in 1929, the PRI's combination of formal corporatism and informal clientelism channeled demand-making into sanctioned venues, limited alternative organizing, and reinforced state power by incorporating dissident groups and leaders. Originally focused on social sectors important to a largely agrarian society with a violent legacy, the PRI created a corporatist structure to incorporate peasants, labor, and the military (Hamilton 1982). Over time, and with increasing urbanization, the importance of the military dropped, while that of urban groups increased. In response, the PRI created an organization that united disparate groups ranging from urban middle-class professionals to squatter communities (Davis 1994). By channeling participation into mass organizations, the party created structures to address popular needs and maintain legitimacy.

During the postwar period, the PRI pursued economic modernization by implementing import substitution industrialization policies (Dussel Peters 2000). Like many nations, Mexico coupled protectionist trade policies with active investment in selected infrastructure. Politically, import substitution industrialization (ISI) reinforced corporatism and clientelism by producing significant economic growth and rewarding Mexico's working and middle classes, generating both the skills to manufacture new goods and the economic wherewithal to consume them.[5] Although the fruits of this growth were not shared equally, the Mexican working and middle classes prospered in large part because of the political decisions made to maintain loyalty to the state. For example, labor legislation increased the share of income devoted to the middle earning 55 percent of the population (Dussel Peters 2000). Additionally, the middle and working classes saw substantial openings in the labor market due to the expansion of private industry and the growth of the Mexican state.

The state also augmented material quality of life and eased the pressures of urbanization with substantial subsidies of food, fuel, transportation, and urban development. The middle class enjoyed ample wages, urban amenities, credit opportunities, and the availability of low-wage domestic services. PRI social policy simultaneously improved nutrition, housing, and public services for the poor and working class. As a result, education levels, standard of living, and life expectancy rose. During the late 1970s, 50 percent of the industries paid sufficiently high wages that their employees' households could subsist on one wage (Levy and Bruhn 2001; Escobar Latapí and Roberts 1991).

Despite governmental corruption, the expanding economy allied urban groups to the PRI in election after election. Although the PRI ruled in an antidemocratic fashion, Mexico's economic growth allowed the ruling party sufficient patronage spoils to integrate large portions of Mexican society. Economic slowdowns in the 1970s, however, provided material spurs to the political demands of an incipient democratization movement. The debt crisis diminished the government's ability to respond to cries for democracy with expanding social welfare spending and minimal openings to alternative parties.

The Democratization Movement

As Mexico's economy worsened, PRI legitimacy waned. Earlier, even when opposition political parties or social movements protested electoral fraud or repression, the PRI maintained a crucial level of popular support. This support was gained through inclusive social policy and cooptation, as well as through protectionist economic policies that helped both governmental and private industry employees. All of these strategies required resources available in an expanding economy, distributed by a state based, at least in part, on resolving social needs.[6]

As the economy contracted, and more state resources were devoted to debt service, economic inclusion through favorable labor policy and neighborhood patronage became untenable. The imperatives of neoliberal globalization prioritized debt payment, privatization, and dismantling protectionist industrial policy. The results of such policies impoverished much of the PRI's social base. For example, wages declined precipitously for Mexican workers, with annual decreases ranging between 7.7 to 12.3 percent in an almost uninterrupted decline that lasted from 1982 through 1997. The number of households falling below the official poverty line increased, following both the drop in wages and increases in unemployment. Finally, income inequality worsened even during temporary periods of economic growth (Portes and Hoffman 2003; Friedmann, Lustig, and Legovini 1995; Lustig 1998; Gonzàlez de la Rocha 2001; Boltvinik 2003; Alarcón 2003).

Neoliberal policies left Mexicans with lower wages, limited access to social welfare benefits, lower physical quality of life, fewer jobs, and increasing levels of inequality. These policies also made it impossible for the state to maintain power using decades-old strategies of incorporation. Thus, important foundations of the PRI regime failed. Nascent and long-standing political parties joined with other forms of citizen opposition to build a movement aimed at creating democracy.

The democratization movement eventually grew to include, among others, independent unions (Cook 1990; Foweraker 1993; LaBotz 1988; Stevens 1974), indigenous movements (Collier 1999; N. Harvey 1994, 1998), community organizations (Alonso 1986; Ramìrez Sáiz 1986; Tavera 1999; Safa Barraza 2001), farmers and middle-class debtors (Williams 2001), and NGOs (Fox 1992; Aguayo Quezada 1998; Aguayo Quezada and Parra Rosales 1997; Ramìrez Sáiz 2006; Olvera 2001). These organizations worked to change the politics and economy of Mexico with the aim of increasing citizen participation. They worked singly and in coalitions, inside conventional political channels and outside them (Cornelius, Eisenstadt, and Hindley 1999; Rodriguez and Ward 1992, 1994; Ward and Rodriguez 1999).

The urban poor and working class largely pushed their agenda through neighborhood groups. The PRI had long exchanged a panoply of social goods, such as jobs, housing, electricity, potable water, and sewers, for political support, establishing patronal relationships with their neighborhood clients. As the economic crisis unraveled, the Mexican political system's capability to resolve the needs of poor people and the way these people articulated their demands changed. Democratic rhetoric newly framed the demands for urban services; clientelism was no longer a pragmatic exchange to solve urban problems, but an affront to their citizenship.[7] Building on new conceptions of citizenship rights, urban political organizations extended their demands to human rights and fair elections. The new democratic rhetoric often emerged as a result of contact with other organizations (Shefner 2006).

The mobilization of the urban poor attempted to disrupt or pressure institutions of power. Demonstrations and rallies commonly targeted state- and municipal-level offices and agencies charged with addressing urban needs. In addition to pressuring government officials through mass mobilizations, neighborhood groups ran candidates for local office. Urban organizations also expressed solidarity and support for other movements, including those advocating for indigenous rights, independent unions, debtors, peasants, and the Zapatista rebels. Increasingly, the efforts of organizations representing the poor and the working class brought them into contact and coalesced effort with the middle class.

The urban middle class was largely organized by nongovernmental organizations focused on democratization and human rights. Their efforts relied more on legislative and electoral pressure than on mass mobilization, with the notable exceptions of public sector unions and the debtor's movement (Foweraker 1993; Williams 2001). Middle-class organizations frequently worked in the electoral arena, campaigning or running candidates for office. Nonpartisan strategies in the electoral arena included organizing electoral observation campaigns and legislative initiatives.

The early efforts of NGOs in the democratization movement, according to one observer and activist, were devoted to "organizing and training marginal or vulnerable sectors of the population" (Aguayo Quezada 1998, 169). Broad-based fronts and coalitions among the middle class and the urban poor and working class formed in the early 1980s to protest against austerity policies and advocate for better urban services (Moctezuma 1984; Carr 1986). The creation of these alliances were "important in shaping broad political fronts which joined parties and social organizations in attempts to collaborate around shared interests transcending sectoral demands" (Tamayo 1990, 126). Neighborhood, community, and peasant organizations recognized that their battles extended beyond their locale and joined with other groups to push the common agenda of democratization.

Protest against electoral fraud joined middle-class and poor actors in response to state elections in Nuevo Leon and Chihuahua in 1985 and in San Luis de Potosi in 1991. Mobilization strategies included disruptive confrontations such as barricades and demonstrations, with hunger strikes immediately following the events. The strategic focus turned further toward electoral activities after 1988.

In the 1988 Mexican presidential election, the PRI candidate was nearly defeated by Cuauhtémoc Cárdenas representing an opposition front combining several political parties and social movement organizations. Cárdenas lost the election to the PRI candidate, Carlos Salinas de Gortari, only after the computerized vote count mysteriously shut down while the opposition candidate was winning. The widely accepted belief that Cárdenas had been defrauded led many activists to recognize that without greater focus on electoral justice, little change would be possible in Mexico.

The formation of the Partido de la Revolución Democrática, (Democratic Revolutionary Party, or PRD) provided a venue with which to institutionalize many activists' efforts, and gains were made in elections at local and state levels. Subsequently, the democratization movement increasingly focused on electoral activism (Ramìrez Sáiz 2006; Aguayo Quezada and Parra Rosales 1997, Aguayo Quezada 1998). The PRD's local strategy built on its social movement links by opening its registration to entice social movement activists to run for election. This inclusion of movement activists had the dual impact of diminishing local social movement struggles and increasing the priority of party work and commitment. The electoral strategies of the democratization movement intensified further as activists initiated popular education campaigns and organized voter turnout and voting observation campaigns.

Middle-class NGOs continued to seek issues and venues on which they could work with the organized poor. One of these was the Alianza Cívica, an organization of NGOs focused explicitly on policing Mexico's elections. The Alianza organized eighteen thousand Mexicans, many from independent neighborhood associations. During the 1994 presidential elections, citizens representing the Alianza Cívica monitored voting and pursued violations at more than ten thousand polling places (Aguayo Quezada and Parra Rosales 1997; Olvera 2001).

Another issue of convergence for the democratization movement emerged in 1994: the Zapatista's challenge to the Mexican political hierarchy. Zapatista rhetoric linking Mexico's poverty to its lack of democracy and indigenous representation resonated with democratization movement activists. But the movement's ability to support and protect the Zapatistas through mass mobilization was more significant than the rebellion itself. Within three months of the short-lived rebellion, "400 Mexican NGOs in 11 networks and 100 international NGOs conducted diverse missions in Chiapas" (Chand 2001, 226). Although many found the Zapatistas irresistibly romantic, the Ejercito Zapatista de Liberacion Nacional's (EZLN's) political influence was limited. Much more important than the presence of the Zapatistas and the poetry of their most prominent leader, Comandante Marcos, was how the indigenous movement provided an issue around which the democratization movement consolidated.

Over time, party building overwhelmed mass mobilization and disruption. Despite its strong showing in 1988, the PRD proved vulnerable. In contrast, the party positioned to the right of the PRI, the PAN (Partido Acción Nacional, or National Action Party), became an increasingly viable competitor for power. The party's structure had been institutionalized for decades, and it won increasing numbers of seats in local and state offices.

In large part, the PAN's victories were due to the democratization movement. In response to charges of fraud and unfair elections, President Salinas de Gortari replaced governors from many states during his six-year regime. When new officials were affiliated with non-PRI parties, however, they came most frequently from the conservative opposition, the PAN. The PRD also suffered more direct repression, reporting the loss of more than 250 militants to repression during the Salinas presidency. Simultaneously, the PRD's capacity as a political contender was further damaged by intraparty squabbles after local and state elections during the 1990s fragmented the party along pre-existing fault lines (Bruhn 1997).

With their longer history and recent electoral wins, the PAN was poised to win federal elections. The PAN's long-standing opposition contrasted with the PRD's recent history and internal divisions. The new party was also subjected to propaganda warning of the instability of a leftist government. The result was the *voto útil* (useful vote), a decision made by many voters in 2000 that the primary goal was to rid the nation of the PRI.

The Mexican democratization movement's goal of political change was a structural result of the movement's composition. With the debt crisis, neoliberal policy constrained the state from distributing patronage as effectively. Quality of life deteriorated for the middle class, while survival of the poor and working class became increasingly tenuous. One result was that these actors formed coalitions that demonstrated significant power against the government. As the state became the instrument of hardships, it became the target of the democratization movement. In 2000, PAN candidate Vicente Fox won the presidency, and the Mexican legislature was split by the three most powerful parties.

Civil Society or Class Society?

After an extended struggle, a movement based on coalesced yet disparate social sectors won victory demonstrated by the transition in electoral politics. Yet the democratization struggle provides another way in which class issues are incorrectly ignored by the discourse of civil society (Cohen and Arato 1992). The democratization movement was made up of separate groups with different class locations and interests, which at times converged, yet often contradicted. By lumping all within civil society, specific interests and orientations, many best understood with class analysis, are obscured.

Examining the Mexican democratization struggle is useful for documenting a coalesced effort at political change that could not have reached its level of success without that character of coalition. No single sector in Mexico could have achieved democratization; it had to be a product of struggle by multiple groups. Yet as much as reading this effort as a civil society struggle reveals, it obscures more.

First, the impetus for the democratization movement was as much economic as political. Politically, the Mexican system was deeply corrupt, using fraudulent elections, selective repression, and clientelist vote buying with great facility. Additionally, the government was extremely effective in keeping challengers at bay through strategies that weakened the opposition by creating small parties that favored the PRI, or buying off individual leaders. But it was two decades of neoliberal policy that coalesced the opposition, given the widespread damage imposed on Mexico's citizens. The middle class could not find credit for their business as interest rates on their loans skyrocketed. Even worse, opening the market to international competition meant that many small businesses were forced out of the market. With diminishing patronage rewards in neighborhoods, or wage declines even among previously privileged occupations and industries, the living conditions of the poor and working class became even more unsustainable. Finally, whether through NAFTA or other agreements, years of neoliberal policy endangered peasants as privilege was increasingly accorded to agribusiness.

Second, the democratization movement was made up of different groups that were consistent in their disgust with the PRI, but with different class-based grievances stemming from the specific damages that neoliberal policies inflicted on them. Peasants suffered declining prices for some commodities, while prices increased for the urban poor. Security of landholding diminished for the peasants, especially after President Salinas's *ejido* legislation allowed formally communal land to be sold (Austin 1994). The low prices suffered by the peasants could only be resolved by raising prices for the urban working class. Similarly, the diminishing of land availability forced peasants to migrate to the cities, where they added to both the scarcity of jobs and pressured urban services in peripheral communities. Similarly, middle-class business suffered from diminished credit, for which they competed with the peasants. One way for the middle class to regain an advantage for their businesses would be to reduce wages, further straining the working poor. Thus, although different sectors coalesced on issues of political governance, the way to ameliorate the effects of the neoliberal policies individual groups suffered most may have conflicted with the class standing of their political allies.

Class stratification brought with it hierarchical control over strategy. Class privilege, accompanied by higher status, helped mold strategy in ways that reinforced hierarchical standing.[8] For example, Alianza Cívica has been celebrated as a broad and inclusive coalition. The mass of observers were drawn from local community organizations. The organization would not have been nearly as successful without these community activists, as they possessed the local knowledge required to spot those illegitimately pressuring voters. Yet the activists devising the strategy and pursuing legal recourses possessed significantly more education and were of much higher class standing than the average poll watcher.

Finally, the strategy of democratization will not resolve economic grievances as fully as political grievances. Democratization need not resolve class hierarchy. If the political alternatives that are chosen neither articulate nor pursue alternatives to systems that exacerbate class inequality, there is little reason to expect those levels of inequality to decrease. Democratization is about distribution of political power, but if political power mirrors economic power to a large extent, little genuine change may occur. Democratization of formal political institutions may do little to eradicate class inequalities or challenge class rule.

Thus, focusing on the civil society experience can obscure important elements of who are mobilized by certain movements, and why. As Cohen and Arato (1992, 2) noted, "The current 'discourse of civil society' . . . focuses precisely on new generally non-class-based forms of collective action oriented and linked to the legal, associational, and public institutions of society." The willful ignoring of class is the problem with much civil society analysis, especially that which critiques neoliberalism. Neoliberal policy was created by those championing class interests within the developmental project and has very different effects on constituencies who must be defined by class.

Democratization of formal political institutions may do little to eradicate class inequalities or challenge class rule.

Certainly those whose mobilization cannot be directly linked to class locations and neoliberalism are important to recognize and understand in their own terms. The critique launched at orthodox Marxists for ignoring or diminishing the importance of struggles to ameliorate injustices based on ethnic or gender inequalities helped researchers recognize a plethora of social ills and multiple kinds of political efforts. Yet many struggles that are not articulated in class terms, such as those of indigenous peoples, still have class implications. For example, it was not only the disruption of indigenous traditions of landholding and farming in Chiapas that were the roots of the Zapatista rebellion. It was the expansion of corporate farming interests that disrupted these ways of life. These powerful sectors come bearing class-defined interests and act in ways that further those interests. Neoliberalism allowed these sectors to further marshal state power to pursue their interests. Thus, even if mobilized groups do not articulate their opposition in class terms, the struggle to impose and resist neoliberalism must be understood with class in mind.

Conclusion: The Strata of Civil Society

Civil society analysis, I argue, obscures many of the political dynamics and relationships we are most interested to uncover. In this conclusion, I summarize the shortcomings of this conceptual tool.

First, many researchers forget that civil society must be understood as equally stratified as other ways of conceptualizing society. The concept entices us to examine the unity of society, especially in opposition to oppressive economic models such as neoliberalism, or political evils such as authoritarianism. The false unity allows us to ignore how civil society is riven by strata defined by differences in class, status, ethnicity, and gender among many others. Recognizing this conceptual error has important implications for our better understanding of differentiation of interests, opportunities, and capacities of different groups within a mobilized citizenry. My critique is largely based on the ignoring of class among those who study the intersection of neoliberalism and civil society. I do not seek to deny the multitude of varying social categories, all of which are identified with structured hierarchies and inequality. Nor do I want to return to defining class as the unvaryingly primary division, one supplying some kind of master status above and beyond various other categories.

Many researchers forget that civil society must be understood as equally stratified as other ways of conceptualizing society.

Instead, I want to emphasize that if we are looking at organized efforts to resist, change, or even overturn hierarchies, we must examine the social bases of those hierarchies. The social basis of the neoliberal project is class. Because neoliberalism is a class project, that project has to be assessed in class terms: how people act from their class positions to impose or resist class pressures. Which particular hierarchy penetrates a specific society at a specific time is a case of historical contingency, to be examined within various cases. Indeed, hierarchical systems intersect in ways that make it difficult to assess the impacts of one over another. But to examine how domination works, we have to identify the social base of individual systems, then assess impacts on disadvantaged groups and their efforts and strategies of responding to the form of domination in their own terms.

Said in a different way, the new social movement researchers were correct: earlier discourses of class analysis indeed failed to capture the actions, motivations, and goals of many different forms of collective action. We have to acknowledge a whole series of oppressive social structures to understand the emergence of multiple types of movements. These movements are defined in large part by identities, whether these are imposed by social structure or embraced by movement participants. These identities are also a result of communities emerging from social hierarchy and oppression. If we are to understand the roots and emergence of different contentious communities, we have to recognize a whole series of oppressions—race, gender, ethnicity, and so on—that characterize current and historical social arrangements. Understanding the multitude of oppressions and contention, however, may be obscured when we expect too much from the civil society concept.

Second, recognizing the strata of civil society may help us understand the dynamics and outcome of strategic efforts at unified struggle. The way civil society works together on shared strategies may build bridges or create fissures, depending on relations among members, ability to recognize hierarchy between groups, and the subsequent possibility of differential outcomes from shared strategy.

Third, recognizing the strata of civil society suggests that we carefully examine coalition strategies. Organizing temporary coalitions around shared goals can make enormous sense when groups are mobilizing to create an opposition and launch an alternative. Yet recognizing the strata of civil society forces us to understand that the successful accomplishment of a coalesced strategy will still yield differential impacts on the members of civil society.

Two deceptively simple questions must be asked when examining coalitions of disparate groups. What is politics for? And how does the answer to this question differ for different groups? The fact that protesting groups coalesce in answer to shared injuries stemming from globalization does not make their group differences shrink. Instead, groups suffer injuries from globalization differently because of their own peculiarities, whether they are defined by class, other divisions, or the intersections of class and other hierarchically based cleavages. Although groups make strategic choices to coalesce around shared injuries stemming from globalization, the specifics of those injuries, the differences of resources upon which they may draw, their varied levels of social power, all continue to make their experiences of globalization and unifying against globalization distinctive. The question must remain open: do the benefits of common action address the needs of certain coalesced groups more than others? Similarly, how do internal hierarchies influence the aims of coalitions?

These questions and their answers suggest that the differentiation within civil society is sufficiently great that it is equally important to look at the strata as at the whole when we think theoretically and empirically about popular action, and pragmatically when we work with those groups.

After twenty-five years of obsession with a holistic analysis of civil society, what changes can we make to strengthen our research? One change is to mediate large scale conceptualizing with specificity. Clearly, we must look at the complex intersections of structured inequalities. The hardships imposed by structural positions, and the subsequent ways that resistance is generated and alternatives are articulated depend on aggrieved social groups' resources, culture, power, allies, and so on. The more we understand these differences, the better placed we are to understand such struggles. But to trace, understand, and aid particular groups, we have to understand their actions and potential in terms specific to them and the systems against which they struggle. In both theoretical and empirical terms, the more we continue to use the undifferentiated concept of civil society, the more we commit the same kind of one-size-fits-all analytic error for which we criticize neoliberal policy makers.

Notes

1. Cohen and Arato (1992, 29) noted also that civil society is spoken of as enjoying "resurrection . . . rebirth, reconstruction, or renaissance."

2. Slater (1985) and Alvarez, Dagnino, and Escobar (1992) are two of the best-known applications of new social movement theory to Latin America.

3. The Centre for Civil Society at the London School of Economics suggests that the popularity of the concept has more to do with the academic recognition that the "third sector" must be analyzed in conjunction with traditional examinations of state and market to understand its impact on governance, economics, and culture (see http://www.lse.ac.uk/collections/CCS/what_is_civil_society.htm).

4. See D. Harvey (2005, chap. 2) for a good description of the concerted effort by the capitalist class to build a neoliberal consensus.

5. Annual increases in gross domestic product ranged from 5.1 to 7.6 percent from 1950 to 1969 (Lustig 1998).

6. I do not mean to romanticize the Partido Revolucionario Institucional (Institutionalized Revolutionary Party, or PRI) state but to demonstrate genuine differences in economic policy from the 1950s to early 1970s and the 1980s and 1990s, and how these economic policies had political ramifications.

7. For more on neighborhood efforts toward democratization, see Shefner (1999, 2000, 2001); Ramìrez Sáiz (1986, 2006).

8. For more on how different groups worked together, see Shefner (1999, 2006).

References

Aguayo Quezada, Sergio. 1998. Electoral observation and democracy in Mexico. In *Electoral observation and democratic transitions in Latin America*, ed. Kevin Middlebrook. San Diego: Center for U.S.-Mexico Studies, University of California, San Diego.

Aguayo Quezada, Sergio, and Luz Paula Parra Rosales. 1997. *Las Organizaciones No Gubermentales de Derechos Humanos en Mexico: entre la democracia participativa y la electoral*. México, D.F.: Academia Mexicana de Derechos Humanos.

Alarcón, Diana. 2003. Income distribution and poverty alleviation in Mexico A comparative analysis. In *Confronting development: Assessing Mexico's economic and social policy challenges*, ed. Kevin Middlebrook and Eduardo Zepeda. Stanford, CA: Stanford University Press.

Alonso, J., ed. 1986. *Los movimientos sociales en el valle de Mexico*. Mexico, D.F.: CIESAS.

Alvarez, Sonia E., Evelina Dagnino, and Arturo Escobar, eds. 1998. *Culture of politics, politics of cultures: Re-visioning Latin American social movements*. Boulder, CO: Westview.

Austin. 1994. The Austin Memorandum on the Reform of Article 27 and its impact upon the urbanization of the Ejido in Mexico. *Bulletin of Latin American Research* 13 (3): 327-35.

Babb, Sarah. 2001. *Managing Mexico: Economists from nationalism to neo-liberalism*. Princeton, NJ: Princeton University Press.

Blair, Harry. 1997. Spreading power to the periphery: A USAID assessment of democratic local government. Washington, DC: USAID.

Boltvinik, Julio. 2003. Welfare, inequality, and poverty in Mexico, 1979-2000. In *Confronting development: Assessing Mexico's economic and social policy challenges*, ed. Kevin Middlebrook and Eduardo Zepeda. Stanford, CA: Stanford University Press.

Bruhn, Kathleen. 1997. *Taking on Goliath*. University Park: Pennsylvania State University Press.

Carr, Barry. 1986. The Mexican left, the popular movements, and the politics of austerity, 1982-1985. In *The Mexican left, the popular movements, and the politics of austerity*, ed. B. Carr and R. A. Montoya. Monograph Series, 18. San Diego: Center for U.S.-Mexican Studies, University of California, San Diego.

Centeno, Miguel Angel. 1997. *Democracy within reason: Technocratic revolution in Mexico*. 2nd ed. University Park: Pennsylvania State University Press.

Chand, Vikram. 2001. *Mexico's political awakening*. South Bend, IN: Notre Dame University Press.

Cohen, Jean, and Andrew Arato. 1992. *Civil society and political theory*. Cambridge, MA: MIT Press.

Collier, George. 1999. *Basta! Land and the Zapatista rebellion in Chiapas*. Oakland, CA: Food First Books.

Cook, Maria Lorena. 1990. Organizing opposition in the teachers movement in Oaxaca. In *Popular movements and political change in Mexico*, ed. Joe Foweraker and Ann Craig. Boulder, CO: Lynne Rienner.

Cornelius, W. A., T. Eisenstadt, and Jane Hindley. 1999. *Subnational politics and democratization in Mexico*. San Diego: Center for U.S.-Mexican Studies, University of California, San Diego.

Dagnino, Evelina. 1998. Culture, citizenship, and democracy: Changing discourses and practices of the Latin American left. In *Cultures of politics, politics of cultures: Re-visioning Latin American social movements*, ed. Sonia E. Alvarez, Evelina Dagnino, and Arturo Escobar. Boulder, CO: Westview.

Davis, Diane. 1994. *Urban leviathan: Mexico City in the twentieth century*. Philadelphia: Temple University Press.

Diamond, Larry, Jonathan Hartlyn, Juan Linz, and Seymour Martin Lipset, eds. 1999. *Democracy in developing countries: Latin America*. 2nd ed. Boulder, CO: Lynne Rienner.

Dussel Peters, Enrique. 2000. *Polarizing Mexico: The impact of liberalization strategy*. Boulder, CO: Lynne Rienner.

Escobar Latapí, Agustín, and Bryan R. Roberts. 1991. Urban stratification, the middle classes, and economic change in Mexico. In *Social responses to Mexico's economic crisis of the 1980s*, ed. Mercedes González de la Rocha and Agustín Escobar Latapí. San Diego: Center for U.S.-Mexican Studies, University of California, San Diego.

Foweraker, Joe. 1993. *Popular mobilization in Mexico: The Teachers' Movement, 1977-87*. Cambridge: Cambridge University Press.

Fox, Jonathan. 1992. The politics of food in Mexico: State power and social mobilization. Ithaca, NY: Cornell University Press.

Friedmann, Santiago, Nora Lustig, and Arianna Legovini. 1995. Mexico: Social spending and food subsidies during adjustment in the 1980s. In *Coping with austerity*, ed. Nora Lustig. Washington, DC: Brookings Institution.

Gomá, R. G., R. González, S. Martí, L. Peláez, M. Truñó, P. Ibarra, M. J. Monteserín, and A. Blas. 2003. Participation, public policies, and democracy. In *Social Movements and Democracy*, ed. Pedro Ibarra. New York: Palgrave.

Gonzàlez de la Rocha, M. 2001. From the resources of poverty to the poverty of resources? The erosion of a survival model. *Latin American Perspectives* 28 (4): 72-100.

Hamilton, Nora. 1982. *The limits of state autonomy: Post-revolutionary Mexico*. Princeton, NJ: Princeton University Press.

Harris, Richard L., and Melinda J. Seid. 2000. Critical perspectives on globalization and neo-liberalism in the developing countries. *Journal of Developing Societies* 16 (1): 1-26.

Harvey, David. 2005. *A brief history of neo-liberalism*. New York: Oxford University Press.

Harvey, Neil. 1994. *Rebellion in Chiapas*. San Diego: University of California Press.

———. 1998. The Chiapas rebellion: The struggle for land and democracy. Durham, NC: Duke University Press.

Hedman, E.-L. E. 1997. Constructing civil society: Election watch movements in the Philippines. In *Social movements in development: The challenge of globalization and democratization*, ed. Staffan Lindberg and Árni Sverrisson. New York: St. Martin's.

Hollifield, J. F., and C. Jillson, eds. 2000. *Pathways to democracy: The political economy of democratic transitions*. New York: Routledge.

Jelin, Elizabeth. 1997. Emergent citizenship or exclusion? Social movements and non-governmental organizations in the 1990s. In *Politics, social change, and economic restructuring in Latin America*, ed. William C. Smith and Roberto P. Korzeniewicz. Boulder, CO: North-South Center Press and Lynne Rienner.

Keane, John. 2003. *Global civil society?* Cambridge: Cambridge University Press.

La Botz, Dan. 1988. *The crisis of Mexican labor*. New York: Praeger.

Levine, Daniel H., and Brian F. Crisp. 1999. Venezuela: The character, crisis and possible future of democracy. In *Democracy in developing countries: Latin America*, 2nd ed., ed. Larry Diamond, Juan J. Linz, Seymour Martin Lipset, and Jonathan Hartlyn. Boulder, CO: Lynne Rienner.

Levy, Daniel, and Kathleen Bruhn. 2001. *Mexico: The struggle for democratic development*. Berkeley: University of California Press.

Lustig, Nora. 1998. *Mexico: The remaking of an economy*. 2nd ed. Washington, DC: Brookings Institution.

Moctezuma, Pedro. 1984. El movimiento urbano popular mexicano. *Nueva Antropologia* 6 (24): 61-87.

Olvera, Alberto. 2001. Movimientos Sociales Prodemocráticos, Democratización y Esfera Pública en Méxivo: el caso de Alianza Cívica. Xalapa, Veracruz, Mexico: Instituto de Investigaciones Históricao-Sociales.

Portes, Alejandro, and Kelly Hoffman. 2003. Latin American class structures: Their composition and change during the neo-liberal era. *Latin American Research Review* 38 (1): 41-82.

Putnam, Robert D. 2000. Bowling alone: The collapse and revival of American community. New York: Simon & Schuster.

Pye, Lucian. 2000. Democracy and its enemies. In *Pathways to democracy: The political economy of democratic transitions*, ed. James F. Hollifield and Calvin Jillson. New York: Routledge.

Ramìrez Sáiz, Juan Manuel. 1986. *El Movimiento Urban Popular en Mexico*. Mexico, D.F.: Siglo XXI.

———. 2006. Informal politics in the Mexican democratic transition: The case of the People's Urban Movement. In *Out of the shadows: Political action and the informal economy in Latin America*, ed. Patricia Fernández-Kelly and Jon Shefner. University Park: Pennsylvania State University Press.

Robinson, William. 1996. *Promoting polyarchy: Globalization, US intervention, and hegemony*. Cambridge: Cambridge University Press.

Rodriguez, Victoria, and Peter Ward. 1992. *Policymaking, politics, and urban governance in Chihuahua*. San Diego: Center for U.S.-Mexico Studies, University of California, San Diego.

———. 1994. *Political change in Baja California*. San Diego: Center for U.S.-Mexico Studies, University of California, San Diego.

Roxborough, Ian. 1997. Citizenship and social movements under neo-liberalism. In *Politics, social change and economic restructuring in Latin America*, ed. William C. Smith and Roberto Patricio Korzeniewicz. Miami, FL: North-South Center Press.

Rucht, Dieter. 1999. The transnationalization of social movements: Trends, causes, problems. In *Social movements in a globalizing world*, ed. Donatella della Porta, Hanspieter Kriesi, and Dieter Rucht. London: St. MacMillan Press.

Safa Barraza, Patricia. 2001. *Vecinos y Vecindarios en la ciudad de Mexico*. Mexico City: CIESAS.

Shefner, Jon. 1999. Sponsors and the urban poor: Resources or restrictions? *Social Problems* 46 (3): 376-97.

———. 2000. Austerity and neighborhood politics in Guadalajara, Mexico. *Sociological Inquiry* 70 (3): 338-59.

———. 2001. Coalitions and clientelism in Mexico. *Theory & Society* 30:593-628.

———. 2006. Do you think democracy is a magical thing? From basic needs to democratization in informal politics. In *Out of the shadows*, ed. Patricia Fernandez-Kelly and Jon Shefner. University Park: Pennsylvania State University Press.

Shefner, Jon, George Pasdirtz, and Cory Blad. 2006. Austerity protests and social immiseration: Evidence from Mexico and Argentina. In *Latin American social movements*, ed. Hank Johnston and Paul Almeida. Lanham, MD: Rowman & Littlefield.

Slater, David. 1985. *New social movements and the state in Latin America*. Amsterdam: CEDLA.

Stevens, Evelyn. 1974. *Protest and response in Mexico*. Cambridge, MA: MIT Press.

Tamayo, Jaime. 1990. Neo-liberalism encounters neocardenismo. In *Popular movements and political change in Mexico*, ed. J. Foweraker and Ann L. Craig. Boulder, CO: Lynne Rienner.

Tavera. L. 1999. *Social movements and civil society: The Mexico City 1985 Earthquake Victims Movement*. Doctoral diss., Department of Sociology, Yale University, New Haven, CT.

Walton, John, and Charles Ragin. 1990. Global and national sources of political protest: Third world responses to the debt crisis. *American Sociological Review* 55 (6): 876-90.

Walton, John, and David Seddon. 1994. *Free markets and food riots*. Oxford, UK: Blackwell.

Ward, Peter, and Victoria Rodriguez. 1999. *New federalism and state government in Mexico*. San Diego: Center for U.S.-Mexico Studies, University of California, San Diego.

White, Gordon. 1996. Civil society, democratization and development. In *Democratization in the south: The jagged wave*. Manchester, UK: Manchester University Press.

Williams, Heather. 2001. Social movements and economic transition: Markets and distributive conflict in Mexico. Cambridge: Cambridge University Press.

Yúdice, George. 1998. The globalization of culture and the new civil society. In *Cultures of politics, politics of cultures: Re-visioning Latin American social movements*, ed. Sonia E. Alvarez, Evelina Dagnino, and Arturo Escobar. Boulder, CO: Westview.

Zermeño, Sergio. 1997. State, society and dependent neoliberalism in Mexico: The case of the Chiapas uprising. In *Politics, social change and economic restructuring in Latin America*, ed. William C. Smith and Roberto Patrocinio Korzeniewicz. Miami, FL: North-South Centre Press.

SECTION THREE

Regionalization and the Foray on Primary Goods

This article analyzes the benefits and costs of financial globalization. While most attention has been placed on the opportunity to obtain additional capital, the benefits from incorporating international norms are also highlighted. The article examines the trends in capital flows, both from public sector institutions and private investors, placing special emphasis on foreign direct investment and remittances. Major problems identified are the skewed distribution of foreign investment—not only among regions and countries, but also among types of firms—as well as its volatility. The article concludes with a set of policy recommendations to spread the benefits of foreign capital and to make it more productive.

Keywords: globalization; financial flows; foreign direct investment (FDI); remittances; capital volatility

The Globalization of Capital Flows: Who Benefits?

By
BARBARA STALLINGS

T he past several decades of global change have brought multiple issues into high profile, including sharper economic and geographic polarization, heightened levels of inequality within developed and developing nations, and new patterns of regionalization.[1] An important cause of the growing international and intranational differentiation is the role of capital flows. Globalization and liberalization have led to greater mobility of capital, but not all regions, countries, or firms have been recipients in equal measure. Also, while capital flows can provide significant benefits, they also pose many challenges.

Barbara Stallings is William R. Rhodes Research Professor and director of the Watson Institute for International Studies at Brown University. She is also editor of Studies in Comparative International Development. *Previously she was a professor of political economy at the University of Wisconsin–Madison and director of the Economic Development Division of the United Nations Economic Commission for Latin America and the Caribbean in Santiago, Chile. She works on issues of development strategy and finance in Latin America and East Asia. Her most recent book is* Finance for Development: Latin America in Comparative Perspective *(Brookings Institution Press, 2006).*

DOI: 10.1177/0002716206297918

202

This article looks at both the positive and negative aspects from the particular viewpoint of developing countries. The first section discusses definitions of globalization and liberalization and asks why countries would liberalize. The second section examines the characteristics of capital flows, comparing public and private sources and noting the reduction of the first and the expansion of the second in recent years. A traditional type of capital flow (foreign direct investment, or FDI) is also compared with a newer one (remittances). The third section analyzes the recipients of capital flows or the question of who has access among regions, countries, and firms. The fourth section considers capital volatility, contrasting short-term and long-term investments. The concluding section discusses the balance sheet of winners and losers and asks how the benefits of financial globalization might be spread more evenly. Overall, the article argues that if the benefits of globalization are to be preserved, the complex problems created or exacerbated by globalization must be substantially mitigated, even though they can never be completely resolved.

Globalization and Liberalization

A vast number of studies have been published in recent years about the advantages and disadvantages of globalization and economic liberalization. While proponents argue that these processes will speed up growth and help to create jobs and reduce poverty, critics charge that the problems created often outweigh the benefits, especially for countries and groups at the bottom of the income ladder.[2] But what is meant by globalization and liberalization, and what is the relationship between the two? Why would governments, even those who claim to represent progressive ideas, liberalize their economies?

Globalization, according to the definition used in this article, refers to the increasing integration of the world through transnational flows of goods, capital, ideas, and norms. People have generally been less mobile, although immigration has accelerated in recent years for economic, social, and political reasons. Thus, globalization is not a purely economic phenomenon even if the basic framework is economic.[3] A crucial aspect of globalization is that the flows will take place regardless of whether any individual developing country participates. Thus, from the developing country perspective, globalization can be considered an exogenous set of variables.

Liberalization is, in some ways, the opposite side of the coin. It consists of the removal of barriers—economic, political, and legal—to transnational flows over their borders by individual developing countries. Unlike globalization, it is an internal process and represents the decision to take part in globalization. It is important, however, to mention two caveats to these definitions. First, if most countries are closed economically and ideologically, then globalization will be seriously hobbled. Second, the "decision" to participate may be promoted by powerful actors already involved in globalization and thus some degree of manipulation may be involved. Likewise, not all citizens of a given country may be in agreement with a decision by their government to liberalize.

If we take globalization as a given, why have most governments decided to participate in it, that is, to liberalize their economies? Unless the decision is totally against their will, which is highly unlikely, they liberalize because they think they will benefit. Looking at examples from the financial sector, we can identify several potential benefits.[4] The one most discussed is greater access to capital, which can help increase growth through higher investment rates, better technology, and entrée to foreign markets. This benefit could accrue either though FDI, which almost always involves some increased investment, or through access to long-term loans and other finance through international capital markets.[5]

[Governments liberalize their economies] because they think they will benefit [through] greater access to capital, . . . better technology, and entrée to foreign markets.

Equally important, however, globalization involves the spread of norms and institutions. In the financial area, through organizations such as the Bank for International Settlements (BIS) and the International Monetary Fund (IMF), better regulation and supervision have been promoted as have more independent central banks. More generally, improved corporate governance of both financial and nonfinancial firms—particularly with respect to greater transparency and increased availability of information—brings benefits to shareholders and the general public alike.[6]

Set against these potential benefits are costs that can also be large. One of those costs is increasing inequality across and within nations as some countries and some groups get access to large amounts of capital while others are shut out. Increased inequality, in turn, not only leads to wasted resources but also is likely to increase instability and thus further the gap between those who are considered good and poor credit risks. Ironically, the other potential cost that many experts highlight—that resulting from the volatility of capital flows—tends to be concentrated among countries that do have access to capital.[7] In this sense, poorer countries are protected. Volatility, arising from large surges of capital moving across borders in both directions, makes it difficult to manage an economy and, in the worst of cases, can result in extremely damaging crises. These two problems—inequality and volatility—can potentially undermine globalization itself if they are not dealt with adequately.

Characteristics of Capital Flows

Before we can analyze winners and losers of financial globalization and liberalization, we have to study the characteristics of capital flows and their trends over recent years. Figure 1 provides an overview of total global capital flows to developing

FIGURE 1
TOTAL NET CAPITAL FLOWS TO DEVELOPING COUNTRIES

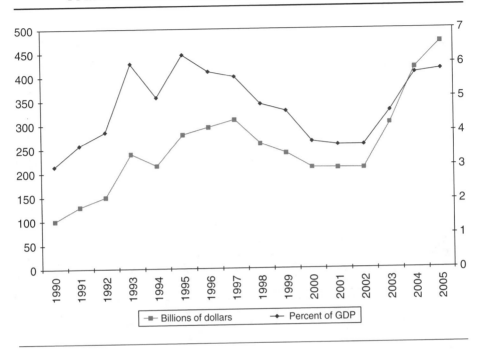

countries in the past decade and a half. The lighter line represents billions of dollars, and the darker one shows flows as a percentage of GDP. The lines are similar; combined they tell a story about the rapid surge of capital flows into developing countries in the early part of the 1990s, followed by a drop through the first part of the current decade and then a recent turn back up to reach a peak of US$470 billion in 2005 (nearly 6 percent of GDP).[8] All three subperiods reflect trends in the broader international political economy. The early surge came as a response to the end of the debt crisis of the 1980s as well as the perceived greater stability in developing economies. The drop in the second half of the 1990s occurred in large part as a reaction to the Mexican and Asian crises. As these crises were gradually overcome, capital again began to move into the developing world.

While Figure 1 shows an overall picture of capital flows, it is important to disaggregate them to understand the mechanisms at work as well as the consequences for recipients. One important distinction is the difference between public capital flows—that is, disbursements coming from governments and multilateral organizations—versus private flows. It is fascinating to observe that in 1990, public and private capital flows to developing countries were nearly identical, about US$50 billion each. What a difference fifteen years have made. Public capital has not even stayed constant; it has fallen in nominal terms and net flows are now negative. (It should be noted that grants have been increasing in a modest way.

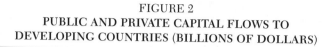

FIGURE 2
PUBLIC AND PRIVATE CAPITAL FLOWS TO
DEVELOPING COUNTRIES (BILLIONS OF DOLLARS)

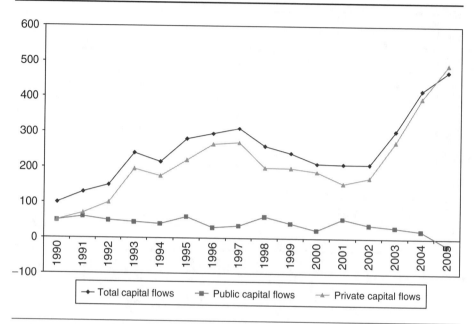

Given balance-of-payments rules, however, they are not included as part of capital flows.) Meanwhile, private flows increased sharply until about 1997, falling off but then increasing over the past few years to reach a new high of nearly US$500 billion in 2005. It is clearly private investors who are playing the dominant role in spurring capital mobility, both the inflows and outflows. The significance of this fact will become apparent later when we see the distribution of public and private flows among different groups of developing countries (see Figure 2).

Another distinction looks within the private investor category to focus on different types of capital involved in the transfers. FDI is regarded at present as the most positive of all capital flows since it is thought to be the most stable type and to provide positive externalities in the form of access to foreign markets and to technology. It is interesting that this view is just the opposite of that prevailing in the 1970s, when many FDI projects in developing countries were nationalized because they were seen as displacing local capital and extracting capital from the country in the form of profit remittances. Figure 3 shows how significant FDI has become both in terms of billions of dollars and percentage of GDP. In 2005, it reached US$240 billion (3 percent of GDP), a nearly tenfold increase from US$25 billion (0.5 percent of GDP) in 1990. Thus, FDI now represents approximately half of total capital flows.

Finally, Figure 4 introduces a newly significant type of foreign resources. Remittances from workers who have gone abroad to work have been important for

FIGURE 3
NET FOREIGN DIRECT INVESTMENT (FDI) FLOWS TO
DEVELOPING COUNTRIES

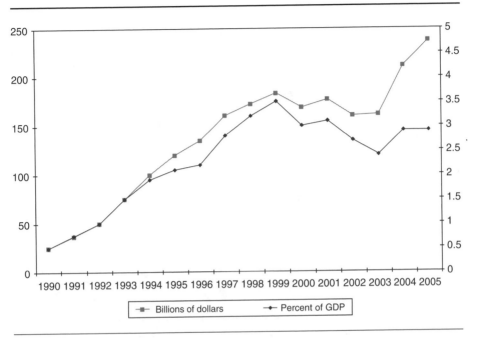

some countries for a long time, but recently they have ballooned to become a major source of foreign exchange.[9] In 2004, the last year for which complete estimates are available, remittances to developing countries totaled US$167 billion. In Latin America alone in 2005, the amount was nearly US$50 billion. In many of the smaller economies of Central America and the Caribbean, remittances amount to more than 10 percent of GDP.[10] As we will see later, one of the reasons that these flows are important is that they are distributed among countries and households in a very different way than other private capital flows. To see the significance of remittances, Figure 4 compares them with FDI flows. There it can be seen that the former had become almost as important as the latter a couple of years ago although the gap has widened somewhat since 2003 with the recent surge in FDI.[11]

Access to Foreign Capital

While there is general—even if not total—agreement that foreign capital can have a positive impact on the development process, we have also seen that two central arguments are made about the negative aspects of these flows. In this section, we discuss the issue of skewed access to foreign capital; in the next one we discuss the problems of volatility.

FIGURE 4
REMITTANCES AND FOREIGN DIRECT INVESTMENT (FDI)
TO DEVELOPING COUNTRIES (BILLIONS OF DOLLARS)

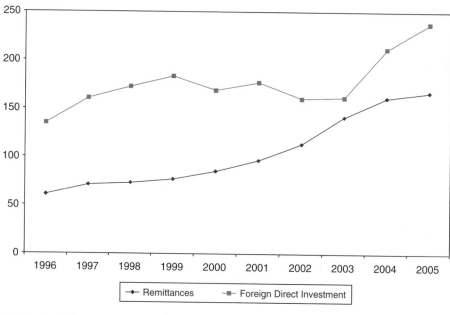

   Who is getting access to foreign capital and of what kind? We can think of several categories of potential beneficiaries: all developing countries, certain regions, certain countries, and certain types of firms. Table 1 shows what regions of the world get access to capital and of what types. The data are flows for the year 2004; they include both dollar amounts and percent of GDP since the former can give some misleading impressions. Thus, the largest recipient by dollar amount is Eastern Europe, but Sub-Saharan Africa obtains nearly twice as much as a share of GDP.
   For all regions except Sub-Saharan Africa, private flows are many times larger than public monies. Among private sector flows, FDI is generally much more important than flows from the capital markets. Within the public sector category, grants are the dominant positive flow. In every case except Africa and South Asia, official loans are actually negative as bilateral and multilateral sources receive more money in repayments than they lend out. Reliance on public sector flows has advantages, in that they are generally more stable, but as we have seen, they have been declining over time while private sector flows have been expanding rapidly.
   Another way of looking at the allocation issue is by country. Tables 2 and 3 do so with a focus on the distribution of FDI in comparison to remittances. FDI

TABLE 1
REGIONAL DISTRIBUTION OF TOTAL NET CAPITAL FLOWS, 2004
(BILLIONS OF DOLLARS)

	East Asia	Eastern Europe	Latin America	Middle East	South Asia	Africa
Grants	2.7	9.0	3.2	4.0	4.3	24.2
Official loans	−7.9	−1.8	−5.7	−2.2	1.8	1.4
Private flows	83.6	74.6	50.7	6.7	16.9	15.4
Foreign direct investment (FDI)	63.6	37.6	42.4	4.1	6.5	11.3
Capital markets	20.0	37.0	8.3	2.6	10.4	4.1
Total	78.4	81.8	48.2	8.5	23.0	41.0
As percentage of GDP	3.5	5.0	2.7	1.8	2.8	9.3

SOURCE: Calculated from regional tables in World Bank (2005, vol. II, pp. 6-29).

TABLE 2
CONCENTRATION OF FOREIGN DIRECT INVESTMENT (FDI) FLOWS TO
DEVELOPING COUNTRIES, 2004

Country	Amount	Percentage	Cumulative
China	56.0	33.8	33.8
Brazil	15.3	9.2	43.0
Mexico	14.1	8.5	51.5
Russia	7.8	4.7	56.2
Chile	5.6	3.4	59.6
India	5.3	3.2	62.8
Poland	4.7	2.8	65.6
Czech Republic	3.8	2.3	67.9
Others	52.9	32.0	100.0
Total	165.5	100.0	

SOURCE: Calculated from World Bank (2005, vol. I, p. 145).

flows are highly concentrated, as can be seen in Table 2. Eight countries alone get more than two-thirds of all foreign direct investment. China receives about one-third of the total, while Brazil and Mexico also figure prominently as destinations of FDI flows. Over the past decade and a half, Russia and two Eastern European economies have joined the group, as have Chile and India.[12]

Table 3, by contrast, shows the allocation of remittances. While the concentration of remittances is lower than FDI, it is still high. In this case, eight countries receive about half of all remittances. In most cases, however, the list of countries is very different. India leads the list as a recipient of remittances, followed by

TABLE 3
CONCENTRATION OF REMITTANCES TO DEVELOPING COUNTRIES, 2004

Country	Amount	Percentage	Cumulative
India	23.0	18.3	18.3
Mexico	17.0	13.5	31.8
Philippines	8.1	6.4	38.2
China	4.6	3.7	41.9
Pakistan	4.1	3.3	45.2
Morocco	3.6	2.9	48.1
Bangladesh	3.4	2.7	50.8
Colombia	3.1	2.5	53.3
Others	58.9	46.8	100
Total	125.8	100	

SOURCE: Calculated from World Bank (2005, vol. I, p. 136).

Mexico, the Philippines, China, Pakistan, Morocco, Bangladesh, and Colombia. Thus, only China, India, and Mexico are on both lists. It is reasonable to expect that the impact of the two kinds of flows is very different as well. FDI and remittances go to substantially different kinds of places. As a general rule, FDI is attracted to dynamic countries with higher per capita incomes, while remittances tend to go to poorer countries that cannot provide enough jobs for their workers at home. At the household level, the two types of flow are also very different. Recent World Bank research offers an optimistic vision of the advantages of remittances, which are found to help reduce poverty; smooth household consumption; ease working capital constraints; and increase household expenditure on education, health, and entrepreneurship.[13]

Finally, in an assessment of capital flows, it is important to consider production units, where size is a crucial determinant of access to finance. Large firms have easy access to foreign capital, both through FDI and the international capital markets. Medium, small, and micro firms, by contrast, have much greater difficulty in obtaining capital to finance their operations. While they cannot resort to international markets, medium-sized firms may be able to tap local financial markets, depending on how individual countries' markets are structured, what kinds of norms regulate the allocation of capital, and the existing resources available to mobilize investments. Small and micro firms are limited to finance from banks and other local lenders, in addition to retained earnings. This means they will grow more slowly, and the gap between them and their larger counterparts is likely to increase. This is very important since small firms tend to create the majority of jobs, especially in developing economies.

Using data from a survey by the World Bank in 2000, which asked small entrepreneurs in various regions about the major obstacles they face in conducting business (see Table 4), we can get some idea about the general problem of finance for small firms, but also how it varies to some extent by region. In East

TABLE 4
ACCESS TO FINANCE FOR SMALL FIRMS IS MAJOR OBSTACLE

Region	Percentage Agree
East Asia Pacific	33.5
Eastern Europe	26.0
Latin America	43.8
South Asia	41.9
Sub-Saharan Africa	40.2

SOURCE: World Bank, *World Business Environment Survey 2000*, online database; http://info
.worldbank.org/governance/wbes/.

Asia and Eastern Europe, less than a third of those interviewed said that finance
is a major obstacle, whereas in Latin America, South Asia, and Sub-Saharan
Africa, more than 40 percent of small businesspeople see access to capital as a
major obstacle to conduct operations.

Volatility of Capital Flows

Volatility is a second aspect of capital flows that has been heavily criticized by
those who question the benefits of globalization.[14] The issue here is that funds can
move in and out of countries with great rapidity, making it difficult for the authorities to manage macroeconomic policy. This is especially problematic in developing
countries since their economic size tends to be small in comparison with the
increasingly large flows of international finance. In the worst of cases, this volatility
can contribute to financial crises that can be devastating for developing economies.
Many experts, for example, have argued that such volatility was an important contributor to both the Mexican and Asian financial crises of the 1990s.[15]

Private financial flows are volatile by nature, depending as they do on the
changing opinions of investors about the creditworthiness of individual borrowers but also about the characteristics of the markets as a whole. Nonetheless,
some types of private flows are believed to be more volatile than others. At present, most experts regard FDI as the least volatile flows since it is thought to be
difficult to withdraw tangible physical investments. Others have begun to question this argument, however, suggesting that the use of derivatives may make
FDI quite similar to other flows in terms of volatility.[16]

While expert opinion may vary with respect to FDI, almost all consider short-
term flows to be the most volatile of all. Table 5 provides an idea of the pattern
of short-term flows and the damage they can cause. It shows Latin America
before and after the Mexican financial crisis of 1994-1995 and East Asia before
and after the 1997-1998 crisis. The table depicts short-term bank loans compared
to longer-term debt securities. As may be seen, even in Latin America—a less
dramatic case than East Asia—the turnaround in terms of short-term flows in
the two years before and after the crisis was considerable. The trend was from a

TABLE 5
SHORT-TERM FOREIGN CAPITAL FLOWS DURING CRISES
(BILLIONS OF DOLLARS)

	Latin America		East Asia	
	1993-1994	1995-1996	1995-1996	1997-1998
Bank loans	14.9	−0.1	51.3	−60.4
Debt securities	5.6	1.3	5.2	4.3
Total	20.5	1.4	56.4	−56.2

SOURCE: BIS-IMF-OECD-World Bank, Joint Statistics on External Debt, online database; http://www.oecd.org/site/0,2865,en_21571361_31596493_1_1_1_1_1_,00.html. BIS = Bank for International Settlements.

moderately large positive number to a small negative number. Debt securities, by contrast, moved in the same direction, but the numbers remained positive. East Asia presents a far more drastic picture: a very large short-term capital inflow in the two years right before the crisis turned into an enormous outflow in the two years after financial upheaval. In that case, debt securities were not very large compared to the short-term flows but remained at more or less the same level throughout the transition. In the Asian countries, the balance shifted by more than a hundred billion dollars over a four-year period.

One argument that has long been made in favor of more public sector financing for developing countries is that it is less volatile than its private sector counterpart. Indeed, some public loans are explicitly countercyclical in the sense that they are offered when a borrowing country is in trouble and other lenders have withdrawn. The IMF is the main example of an institution that is designed to serve this function, but the World Bank and the regional development banks also engage in some countercyclical lending. The argument cannot be carried too far, however, especially with respect to some bilateral financing. Governments of lending countries can also be quite fickle in their willingness to support "foreign aid" to developing economies. In addition, as we have already seen, the long-term trend of public sector loans has been declining and is now negative on a net basis. Those that rely on these funds are therefore in a vulnerable situation.

Can Benefits Be Spread More Evenly?

We are now in a position to present a balance sheet of the positive and negative aspects of financial globalization.

(1) Some regions (especially East Asia, Eastern Europe, and some countries in Latin America) have been able to attract a large volume of private capital flows, which can potentially help increase growth and provide resources for development of human capital. Other regions (Sub-Saharan Africa, South Asia, and the non–oil exporters in the Middle East) have to rely on declining supplies of public sector

capital. Newer flows, especially remittances, are beginning to provide enhanced opportunities to countries and regions that have not always been favored by traditional capital flows.

(2) Some firms and households have also been able to take advantage of the burgeoning quantities of private capital. At the firm level, these are almost exclusively large, well-established companies—including state-owned firms. Some relatively well-off households are beginning to get access to mortgage finance and consumer credit that are often provided directly by foreign banks or indirectly as local banks borrow abroad and on-lend at home. Poorer households have been assisted in some cases by remittances from family members working abroad.

(3) The spread of international financial norms—including better regulation and supervision of banks and financial markets, greater transparency, and wider diffusion of information—has been beneficial to all kinds of borrowers in ways that are often overlooked. There is increasing evidence that countries with good corporate governance in the financial and nonfinancial sector have deeper financial markets and greater opportunities for new borrowers to obtain access.

(4) Volatility undermines the value of financial flows for almost all recipients. The tendency for these flows to come in surges and withdraw just as quickly makes it much more difficult to manage economies in a sensible way and, in especially complicated situations, can even provoke financial crises. These retard economic growth for years, in part because the financial sector itself is severely damaged.

The policy question at the heart of this article is how to spread benefits in ways that are more equitable and more productive than those existing at present.

The policy question at the heart of this article is how to spread benefits in ways that are more equitable and more productive than those existing at present. What are the tools available to achieve that goal? If public officials and policy makers want to promote foreign capital, there are some things they can do to make their countries more attractive. Political stability is a top item on that list. More transparency in financial transactions, the result of institutional norms directed at governing capital flows, is another priority. Yet rapid growth is probably the single most important characteristic of countries gaining the favor of foreign investors. Is foreign capital itself creating a positive cycle in terms of growth? For some countries, like China and Chile, that certainly appears to be the case. For many countries, however, external finance has not helped growth. This is not necessarily because capitalists are not playing by the rules but because states have not created suitable conditions for attracting foreign investments. Recent research has tried to identify characteristics that increase the chances of foreign capital having a positive impact, but some circularity is involved since these are the same characteristics that foreign investment is supposed to promote.[17]

The skewed distribution of foreign finance among regions and countries actually embodies two different sets of problems. For those countries with ready access to private flows, debt buildup as well as volatility are serious concerns. Prudent debt management is probably easier to deal with than volatility. In Latin America, however, Chile, Colombia, and Brazil have used economic measures to slow down the inflow of capital, which, in turn, cushions the blow of subsequent outflows. To be effective, however, these measures must be accompanied by sound macroeconomic policies.[18] Another kind of problem exists for countries that must rely on public funds. While grants have been increasing, public sector loans have been falling and, as noted above, are now negative in net terms. It behooves the multilateral agencies, who are at the heart of this problem, to study ways to maintain a positive loan flow.

The article contends that it is not enough to worry about which countries gain access but also about the kinds of firms that have access to capital. This is not just a question of social justice but also of employment and economic growth. How to increase access for smaller firms leads into the debate about the role of the government in the financial sector. New theories of banking decry the continued existence of public sector banks, suggesting that the way to get finance to the people who really need it is to rely exclusively on private institutions. While this may often be true, public banks can fulfill some functions that are complementary to the role played by the private sector. One concerns finance for small firms, where interesting examples exist of "second-tier" public banks that intermediate between international sources of capital (public and private) and small borrowers via private banks.[19]

All of these issues—the productivity of foreign capital in terms of increasing growth, the problem of volatility, and the question of who has access to capital—are in urgent need of solution. If positive responses cannot be found, the benefits associated with globalization in general, not just financial globalization, may be called into question.[20] Since even the sharpest critics agree that globalization is potentially a great benefit for developing countries, its curtailment is not in their interest. It is important, then, for developing country governments to work together with their counterparts in developed countries and with international organizations to look for creative solutions.

Notes

1. Some of the ideas in this article were developed earlier in Stallings (2002).

2. On the positive side, see Bhagwati (2004) and Wolf (2004). For a more critical approach, see Rodrik (1997, 1999) and Stiglitz (2002, 2006). A study that tries to present a balanced, empirical analysis for the case of Latin America is Stallings and Peres (2000); a similar but broader work that focuses on winners and

losers is de la Dehesa (2006). A useful analysis comparing current globalization with the past is Bordo, Eichengreen, and Irwin (1999).

3. For a definition of globalization that brings in noneconomic variables, see Rosenau (1997). A useful multidisciplinary treatment of globalization is Held et al. (1999); on governance of globalization, see Held and McGrew (2002).

4. Financial globalization has become arguably the most contentious aspect of globalization. A number of recent publications by high-profile economists have debated the merits and demerits. See, for example, Stiglitz (2002), Prasad et al. (2003), Kose et al. (2006), and Mishkin (2006).

5. Perhaps the most enthusiastic proponent of financial globalization as a source of growth and prosperity in developing countries today is Frederic Mishkin. See his arguments on the subject in Mishkin (2006).

6. On corporate governance and the role of the international financial institutions, see Stallings (2006, chap. 4).

7. See, for example, Ffrench-Davis (2001) on problems of successful economies.

8. These flows are nonetheless smaller than those of the late nineteenth and early twentieth centuries. As measured by current account deficits, several important capital importers then were bringing in more than 10 percent of GDP (see Bordo, Eichengreen, and Irwin 1999).

9. It should be noted that, in terms of the balance of payments, remittances (like grants) are not considered part of the capital account but are located in the current account. Thus, they are not included in the overall capital flows shown in Figure 1.

10. For data, see World Bank (2006b) and Fajnzylber and López (forthcoming).

11. This graph is based on World Bank data. Data from the United Nations Conference on Trade and Development (2006) show a bigger gap between the two.

12. Foreign direct investment (FDI) to developing countries in 2005 was about 25 percent of total FDI. That is, the large majority of FDI goes to developed economies (calculated from World Bank, 2006a, vol. I, Table 2.6).

13. See World Bank (2006b, chap. 5). A great deal of research has been done on remittances in the past few years. In addition to the World Bank document, see, for example, see Terry and Wilson (2005) and Fajnzylber and López (forthcoming).

14. Among those who criticize financial globalization, volatility is a major target of their analyses. See, for example, Stiglitz (2002, esp. chap. 3), Ocampo and Martín (2003), Ffrench-Davis and Griffith-Jones (2004), and Calvo (2005).

15. On Mexico, see Calvo and Mendoza (1996); and Sachs, Tornell, and Velasco (1996). Amidst the vast literature spawned by the Asian crisis, see overviews in Lindgren, García, and Saal (1999); and Lee (2003). Stallings (2006, chap. 2) compared the two.

16. An early argument that questioned the difference between FDI and other flows was Claessens, Dooley, and Warner (1995). A more recent analysis that concentrates on the role of derivatives is Griffith-Jones and Dodd (2006).

17. See, for example, the discussion in Kose et al (2006).

18. These types of measure are very controversial, but they have gained wider acceptance, even at the international financial institutions.

19. Stallings (2006, chap. 9) discussed examples in Latin America and East Asia, where public sector banks have successfully complemented private sector activities.

20. The new chairman of the Federal Reserve recently issued a warning along these very lines.

References

Bhagwati, Jagdish. 2004. *In defense of globalization.* New York: Oxford University Press.

Bordo, Michael D., Barry Eichengreen, and Douglas A. Irwin. 1999. Is globalization today really different than globalization a hundred years ago? Working Paper 7195, National Bureau of Economic Research, Cambridge, MA.

Calvo, Guillermo. 2005. *Emerging capital markets in turmoil: Bad luck or bad policy?* Cambridge, MA: MIT Press.

Calvo, Guillermo, and Enrique Mendoza. 1996. Mexico's balance of payments: A chronicle of death foretold. *Journal of International Economics* 41 (3-4): 235-64.

Claessens, Stijn, Michael Dooley, and Andrew Warner. 1995. Portfolio capital flows: Hot or cold? *World Bank Economic Review* 9 (1): 153-74.

de la Dehesa, Guillermo. 2006. *Winners and losers in globalization.* Oxford, UK: Blackwell.

Fajnzylber, Pablo, and J. Humberto López. Forthcoming. *Close to home: The development impact of remittances in Latin America.* Washington, DC: World Bank.

Ffrench-Davis, Ricardo, ed. 2001. *Financial crisis in successful emerging economies.* Washington, DC: Brookings Institution.

Ffrench-Davis, Ricardo, and Stephany Griffith-Jones, eds. 2004. *From capital surges to drought: Seeking stability in emerging economies.* New York: Palgrave Macmillan.

Griffith-Jones, Stephany, and Randall Dodd. 2006. *Chile's derivatives markets: Stabilizing or speculative impact?* Santiago, Chile: UN Economic Commission for Latin America and the Caribbean.

Held, David, Anthony McGrew, David Goldblatt, and Jonathan Perraton. 1999. *Global transformation: Politics, economics, and culture.* Stanford, CA: Stanford University Press.

Held, David, and Anthony McGrew, eds. 2002. *Governing globalization.* New York: Polity.

Kose, M. Ayhan, Eswar Prasad, Kenneth Rogoff, and Shang-Jin Wei. 2006. Financial globalization: A reappraisal. Working Paper 6/189, International Monetary Fund, Washington, DC.

Lee, Chung H., ed. 2003. *Financial liberalization and economic crisis in Asia.* London: Routledge.

Lindgren, Carl-Johan, Gillian García, and Matthew I. Saal. 1999. *Financial sector crisis and restructuring: Lessons from Asia.* Occasional Paper 188. Washington, DC: International Monetary Fund.

Mishkin, Frederic. 2006. *The next great globalization: How disadvantaged nations can harness their financial systems to get rich.* Princeton, NJ: Princeton University Press.

Ocampo, José Antonio, and Juan Martín, eds. 2003. *Globalización y desarrollo: una reflexión desde América Latina y el Caribe.* Bogotá, Colombia: Alfaomega.

Prasad, Eswar, Kenneth Rogoff, Shuang-Jin Wei, and M. Ayhan Kose. 2003. *Effects of financial globalization on developing countries.* Occasional Paper 220. Washington, DC: IMF.

Rodrik, Dani. 1997. *Has globalization gone too far?* Washington, DC: Institute of International Economics.

———. 1999. *The new global economy and developing countries: Making openness work.* Washington, DC: Overseas Development Council.

Rosenau, James. 1997. The complexities and contradictions of globalization. *Current History* 96 (613): 360-64.

Sachs, Jeffrey, Alfredo Tornell, and Andrés Velasco. 1996. The Mexican peso crisis: Sudden death or death foretold? *Journal of International Economics* 41 (3-4): 265-83.

Stallings, Barbara. 2002. Globalization and liberalization: The impact on developing countries. In *States, markets, and just growth: Development in the 21st century,* ed. Atul Kohli, Chung-In Moon, and George Sorensen. Tokyo: United Nations Press.

———. 2006. *Finance for development: Latin America in comparative perspective.* With Rogerio Studart. Washington, DC: Brookings Institution.

Stallings, Barbara, and Wilson Peres. 2000. *Growth, employment, and equity: The impact of the economic reforms in Latin America and the Caribbean.* Washington, DC: Brookings Institution.

Stiglitz, Joseph. 2002. *Globalization and its discontents.* New York: Norton.

———. 2006. *Making globalization work.* New York: Norton.

Terry, Donald F., and Steven R. Wilson, eds. 2005. *Beyond small change: Making migrant remittances count.* Washington, DC: Inter-American Development Bank.

United Nations Conference on Trade and Development (UNCTAD). 2006. *Trade and development report, 2006.* Geneva, Switzerland: United Nations.

Wolf, Martin. 2004. *Why globalization works.* New Haven, CT: Yale University Press.

World Bank. 2005. *Global development finance 2005: Mobilizing finance and managing vulnerability.* Washington, DC: World Bank.

———. 2006a. *Global development finance 2006: The development potential of surging capital flows.* Washington, DC: World Bank.

———. 2006b. *Global economic prospects 2006: Economic implications of remittances and migration.* Washington, DC: World Bank.

Trading Impressions: Evidence from Costa Rica

The case of indigenous artisans in Costa Rica trying to succeed in the global markets for handicrafts and international tourism demonstrates that the public narratives of the country's character circulated by their national government and other institutional actors impose severe constraints on artisans and other economic actors. Market opportunities and socioinstitutional constraints arise not only from the beliefs that people within a national territory have about themselves but also from the roles that outsiders recognize as appropriate to a people within a given territory. The Costa Rican case suggests that the promises and pitfalls of the NAFTA free trade agreement cannot be understood adequately by solely examining the structural conditions of each country. Instead, the uneven spread of benefits and liabilities will depend, in part, on how nation-states and their subnational communities are framed in the imaginations of the global marketplace.

Keywords: international tourism; handicrafts; Costa Rica; Chorotega; impression management; embeddedness

By
FREDERICK WHERRY

The impressions that global buyers have about different countries have important implications for international tourism and local cultural industries. According to the neoliberal market paradigm, countries possessing cultural riches—such as historically significant sites and craft traditions embodied in such cultural commodities as ceramics, wood carvings, baskets, and the like—should be able to thrive in free trade regimes such as the North American Free Trade Agreement (NAFTA). However, this article demonstrates that culture cannot be used as a tool by all countries in the same way. International buyers have to believe that the roles local tourism and cultural industries play are suitable for the players and their stage. This problem of belief in the part that local cultural agents play explains, in part, the difficulties encountered by indigenous artisans in Costa Rica trying to succeed in the global markets for handicrafts and international tourism.

DOI: 10.1177/0002716206296818

Although Costa Rica leads Central America in the revenues generated from international tourism, indigenous Costa Rican artisans who predictably would benefit from these large flows of tourists find themselves in receipt of few tourist dollars and little government support. The tourists do not patronize indigenous artisans because most tourists do not know that these artisans exist, and international awareness of what cultural riches a country possesses has depended historically on the public narratives that government officials disseminated in international forums such as the World's Fair and other international gatherings. In *Ethnic and Tourist Arts: Cultural Expressions from the Fourth World* (1976, 310-11), Nelson H. H. Graburn reminded us of the important role that national governments play in amplifying public narratives by promoting sectors of the economy that tell the right story about the country's character. Take Mexico, for example:

> The government concerns include ... promoting a favorable image of regional Mexico. ... Mexico has long differentiated itself from European Spain and from other Latin American countries; it has glorified the arts of the conquered civilizations ... [and] supports many exhibitions, collections, and museums. (pp. 117-18)

When the Mexican government proudly supports expressions of *indigenismo*, "that which is Indian and not European" (p. 115), it is both promoting the country's national image as distinctly as possible from that of the European invader and using this distinction to make more salient the richness of its cultural hybrids. The Mexican government uses export incentives as a means to manage the impression that its polity has of itself and that outsiders have of its polity—different but proud of it.

Countries such as Ghana have used these cultural differences embodied in commodities to respond to global economic pressures and to domestic political exigencies. Shea butter, an indigenous commodity, became popularized through The Body Shop's and L'Occitane's advertisements of Ghanaian and other west African women gathering shea nuts, pulverizing them, and putting the lotion to traditional uses, just as these women have done for generations. President J. J. Rawlings offered strong state support to shea nut producers in northern Ghana in response to pressures from economic interests within and outside of the nation-state and as a means to satisfy the conditions of structural adjustment imposed by the international financial institutions (Chalfin 2004). At the same time, Rawlings recognized that incorporating the indigenous commodities of the north into the

Frederick Wherry is an assistant professor of sociology and a faculty associate at the Center for Southeast Asian Studies at the University of Michigan. He straddles the fields of economic sociology and the sociology of culture in his investigations of culture, markets, and comparative international development. This article is based on material from his book, Global Markets and Local Crafts: Thailand and Costa Rica Compared *(forthcoming), Johns Hopkins University Press, which examines how international tourism and the global market for handicrafts have affected the economic development of communities where most of the residents earn their living directly or indirectly from handicraft sales in Thailand and Costa Rica. He is currently completing an ethnographic monograph, "Art Night and Business Days in the Barrio: Philadelphia's Golden Block," that investigates how an ethnic enclave is using its culture to revitalize the local economy in postindustrial Philadelphia.*

public narrative of what it means to be Ghanaian would facilitate the political incorporation of the region into the rest of Ghana. The state's involvement with shea nuts and shea butter satisfied material, political, and ideational interests.

Likewise, in his prescient analysis of handicraft merchants in Otavalo, David Kyle (2000) observed that the deference tourists gave to artisans presumed to be authentic depended not on an assessment of historical accuracy but rather on the social accumulation of cultural cachet afforded to some groups but not others. Although the artisans in Azuay create authentic crafts while some of the handicraft merchants in Otavalo sell inventory from other Latin American groups, the artisans in Azuay have failed to convince foreigners of the authenticity of their crafts. Attempts in the 1980s by the Ecuadorian government to correct the false notion that the products from Azuay are not authentic were rationalized away by international tourists and other buyers who object that such news breaches what everyone knows to be true. Confronted with the breach between what the individual expects another to do given the situation and how the other behaves— what Harold Garfinkel (1967) called a breaching experiment—the confronting individual tries to "fix" the problem (the non-sense) through polite conversational redirections meant to spare all involved the embarrassment of exposed ignorance or manifest abnormality. By contrast, the Otavalans are given the benefit of the doubt as being authentic—"nearly anything they [the Otavalans] sell is considered by foreigners as socially noble and culturally 'authentic' " (Kyle 2000, 192).

That so-called economic behavior is socially relevant and socially conditioned is well known. In *Economy and Society*, Max Weber identified transcendental beliefs (based in cultural traditions or religious belief) and social conventions (collective practices and rituals) as two orienting factors for economic life (Weber 1914/1978). Institutionally oriented studies in sociology have demonstrated how collective understandings shape the institutions that, in turn, affect economic outcomes (Biggart and Orrú 1997; Biggart and Guillén 1999; Powell and DiMaggio 1991). Collective understandings about the national identity and the way that exports represent that identity inform the country's cultural tool kit—"symbols, stories, rituals, and world-views, which people may use in varying configurations to solve different kinds of problems" (Swidler 1986, 273). The tool kit shapes the strategies that actors are likely to pursue as well as the manner of pursuit.

Similar to Biggart and Guillén's account of how institutional logics organize industries within a country, this article highlights how historical events and the understandings that result from them influence "the types, availability, and legitimacy of actors [and symbols]" (Biggart and Guillén 1999, 728) in the economy for cultural commodities. The government's public narratives reveal how it interprets the meanings (sign-vehicles) carried by economic action, such as what it means to export cultural commodities depicting western traditions rather than (or in conjunction with) indigenous commodities evoking images of the wild, abundant jungle and its indigenous inhabitants. Public narratives reflect the response of the nation-state to the society of world opinion, the response of world society to the nation's performance, and the adjustments made by the nation-state in response to how the performance is being taken (e.g., Goffman 1959).

The nation-state's public narratives offer collective understandings within the nation-state about its own social identity compared with the social identities of other nation-states and shape commercial opportunities for handicrafts and other local products in such countries as Ecuador (Colloredo-Mansfeld 2002; Kyle 2000; Meisch 2002), Mexico (Carruthers 2001; Cohen 1998; García Canclini 1990), Guatemala (Little 2002; Pérez Sáinz 1997; Peréz-Sáinz and Andrade-Eekhoff 2003), Indonesia (Alexander and Alexander 2000; Causey 2003), Mali (Rovine 2001), Ghana and west Africa (Chalfin 2004), Nigeria (Allen 1983), Costa Rica (Wherry 2006), throughout Central America, and across the globe. Moreover, as Bandelj (2002) demonstrated in her study of foreign direct investment, even in the seemingly noncultural sectors of economic life, public narratives about the character of a people influence the investors' overall country assessments that have important consequences for regional and national economies. The public narratives of nation-states condition the likelihood that a country's capitalists will pursue opportunities in the global handicraft market and that international actors will validate those pursuits with financial transactions. In other words, it is not enough to possess stocks of symbolic capital; the capitalist inherits a collective understanding (orientation) of the uses (appropriation) to which different types of symbolic capital ought to be put. Not only are the former agricultural workers being pushed out of farm, factory, and protected government employment while nonetheless being pulled into handicraft production and tourist services, but also both the workers and the capitalists "see" the production of some types of cultural commodities as a means to protect cultural traditions and to validate a favorable public identity narrative for themselves.

Portes (2006) has argued that the goals that economic institutions have and the appropriate means for pursuing those goals have been missed in past studies of institutions and economic development. Charting a course between culture and structure (Zelizer 2005) enables the social scientist to pinpoint the deep structure of inequality, the social roles and statuses of different nation-states, and other relevant economic institutions as well as the relative statuses that emerge from the interstate and interterritorial comparisons of prestige and stigma symbols. This enduring set of status perceptions orients the course of the country's economic development. These perceptions sometimes divert economic development energies away from those stocks of symbolic capital easily appropriated but socially stigmatized. At other times, these perceptions may intensify the state's motivation to support material culture and to protect cultural traditions in order to promote both economic development and a favorable social identity of the nation-state.

This article uses qualitative and historical materials to sketch the emergence of disadvantage for Costa Rican artisans entering in the global market for handicrafts. The facile account that "those who can, do" will not do; the opportunity to perform in the marketplace does not depend on the individual's character but on the cultural politics and public narratives of the nation-state engaged in symbolic contests for status in the global community. I focus on international tourism and local cultural industries because of their size and their growing significance in Costa Rica and other countries around the world. In 2001, tourism revenues accounted for 7.8 percent of GDP in Costa Rica. In 2004, tourism receipts world-wide totaled US$623 billion, with Costa Rica accounting for US$1.58 billion (United Nations World Tourism Organization 2005). Local cultural industries also contributed greatly to national economies worldwide. According to the data-base of artisanal products maintained by the World Trade Organization and the United Nations Commission on Trade and Development, in 2003 the global export of wooden furniture generated US$14.6 billion; ceramics, US$1.4 billion; candles and tapers, US$1.4 billion; and artificial flowers, US$1.3 billion. Costa Rica accounts for less than one percent of these totals, but other developing and advanced countries account for five, ten, and more than ten percent of these totals. Perhaps because of Costa Rica's weakness in this sector, the database does not include information on export flows from Costa Rica for the aforementioned commodities. Most commentators attribute Costa Rica's weakness in cultural commodity exports to seemingly objective facts. In their view, Costa Rica simply does not have indigenous peoples or crafts.

[T]he opportunity to perform in the marketplace does not depend on the individual's character but on the cultural politics and public narratives of the nation-state engaged in symbolic contests for status in the global community.

History begs to differ. The Chorotegas are one of ten indigenous groups cur-rently recognized by the Costa Rican National Commission on Indigenous Affairs (Tenorio Alfaro 1988). It has not been established precisely when the Chorotegas came to settle in the Nicoya peninsula (Corrales Ulloa 2002, 21-29), but their pottery hierographs link them to Mesoamerican and Mayan civilizations. Scholars disagree on which civilizations have most influenced the indigenous peoples of the Nicoya peninsula in northwest Costa Rica (Scott 1999). The indigenous cul-tures of Nicoya were either (1) a peripheral element of the Olmec empire (Lowe 1989; Sharer 1989; Soustelle 1984), (2) an outpost of the Maya (Lines 1978), or (3) a trading zone in which neither group dominated (Pohorilenko 1981).

The description of northwest Costa Rica as a trading zone where no one group dominated emphasizes Nicoya's contested place within Mesoamerica. Based on his analysis of fifteen pre-Columbian artifacts found in Costa Rica, Anatole

Pohorilenko (1981, 310-11) argued that "the presence of Olmec-related material found in Costa Rica does not warrant the incorporation of the Nicoya Peninsula within the Mesoamerican cultural sphere." Pohorilenko added that some of the Olmec pieces found their way into Costa Rica through trade with the Maya and that some of the Olmec-style glyphs became incorporated into Costa Rican artifacts before the arrival of the Olmec. Costa Rica remains a contested cultural space in the periphery of Mesoamerica (Creamer 1987). To climb out of the periphery of the world system, the Costa Rican state obscured these indigenous contributions to the national identity and thereby disabled handicraft artisans and others who might have benefited from the market for ethnic commodities. Costa Rica lacks neither the indigenous peoples nor their crafts but rather their recognition by international operators.

Costa Rica lacks neither the indigenous peoples nor their crafts but rather their recognition by international operators.

In its early days, Costa Rica was known for its indigenous peoples and their crafts. In 1892, the World's Fair commemorated Columbus' discovery of the Americas. At the Columbian Historical Exhibition, signs of the premodern abounded. The archeological artifacts on display included works from Mexico, Guatemala, Nicaragua, Costa Rica, Columbia, Ecuador, and Peru. For today's international traveler, the inclusion of Costa Rica as a major contributor of archeological artifacts might come as a surprise, since those cultural contributions have been largely erased in public discussions. However, one should remember that Costa Rica contributed several thousand pieces to the exhibition, and the experts at the Fair praised the Costa Rican exhibition for being well organized, original, and tasteful in its ornamentation (Hough 1893; de Peralta and Alfaro 1893).

The World's Fairs offer strategic research materials for understanding how countries get framed as being rich (or poor) in particular cultural traditions because such representations were the manifest function of the fairs. The World's Fairs began in 1851 when Great Britain, at the height of its industrial revolution, hosted the event in London's Crystal Palace, designed by Sir Joseph Paxton reportedly ten days before the opening night of the fair. With more than a million feet of glass slated across iron limbs, the Crystal Palace conveyed the power of the great colonizers of the West and the cultural differences existing between the West and the others. Some 6.2 million visitors came to the fair to witness its thirteen thousand exhibitions. The Western countries boasted of their technological progress; the non-Western countries entertained Western spectators with their careful reconstructions of disorderly bazaars where even the dirt, peeling plaster, and scuff marks on the originals reappeared vibrantly on the copies. Donkeys and their stink along with half-clad villagers donning exotica in their supposed simplicity offered definitive proof of the new world order in which the race to economic and social progress belonged to the "naturally" gifted and the strong (Breckenridge 1989; Karp and Lavine 1991; Mitchell 1989).

Christopher Columbus's "discovery" of the Americas marked the Costa Ricans and their neighbors with a designation they could not shake—the formerly colonized. The colonial period in Costa Rica began in the early 1500s, after Christopher Columbus landed on its Caribbean coast in 1502. In 1522, Captain Gil González called this region "the rich coast" because he believed that great gold deposits awaited exploitation; and in 1539, the Spaniards officially named the territory Costa Rica (Biesanz, Biesanz, and Biesanz 1999). Ironically, Costa Rica did not enjoy the natural abundance of gold and other natural materials that its neighbors offered for extraction. As the "poorest" of the Spanish holdings in Central America, and the territory with the lowest stocks of "naturally" endowed wealth, Costa Rica encountered less coercion from the Spaniards relative to the forced extraction experienced in other parts of the Central American isthmus. Costa Rica's supposed misnomer gave the country a great deal of autonomy and a historical claim to being unlike its neighbors.

Along with its misnomer emerged at least two "public narratives . . . to explain [Costa Rica's] place . . . in the flow of history" (Somers and Block 2005, 280). First, the "agrarian democracy thesis" refers to the notion that agrarian egalitarianism laid the foundations for democracy in Costa Rica. Political participation is easier in Costa Rica compared to other Latin American countries because wealth was more evenly distributed among the population during colonization, giving more of its citizens a material stake in the well-being of the polity. The same land distribution patterns created a more civil, cooperating set of citizens. For example, to the extent that land was more evenly distributed, large plantations could not define the economic landscape. To realize economies of scale, medium-sized and larger farms had to cooperate with one another and with small landholders. The rural, modest, cooperating folk therefore became the dominant image of the Costa Rican character.

This public narrative has made its way into the handicrafts of Costa Rica. The most successful community of handicraft artisans resides in the Central Valley in the town of Sarchí, but they are not associated with Costa Rica's indigenous past. Quite the contrary, these artisans produce brightly decorated oxcarts and other folks arts that represent the agrarian democracy thesis. The oxcarts were used to transport coffee and other agricultural products and the bright colors reflect the lush flora inspiring these hard-working people in their land of plenty.

These images are powerful in that they validate the choices that artisans make and the policies that the state chooses to deploy in their support (and in support of itself through the success of these artisans). Marc Edelman and Mitchell A. Seligson (1994) argued that the agrarian democracy thesis overstates the initial conditions found in Costa Rica, yet the historical validity of the narrative matters less than the belief and its visible manifestation in everyday life.

The second public narrative that persists is that of Costa Rica as a white, European country situated in the middle of Central America. Indeed, U.S. President Taft validated the myth when he famously referred to Costa Rica as the Switzerland of Central America: a stable, social democracy that remained neutral when its neighbors quarreled. With Taft's declaration, the world audience of nations had recognized Costa Rica to be just like a European nation. And under General Tomás Guardia's administration (1870-1882), policies were implemented to make the myth accord more closely with reality. Drawing inspiration from the characters of Greco-Roman mythology, Guardia and his followers became known as "The Olympians." They envisioned a racially pure (white) nation and aspired to civilization's highest standards of secular education, hygiene, science, and patriotism (Molina and Palmer 1990, 65-66). Although the Costa Rican state took antiracist positions in the United Nations, its municipal governments practiced widespread racial discrimination against those lacking *piel claro*, light-complexioned skin (Bourgois 1986; Harpelle 1993; Purcell and Sawyers 1993). The state's self-image as an enlightened nation precluded promoting sectors of the economy or elements of cultural life that might have drawn the attention of outsiders (or of Costa Rican citizens, for that matter) to the exotic or indigenous elements of the past; this included the promotion of cultural tourism and the development of the ethnic handicraft market.

Costa Rica's public narratives obfuscated its indigenous cultures. The narratives emphasized how business people within and outside of the nation-state framed their evaluations of the cultural goods therein produced. Margaret Somers and Fred Block (2005) highlighted the importance of public narratives in their study of government policies and the principles justifying them: "Every nation has a story—a public narrative it tells to explain its place . . . in the flow of history, to justify its normative principles, to delineate the boundaries of rational political decision-making, and to give meaning to its economic policies and practices" (p. 280). These narratives matter for the local promotion and export strategies of nation-states as well as for local entrepreneurs trying to discern what dramaturgical parts their enterprises might plausibly play. The plausibility of their economic roles in the global economy is ideationally embedded.

Economic Logics Framed by Public Narratives

Macroeconomic changes in the economy spur reactions from the nation-state, private industry, and private citizens in their efforts to fend off threats and to take advantage of opportunities. However, how actors and institutions make sense of their maneuvers and how this sense-making informs the goals they pursue and the means of pursuit are the processes of ideational embeddedness. Therefore, we will review the economic history of Costa Rica to identify how the Costa Rican government relied on its public narratives to choose, confer sense, and describe the elements within its territories susceptible of being considered valuable for the type of place that Costa Rica is. In other words, the stocks and beauty of indigenous crafts in Costa Rica's Nicoya peninsula were not reason enough for their export promotion in the eyes of the state. The Costa Rican state pursued economic strategies framed by its public narratives of social democracy, its cultural similarities to Western European norms and practices, and its obligations to and affinities with the international financial institutions. In the rush to leave the reputation of backwardness behind, Costa Rica did what it could to become a fully industrialized country in both a material and ideational sense.

To leave the (accusation of) backwardness behind, in 1963 Costa Rica joined the Central American Common Market (CACM), which imposed high tariffs on goods coming from outside of Central America but low ones on goods produced and sold within the region. As part of the import substitution industrialization (ISI) strategy, government incentives and import duties created a greenhouse to promote local industries while protecting them from competition. As developed by Raúl Prebisch at the Latin American Economic Commission (ECLAC), the ISI strategy would speed the country's approach to industrialization.

Reaping the benefits of readily available loans from international finance institutions and of 1977 coffee prices on the world market that stood at four times their 1975 levels, the Costa Rican state offered a win-win solution for exporters and workers. Agricultural exporters who feared the volatility of the market for their products were happy to diversify their economic base. Moving into other export markets and becoming more integrated with their neighboring countries lessened their risks and increased their payoffs for market participation. Workers were happy because the state employed a fifth of the workforce and produced nearly a quarter of all goods and services (Edelman 1985, 38). The country would soon learn that it was skating on thin ice.

In 1979, Costa Rica was jolted for a second time in that decade by an oil price hike. Two years later, Costa Rica defaulted on its debt. A year later, so did Mexico. After Mexico coughed, so to speak, the rest of Latin America caught the cold. In the meantime, the military struggles within the Central American isthmus undermined the cooperative trade agreements among the Central American states by restricting the movement of goods, services, and capital (Fallas Venegas 1989). Strapped with a large debt and lacking enough buyers in the world market able to pay for Costa Rican products, the neoliberal factions within the country declared the social democracy over. The neoliberal technocrats tried to convince the electorate that Costa Rica's domestic policies were governed from without. If the country's international economic position was weak, the state lacked the funds to implement social legislation. With state funds growing scarcer, it was time to dismantle the as much of the welfare state as institutional inertia would allow.

By 1982, inflation was nearly 100 percent and the currency devaluation was 450 percent compared to 1980 levels. The nation's 3 percent GDP growth in 1978 fell to a nadir of –9.8 percent four years later (Edelman 1985, 40). Meanwhile, "the cost of servicing the debt had risen from a manageable US$60 million in

1977 to US$510 million in 1982" (Wilson 1998, 153). Costa Rica had no choice but to turn to the International Monetary Fund (IMF).

Costa Rica appealed to the IMF for a bailout loan in 1981. In return for the bailout, the government agreed to devalue its currency, decrease spending on social programs, remove price controls, reform the tax code, and increase tax collections. The conditions of the loan exceeded the expectations of the Costa Rican electorate. President Carazo "expelled the IMF's Costa Rica mission, stating that given the choice 'between eating and paying the external debt, we cannot accept anything other than the first option' " (Carazo Odio 1989, 392, quoted in Wilson 1998, 105).

Carazo's position was untenable. Without loans from the international financial institutions, the government fell apart. In 1982, Luis Alberto Monge took control, imposing the orthodox economic stabilization measures required by the IMF. With external loans now flowing into the government's coffers and with the approval of the core countries, Monge saw results. The fiscal deficit fell from 17.4 percent in 1980 to 14 percent in 1981. Costa Rica's GDP grew by 7 percent in 1984 (Wilson 1998, 116).

The country's import substitution strategy had exhausted its possibilities. To revive Costa Rica's economic health, the nation turned to export-oriented industrialization. In the early 1990s, export promotion in Costa Rica relied on three policy regimes: export-processing zones (EPZs), drawbacks, and export contracts. The EPZs were located in nine sites across Costa Rica. Within the zone, a firm could import and export financial capital as well as industrial inputs without paying customs duties. With approval, these firms could also sell up to 40 percent of their products in local markets. There are no requirements for local inputs or for national value-added imports (Clark 1995). The working conditions within these processing zones have deteriorated, rendering them almost indistinguishable from the wage and working conditions in the informal economy (Peréz-Sáinz 1996).

These export regimes affected state-society coalitions by strengthening some civil society groups while debilitating others. A significant group within the upper classes favored the neoliberal turn. They hoped that their products would find lucrative foreign markets. They also disparaged the growing public sector. Ironically, those industrialists who had benefited from the special protections of the ISI platform identified with the upper classes, who were most likely to benefit from laissez-faire trade.

The irony did not end there. José María Figueres, the president from 1994 to 1998 and the opponent of market-driven policies, soon learned the limits of state sovereignty. Although his Liberation Party (PLN) won the elections based on his opposition to the IMF–World Bank austerity measures, he could not obtain loans from international lenders after taking office. After public opinion turned against Figueres, he struck a deal with Rafael Calderon, the former president and leader of the conservative Christian Socialists Party. On April 28, 1995, Figueres and Calderon signed a pact that would reduce the government deficit, eliminate some social services, deregulate the market, and privatize some state-run industries. The

Calderon-Figueres pact dismantled the apparatus on which the poor had heavily relied and created a new set of economic opportunities.

The benefits of economic openness showed themselves with the advent of Intel. Instead of relying on low-cost labor (with which Costa Rica could not compete in the global economy), the national economy turned to the more lucrative knowledge economy. In 1997, Intel (the computer microprocessor producer) did not have a plant in Costa Rica, and textile exports accounted for the lion's share of exports at US$788 million, with bananas and coffee trailing at US$560 and US$391 million, respectively. Two years later, Intel accounted for "8 percent of Costa Rica's GDP and about 40 percent of the country's export value" (Luxner 2000, 3). In 1999, Intel's microchips surpassed by almost 100 percent the export value of textiles, bananas, and coffee combined. And in 1998 and 1999, Costa Rica's GDP growth increased to 8 and 8.3 percent compared with the average for Latin America of 2.3 and 0.3 years in the same time period. Intel accounted for 3.5 percent of GDP and almost 40 percent of exports in 2000 (Swenson 2001, 45). When Intel entered Costa Rica, the country's position in the global economy fundamentally changed.

In addition to becoming a knowledge economy, Costa Rica had already transformed itself into a tourist economy. While the 1990s saw the decline of low-cost manufacturing jobs, it also witnessed the creation of new economic opportunities in tourism. With the few financial resources the state had at its disposal, it could promote tourism by simply offering tax breaks to tour operators within the country. Before the 1990s, Costa Rica was not well known as a major vacation spot. It had retained its reputation from the colonial days as a country whose resources belied its name: there was no gold and there were indigenous peoples populating the territory.

The increased tourism of the 1990s brought the state into contact with travelers who brought in money along with preconceived notions about the environmental (primarily) and cultural (secondarily) riches the country held. Tourism brought in US$600 million in foreign exchange in 1995. Between 1984 and 1994, tourism increased by 178 percent. Over that ten-year period, North American tourists increased from 88,360 to 332,602 persons, representing a 276 percent increase (Costa Rican Tourism Board 2000). Tourism became a mainstay of the economy. In 1991 the revenue from tourism accounted for nearly one-fifth of the value generated by exports. While the tourism sector declined relative to other exports with the advent of Intel, the total revenues garnered by the tourism sector continued to climb. By 1999 tourism generated $US917 million. In the Institute for Costa Rican Tourism's survey of 1500 international tourists to Costa Rica in 1999, a significant proportion of tourists came to enjoy the beaches or to engage in ecotourism, but the survey neither found nor inquired about tourists coming to see cultural heritage sites or to visit folk and indigenous handicraft artisans (Costa Rican Tourism Board 2000). The potential for Costa Rican handicraft artisans to enter global markets has been limited by the state's inability to see them as legitimate competitors in the (modern) global market. The state sees itself promoting industries that might have a comparative advantage in the global market but the state does not recognize the latent function that participation in the global market serves—to distinguish the nation as modern, progressive, and progressing.

If the presence of material culture were sufficient for a state to promote cultural commodities, Costa Rica would be well known for its indigenous crafts. In the late 1800s, Costa Rica demonstrated that it possesses stocks of material culture when it participated in the World's Fair. Then a leader in material culture, the country now has transformed itself into a "green" leader with environmental riches. The state's political and economic history helps us better understand why a reputation for indigenous cultures did not take hold.

Exotic traditions are de-emphasized as the state highlights its movement from its traditional roots into its proper place as a modern, enlightened society.

An Assimilated Identity

In the case of Costa Rica, the assimilated orientation leads states to mimic the cultural institutions found in core countries. Exotic traditions are de-emphasized as the state highlights its movement from its traditional roots into its proper place as a modern, enlightened society. The museums, schools, and tourism organizations do not highlight indigenous groups or local traditions that appear to be backward or, in some other way, embarrassing. As Bourdieu (1990) rightly pointed out, being in the position to act must be coupled with having the disposition to act in a particular way; if the markets are relatively free but the disposition of nation-states and entrepreneurs are so disinclined, cultural goods that might be lucrative are not likely to be exported and the unassuming audience for such goods will not be ready or willing to consume. Such orientations may work well for countries in the core of the world system that are relatively wealthy, with a diversified economy, and with a great deal of political autonomy from external dictates. More diversified economies have positive spillovers in shipping and in communications technologies that aid cultural industries in distributing their products. Such countries also have a "business reputation" for reliability and a "cultural reputation" that is widely recognized. However, countries in the periphery and in the semiperiphery find themselves engaged in ideological battles about their intrinsic cultural wealth. These structural positions of advantage or disadvantage interact with the orientation of nation-states to structure the opportunities available in the handicraft market.

Conclusions: Forces and Frames in Global Cultural Markets

The state's orientation toward indigenous cultures changes over time, and it may arise from the same set of circumstances that lead the state to promote indigenous cultural industries. In other words, changes in the global economy (material conditions) might unleash new opportunities for cultural industries by providing a ready set of consumers for the product while making it more difficult for producers in other sectors of the economy to survive. The state simply abandons the losing horse for the winning one. If this were the only explanation, we would return to the truism: the most creative countries succeed in the creative sectors of the economy. Similarly, path dependency arguments would note the cumulative advantages of already operating in the creative economy where a country's entrepreneurs have already learned the ropes and built the right connections with distributors around the globe. To account for these competing explanations, one would need more comparative cases to see whether the state's orientation toward cultural heritage preceded the state's promotion of cultural commodity exports, all other things being equal. One would also have to account for negative evidence: What happens when one sees an acculturated state ignore opportunities in the cultural economy? Would such a state be said to lack the pertinent evidence for promoting the sector? Would such a state simply lack the organizational capacity to do what it would have done otherwise? Such questions themselves warn of the circular reasoning that one's commitment to a particular theory can bring about. What this article has done is to take a clear-cut case of the state's orientation toward culture as an ideal type for building a theory about the likelihood of the state supporting some types of cultural commodity exports over other available ones.

This article has explored the historical construction of the impressions that Western buyers as well as Costa Rican citizens have about their country's cultural character. These definitions of the situation orient the course of the country's economic development and reinforce the other sources of state power. In the Costa Rican case, I have argued that the government's fear of being associated with a stigmatized identity has sometimes diverted economic development energies away from those stocks of symbolic capital associated with indigenous peoples that might have been easily appropriated. Therefore, to understand the success of artisans in global markets, it is not enough to think about the individual qualities of the artisans or of the particular cultural contributions of their group to world culture; one must also think about the public culture that makes the promotion of particular cultural sectors of the economy thinkable. How a nation's identity is framed affects the likelihood that capital, labor, and knowledge will be mobilized in the service of particular cultural and noncultural productions.

References

Alexander, Jennifer, and Paul. Alexander. 2000. From kinship to contract? Production chains in the Javanese woodworking industries. *Human Organization* 59:106-16.

Allen, Rob. 1983. The myth of a redundant craft: Potters in Northern Nigeria. *Journal of Modern African Studies* 21:159-66.

Bandelj, N. 2002. Embedded economies: Social relations as determinants of foreign direct investment in Central and Eastern Europe. *Social Forces* 81:411-44.

Biesanz, Mavis Hiltunen, Richard Biesanz, and Karen Zubris Biesanz. 1999. *The Ticos: Culture and social change in Costa Rica*. Boulder, CO: Lynne Rienner.

Biggart, Nicole Woolsey, and Mauro F Guillén. 1999. Developing difference: Social organization and the rise of the auto industries of South Korea, Taiwan, Spain, and Argentina. *American Sociological Review* 64:722-47.

Biggart, Nicole W., and Mark Orrú. 1997. Societal strategic advantage: Institutional structure and path dependence in the automotive and electronics industries of East Asia. In *State, market, and organizational form*, ed. A. Bugra and B. Usdiken, 201-39. Berlin: Walter de Gruyter.

Bourdieu, Pierre. 1990. *The logic of practice*. Cambridge, UK: Polity Press in association with Basil Blackwell.

Bourgois, Philippe. 1986. The black diaspora in Costa Rica: Upward mobility and ethnic discrimination. *New West Indian Guide* 60:149-66.

Breckenridge, Carol A. 1989. The aesthetics and politics of colonial collecting: India at world fairs. *Comparative Studies in Society and History* 31:195-216.

Carruthers, David V. 2001. The politics and ecology of indigenous folk art in Mexico. *Human Organization* 60:356-66.

Causey, Andrew. 2003. *Hard bargaining in Sumatra: Western travelers and Toba Bataks in the marketplace of souvenirs*. Honolulu: University of Hawaii Press.

Chalfin, Brenda. 2004. *Shea butter republic: State power, global markets, and the making of an indigenous commodity*. New York: Routledge.

Clark, Mary A. 1995. Nontraditional export promotion in Costa Rica: Sustaining export-led growth. *Journal of Inter-American Studies and World Affairs* 37:181-223.

Cohen, Jeffrey H. 1998. Craft production and the challenge of the global market: An artisans' cooperative in Oaxaca, Mexico. *Human Organization* 57:74-82.

Colloredo-Mansfeld, Rudi. 2002. An ethnography of neoliberalism: Understanding competition in artisan economies. *Current Anthropology* 43:113-37.

Corrales Ulloa, Francisco. 2002. *Los Primeros Costarricenses*. San José: Museo Nacional de Costa Rica.

Costa Rican Tourism Board. 2000. *Costa Rica: Ingresos por Turismo*. San José, Costa Rica: Imprenta Nacional.

Creamer, Winifred. 1987. Mesoamerica as a concept: An archaeological view from Central America. *Latin American Research Review* 22:35-62.

de Peralta, Manuel M., and D. Anastasio Alfaro. 1893. Etnología Centro-Americana catálago razonado de los objetos arquelógicos de la República de Costa Rica en la Exposición Histórica Americana de Madrid—1892. In *The World's Fair, being a pictorial history of the Columbian Exposition with a description of Chicago*, ed. W. E. Cameron. Boston: MacConnell Brothers & Co.

Edelman, Marc. 1985. Back from the brink. *NACLA Report on the Americas* 19:3.

Edelman, Marc, and Mitchell A. Seligson. 1994. Land indequality: A comparison of census data and property records in twentieth-century southern Costa Rica. *Hispanic American Historical Review* 74:445-91.

Fallas Venegas, Helio. 1989. Economic crisis and social transformation in Costa Rica. In *The Costa Rican reader*, ed. M. Edelman and J. Kenen, 193-97. New York: Grove Weidenfeld.

García Canclini, Nestor. 1990. *Culturas híbridas: estrategias para entrar y salir de la modernidad*. Mexico, D.F.: Grijalbo: Consejo Nacional para la Cultura y las Artes.

Garfinkel, Harold. 1967. *Studies in ethnomethodology*. Englewood Cliffs, NJ: Prentice Hall.

Goffman, Erving. 1959. *The presentation of self in everyday life*. Garden City, NY: Doubleday.

Graburn, Nelson H. H. 1976. *Ethnic and tourist arts: Cultural expressions from the fourth world*. Berkeley: University of California Press.

Harpelle, Ronald N. 1993. The social and political integration of West Indians in Costa Rica, 1930-1950. *Journal of Latin American Studies* 25:103-20.

Hough, Walter. 1893. The ancient Central and South American pottery in the Columbina Historical Exhibition at Madrid in 1892. In *The World's Fair, being a pictorial history of the Columbian Exposition with a description of Chicago*, ed. W. E. Cameron. Boston: MacConnell Brothers & Co.

Karp, Ivan, and Steven Lavine. 1991. *Exhibiting cultures: The poetics and politics of museum display.* Washington, DC: Smithsonian Institution Press.

Kyle, David. 2000. *Transnational peasants: Migrations, networks, and ethnicity in Andean Ecuador.* Baltimore: Johns Hopkins University Press.

Lines, José A. 1978. Distribución racial. *Esbozo Arqueologico de Costa Rica* 24:217-22.

Little, Walter E. 2002. Selling strategies and social relations among mobile Maya handicrafts vendors. *Research in Economic Anthropology* 21:61-95.

Lowe, Gareth W. 1989. The heartland Oec: Evolution of material culture. In *Regional perspectives on the Olmec*, ed. R. J. Sharer, 33-67. New York: Cambridge University Press.

Luxner, Larry. 2000. Microchips with macro power. *Américas ¡Ojo!* 52 (November): 3-4.

Meisch, Lynn. 2002. *Andean entrepreneurs: Otavalo merchants and musicians in the global arena.* Austin: University of Texas Press.

Mitchell, Timothy. 1989. The world as exhibition. *Comparative Studies in Society and History* 31:217-36.

Molina, Ivan, and Steven Palmer. 1990. *The history of Costa Rica.* San José: Editorial de la Universidad de Costa Rica.

Peréz-Sáinz, Juan Pablo. 1996. *Neoinformalidid en Centroamérica.* San José, Costa Rica: FLACSO.

———. 1997. Guatemala: The two faces of the metropolitan area. In *The urban Caribbean: Transition to the new global economy*, ed. A. Portes, C. Dore-Cabral, and P. Landolt. 124-51. Baltimore: Johns Hopkins University Press.

Peréz-Sáinz, Juan Pablo, and Katharine Andrade-Eekhoff. 2003. *Communities in globalization: The invisible Mayan Nahual.* Lanham, MD: Rowman & Littlefield.

Pohorilenko, Anatole. 1981. The Olmec style and Costa Rican archaeology. In *The Olmec and their neighbors: Essays in memory of Matthew W. Stirling*, ed. E. P. Benson, 309-27. Washington, DC: Dumbarton Oaks Research Library and Collections.

Portes, Alejandro. 2006. Institutions and development: A conceptual reanalysis. *Population and Development Review* 32:233-62.

Powell, Walter W., and Paul DiMaggio. 1991. *The new institutionalism in organizational analysis.* Chicago: University of Chicago Press.

Purcell, Trevor, and Kathleen Sawyers. 1993. Democracy and ethnic conflict: Blacks in Costa Rica. *Ethnic and Racial Studies* 16:298-322.

Rovine, Victoria. 2001. *Bogolan: Shaping culture through cloth in contemporary Mali.* Washington, DC: Smithsonian Institution Press.

Scott, John F. 1999. *Latin American art: Ancient to modern.* Gainesville: University of Florida Press.

Sharer, Robert J. 1989. The Olmec and the southeast periphery of Mesoamerica. In *Regional perspectives on the Olmec*, ed. R. J. Sharer and D. C. Grove, 247-71. Cambridge: Cambridge University Press.

Somers, Margaret R., and Fred Block. 2005. From poverty to perversity: Ideas, markets and institutions over 200 years of welfare debate. *American Sociological Review* 70:260-87.

Soustelle, Jacques. 1984. *The Olmecs: The oldest civilization in Mexico.* Garden City, NY: Doubleday.

Swenson, James. 2001. A central American standout. *LatinFinance*, July, p. 45.

Swidler, Ann. 1986. Culture in action: Symbols and strategies. *American Sociological Review* 51:273-86.

Tenorio Alfaro, Luis Alberto. 1988. *Reservas Indígenas de Costa Rica.* San José, Costa Rica: Comisión Nacional de Asuntos Indígenas.

United Nations World Tourism Organization (UNWTO). 2005. *World tourism: Highlights.* Madrid, Spain: UNWTO.

Weber, Max. 1914/1978. *Economy and society: An outline of interpretive sociology.* Edited by Guenther Roth and Claus Wittich. Berkeley: University of California Press.

Wherry, Frederick F. 2006. The nation-state, identity management, and indigenous crafts: Constructing markets and opportunities in Northwest Costa Rica. *Ethnic and Racial Studies* 29:124-52.

Wilson, Bruce M. 1998. *Costa Rica: Politics, economics, and democracy.* Boulder, CO: Lynne Rienner.

Zelizer, Viviana A. 2005. Circuits within capitalism. In *The economic sociology of capitalism*, ed. V. Nee and R. Swedberg, 289-322. Princeton, NJ: Princeton University Press.

Globalizing Restricted and Segmented Markets: Challenges to Theory and Values in Economic Sociology

By
DONALD W. LIGHT

Studies of globalization and immigration will benefit by taking into account the relationship between goals, means, and outcomes. In this article, the author introduces the term *pernicious competition* as an alternative to the better known concept of *market failure* to more accurately describe what happens when vital human needs are not efficiently met as a result of global competition. The extended protections of intellectual property in new free trade agreements are an example of market segmentation being used to raise the prices of and reduce access to vital drugs for treating patients with HIV-AIDS. Vital public goods and services should be made distinct from technical public goods so that the dangers of pernicious competition in markets that benefit dominant suppliers or buyers can be identified and the concept of a moral economy can be developed.

Keywords: economic sociology; globalization; public goods; markets; market ethics; HIV-AIDS; CAFTA

The efforts by the world's most powerful corporations to develop global markets have spawned a substantial sociological and economic literature on how transnational markets form, what stages characterize market development, and what rules of exchange are most effective. As the authors of a prominent article put it, "The central question is . . . what kinds of rules and structures promote market activity and what kinds stifle it" (Fligstein and Stone Sweet 2002, 1212). That question, however, assumes that market activity is, in general, socially beneficial

Donald W. Light has been a collaborating researcher with Alejandro Portes at the Center for Migration and Development and a fellow at the Netherlands Institute for Advanced Study in 2006-2007. He is a sociologist and professor of comparative health care at the University of Medicine and Dentistry of New Jersey. This article is part of a set on myths and injustices in international trade.

NOTE: Special thanks to Alejandro Portes and Patricia Fernández-Kelly for supporting this work at the Center for Migration and Development at Princeton University.

DOI: 10.1177/0002716206296960

and that more market activity is even more advantageous as part of the grand globalization blueprint for a better society.

Nevertheless, as Robert K. Merton (1936) observed in the inaugural volume of the *American Sociological Review*, a preoccupation with immediate intended goal(s) may create a blindness to wider, secondary, or further consequences, which may have greater impact than the actors' stated goal. Adam Smith (1791/1896) argued famously that each individual's striving to maximize personal gain will maximize the wealth of everyone "by an invisible hand to promote an end which was no part of his intention." Quite a different unanticipated consequence of individuals striving to maximize gain can occur when a viable export market is created for grain in a low-income country: farmers sell their crops to exporters and domestic famine results (Sen 1981).

Blindness to unanticipated consequences can also result from strongly held convictions and unexamined beliefs, for example, that the globalization of markets is inherently good and benefits all parties.

Blindness to unanticipated consequences can also result from strongly held convictions and unexamined beliefs, for example, that the globalization of markets is inherently good and benefits all parties. Such widespread understandings may not be warranted. Over the past two decades, the growing integration of markets on a world scale and the parallel implementation of neoliberal economic policies have had uneven effects. Robert Wade (2004) at the London School of Economics has reviewed the evidence and concluded that the growth rate of global gross domestic product (GDP) dropped sharply during the 1980s and again in the 1990s. Although there are disputes about the data used by Wade, it appears that the number of people living in extreme poverty has increased recently, and world income distribution has become more unequal. The absolute income gap between the lowest and highest deciles has also widened considerably. Wade offers a detailed explanation of how the World Bank changed measures and calculations to "prove" that its convictions about competition and benefits resulting from globalization were accurate. This is not solely a matter of perspective; the World Bank case shows that consequences cannot only be unanticipated but also denied or buried.

Merton (1936) identified several other factors that merit consideration in research on a topic such as globalization. One should not assume that actions are clearly purposive, for often the aims are "nebulous and hazy." There is the further problem of differentiating between rhetorical purpose and actual goals, a distinction made still more complex by ex post facto rationalizations after unanticipated consequences occur to make them appear intended. Nor should one assume that consequences are clear, for they are affected by the interplay of the action, the objective situation, and the conditions of action. Even when clear, unanticipated consequences are not necessarily undesirable. Actions can lead to fortuitous results as well.

The conceptual model advanced by Merton (1936) pointed out that different consequences may be reasonably inferred from a situation and a given action. Two other factors that can contribute to not seeing the outcomes of particular policies are limited knowledge and error. Both can lead to accidental effects and both can then lead to ex post facto rationalization to cover up or explain away limited information or mistakes. Finally, a policy and its predicted consequences can become new factors that influence how others act and how the policy's implementation affects its intended consequences.

Alejandro Portes (2000) has extended Merton's analytic framework in valuable ways. First, he introduced the concept of *hidden abode* to designate concealed goals about which social actors may have various levels of awareness. The concept echoes earlier conceptualizations by Antonio Gramsci and Pierre Bourdieu, authors who gave attention to the elusive character of consciousness and the habitual nature of experience. Humans, it appears, find it difficult to identify true motives and objectives. In the case of globalization and the diffusion of neoliberal policies, many advocates point to widespread benefits while holding self interest as a tacit priority.

The hidden abode of concealed goals has also played a central role in globalization and immigration policies because so much deliberation is conducted behind closed doors, and communication about decisions reached is so closely controlled. Secretiveness has been at play in fostering distrust and policy impasse. Thus, even where there is no hidden agenda, the lack of trust among observers and the public at large can change the relationship between policy and outcome.

Second, policies may have latent functions in producing results other than what actors intended, or they may serve alternative and covert purposes. Principal among these is the latent function of purposive action in ordering the world to serve the interests of dominant political and economic groups. The history of the globalization movement provides evidence that one of the aims was to reorder markets and trading rules to benefit global corporations that were running out of markets (Drahos and Braithwaite 2002; Sell 1998, 2003). Portes (2000) observes that the resulting outcome of a given purposive action may emerge from revisions, concessions, and improvisations of means and thus be different from the initial goal. This ironic turn of events seems particularly important to globalization studies—goals may be achieved through improvisation and a lucky turn of events.

Merton's and Portes's contributions to the study of the relationship between goals, means, and outcomes are relevant to the research on international economic and immigration policies. For example, contrary to its explicit mandate, the North American Free Trade Agreement (NAFTA) did not open labor markets; instead it segmented them, with surprising and sometimes deleterious effects (Massey, Durand, and Malone 2002). More widely, globalizing trade agreements, structured largely around the interests of large corporations, have had the inadvertent side effect of eliminating jobs, increasing unemployment, fomenting inequality, stirring crime, and weakening the capacity of small businesses to participate in international markets (Portes and Roberts 2005).

In markets dominated by products protected by patents and copyrights, globalization has meant requiring all participating nations to accept the longest and strongest patent and copyright protections from free market price competition, usually many years longer and demanding than necessary to make a profit (Drahos and Braithwaite 2002; Sell 1998, 2003). This forestalls competition. That is, whether acknowledged or concealed, a major goal of globalization from the start has been to universalize highly *restricted* markets in which suppliers control the prices and terms of trade. In the case of drugs for AIDS, cancer, and other life-threatening illnesses, access on the part of needy populations is put in jeopardy. This darker side of the so-called free market (which can never be free of rules, procedures, and structures) requires a more complete research agenda aimed at analyzing both the manifest and latent terms and structures that promote market activity and also the consequences for all parties affected.

Pernicious Competition and Globalization

One impediment to good theory and research is using terms like *market, capital, property,* and *competition* uncritically, as if they were natural and obvious. The term *competition,* for example, embodies the radical proposition that if all parties pursue their own best interests, the results will benefit everyone, and the wealth of nations will increase. As used by many economic sociologists and economists, market competition tacitly assumes that it is beneficial. In the neoclassical economics framework, markets self-regulate and tend toward equilibrium, balancing out the interests of buyers and sellers. Interferences—for example, cumbersome government regulations or other mechanisms impeding competition—produce market failure. In that framework, disparities in the access to goods and services are explained as the result of insufficient information, limited competitive capacity, or external market disruptions.

Competition, however, can only benefit society under strict conditions designed to limit the clever, untrustworthy actions of opportunistic individuals and channel them to the benefit of others (Hsiao 1995; Light 2000; Rice 2003). There must be many buyers and sellers whose relations are independent from one another so that market transactions cannot be influenced by one or more

TABLE 1
STRUCTURAL AND ORGANIZATIONAL CONDITIONS FOR
BENEFICIAL AND PERNICIOUS COMPETITION

Beneficial Competition	"Market Failure" as Pernicious Competition
Buyers: sovereign, maximize clear preferences using good info, shop frequently	Buyers: embedded in relations, mixed preferences, partial info, shop infrequently
Product or service sought is clear	Product or service sought is unclear
Prices clear, known in advance	Product or service sought is unclear
Free, accessible information on features, limitations, or dangers	Partial, incomplete, garbled, or unreliable information
Information is free, easy to get	Information is costly, difficult to obtain
Many buyers and sellers	Few buyers and/or sellers
No relation to each other	Historical, cultural relations, overt or covert
Can purchase from full array of providers	Purchase from limited array
No barriers to entry or exit	Barriers to entry and exit
Market signals quick; markets clear quickly	Market signals and change are slow, muddled
No externalities. No harms (or benefits) to other parts of society not captured in market transactions.	Externalities, often by design, in the market, services or products.

parties to the detriment of others. Information on everything buyers need to know to buy smart and drive the value chain must be complete and free. Transactions must clear quickly. Easy entry of new competitors and prompt exit of unsuccessful competitors are essential. Perhaps the most important require-ment pertinent to promoting humane societies is that there are no externalities, an economic term that may be defined as effects on groups, organizations, insti-tutions, or the environment not specifically part of what is being bought, sold, or contracted for. Even if all these conditions are met (and they usually are not), caveat emptor rules the market, and competitive actions require constant moni-toring. Pursuing self-interests also fosters distrust, exacerbates inequalities, and dismantles communities.

When one or more of the strict conditions is not met for competition that ben-efits society as a whole, economists invoke market failure. Yet market failure is not like engine failure. The market does not sputter and roll to the side of the road. Rather, it roars ahead, with sellers able to exploit buyers and consumers. I sug-gest that this process be labeled *pernicious competition* and that we undertake empirical research on its macro and micro forms. Table 1 identifies ten condi-tions pertaining to beneficial and pernicious competition. That synthesis can pro-vide a research framework for measuring the structural specificities of each condition and its effect on all relevant parties in different domains of globalization, particularly with respect to externalities such as the family and economic security.

[M]arket failure is not like engine failure. The market does not sputter and roll to the side of the road. Rather, it roars ahead, with sellers able to exploit buyers and consumers.

Research on the externalities of globalization would provide the kind of holistic assessment necessary for truly beneficial economic policies to develop. While advocates of globalization invoke the vision of beneficial competition and ostensibly seek to break down trade barriers, they often do so in ways that concentrate market power in the hands of large corporations and the governments beholden to them (Sell 2003; Stiglitz 2002). Thus, one must look quite concretely at *who benefits; who suffers; and how the fabric of family, community, and urban life are affected* when particular policies are applied. The central research question, then, is, "What kinds of rules and structures promote what kinds of market and organizational activities; and what effects do these have on parties affected by them?"

Let us consider, for example, the patenting of plant life and seeds that turns traditional practices—like saving seeds for next year's crops, creating hybrid plants to improve crops, and exchanging plants and seeds, that is, behaviors that farmers throughout the world have been relying on for thousands of years—into illegal activities and forces them to buy seed every year at monopoly prices from one of the seven multinationals that have been rapidly patenting all crops (Barton and Berger 2001). Those corporations are integrating their global markets and expanding them within legally acquired rights that outlaw the local practices of family farmers (Bloque Popular Centroamericano, Alliance for Responsible Trade, and Hemispheric Social Alliance 2004). The resemblance of such practices to those that coincided with primitive accumulation in the early stages of capitalist development is inescapable (see Harvey 2007 [this volume]).

Likewise, free trade agreements that prohibit governments from using programs, laws, and support systems to preserve family farms in the name of free trade and integrated markets ignore both their extensive sociocultural benefits and the unequal terms on which agribusinesses compete with family farms (Galian 2004). Such new policies thus contribute to the expansion of a transnational ruling class (Robinson and Harris 2000).

FIGURE 1
GLOBALIZATION:
MAPPING INTEGRATION AND SEGMENTATION OF MARKETS

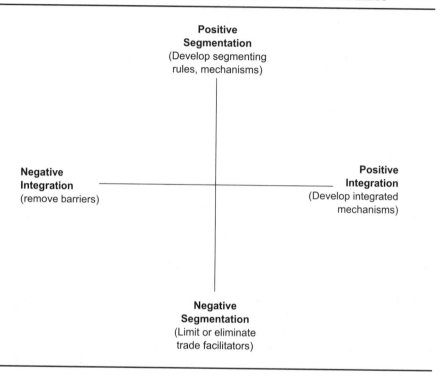

**Positive
Segmentation**
(Develop segmenting
rules, mechanisms)

**Negative
Integration**
(remove barriers)

**Positive
Integration**
(Develop integrated
mechanisms)

**Negative
Segmentation**
(Limit or eliminate
trade facilitators)

Globalizing Market Segmentation

Globalization research and theory must recognize that globalization entails not only negative and positive forms of market integration (Fligstein and Stone Sweet 2002; Scharpf 1996) but also negative and positive forms of market segmentation. Thus, if negative integration involves removing barriers, negative segmentation involves removing facilitators to freely traded goods. If positive integration refers to improving or creating enabling mechanisms, positive segmentation refers to improving or creating obstructing mechanisms. Figure 1 provides a visual space within which to consider various combinations when assessing a given set of market policies.

Examples of market segmentation and control by multinational corporations are the expanded terms for patents in the Central American Free Trade Agreement (CAFTA), one of several bilateral accords the U.S. government crafted after becoming frustrated with protests and concessions over its terms at global meetings, especially as they apply to seeds, agricultural pesticides and fertilizers, and prescription drugs (Sell 2003). First, the expanded regulations limit or eliminate existing conditions and practices that allow patent drugs at lower prices to be exported to the U.S. market or allow its trading partners to import cheaper versions from countries like India and Brazil that produce high-quality drugs at low cost. Besides creating a new ring of legal barriers to the free trade of patented drugs—similar to the way cell phones replete with patented features are freely traded—the new free trade agreements require countries to alter their price-setting boards for greater participation by drug companies. In other words, while the explicit objective of free trade agreements is to emancipate markets and foster competition, their hidden abode is geared to maintain a position of dominance even when competition is impeded.

Those trade agreements also extend protections from normal price competition beyond the twenty years of American patents. The champion of global free trade, Jagdish Bhagwati (2004, 184), bemoaned the protection that these patents extend as involving "a period so long that few economists of repute can be found who would call [such practices] efficient." The new round of U.S. free trade accords forces trading partners to charge their own patients and health care systems higher prices for several years longer (Public Citizen 2004; Shaffer and Brenner 2004). Extended periods of protection from free market price competition allow companies to fix or set prices when they otherwise could not. Thus, price fixing, which violates U.S. antitrust law, suddenly becomes lawful. Sociologists have missed this point when distinguishing between illicit and authorized means—powerful corporations can endeavor to change the law to make formerly illegal practices legal and the previously authorized practices of others illegal. In this case, the repercussions are extensive; they affect not just one country but all trading partners who are asked to sign a free trade agreement or face trade sanctions from the world's largest market.

My investigation into the new requirements to extend monopoly prices, inhibit international trade, and weaken the regulatory bodies that weigh public health needs in pricing drugs was prompted by alarms sounded by medical teams who treat patients with AIDS, cancer, and other deadly diseases (Medecins Sans Frontieres 2003). They petitioned and protested that if CAFTA were signed, vital drugs would no longer be affordable to those who most need them.

There are 1.9 million people living with HIV/AIDS in Latin America and the Caribbean. Competition from generic forms of patented drugs has reduced prices by 80 to 90 percent in countries where they have been allowed to flourish.[1] The most successful initiative to dispense medicines among needy patients affected with HIV/AIDS was implemented in Brazil; but had the current free trade agreement been in place, "it is doubtful that the program would ever have been possible and Brazil may not have been able to achieve its spectacular success: 90,000 AIDS deaths averted, 60,000 cases prevented, and 358,000 AIDS-related hospitalizations avoided between 1996 and 2002, leading to government savings of more than US$2 billion during the same period" (Medecins Sans Frontieres 2003, 8). As free trade agreements were being rolled out in 2002 and 2003, the AIDS group, Health GAP, wrote, "The new rules would far surpass the standard already established [for protecting IP rights of pharmaceutical companies] by the World Trade Organization's Agreement on Trade-Related Aspects of Intellectual Property Rights (TRIPS)" (Health GAP 2003).

To summarize, the new free trade accords institute "rules and structures [to] promote market activity" (to quote Fligstein and Stone Sweet [2002] again) that in the case of prescription drugs force other (usually small) countries to replace their rules and structures designed to provide medical services for all in need to those designed to maximize profits of multi-billion-dollar pharmaceutical corporations backed up by the U.S. Congress. The ethical issues are substantial when the products involved are drugs for treating patients with cancer, diabetes or HIV-AIDS, and the prices in segmented markets can be fifty times greater than in the free trade market. For example, the price of AZT for AIDS patients in Central America under its new free trade agreement could rise from about $200 a year to $10,000 per patient-year (Medecins Sans Frontieres 2003).[2]

Is Market Segmentation of Patented Drugs Necessary?

Americans have been up in arms against the high prices they pay for patent-protected drugs, and they have been crossing borders or using the Internet to buy patented drugs more cheaply—free trade made illegal by the laws put in place. Their actions extend Albert Hirschman's (1970) concept in *Exit, Voice and Loyalty* in sociologically meaningful ways (Light et al. 2003). Industry leaders protest that such practices threaten their available assets for research to discover breakthrough new medicines to reverse disease and postpone death (Pharmaceutical Research and Manufacturers of America 1999). As Glaxo Smith Kline's motto puts it, "Today's medicines pay for tomorrow's miracles." Moved by such appeals, prominent government leaders such as the director of the Food and Drug Administration (FDA) and the under-secretary of commerce vigorously argued on behalf of the pharmaceutical industry that prices in other major research countries are too low to recover their huge research and development (R&D) investments. Such countries are thus envisioned as free riders that cause American prices to be higher. The logical conclusion of this fallacious argument is that free trade agreements are needed to force other nations to raise their prices toward American levels and to block patented drugs being exported at lower prices to the United States. Fairness, not profits, is the stated goal: to stop opportunistic free riders and make them pay their fair share.

Yet the best available evidence, including industry data, contradicts that rationale:

- European prices allow companies to recover all European R&D costs every year, with profits. There is no free riding nor any good evidence that lower European Union prices cause higher U.S. prices (Light and Lexchin 2005).
- Pharmaceutical R&D investments in Europe have been rising for years, not falling. European R&D is robust and discovers new drugs regularly.

- The free-riding argument makes no economic sense in the first place for products sold worldwide. It is an example of myth-making on an international scale.
- U.S. prices are higher just because they are allowed to be in price-protected U.S. markets, which industry advocates characterize as free markets. Uniquely, companies raise prices each year as new drugs get older.
- Drug companies average 12 percent of revenues for R&D, not 18 percent. Net of tax subsidies, the figure is about 7.4 percent, and about 1.3 percent of sales is budgeted for basic research to discover "tomorrow's miracles."
- Eighty-five to 89 percent of "new drugs" and "innovation" are judged to offer little or no therapeutic advantage over existing drugs. Drug companies are discovering very few breakthrough drugs.
- 84.2 percent of global funds for basic research to discover new drugs come from public sources (Light 2006). Global policy should capitalize on this, and markets for vital public goods need to be designed and promoted. (Here is a creative opportunity for economic sociologists.)

Alert readers will have noticed that the free-rider argument has little if anything to do with any country in Central America, or Latin America, or Africa, or Asia (save Japan), or Eastern Europe, because little R&D is done outside a small circle of affluent countries. Thus the unfair free-rider argument, although irrelevant for those countries, deflects the attention of Congress from the hidden goal of segmenting patented goods from free market competition and controlling their sale to maximize corporate price controls and profits.

The new techniques go well beyond patent rights for twenty years, and therefore I call them *techniques for exclusive market control*. Frederick M. Abbott (2004), a distinguished professor of international law, explained for the Friends World Committee at the Quaker United Nations Office, Frederick M. Abbott (2004), a distinguished professor of international law, how these techniques work. The terms inscribed in CAFTA force trading countries to give up the right to cheap versions of patented drugs "to protect public health" and "to promote access to medicines for all." Generic producers are prohibited for five years from using as part of their application the data gathered to get a patented drug initially approved, independent of when the patent expires, so that generic medicines are prohibited from being used even for public health services. "*A restriction on marketing approval becomes another form of monopoly, here granted in ways that the TRIPS Agreement does not require*" (p. 7, italics in original). Drug companies can register for market protection "a chemical entity that is quite old and well known, provided that it was not previously registered in that CAFTA Party" (p. 8). The net effect of these regulations "is to create a web of restrictions and uncertainties that will have a powerful chilling effect on . . . the introduction of third part (generic) medicines that are not under patent" (p. 9) because the rules for market approval enable drug companies to evergreen (continuously renew) their exclusive market control over price and sales. Sick patients will suffer and very sick patients will die; but that is an "externality" to market contracts.

An irony inherent in the conceptual observations by Merton (1936) and Portes (2000) about the relationships between goals, means, and outcomes is making international patents an exception to removing trade barriers by using globalization to raise and extend trade barriers. The champion of globalization, Jagdish Bhagwati (2004, 182-90), turns livid when he describes how pharmaceutical executives worked with U.S. government officials to force Mexico to agree to intellectual property protections (IPP) as a condition for their being admitted to the North American Free Trade Agreement. They then pressed to make the segmentation of markets for IPP products a pillar of the new World Trade Organization, thus "turning it away from its trade mission and rationale and transforming it into a royalty collection agency." Now, Bhagwati observes, every other special interest wants to have its privileged terms enforced by trade sanctions too. Except for the unique case of the EU as an integrated market, is market restriction and segmentation rather than integration a growing hidden abode of globalization as Bhagwati fears?

Reconceptualizing Public Goods and Services

Treating drugs for seriously ill patients as private goods and the object of market segmentation raises a deeper issue to which economic sociologists could contribute: what is a public good? The term has been defined by economists in a way that obscures—and even excludes—the deep moral nature of such a concept, concealing the ways in which such goods are socially constructed. As the *Encyclopedia from the Library of Economics and Liberty* explains, public goods, such as a fireworks display, cannot exclude nonpayers and can be enjoyed or consumed by anyone without reducing the consumption by others (Cowen 2006). The strong implication is that anything else without these two attributes of being nonexclusive and nonrivalrous is a private good. But what about goods and services, like essential medicines, that have neither of these technical qualities but are vital to the public? If they are not public goods but more than private goods, how shall we conceptualize them and name them?

A hidden goal of large corporations and conservatives behind globalization— even a requirement under World Trade Organization rules and governance—is to privatize public services and thus to open up huge new markets in privatized public services (Pollock and Price 2003). The term *public good* prevents us from having a word for goods and services deemed vital to a well-functioning and good society that are not technically what economists call public goods. Sociology can make a valuable contribution by doing research to show how most public goods and services are not inherently so but socially and culturally constructed realities adhering to norms and conventions shared, often informally, by the collectivity. Comparative and historical research can identify how different societies have defined and organized the same goods to have more or less of the technical attributes that economists claim are characteristic of public goods.

For example, streets are constructed as a public service, although they could be built as private causeways or toll roads. Parks too can be public, exclusively private, or accessible only to those who pay. In other words, societies make subtle distinctions between goods that must be shared by the many to promote efficiency and those that can be retained in the private domain to benefit only a few. Research on such distinctions should be complemented with studies of what goods and services are vital to a fair and just society, like the compelling case for universal health care, even when only a fraction of services can be characterized as public assets. Such vital goods and services usually do not meet the demanding requirements for beneficial competition, so that privatizing them produces unfree markets and pernicious competition. For these reasons, a new term is needed, *vital public goods and services*, as distinct from *technical* public goods and services.

Distinguishing between vital and technical public goods leads to a new sociological insight about the latter: they often are not *inherently* nonrivalrous and nonexclusive but socially and economically constructed to be so. A fireworks display can be in a stadium and not too high, or in the town square. Fire and police departments are often considered as examples of pure public goods.[3] But fire brigades used to work by private subscription, and private policing has a long history as well. Public schooling, much of sanitation, potable water, garbage collection, health care services, and certainly drugs are technically *not* public goods, except to the extent that they are socially designated by societies so that they work in nonexclusive, nonrivalrous ways. In the case of drugs, we might consider the carefully developed list of what the World Health Organization calls Essential Medicines as vital public goods, even though they are not technically public goods. This is but one illustration of how economic sociologists can use historical and culture frameworks to provide not only powerful assessments of hidden and latent aspects of globalization but also informed visions of what a good society and moral economy would look like (Bellah and Madsen 1991; Block 2006).

Notes

1. Readers may need a sense of proportion. Based on international data, it appears that a year's supply of AZT can be manufactured for $100. Although nearly all the research and development was paid for by the public, U.S. prices were launched at $10,000 or one hundred times cost and have been held to that level. Thus, a 90 percent discount is $1,000, ten times cost. This is not atypical. Common patented drugs priced at $5.00 each can be manufactured for $0.05 each at facilities that meet Food and Drug Administration (FDA) standards for quality.

2. Under years of protest and pressure against initial World Health Organization terms for intellectual property protections (IPP) products, concessions have been made when a country declares a public health crisis, though what constitutes such a crisis and how often exemptions would be made are unclear.

3. If critics argue that it is the fire, not the fire brigade, that is the "public good" because it can be contagious and ignite adjacent buildings, they run into analogous theoretical problems that reflect sociological realities. Would this argument mean that fires of homes in widely separated lots owned by the affluent are private goods because noncontagious, and should not be ministered by the town fire department?

References

Abbott, Frederick M. 2004. *The Doha Declaration on the TRIPS Agreement and Public Health and the contradictory trend in bilateral and regional free trade agreements*. Geneva, Switzerland: Friends World committee for Consultation (Quakers).

Barton, John H., and Peter Berger. 2001. Patenting agriculture. *Issues in Science and Technology* 17 (4): 43-50.

Bellah, Robert M., and R. Madsen. 1991. *The good society*. New York: Knopf.

Bhagwati, Jagdish. 2004. *In defense of globalization*. London: Oxford University Press.

Block, Fred. 2006. A moral economy. *The Nation*, March 20.

Bloque Popular Centroamericano, Alliance for Responsible Trade, and Hemispheric Social Alliance. 2004. *Why we say no to CAFTA*. Bloque Popular Centroamericano, Alliance for Responsible Trade, and Hemispheric Social Alliance.

Cowen, Tyler. 2006. *The concise encyclopedia of economics*. The Library of Economics and Liberty, http://www.econlib.org/library/ENC/PublicGoodsandExternalities.html.

Drahos, Peter, and John Braithwaite. 2002. Intellectual property, corporate strategy, globalisation: TRIPS in context. *Wisconsin International Law Journal* 20:451-80.

Fligstein, Neil, and Alec Stone Sweet. 2002. Constructing politics and markets: An institutional account of European integration. *American Journal of Sociology* 107:1206-43.

Galian, Carlos. 2004. *CAFTA: The nail in the coffin of Central American agriculture*. Washington, DC: Oxfam International.

Harvey, David. 2007. Neoliberalism as creative destruction. *Annals of the American Society of Political and Social Science* 610:22-44.

Health GAP. 2003. *The Central America Free Trade Agreement, access to AIDS medicines, and intellectual property*. New York: Health GAP (Global Access Project).

Hirschman, Albert O. 1970. *Exit, voice and loyalty: Responses to decline in firms, organizations and states*. Cambridge, MA: Harvard University Press.

Hsiao, William C. 1995. Abnormal economics in health sector. *Health Policy* 32:125-39.

Light, Donald. 2000. The sociological character of markets in health care. In *Handbook of social studies in health and medicine*, ed. G. Albrecht, R. Fitzpatrick, and S. C. Scrimshaw, 394-408. London: Sage.

———. 2006. Basic research funds to discover important new drugs: Who contributes how much? In *Monitoring the financial flows for health research 2005: Behind the global numbers*, ed. M. A. Burke, 27-43. Geneva, Switzerland: Global Forum for Health Research.

Light, Donald W., Ramon Castellblanch, Pablo Arrendondo, and Deborah Socolar. 2003. No exit and the organization of voice in biotechnology and pharmaceuticals. *Journal of Health Politics, Policy and Law* 28:473-507.

Light, Donald W., and Joel Lexchin. 2005. Foreign free riders and the high price of US medicines. *BMJ* 331:958-60.

Massey, Douglas S., Jorge Durand, and Nolan J. Malone. 2002. *Beyond smoke and mirrors*. New York: Russell Sage Foundation.

Medecins Sans Frontieres. 2003. *Trading away health: Intellectual property and access to medicines in the Free Trade Area of the Americas (FTAA) Agreement*. Paris: Medecins Sans Frontieres.

Merton, Robert K. 1936. The unanticipated consequences of purposive social action. *American Sociological Review* 1:894-904.

Pharmaceutical Research and Manufacturers of America (PhRMA). 1999. *Why do prescription drugs cost so much . . . and other questions about your medicine*. Washington, DC: PhRMA.

Pollock, Allyson M., and David Price. 2003. The public health implications of world trade negotiations on the general agreement on trade in services and public services. *Lancet* 362:1072-75.

Portes, Alejandro. 2000. The hidden abode: Sociology as analysis of the unexpected. *American Sociological Review* 65:1-18.

Portes, Alejandro, and Bryan R. Roberts. 2005. The free-market city: Latin American urbanization in the years of the neoliberal experiment. *Studies in Comparative International Development* 40:43-82.

Public Citizen. 2004. *CAFTA and access to medicine*. Washington DC: Public Citizen.

Rice, Thomas. 2003. *The health care of economics reconsidered*. Chicago: Health Administration Press.

Robinson, William I., and Jerry Harris. 2000. Towards a global ruling class? Globalization and the transnational capitalist class. *Science & Society* 64:11-54.

Scharpf, F. 1996. Negative and positive integration in the policy economy of European welfare states. In *Governance in the European Union*, ed. G. Marks, F. Scharpf, P. Schmitter, and W. Streeck. London: Sage.

Sell, Susan K. 1998. *Power and ideas: North-south politics of intellectual property*. Albany: State University of New York Press.

———. 2003. *Private power, public law*. New York: Cambridge University Press.

Sen, Amartya. 1981. *Poverty and famines*. New York: Oxford University Press.

Shaffer, Ellen R., and Joe Brenner. 2004. *The U.S.-Central American Free Trade Agreement*. Pp. 1-2. San Francisco: Center for Policy Analysis on Trade and Health (CPATH).

Smith, Adam. 1791/1896. *An inquiry into the nature and causes of the wealth of nations*. 6th ed. London: G. Bell & Sons.

Stiglitz, Joseph E. 2002. *Globalization and its discontents*. New York: Norton.

Wade, Robert Hunter. 2004. Is globalization reducing poverty and inequality? *World Development* 32:567-89.

From Managed to Free(r) Markets: Transnational and Regional Governance of Asian Timber

By
PAUL K. GELLERT

On the basis of research conducted in Indonesia, the author investigates a key transition in the production of timber for export. The analysis is based on a rich literature focusing on commodity chains. In addition to economic factors, the author gives attention to structures of governance, including the formation and dissolution of political alliances and coalitions. From the late 1980s through 1998, Indonesian plywood producers consolidated power in a state-supported domestic oligopoly, forged a transnational alliance that circumvented the power of Japanese trading houses, and supported domestic accumulation. The Asian crisis of 1997 to 1998 and structural adjustments imposed by the International Monetary Fund radically transformed Indonesia's options, diminishing its capacity to compete, as China emerged as a major producer of wood-related products. The Indonesian case may well illustrate processes of market remarginalization resulting from the implementation of neoliberal policies.

Keywords: Indonesia; commodity chains; plywood production; forestation and deforestation; transnational alliances and markets

Indonesia's economy suffered terribly during the Asian crisis of 1997 to 1998 as its currency exchange rate tumbled and GDP, exports, and foreign investments declined. The people of Indonesia also experienced pain as high inflation and unemployment coupled with high debt levels riveted the nation. During the crisis, the Indonesian government signed onto an International Monetary Fund (IMF) structural adjustment package worth US$43 billion. As with most structural adjustments around the world, this Washington Consensus approach included a tightened monetary policy, and the liberalization of trade and investment aimed at economic recovery. Recovery in Indonesia, however, has been slower than in other Southeast Asian countries. After several decades of impressive and widely touted growth rates of about 6 percent annually and the expansion of manufacturing exports (World Bank 1993), Indonesia's economy seemed poised to revert to old patterns of

DOI: 10.1177/0002716206297462

export relying on natural resources and agricultural commodities (Gellert 2005). Yet investment and growth have not been sufficient to overcome the serious debt and unemployment problems plaguing the country (Toemion 2002, cited in Rao 2002).

In the past couple of decades, neoliberalism has spread throughout many nations and regions in the world. The extension of that economic and political perspective will continue to have an extensive and important impact on the global distribution of benefits and movements of capital, goods, and people. The predominant focus of the literature on contemporary patterns of globalization has focused on manufacturing and services sectors (e.g., Dicken 2003). Within this literature, an important thread has been the analysis of global commodity or value chains. In other words, globalization currently entails not only the opening of markets but also a reconfiguration of production patterns joining disparate areas of the world.

Neoliberalism and changes in the scale of governance affecting commodity trade and markets continue to be of the utmost significance in the current period. National states as well as local governments play a part in globalization. Understanding that trend as a set of processes, therefore, is crucial (see Heynan and Robbins 2005; McCarthy and Prudham 2004). In many studies both laudatory and critical, neoliberalism is assumed to be an event that occurs once and completely transforms the people, governments, and other actors and activities under its sway. More nuanced studies have begun to recognize the limits, resistances, and frictions that prevent the full extension of neoliberal ideas and practices (Tsing 2004). Indeed, it may well be the case that illiberal forms of governance are coming to dominate polities such as Indonesia even as economic liberalization takes place (Robison 2006; Shefner 2007 [this volume]).

Students of globalization are increasingly shifting attention toward natural resources and raw materials (Bridge 2004; Bunker and Ciccantell 2005). The liberalization of exports in the natural resource sector is one of many ironies in structural adjustment packages that purport to modernize economic activity. A focus on agricultural and mining assets is also part of bilateral, multilateral, and regional free trade agreements currently proliferating in Asia and around the world. Those accords take little cognizance of the specificity of natural staples in each geographical area or the means necessary to transform primary inputs into commodities, to say nothing about the challenges involved in downstream processing or the degradation of the environment resulting from continued extraction.

This article explores the impact of liberalization on a politically organized and regimented commodity chain. After briefly reviewing the state of the relevant

Paul K. Gellert is an assistant professor in the Department of Sociology at the University of Tennessee. His research focuses on the political economy of timber, other natural resources, and development in Indonesia in relation to Japan, China, and the Asia-Pacific region. Recent publications include "The Seductive Quality of Central Human Capabilities: Sociological Insights into Nussbaum and Sen's Disagreement," in Economy and Society; *and "The Shifting Natures of 'Development': Growth, Crisis, and Recovery in Indonesia's Forests," in* World Development.

NOTE: The author gratefully acknowledges an Abe Fellowship of the Japan Foundation Center for Global Partnership (CGP) for its generous support of the research on which the article is based.

literature, including value chains and production networks, I focus on the construction of a particular linkage in the tropical timber chain between Indonesia and Japan in the decade from 1988 to 1998. In the third section, I examine the dismantling of the transnational political alliance that originally enabled the link to be formed as a direct result of IMF-led structural adjustment and the cementing of a neoliberal, free market, form of governance.

The fourth section raises some complications for a linear analysis of a change from market liberalization to environmental degradation. Complex mechanisms, including the depletion of timber stands, the diversion of resources to other end products and institutional factors such as the political decentralization and reform of the Indonesian forestry agencies, and the regional and global ascent of Chinese production and export facilities, have contributed to the (contested) demise of the Indonesian plywood industry (Barham, Bunker, and O'Hearn 1994). The disquieting conclusion of this paper is that the end of the plywood era in Indonesia will likely lead to expanded forest conversion and more intense processes of "accumulation by dispossession" (Harvey 2003, 2007).

Global Commodity Chains and Globalization

Globalization entails a functional integration among internationally dispersed activities (Dicken 2003; Gereffi 1994). From its roots in the world-systems tradition, global commodity chain (GCC) analysis attempts to understand the international division of labor by focusing on the production and exchange of specific commodities over time. Put differently, students of globalization and commodity chains pinpoint all main stages in the process of production, noting, in addition to their function as part of the whole, their physical locations, thus showing spatial and distributive dimensions. The components of a single T-shirt or television set may travel around the world before becoming part of the finished product. In recent years, the study of global production processes has reached maturity. Recognizing that "the global commodity chain construct has inspired and oriented a spate of recent scholarship," a good number of analysts have recently offered review articles or summary statements of global commodity chains (Bair 2005, 153), global value chains (Gereffi, Humphrey, and Sturgeon 2005), or global production networks (Henderson et al. 2002; Hess and Yeung 2006).

As Gereffi, Humphrey, and Sturgeon (2005, 81) observed, "The key insight is that coordination and control of global-scale production systems, despite their complexity, can be achieved without direct ownership" (see also Hughes 2000; Henderson et al. 2002; Dicken et al. 2001). Initially, Gereffi (1994) divided commodity chains into buyer-driven and supplier-driven types. More recently, building on work with colleagues in the global value chains framework, Gereffi, Humphrey, and Sturgeon (2005) delineated five analytical types of governance structures on a spectrum that ranges from markets to hierarchies with modular, relational, and captive value chains in between. They hypothesized that patterns of governance will be determined by three factors: complexity of transactions, codifiability of information, and the capabilities of suppliers "regardless of the institutional context in which they are situated" (p. 99).

This revised theoretical approach offers a more nuanced understanding of value chain governance, allowing us to see the movement of timber exports from Indonesia through liberalization from relational value chains, in which there were complex dependencies between buyers and sellers to market transactions where the costs of switching partners are lowered. Although this momentous change has consequences for economic development, the role of the state and interstate agreements on trade liberalization have garnered scant notice. By contrast, power asymmetries in the global value chain between buyers and suppliers, that is firms, have captured most of the attention (Gereffi, Humphrey, and Sturgeon 2005, 87-88). States (public institutions) appear to affect the governance structure only insofar as grades and standards are codified with their assistance. Yet more is involved. This article takes its cue from Bair's (2005) conclusion that global commodity chain analysis should pay closer attention to larger institutional and structural environments if we are interested in understanding the contours of uneven development.

How firms in developing nations can gain access to markets in developed countries may be less important than how to negotiate the terms of that access.

How firms in developing nations can gain access to markets in developed countries may be less important than how to negotiate the terms of that access. When we are considering natural resources, other raw materials, or "producer-oriented industries" (Gerlach 1992), rather than direct consumer-oriented commodities, countervailing pressure can tap the sources of inputs (Bunker and Ciccantell 2005; Ribot and Peluso 2003). Under such conditions, terms of access and the distribution of benefits become top priorities. Multiple factors are causally linked to a shifting global trade architecture, coordination among various producers inside particular exporting areas (states, regions, nation-states, supranational regions), and the politics within exporting nations, for example, contestations over scale (Heynan and Robbins 2005; Smith 2004; Swyngedouw 1997, 2004). Gereffi, Humphrey, and Sturgeon (2005, 100) focused on "the benefits of access and the risks of exclusion" for firms, but it is also worth considering the risks of access and benefits of exclusion for governments, public interest groups, and environmental advocates (see, e.g., Dove 1996).[1]

Regions and Regionalism in Asia

When focusing on terms of access, the changing governance structure of commodity chains needs to be seen also in the context of broader shifts in regionalism at the continental level. During the years of the economic "miracle" growth of the Asian newly industrializing economies, the dominant literature emphasized "flying geese" and predicted, in line with modernization theory, the progressive development of the smaller geese into larger, healthier ones. Nevertheless, as Bernard and Ravenhill (1995) observed, even at the time, the geese in Southeast Asia developed as part of a regional whole and amid relations that did not imply further development. As time has shown, the dependency relations in Southeast Asia have only become more pronounced in recent years. In other words, to assess the development of a particular country, it is best to take into consideration its position vis-à-vis neighboring nations.

When taking regional ties into consideration, it is possible to see that gone are the days of dominance on the part of multilateral treaties such as the North American Free Trade Agreement (NAFTA) or the Free Trade Area of the Americas (FTAA). The political agenda for free trade fractured after the failure of the Seattle 1999 World Trade Organization (WTO) summit. Now analysts are cataloguing various bilateral, regional, and multilateral agreements that affect trade and development. Crosscutting the analysis of commodity chain governance, therefore, are efforts to understand the regional and multilateral negotiations over free trade and open markets.

What is most crucial in these multiplying arrangements about free trade? Pekkanen (2005) argued that Japan has shifted over time away from bilateral arrangements, especially with the United States, to participation in the multilateral WTO in the 1990s. More recently, Japan has turned to regional alternatives through a series of bilateral accords known as Economic Partnership Agreements (EPAs), beginning with Singapore in 2002. Malaysia, Thailand, the Philippines, and, finally in 2006, Indonesia, followed in the creation of EPAs with Japan.

Free trade agreements, whether bilateral or multilateral, like the governance of commodity chains, are basically concerned with the hierarchy of power within the global system. The proliferation of pacts with Japan is partly explained by the search for three objectives: stabilizing trade, diminishing commercial volatility, and gaining rapid market access and protection of investments (Pekkanen 2005, 78-79; see also Krauss 2003; Dent 2003). Japan's "preferential" regional approach to trade can also be viewed as a reaction to China's growing influence in the region and the focus of leaders in that gigantic nation on regional free trade agreements within Asia. Notably, one such treaty was signed with the Association of Southeast Asian Nations (ASEAN) in 2001. When fully implemented, it will create the world's largest free trade area, with a combined GDP of US$2.2 trillion, trade of US$1.23 trillion, and a population of 1.7 billion people. At the same time, ASEAN member nations individually are more willing to engage Japan bilaterally as a counterweight to China at a time when Japanese hegemony is no longer feared (Pekkanen 2005, 97).

Taken together, the actions of China and Japan bear similarities to NAFTA in the American hemisphere, which entailed a broad reconfiguring of access to raw materials to bolster the position of the United States as a global dominant power (Ciccantell 2001). Within Asia, a similar pattern emerges: the causal thrust of economic integration involves access to raw materials. The most important element in that power dynamic is the struggle for rising hegemon(s), or competing ones, to reconfigure the right to use and transport key primary goods (Ciccantell and Bunker 2004; Bunker and Ciccantell 2005). The case of timber presented in the remainder of this article provides a window onto these processes in the case of one less critical sector.

Free trade agreements, whether bilateral or multilateral, like the governance of commodity chains, are basically concerned with the hierarchy of power within the global system.

Producing a Timber Commodity Chain: National and Transnational Alliances

From the late 1980s through 1998, Indonesian plywood producers consolidated a state-supported domestic oligopoly, forged a transnational alliance that circumvented the power of Japanese trading houses, and supported Indonesian private accumulation (Gellert 2003). In effect, the Indonesian case exemplified a negotiated governance structure over the timber commodity along the lines Gereffi, Humphrey, and Sturgeon (2005) used to describe relational value chains in which—as scholars in the global production network literature emphasize (Hess and Yeung 2006)—particular, culturally based relationships are established that are important to market functions. During the period under consideration, political consistency created stable conditions for accumulation based on the extraction of timber and other resources while state ideology promoted steady forest management.

After a decade of log exports, the New Order government of President Suharto, in alliance with largely Chinese-Indonesian firms, moved to industrialize on the basis of the downstream production of plywood (Dauvergne 1997; Ross 2001). A joint ministerial decree that banned log exports by 1985, in tandem with financial subsidies, led plywood processing mills to increase fivefold to 101 by 1985 and to 132 by 1990, with a capacity of 12.6 million cubic meters (m^3)

(Barr 2001). Exports grew from less than 1 million m^3 in 1980 to more than 9 million m^3 in the early 1990s, amounting to about 80 percent of world trade in tropical plywood (Dauvergne 1997, 78, Table 9). Forest-based exports (plywood, furniture, and pulp) totaled more than $9 billion per year in the mid-1990s (World Bank 2001, 6).

During that stretch of time, the concentration of ownership and control in the plywood sector increased under the tight organizational authority of the Indonesian Wood Panel Association, Apkindo, and its leader, Suharto confidant Mohamad (Bob) Hasan. Apkindo overtook and determined export destinations, quantities, and prices, and penalized companies that attempted to evade its jurisdiction (Dauvergne 1997; Barr 1998). In addition, Hasan leveraged domestic organizational control into significant market shares in Japan and other important locations. In Japan, Hasan formed an alliance with a small trading company to circumvent the purchasing and market clout of the dominant *sogo sosha* (general trading companies) (Gellert 2003; Gerlach 1992). This transnational alliance created an exclusive purchasing arrangement and added fees onto the buying price at a time when Indonesian exports controlled more than three-quarters of the market for tropical plywood. Disproportionate benefits accrued to Hasan himself. That brought about complaints from importers and, on rare occasion, Indonesian exporters (Barr 1998). To be sure, this governance structure did not represent "ascent" by Indonesia in the global division of labor—that still remains a developmentalist illusion (Gellert 2003; Arrighi 1990). Yet the alliances forged by the Suharto government gave Indonesia a signal role in the regional market, raising hopes that revenues derived from plywood exports could be applied to bolster national development. Those hopes, however, were dashed in the late 1990s.

Neoliberalism, Structural Adjustment, and Postcrisis Tendencies toward Freer Markets

Between 1998 and 2005, the Asian financial crisis and then structural adjustment imposed by the IMF caused the liberalization of the timber trade and the dismantling of the political alliance underpinning that industry in the preceding period (Gellert 2005). While initially expected to cause an open-access disaster of Indonesian resources, the outcome of the liberalization process had contradictory effects on the political economy of the region, especially in Indonesia and Japan. Despite industrial association efforts, continued decline in the resource base of Indonesia and shrinking demand in Japan negatively affected Indonesia's plywood industry. Simultaneously, vastly increased demand from Chinese markets has put new but different pressures on Indonesian forests. While Japanese importers had adapted to an earlier pattern of Indonesian downstream exports and bought large amounts of plywood, Chinese importers were more interested in raw logs, which the Indonesian government had made illegal. Also, whereas the Japanese government has moved toward "greening" its imports and its image, the Chinese remain relatively insensitive to the environmental impacts of trade. This has given China a ruthless competitive advantage.

The forms of governance established in the late 1980s and early 1990s in the plywood commodity chain between Indonesia and Japan were dismantled during and after the Asian financial crisis of 1997 to 1998. The IMF-led structural adjustment package systematically eroded the power of Apkindo but also indirectly accelerated a transition to a neoliberal, ungoverned, or market-oriented chain. Rather than a shift from producer-driven to buyer-driven chain governance structures, there has been a commodity-based transition to supply raw materials to competing hegemonic powers within a still-competitive world-system structure. In other words, the previous era provided a modicum of protection in the production of plywood through the application of government-established boundaries to the exploitation of natural resources. Under present conditions those boundaries have become contested at many levels, leaving Indonesian producers vulnerable to the penetration of powerful competitors.

The dismantling of the governance structure at the hands of the IMF took on different forms at the two end poles of the chain. In Indonesia, Apkindo was disempowered as its joint marketing boards (JMBs) were stripped of their authority over export destinations and prices. The JMBs thereby became more like industrial information gathering bodies, although how much of their information was shared back with the companies is unclear. On the Japanese side of the ocean, Nippindo attempted to survive in a more competitive environment. Nevertheless, after several years of competing again with *sogo sosha* and other direct buyers of Indonesian plywood, Nippindo, as well as its Japanese parent company Kanmatsu, collapsed into bankruptcy in April 2005.[2] This opened the gates for other agents to tap into Indonesia's depleting resource base.

After years of dominating the Japanese market, Indonesian plywood appeared to be slowly recovering from the crisis that affected Japanese demand but is now in a rapid phase of decline. An assessment of trade on a monthly basis shows that, in September 2004, the volume imported from Malaysia for the first time exceeded that from Indonesia. By 2005, Japan was buying more plywood from Malaysia than from Indonesia on an annual basis. And by the first half of 2006, imports from Indonesia had dropped to only 36 percent of the total (Japan Wood Products Information and Research Center [JAWIC], September 2006).[3]

Overall Japanese demand for solid wood products (logs, lumber, and structural panels) does not appear to have declined significantly in recent years. As in the United States, the primary use for wood panels in Japan is for home construction. Therefore, housing starts are a good indicator of the demand for wood products in the whole economy. In 2004, Japanese housing starts increased by 3 percent to 1.19 million units, reaching nearly the level of 2000 housing starts. Wood construction of various sorts continues to equal more than 40 percent of homes. Although demand remains vigorous, the providers of raw materials are now different and more numerous.

New players have changed the economic geography of solid wood production and trade. Most important, China has jumped into the global scene as a significant producer and exporter of panels. Indonesia has lost market share to Malaysia and China, both of which have been denounced by nongovernmental organizations and activist groups for their involvement in the illegal logging trade. Chinese ply-wood exports reached 5 percent of Japan's market in 2005 and 9 percent in 2006. China's growing importance as an importer and exporter of timber is the dominant trend affecting the industrial firms and forests of Indonesia at present.

The massive floods that occurred along the Yangtze River in southwest China in 1998 caused the loss of more than twenty-five hundred lives and were the most costly since the 1950s. Despite significant forestation programs in that country, loggers continued to harvest natural woodlands up until that time. In the ensuing months, China's government implemented an effective logging ban in seventeen provinces in the Yangtze region (Lang 2002). Authorities reduced logging domes-tically from a peak of 67 million m^3 in 1995 to (still very significant) 48 million m^3 in 2003 (Lang and Chan 2006, 170). The result of the ban, however, was to shift the demand for wood in China to sources in the rest of Asia. Significantly, in 1999, as it prepared to enter the WTO, China reduced import tariffs and loosened restrictions on export licenses for forest industries (Lang and Chan 2006, 173-74).

The organization and profits of the Indonesian timber industry are being rescaled by this boom in Chinese imports (International Tropical Timber Organization [ITTO] 2004; Sun, Katsigris, and White 2004). Such imports may be part of China's world-historical rise as a global hegemonic power (Bunker and Ciccantell 2005), but whether or not that country actually becomes a hegemon, the impact on Indonesia is already profound. Between 1997 and 2003, the total volume of Chinese forest-product imports (in round-wood equivalents [RWE]) grew two and a half times from 40 million m^3 to more than 106 million m^3 (Sun, Katsigris, and White 2004, Figure 1).[4] With a domestic ban placed on logging in southwest China following the floods of 1998, China has become the world's lead-ing importer of industrial round-wood (i.e., logs) with 2002 imports more than 24 million m^3. An additional 7.7 million m^3 RWE was imported as sawn wood. In 1999 Chinese imports surpassed domestic timber production, and total wood imports now are more than 100 million m^3 RWE (Lang and Chan 2006, Figure 3). By value, total Chinese forest product imports have moved from seventh to sec-ond in the world (Sun, Katsigris, and White 2004, 2).

Against the context of China's rapidly expanding market, Indonesian exports are being reperipheralized in two ways. First, there is a push "backward" to raw logs and away from the regime of plywood exports during the Suharto-Hasan era. The legal opening for log exports from Indonesia under the IMF adjustment policy of 1998 led to a large jump in exports to China. Then, in 2002, after the log export ban was reinstated in October 2001 (officially, a log export "moratorium"), China still reported log imports from Indonesia in excess of 1 million m^3. Trade analysts and investigative reports indicate a continued flow of raw logs in more recent years. In its 2004 annual report, the ITTO further noted that China had imports of nearly 116,000 m^3 in 2003, thereby "supporting the claims of many observers that substantial undocumented or illegal Indonesian log exports con-tinue to exist (ITTO 2004, 15). Most vocally, the Environmental Investigation

Agency (EIA)/Telapak (2005) reported that exports of merbau logs from Papua alone amounted to 300,000 m³ per month or 3.6 million m³ per year.

The dynamics of legal and illegal logging could be analyzed within a commodity chain framework that highlights the particular forms of governance facilitating trade, as well as the benefits accruing to Chinese importers from that process. Nevertheless, such an analysis might miss the broader and equally important dynamic entailing the Chinese reconfiguration of cheap access to raw materials. More recent data demonstrates that up to three-quarters of China's imports of logs and wooden goods are (re)processed into finished products destined for export markets (Sun, Cheng, and Canby 2005; Stark and Cheung 2006). The destinations for such commodities are dominated by the United States (27 percent), Japan (17 percent), and Korea (8 percent) (Stark and Cheung 2006, Figure 2.10).[5]

Second, there is a potential geographical peripheralization of Indonesia as a source of raw wood materials because importers are shifting their attention, most notably, to supplies from the Siberian Far East woodlots. Since 1997, the sources of Chinese log imports have changed dramatically. Whereas in the past almost 80 percent were hardwood logs, mostly tropical in origin, now 65 percent are softwood logs. And the most significant part of the new softwood imports is from Russian (e.g., larch) providers. U.S. and Canadian exporters are also increasingly interested in the "vast" Chinese market, which in their minds has acquired mythological proportions, although timber-framed houses are "only a small fraction (<1 percent) of Chinese housing starts" (ITTO 2004, 7).[6] In sawn wood, more than 75 percent of Chinese imports are still hardwood, although Russian softwood is increasing in this category too.

Contradictory and Uncertain Environmental Effects of Liberalization

For many years, Indonesia has been recognized globally as a center of deforestation. The loss of megadiversity in the world's second or third largest national territory of tropical rain forest was widely bemoaned. In a recent and fascinating study that builds on new understandings of fragment ecology and complex matrices of human and environment interaction, Hecht and colleagues (2006) found evidence of forest resurgence in El Salvador. This recovery of woodlands, they argued, is occurring in part due to structural adjustment policies that maintain urban bias and thus undermine investment in the rural and agricultural sectors.

Whether such developments may represent a silver lining, they seem dubious at present in Indonesia. Conversion of forests for palm oil and pulp and paper plantations is rapid, increasing, and heavily encouraged by the Indonesian government. In fact, despite the debacle of earlier cycles of subsidized forest plantations, the current Yudhoyono government appears headed toward renewed subsidies taken from the so-called reforestation fund. More likely than the resurgence of Indonesia as a provider of primary resources is its marginalization as other competitors, especially China, take the front line in the production of primary goods.

Conclusion

Only a decade ago, Indonesia reigned as one of the world's main suppliers of plywood. Its preeminence depended on the forging of political alliances that established legal boundaries, protecting the national resource base and its use for timber from competitive pressures to a large extent. Those alliances were not perfect—they allowed for the concentration of capital and did not redistribute equally or even fairly the benefits derived from timber production. Despite those limitations, the state's entrepreneurial intervention in and monitoring of wood-related products increased Indonesia's capacity to capture market shares at the regional level and funnel revenues toward the expansion of public services.

The financial crisis of the late 1990s created a window of opportunity for international development organizations like the IMF to realign the balance of power among Asian nations and reconfigure access to natural resources.

The financial crisis of the late 1990s created a window of opportunity for international development organizations like the IMF to realign the balance of power among Asian nations and reconfigure access to natural resources. The neoliberal process thus advanced has greatly eroded the capacity of Indonesia to compete at the regional level. Paradoxically, the opening of markets has given an advantage to China, a country that now emerges as the dominant power in Asia, not solely because of its large territory and population but also because of its willingness to adopt the ruthless logic of the market. Indonesia's capacity to compete had depended on managed structures of governance over timber production; China's influence is predicated upon the sheer exploitation of natural resources.

Indonesia's transition illustrates two processes conceptualized in the literature of globalization and commodity chains. One is the extent to which structural adjustment packages can increase the number of competitors vying for position in particular productive processes. In Asia, the tendency has been toward the disappearance of overarching free trade accords and the proliferation of multilateral agreements that protect participants, to some extent, from being crushed by a single dominant party. The other process consists of what Andre Gunder Frank once called "the development of underdevelopment." As neoliberal policies are applied, countries like Indonesia are pushed backward into roles they had sought to overcome; that is, they increasingly become sources of primary goods. The reperipheralization of Indonesia is a paradoxical outcome of economic liberalization, whose ostensible goal has been to increase the likelihood of prosperity by opening markets and facilitating competition.

Finally, it is worth emphasizing that neoliberalism both in Asia and Latin America has entailed the reconfiguration of access to agricultural and mining resources. In that sense, Indonesia is now poised to illustrate what David Harvey calls "accumulation by dispossession." Regrettably, the dispossession is local while the accumulation occurs abroad. The effects of this process upon the natural resources that once made Indonesia the envy of the region may be unimaginable. Then again, the benefits for those controlling the neoliberal agenda are immeasurable.

Notes

1. Particularly ironic is that in the next sentence, the authors discussed "paths of sustainable development" in a mainstream turn of phrase that has little to do with sustainability in an environmental sense.

2. The former CEO, Mazaki, would not make himself available for a follow-up interview in 2005, due to his advanced age, according to his staff.

3. Japan Wood Products Information and Research Center (JAWIC) data show that plywood imports from Malaysia in the first six months of 2006 were 1,171,343 cubic meters (m^3) whereas those from Indonesia were a mere 661,699 m^3. See the JAWIC Web site at http://www.jawic.or.jp/english/publications.html.

4. Round-wood equivalents (RWE) is a calculation based on typical factory recovery rates. For example, it takes about 2 m^3 of raw logs to produce 1 m^3 of plywood. The 2003 figures are preliminary.

5. Figures refer to all wood products except furniture, which itself is a multi-billion-dollar export industry.

6. Interview with timber association official, Washington, D.C., June 2004.

References

Arrighi, Giovanni. 1990. The developmentalist illusion: A reconceptualization of the semiperiphery. In *Semiperipheral states in the world-economy, contributions in economics and economic history*, ed. W. G. Martin, 11-42. New York: Greenwood.

Bair, Jennifer. 2005. Global capitalism and commodity chains: Looking back, going forward. *Competition and Change* 9:153-80.

Barham, Bradford, Stephen G. Bunker, and Denis O'Hearn, eds. 1994. *States, firms, and raw materials: The world economy and ecology of aluminum*. Madison: University of Wisconsin Press.

Barr, C. 1998. Bob Hasan, the rise of Apkindo, and the shifting dynamics of control in Indonesia's timber sector. *Indonesia* 65:1-36.

———. 2001. *Banking on sustainability: Structural adjustment and forestry reform in post-Suharto Indonesia*. Washington, DC: WWF Macroeconomics Program Office and Center for International Forestry Research (CIFOR).

Bernard, Mitchell, and John Ravenhill. 1995. Beyond product cycles and flying geese: Regionalization, hierarchy, and the industrialization of East Asia. *World Politics* 47:171-209.

Bridge, Gavin. 2004. Mapping the bonanza: Geographies of mining investment in an era of neo-liberal reform. *The Professional Geographer* 56:406-21.

Bunker, Stephen G., and Paul S. Ciccantell. 2005. *Globalization and the race for resources.* Baltimore: Johns Hopkins University Press.

Ciccantell, Paul S. 2001. NAFTA and the reconstruction of U.S. hegemony: The raw materials foundations of economic competitiveness. *Canadian Journal of Sociology/Cahiers canadiens de sociologie* 26:57-87.

Ciccantell, Paul S., and Stephen G. Bunker. 2004. The economic ascent of China and the potential for restructuring the capitalist world-economy. *Journal of World-Systems Research* 10 (3): 565-89.

Dauvergne, Peter. 1997. *Shadows in the forest: Japan and the politics of timber in Southeast Asia.* Cambridge, MA: MIT Press.

Dent, Christopher M. 2003. Networking the region? The emergence and impact of Asia-Pacific bilateral free trade agreement projects. *Pacific Review* 16 (1): 1-28.

Dicken, Peter. 2003. *Global shift: Reshaping the global economic map in the 21st century.* New York: Guilford.

Dicken, Peter, Philip F. Kelly, Kris Olds, and Henry Wai-Chung Yeung. 2001. Chains and networks, territories and scales: Towards a relational framework for analysing the global economy. *Global Networks: A Journal of Transnational Affairs* 1 (2): 89-112.

Dove, Michael. 1996. So far from power, so near to the forest: A structural analysis of gain and blame in tropical forest development. In *Borneo in transition: People, forests, conservation and development,* ed. Christine Padoch and Nancy L. Peluso, 41-58. New York: Oxford University Press.

Environmental Investigation Agency (EIA)/Telapak. 2005. *The last frontier: Illegal logging in Papua and China's massive timber theft.* London: EIA/Telapak.

Gellert, Paul K. 2003. Renegotiating a timber commodity chain: The politics of the Indonesia-Japan plywood link. *Sociological Forum* 18:53-84.

———. 2005. The shifting natures of development: Growth, crisis and recovery in Indonesia's forests. *World Development* 33:1345-64.

Gereffi, Gary. 1994. The organization of buyer-driven global commodity chains: How US retailers shape overseas production networks. In *Commodity chains and global capitalism,* ed. Gary Gereffi and Miguel Korzeniewicz, 95-122. Westport, CT: Praeger.

Gereffi, Gary, John Humphrey, and Timothy Sturgeon. 2005. The governance of global value chains. *Review of International Political Economy* 12:78-104.

Gerlach, Michael L. 1992. *Alliance capitalism: The social organization of Japanese business.* Berkeley: University of California Press.

Harvey, David. 2003. *The new imperialism.* Oxford: Oxford University Press.

———. 2007. Neoliberalism as creative destruction. *Annals of the American Academy of Political and Social Science* 610:22-44.

Hecht, Susanna B., Susan Kandel, Ileana Gomes, Nelson Cuellar, and Herman Rosa. 2006. Globalization, forest resurgence, and environmental politics in El Salvador. *World Development* 34:308-23.

Henderson, J., Peter Dicken, Martin Hess, Neil Coe, and Henry W.-C. Yeung. 2002. Global production networks and the analysis of economic development. *Review of International Political Economy* 9:436-64.

Hess, Martin, and Henry W.-C. Yeung. 2006. Whither global production networks in economic geography? *Environment and Planning A* 38:1193-1204.

Heynan, Nik, and Paul Robbins. 2005. The neo-liberalization of nature: Governance, privatization, enclosure and valuation—Editors' introduction. *Capitalism Nature Socialism* 16:5-8.

Hughes, A. 2000. Retailers, knowledges and changing commodity networks: The case of the cut flower trade. *Geoforum* 31:175-190.

International Tropical Timber Organization (ITTO). 2004. *Annual review and assessment of the world timber situation 2003.* Yokohama, Japan: ITTO.

Krauss, Ellis. 2003. The US, Japan, and trade liberalization: From bilateralism to regional multilateralism to regionalism. *Pacific Review* 16 (3): 307-33.

Lang, Graeme. 2002. Forests, floods, and the environmental state in China. *Organization and Environment* 15:119-30.

Lang, Graeme, and Cathy Hiu Wan Chan. 2006. China's impact on forests in Southeast Asia. *Journal of Contemporary Asia* 36:167-95.

McCarthy, James, and W. Scott Prudham. 2004. Neo-liberal nature and the nature of neo-liberalism. *Geoforum* 35:275-83.

Pekkanen, Saadia. 2005. Bilateralism, multilateralism, or regionalism? Japan's trade forum choices. *Journal of East Asian Studies* 5 (1): 77-103.

Rao, J. Mohan. 2002. Globalization, debt and development: Lessons and policy alternatives facing Indonesia. Paper prepared for the 13th Conference of the International NGO Forum on Indonesian Development (INFID), Yogyakarta, 30 September–2 October, 2002. http://infid.be/publication.html.

Ribot, Jesse C., and Nancy Lee Peluso. 2003. A theory of access. *Rural Sociology* 68:153-81.

Robison, Richard. 2006. *The neoliberal revolution: Forging the market state.* New York: Palgrave MacMillan.

Ross, Michael. L. 2001. *Timber booms and institutional breakdown in Southeast Asia.* New York: Cambridge University Press.

Shefner, Jon. 2007. Rethinking civil society in the age of NAFTA: The case of Mexico. *Annals of the American Academy of Political and Social Science* 610:182-200.

Smith, Neil. 2004. Scale bending and the fate of the national. In *Scale and geographic inquiry: Nature, society, and method,* ed. E. Sheppard and R. B. McMaster, 192-212. Malden, MA: Blackwell.

Stark, Tamara, and Sze Pang Cheung. 2006. *Sharing the blame: Global consumption and China's role in ancient forest destruction.* March 28. A report published by Greenpeace International and Greenpeace China. www.greenpeace.org/international.

Sun, Xiufang, Nian Cheng, and Kerstin Canby. 2005. *China's forest product exports: An overview of trends by segment and destination.* Washington, DC: Forest Trends.

Sun, Xiufang, Eugenia Katsigris, and Andy White. 2004. *Meeting China's demand for forest products: An overview of import trends, ports of entry, and supplying countries, with emphasis on the Asia-Pacific region.* Washington, DC: Forest Trends.

Swyngedouw, Erik. 1997. Neither global nor local: Glocalization and the politics of scale. In *Spaces of globalization: Reasserting the power of the local,* ed. K. Cox, 137-66. New York: Guilford.

———. 2004. Scaled geographies: Nature, place, and the politics of scale. In *Scale and geographic inquiry: Nature, society, and method,* ed. E. Sheppard and R. B. McMaster, 129-53. Malden, MA: Blackwell.

Tsing, Anna L. 2004. *Friction: An ethnography of global connection.* Princeton, NJ: Princeton University Press.

World Bank. 1993. *The East Asian miracle: Economic growth and public policy.* New York: Oxford University Press.

———. 2001. *Indonesia: Environment and natural resource management in a time of transition.* Washington, DC: World Bank.

BOOK REVIEW ESSAY

David Harvey. 2005. *A Brief History of Neoliberalism*. Oxford: Oxford University Press. ISBN 0-19-928326-5.

A Brief History of Neoliberalism

Reviewed By
JON SHEFNER

Neoliberal economic thought has predominated policy-making arenas for thirty years, as much in the Global North as in developing nations. The verdict is clear. Globally, neoliberal policy has retarded economic growth, although national and even regional growth spurts have occurred along the way. The growth that has taken place has been uneven geographically and stratified along class lines, with polarization of wealth endemic in nations that have followed neoliberal dictates. For middle classes and below, the results have been unambiguous: declining wages and employment levels and reduced access to services such as health care, education, and others that provide security from the ravages of the market. With such clear evidence available to indict neoliberal thought, how has it remained so hegemonic among policy-making circles?

This question, along with how neoliberalism arrived at its current dominance, is David Harvey's theme in this important book. Harvey argues that capitalist class segments in the United States and the United Kingdom worked together with probusiness intellectuals, using tools of international financial institutions, to forge a message articulating that the enemy of the economy is state intervention, and that the market must be left to resolve social and economic needs. According to Harvey, neoliberals

Jon Shefner is an associate professor of sociology and director of the Interdisciplinary Program in Global Studies at the University of Tennessee. His work examines the relationship of economic deprivation and democratization in Mexico within a comparative study of IMF austerity policies, protest, and regime change. He is the coeditor, with Patricia Fernandez-Kelly, of Out of the Shadows, *a volume that examines the intersection of the informal economy and grassroots political action.*

DOI: 10.1177/0002716206297899

first experimented with the financial problems of New York City, squeezing city government with predictable results of urban decay, unemployment, decline in social services, and crime—coupled with greater generation of polarized wealth. From there, a template emerged which relied on diminishing certain state regulations, liberalizing trade relations, and loosening capital restrictions.

These financial innovations, along with technological advances making production more flexible, reinforced multinational capital's ability to manufacture offshore, exploiting cheaper and more compliant labor and imposing policy on developing states. With legitimation produced by intellectual advocates, the new orthodoxy has provided substantial returns to the wealthy and a reconstitution of class forces within nations as diverse as the United States, the United Kingdom, Sweden, Mexico, and China.

Yet neoliberalism has not been applied without variation, Harvey points out. The degree of application of neoliberal policies has differed by form of state and moments of geopolitical conflict. Indeed, states whose governments have been more moderate in introducing neoliberal reforms have fared better than those that have been vulnerable to full imposition through IMF fiat. Regardless of level of application, however, even nominally leftist or populist parties, such as the Social Democrats in Sweden, New Labour in the United Kingdom, and the Democrats in the United States not only came to believe the rhetoric that "there is no alternative" to neoliberalism but designed and implemented policy that attacked labor while institutionalizing the polarization of wealth and political power.

[S]tates whose governments have been more moderate in introducing neoliberal reforms have fared better than those that have been vulnerable to full imposition through IMF fiat.

The contributions of this book are many. The old debate of instrumental versus structuralist states has not been fully resolved with globalization's new focus on global governance rather than on national states. Indeed, some have argued that states no longer matter in the days of uncontrollable capital, international financial institutions, and technologically driven speed of production. Harvey puts this argument to rest as he demonstrates that states clearly matter in the construction, export, and implementation of neoliberal policy. His documentation of how business-oriented think tanks, government officials, and business organizations colluded to articulate neoliberal thought also resolves the insufficiency of purely structuralist arguments. Government cannot be pushed to abide by capital's needs without active efforts by hegemonic intellectuals in the construction of new ideologies and policy rationales. The power of ideas may not equate with the power of capitalism, but Harvey shows how consent was manufactured by building on postmodern and individually defined conceptualizations of freedom. His argument here is a bit overstated, as authors have demonstrated how Mexico, as one example, welcomed the new orthodoxy above and beyond the imposition of neoliberalism by the IMF, Wall Street, and the U.S. Treasury. The point remains, however, that neoliberal states could not have been constructed without the active cooperation of government, dominant classes, intellectuals, and sympathetic media.

This is not to say that neoliberalism has benefited all capitalist classes equally. Capital does not possess a unified set of interests, as international finance and industrialists had very different interests as globalization progressed. Indeed, as Harvey shows, finance exerted its power with weapons of interest rates and credit availability in its struggle for dominance. The result has been the restoration of class privilege that was minimized during the post-WWII accord between capital and labor.

Harvey, like many of us, is alert to the possibility of global alternatives as the benefits of neoliberalism prove to be illusory. The overextension of U.S. debt poses the possibility of a crash, which could have savage effects nationally and globally. The emergence of a different global hegemon, especially from Asia, could result from a U.S. meltdown or less disruptive changes. Another grim possibility raised by Harvey is the rescue of U.S. hegemony by the pursuit of neoconservative political strategies of militarization, with repressive outcomes both within and without the United States. Other alternatives require active resistance by social movements in targeting the acceleration of inequities brought by neoliberal policy.

Yet Harvey leaves unexplored some other possible alternatives as neoliberalism searches for new markets. Current signs of neoliberal expansion may indeed prove to be cannibalism, as European and U.S. mergers have expanded. Such activity may follow the path of similar events of the 1970s through 1980s, which increased corporate profits, while making many productive jobs redundant. Further evidence comes from recent attempts by the U.S.-based NASDAQ to buy London's FTSE, another effort to add wealth without increasing production. Such events show that business is unwilling to return to the labor-capital accord that defined much of postwar relations in the United Kingdom and United States. New takeover and merger attempts may further demonstrate the fundamental unsustainability of neoliberal policy or may provide sufficient playground that collapse is postponed.

Harvey's hopes for more humane alternatives are based on the proliferation of antiglobalization movements. He recognizes that the wave of resistance began well before the wave of protests that followed the Seattle WTO protests, citing the occasion of protests against IMF austerity measures. Pinning hopes on movements like the Zapatistas in the 2000s, however, may prove as ephemeral as the enthusiasm generated by the Sandinistas in the 1980s. Social movements are playing important roles in resistance to neoliberalism and creating visions of new alternatives, as Harvey suggests. Yet the force of these movements is most likely to be felt in their impact on national states.

Election of governments of the left and center-left in Latin America were spurred by a whole series of organized resistance efforts, including antiausterity protest. In the past, nations like Jamaica and Peru stood alone when they tried to halt the advance of IMF-imposed neoliberal reforms in their nations, and their attempts were crushed. It is the new ability to stand up to the restoration of class privilege, clearly documented as the intent of neoliberal policy makers and intellectuals, that may emerge from a coalition of Latin American and other nations. Indeed, the failure of the Doha round of WTO talks owes a great deal to the formation of such a coalition, which in turn is based on social movement opposition to structural adjustment and other expressions of neoliberalism. The Bolivarian alternative may not excite many citizens outside Venezuela, but the opportunity to create other visions of a just society may result from a wide coalition that halts the spread of variants of neoliberalism. Regardless of which alternative toward social justice is pursued, action requires clear-eyed analysis and diagnosis, which this book provides in admirable detail, elegant style, and comprehensive coverage.

SECTION FOUR

Quick Read Synopsis

QUICK READ SYNOPSIS

NAFTA and Beyond: Alternative Perspectives in the Study of Global Trade and Development

Special Editors: PATRICIA FERNÁNDEZ-KELLY
Princeton University

and

JON SHEFNER
University of Tennessee

Volume 610, March 2007

Prepared by Herb Fayer, Jerry Lee Foundation

DOI: 10.1177/0002716207300035

SECTION ONE: POLITICAL AND ECONOMIC DIMENSIONS OF FREE TRADE

Neoliberalism as Creative Destruction

David Harvey, CUNY Graduate Center

Background   Neoliberalism is a theory proposing that human well-being can best be advanced by the maximization of entrepreneurial freedoms within an institutional framework characterized by private property rights, individual liberty, unencumbered markets, and free trade.

- The role of the state is to create and preserve an institutional framework.
- If markets do not exist (in education, health care, social security, or environmental pollution), they must be created by state action.
- State interventions in markets (once created) must be kept to a bare minimum—the state cannot second-guess market conditions.

NOTE: The creation of neoliberal systems has entailed much destruction, not only of prior institutional frameworks, but also of divisions of labor, social relations, welfare provisions, technological mixes, ways of life, attachments to the land, habits of the heart, ways of thought, and the like.

Why
Neoliberalism?

Toward the end of the 1960s, global capitalism was falling into disarray.
- The embedded capitalism of the postwar period was no longer working.
- The crisis of capital accumulation of the 1970s affected everyone through the combination of rising unemployment and accelerating inflation and discontent was widespread.
- U.S. neoliberal imperialist strategies were articulated through a global network of power relations, which was to permit the U.S. upper classes to exact financial tribute and command rents from the rest of the world as a means to augment their already hegemonic control.

NOTE: Neoliberalism has not proven effective at revitalizing global capital accumulation but it has succeeded in restoring class power—in a conflict between the integrity of financial institutions and bondholders and the well-being of the citizens, the former would be given preference.

Support for
Neoliberalism

In spite of a dismal record of failures, many have been persuaded that neoliberalization is a successful solution for several reasons.
- Neoliberalization has been accompanied by increasing volatility within global capitalism.
- It has been a huge success from the standpoint of the upper classes.
- With the media dominated by upper-class interests, a myth grew saying that certain sectors failed because they were not competitive enough, thereby setting the stage for even more neoliberal reforms.

Class Power

The practices that restored class power are best described as an ongoing process of accumulation by dispossession that grew rapidly under neoliberalism. There are four main elements:
- privatization—the transfer of assets from the public and popular realms to the private and class-privileged domains;
- financialization—deregulation allowed the financial system to become one of the main centers of redistributive activity through speculation, predation, fraud, and thievery;
- the management and manipulation of crises; and
- state redistributions—it does this via privatization schemes and cutbacks in government expenditures meant to support the social wage.

NOTE: The neoliberal state also seeks redistributions through a variety of other means such as revisions in the tax code to benefit returns on investment rather than incomes and wages, promotion of regressive elements in the tax code (such as sales taxes), displacement of state expenditures, and free access to all by user fees (e.g., on higher education) and the provision of a vast array of subsidies and tax breaks to corporations.

Opposition

Neoliberalism has spawned a swath of oppositional movements, many of which are radically different from the worker-based movements that dominated before 1980.
- These movements shift the terrain of political organization away from traditional political parties and labor organizing to a less focused political dynamic of social action across the spectrum of civil society.

- Many of these diverse currents now come together at the World Social Forum in an attempt to define their shared mission and build an organizational structure capable of confronting the many variants of neoliberalism and of neoconservatism.

Conclusion   It is the profoundly antidemocratic nature of neoliberalism that should surely be the main focus of political struggle.

- Institutions with enormous leverage, like the Federal Reserve, are outside any democratic control.
- Internationally, the lack of simple accountability let alone democratic control over institutions such as the IMF, the WTO, and the World Bank, to say nothing of the great private power of financial institutions, makes a mockery of any real concern about democratization.
- The more clearly oppositional movements recognize that their central objective must be to confront class power that has been so effectively restored under neoliberalization, the more they will be likely to cohere.

Liberalism and the Good Society in the Iberian World

Miguel Angel Centeno, Princeton University

Background   Two basic questions motivate this article.

- Has the Iberian political economic legacy been an uninterrupted failure?
- To what extent did Latin America "fail" liberalism?

Liberalism   We can separate the central tenets of liberalism into those having to do with behavioral assumptions and those dealing with institutional expectations.

- Liberalism is based on the primacy of the individual and the rights thereof over and above any collective claims.
- Liberalism assumes cognitive rationality, not necessarily in its extreme microeconomic form, but as a guiding principle for social analysis.
- Liberalism rejects the perfectibility of human beings. The same individuals who are held to be the center of all things are also seen as potentially opportunistic.
- The central problem of liberalism is to secure individual freedom while also allowing social interaction in a world of possible malfeasance.

Creating Order   How does one create order from the various desires and acts of individuals who cannot always be counted upon to be virtuous?

- The solution for liberalism is mutual dependence: we interact with each other because we want something from one another.
- People become specialists to be able to deal with others and extract the highest possible profit for their efforts.
- The role of the state is essentially to serve as a guarantor of contracts.

The State	It is no accident that both liberalism as a doctrine and the state as a political institution arose simultaneously.

- In a variety of ways they are dependent on each other; one makes the other one possible.
- Liberalism relies on the nation-state to balance the recognized economic inequalities that would result from the market with a politically based equality based on citizenship.

Q
R
S

The Iberian World

To what extent can we say that such an outlook as liberalism has been applied in Latin America and the rest of the Iberian world?

- Beginning in the 1970s, the classic tenets of liberalism became increasingly accepted throughout the Iberian world.
- The repeated victory of liberalism in the Iberian world may have much to do with the validity of its ideas and concepts.
  - Influencers adopted the leading theories bandied about in the wake of the Enlightenment and the Age of Revolution.
  - The appeal of liberalism was also fueled by the success of the United States contrasted with the fortunes of Latin America.

Global Pressures

Beginning in 1973, massive global lending allowed almost all countries later to have neoliberal policies to borrow beyond their wildest dreams.

- Such assets were unavailable unless the same countries could maintain their viability as international debtors.
- As debtor nations, they were judged accountable if they were seen as moving toward a neoliberal alternative. In that case, they would be rewarded with more loans.
- As countries opened their markets to satisfy the conditions of their continued access to international cash, they saw previous domestic suppliers of a variety of goods and services disappear.
- Neoliberalism not only justified itself but also appeared to make its adoption irreversible.
- One trend is clear: the erosion of the middle class.

Failure

Overall, the author posits the imposition of Liberal policies a qualified failure.

- *Inequality*—Latin America is the most unequal region on the planet.
- *State incapacity*—that the absence of a legitimate order made the balance between political and economic power, mediated through the law, impossible in the region.
- *Global marginality*—the dependence of most of the Iberian nations rests on external forces.

Conclusion

Pulling the state out of the market, and even public activity, without putting into place a legitimate system to hold rulers and ruled accountable to the same norms, has had perverse consequences in the Iberian World.

- Liberalization on its own does not stabilize or protect property rights although it transfers ownership from the public domain and places more collective decision making in private hands.

- Latin America suggests a need for legal and social reform, not just technocratic solutions.
- Absent strong liberal states we witness the failure of neoliberalism in most Iberian countries: wealth without well-being, governments without laws, markets without contracts, and citizens without rights.

Migration, Development, and Segmented Assimilation: A Conceptual Review of the Evidence

Alejandro Portes, Princeton University

Background

The development model adopted in the immense majority of labor-exporting American countries has not generated opportunities for growth nor economic or social development.

- It has meant the emergence of regressive dynamics: unemployment and job risk, greater social inequalities, loss of qualified workers, productive disarticulation and stagnation, inflation, and greater economic dependency.

NOTE: As a consequence, we experience a convergence between depopulation and the abandonment of productive activities in areas of high emigration. The study of international migration and development has been wracked by the controversy between perspectives that see the outflow of people not only as a symptom of underdevelopment but also as a cause of its perpetuation and those that regard migration both as a short-term safety valve and as a potential long-term instrument for sustained growth.

Consequences of Migration

Certain assumptions and conclusions about the consequences of migration that seem to be agreed upon by proponents of all perspectives are as follows:

- On one hand, the move abroad is economically beneficial for most migrants and their families, and remittances from major labor-exporting countries become a key source of foreign exchange.
- On the other hand, migrant investments in direct productive activities in their home countries have, at best, a modest effect on national economic growth.
- Then, when migrants bring their families with them, the process of depopulation accelerates, as return migration becomes less probable and in the new country the downward assimilation of youths reinforces negative stereotypes about the migrant population, raising the probability of its conversion into an impoverished caste-like minority.

National Development

Theories of national development, in Latin America and elsewhere, have seldom paid much attention to international migration.

- At best, these flows have been treated as a marginal phenomenon—a reflection of the problems of underdevelopment.
- That position is no longer sustainable—the size of expatriate communities and the volume of the remittances that they send home have prompted a

reorientation of theoretical models in which the massive resources put into motion by immigrants take center stage.

- For some authors, remittances can play a key role in resolving past financial bottlenecks and furnishing the necessary resources for long-term development.

Remittances   The author argues that the above rosy predictions are exaggerated—there is no precedent that any country has taken the road toward sustained development on the basis of the remittances sent by its expatriates.

- Depending on remittances, migration can lead to vastly different consequences—economic stagnation, the emptying out of sending places, and the massive loss of talent versus the energizing of local economies, new productive activities, and significant contributions for scientific and technological development.
- While migration inevitably produces a settlement process in the host country, the extent to which the normative pattern is return after temporary stays abroad governs the potential of the movement for strengthening local economies and preventing depopulation.
- Cyclical migrations work best for both sending and receiving societies—returnees are much more likely to save and make productive investments at home; they leave families behind to which sizable remittances are sent.
- More important, temporary migrants do not compromise the future of the next generation by placing their children in danger of downward assimilation abroad.

The Role of   In this area, as in all others pertaining to national development, the role of
the State   the state is decisive.

- The positive relationship between migration and development is not automatic—market forces alone will not establish the connection.
- The proactive intervention of the state to create productive infrastructure in rural areas and scientific/technological institutions capable of innovation are necessary conditions for the developmental potential of migration flows to materialize.
- Countries that simply open their borders, hoping that the "magic" of the market will do the rest, will not reap these benefits.

Borders for Whom? The Role of NAFTA in Mexico-U.S. Migration

Patricia Fernández-Kelly and Douglas S. Massey, Princeton University

Background   The authors give attention to the main factors that resulted in the passage of NAFTA to then investigate Mexican immigration to the United States during approximately the same period that the bilateral treaty has been in effect.

- The application of neoliberal economic policies throughout the hemisphere was a solution to perceived financial crises precipitated by Latin America's external debt of the 1980s.

- U.S. banks supported NAFTA to transform risk into opportunity.
- The tacit purpose of the accord was to improve conditions for the expansion of financial capital, not merely to facilitate trade.
- In the second part of the article, the authors explore the unintended consequences of NAFTA.

The Two Sides of NAFTA

Critics of the North American Free Trade Agreement tend to portray it as a tool of American domination.

- From the point of view of U.S. businesses, NAFTA was a concerted attempt to further preeminence at the hemispheric level.
  - Free trade was an opportunity to reshuffle capitalist forces by defining conditions for the profitable deployment of assets.
- From the point of view of Mexico, the treaty signified an attempt at integration into the global economy through liberalization and the reconfiguration of Mexico's authoritarian state.
  - Free trade represented a breaking away from earlier models of development based on import-substitution industrialization.
- In both countries, NAFTA may be seen as an outcome of earlier attempts to find a solution to the debt crisis of the 1980s.
  - The position taken by U.S. financiers clarifies to a large extent the divided structure of NAFTA, which quickened and codified a twenty-year-long process of economic liberalization during which companies had relocated much of their production to Asia and the U.S.-Mexico border.
  - Mexico's commitment to neoliberalism and free trade was part of a larger vision for national development.

NOTE: The narrow interests of finance capital and the misdirected approach of Mexico's government did less for workers on both sides of the border than for the consolidation of a powerful binational class of professionals, investors, and politicians.

Immigration Policy in the United States

U.S. immigration policies and practices took into account the realities of economic interdependence and the expanded demand for Mexican labor.

- By the end of the twentieth century, two-thirds of all Mexicans knew someone who had been to the United States, and almost 60 percent were socially connected to someone living on American soil.
- Immigration policies started to tighten in 1986, the same year that Mexico entered the General Agreement on Tariffs and Trade (GATT).
- With the passage of the 1986 Immigration Reform and Control Act, the U.S. Congress criminalized the hiring of unauthorized workers by U.S. employers and increased funding for the U.S. Border Patrol.
- In 1993, when the passage of NAFTA was making headlines, the U.S. Border Patrol launched Operation Blockade and Operation Gatekeeper to intercept Mexican workers at two critical entry points.
- The tendency in the years following NAFTA's passage has been toward the growing fusion of all markets, save one: labor.
  - After 9/11, the newly established Department of Homeland Security further tightened immigration measures using the Immigration and Customs Enforcement police (ICE).

• Anti-immigrant fervor reached a climax on December 16, 2005, with the so-called Sensenbrenner Law, which would turn into felonies not just the unauthorized crossing of the border but also the hiring of and provision of services and humanitarian aid to undocumented immigrants.

Border Militarization

The unilateral militarization of the border has been successful in achieving one outcome: it has dramatically increased the costs and risks of border crossing.
• Perhaps the most important but unexpected effect of current immigration policies has been to decrease the likelihood that unauthorized workers will return to their home country.
• Proposed specific measures that would reconcile U.S. immigration policy with the realities have been brought about by the growing economic integration that NAFTA facilitated.

Conclusions

The refusal on the part of the architects of NAFTA to consider labor flows as part of the neoliberal project has given rise to several unintended consequences, all of which are counter to the stated goals of the treaty.
• The reduction of public spending in Mexico, the removal of subsidies to subsistence agriculture, the opening of feed and seed markets, and the commercialization of arable land have had a displacing effect, leading peasants to seek economic opportunities in the United States.
• Increased migration flows have been met in the United States with growing attempts at curtailment.
• Tighter migration policies have grown a finely tuned machine of people smugglers and false document manufacturers.
• The harsher character of U.S. immigration policy is leading to the expansion of the Mexican population in the United States.

SECTION TWO: NAFTA, LABOR AND THE NATIONAL STATE

The Strategic Role of Mexican Labor under NAFTA: Critical Perspectives on Current Economic Integration

Raúl Delgado Wise, Autonomous University of Zacatecas; and James M. Cypher, California State University, Fresno

Background

In this article, the authors present a new theoretical formulation of the Mexican economy under the North American Free Trade Agreement (NAFTA)—*the cheap-labor export-led model.*
• Mexico's new role consists of exporting its cheap labor, not in achieving new high-value-added forms of production through enhanced specialization.

- NAFTA was presented as an antidote to emigration, but what we see is the export of cheap, largely poorly trained labor.

NOTE: The result is a lack of economic continuity, autonomy, and dynamism where the productive apparatus has been dismantled and reassembled to fit the structural requirements of the United States, leaving Mexico in control of certain low-value-added resource-based activities and a range of other pursuits in tourism, finance, and real estate.

NAFTA

NAFTA has exhibited the following effects:
- It has been a losing proposition for workers, small and medium-sized businesses, and, particularly, peasants.
- In the United States, for the working class and portions of the middle class, and for some sectors of business, the impact of NAFTA has been negative.
- At the same time, NAFTA has directly benefited a small set of interests on both sides of the border, especially U.S.-based transnational corporations (TNCs) and Mexico's largest conglomerates.
- The sweeping changes in policy have correlated with massive waves of emigration. This injection of cheap labor has served to indirectly lower reproduction costs and, therefore, the wages of U.S. workers.

NOTE: The widely disseminated vision portraying Mexico's restructuring as a resounding success stands in sharp contrast to the continued growth of emigration, to the degree that Mexico has now become the principal country of emigrants in the world.

Export Model

Analysis serves to show that the export-led model employed in Mexico is characterized through its low capacity to create national employment, the counterpart of which is the blooming of the informal sector, which has accounted for roughly 50 percent of the *growth* in employment in recent years.
- As a direct result of the failure of the model, between 1984 and 2004, the number of households registering at either the poverty level or the extreme poverty level rose from 12,970,000 to 15,915,000.
- This situation has been the nurturing ground for the explosive international migration process that currently characterizes Mexico.

*NAFTA
Support*

The vast restructuring of the Mexican economy via NAFTA could not, and did not, occur without the consent and active participation of Mexico's political class and its industrial elite.
- The business class supported the indiscriminate opening of the economy, and the large conglomerates or *grupos*, particularly those based in Monterrey, had always held a neoliberal/antistate view.
- Economic stagnation in the 1980s had forced many of them to seek growing markets in the international economy. The closest and cheapest option was to export to the vast U.S. market.
- The largest conglomerates eventually became convinced that a new bilateral trade agreement (NAFTA) could circumvent the legal hurdles blocking the U.S. market.

Implications for Mexico

There are many implications for Mexico:

- The labor export-led model gives rise to a process of disaccumulation as the economic surplus is transferred abroad, depriving Mexico of potential multiplier and spread effects.
- Substantial levels of spending by Mexico on education and health care are subsidized inputs into the U.S. transnational production system via the mass of illegal immigrants working in the United States.
- To the above should be added the subsidies and lost tax revenues that the Mexican government has permitted to continue up to the present.
- In Mexico, the labor export-led model has involved collateral costs in terms of deindustrialization and rising unemployment, along with deskilling as industrial workers are forced to shift to the informal sector or to underemployment—dismantling much of the productive apparatus.
- Economic integration under NAFTA, rather than promoting convergence in the development levels of Mexico and the United States, has deepened the asymmetries that exist between the two countries:
  - Whereas in 1994, per capita GDP in the United States was 2.6 times that of Mexico, by 2004 the ratio had increased to 2.9.

NOTE: In the final analysis, socioeconomic development has never been achieved by a nation as a result of exogenous forces. The history of economic development shows that the responsibility for initiating and maintaining a process of economic development depends on endogenous social forces, particularly on the ability of the state to mount and sustain a national project of accumulation rather than searching out and adopting policies that are generators of asymmetric accumulation processes such as NAFTA.

Resistance and Compliance in the Age of Globalization: Indian Women and Labor Organizations

Rina Agarwala, Johns Hopkins University

Background

This study examines the changing relationship between the state and labor as countries throughout the world liberalize their economies and integrate with one another, causing an increase in informal workers, who by definition receive no guaranteed benefits from either an employer or a state.

- States support companies in their decision to use unprotected labor by initiating incentive programs that encourage formally protected workers to leave their jobs, creating free trade zones where firms are not held to labor laws, and contracting public sector services to private sector firms that can hire informally.
- Economic reforms that encourage free trade, increase capital and labor mobility, and heighten global competition have pushed labor movements into a crisis characterized by declining union density and a diminishing ability of workers to influence the state.

Q R S

- This study attempts to better understand workers' role in shaping the current phase of economic and political transitions.
- In a larger sense, this is a study about the changing nature of the relationship between the state and society as nations liberalize their own economies and integrate with others.

NOTE: The main difference between informal and formal workers is that the latter are protected and held accountable by state legislation. Informality disperses production through home-based work, complicates employer-employee relationships, and atomizes labor relationships by eliminating the daily shop floor gathering of workers.

Implications

Informal workers' organizational strategies provide important clues about how they can mobilize in a system with little regulation and blurred employer-employee relations.

- Informal workers are forcing government authorities to acknowledge that they simply cannot live on the below-subsistence wages and unstable employment into which they are currently being forced.
- The study's findings call for a qualification of the prevailing definition of the informal sector.
- This study reasserts class as an important analytical tool with which to examine differences in life chances and resistance against exploitation.
- The findings warrant rethinking state-society relations in the modern era.
  - On one hand, the theoretical framework tested in this study shows that informal workers are most successful in states that have a populist leadership.
  - On the other hand, traditional left-oriented political parties that strive to meet workers' needs, such as the Communist Party of India-Marxist, were found to be least helpful to informal workers.
- This study gives new insights into the role women play in linking the public and private spheres in contemporary labor movements.
- This study makes important contributions to the growing literature on global cities.

Research Needed

This study raises several questions for further research.

- First, how prevalent are these trends in the non-Indian context?
  - The findings from India should be compared in a cross-national perspective to other informal workers' movements around the world.
- How do informal workers' movements vary by sector and industry?
  - Studies across more sectors will provide further insight into how pervasive informal workers' movements are and how they may differ according to conditions of work.
- Future studies should examine workers' movements among the self-employed.
  - Further research into informal workers' movements in a liberalization context is essential to understanding the myriad of problems arising in the implementation of state benefits for workers and differences in organizational structures.

Resistance and Identity Politics in an Age of Globalization

Deborah J. Yashar, Princeton University

Background

Throughout the Americas, indigenous movements have emerged and deployed discourses opposing neoliberalism, condemning privatization, the sale of public lands to private interests (oil, logging, cattle, etc.), and the decline in social services.

- This article is a cautionary tale about the scope of globalization arguments.
- Contrary to the idea that national states may have lost prominence in the age of globalization, the author contends that indigenous movements have emerged where there are
  - challenges to preexisting corporate identities,
  - transcommunity networks to provide the resources for mobilization, and
  - associational spaces to facilitate collective expression.

Social Movements

The burgeoning globalization literature has underscored significant changes in recent years:

- a greater interpenetration of economic markets,
- technological changes that increase the speed and density of global communications,
- a growth of international organizations and networks, and
- the emergence of new norms that span borders.

Globalization Arguments

The author takes up four types of arguments and highlights their limited ability to explain the emergence of Latin America's indigenous mobilization:

- economic globalization,
- globalization of resources and networks,
- globalization of norms, and
- political globalization

NOTE: Each of the above globalization approaches is at first compelling and aptly describes movements that have gained substantial press. There appears to be a descriptive fit between certain aspects of globalization and the campaigns launched by some social movements, but these globalization approaches remain blunt instruments to address the regionwide politicization of ethnic cleavages in general and indigenous movements in Latin America in particular.

Alternative Arguments

The author's own research has led to a set of alternative arguments about the emergence of ethnic politics in Latin America.

- Indigenous movements are claiming and demanding a series of *state-based reforms* to reconfigure citizenship.
- These demands form part of a postliberal challenge since indigenous people demand both respect and incorporation as individual citizens (the liberal promise) and legal recognition as collectively autonomous units (the postliberal challenge).
- To pursue these goals, indigenous movements have voiced their demands through social movement politics.

- As of late, they have also turned to electoral politics to introduce their demands into formal politics.

NOTE: The point to emphasize here is that indigenous people are organizing and articulating ethnic-based agendas that contest the definition and terms of *national* citizenship, both insisting on greater inclusion in the national state and greater autonomy from it.

Supporting Arguments

To elucidate these new patterns of claim-making, the author argues that contemporary indigenous movements in the Americas emerged in the last third of the twentieth century when three factors were at play:
- challenges to local autonomy from changing citizenship regimes,
- transcommunity networks, and
- political associational space.

NOTE: Only where these three factors were present did indigenous people have not only the motive but also the capacity and opportunity to forge regional and national movements.

Conclusion

This article addresses the significance of globalization and the changing international environment as we witness an ever more integrated world economy, transnational networks, international norms, and global hegemony.
- States have modified their restrictions on free markets, reforged international political alliances, confronted new actors that pressure states to reform their relations with citizens, and come up against (de)legitimating discourses to which they are expected to respond.
- Globalization arguments portray striking developments that are occurring at the expense of state sovereignty over domestic affairs.
- In looking comparatively at collective action, we see that the international arena does not simply shape social movements, nor does globalization explain the timing or intensity of movements that emerge.
- Finally, globalization does not provide a handle on which identities become the salient basis for collective action.

NOTE: Though changes are taking place in the international economy, networks, and norms, one should not assume that these descriptive developments have causal significance. For it is unclear why, when, and where these changes do or do not generate collective action or which form collective action is likely to take. The theoretical task for studies of collective action then is to articulate better the structured and contingent relations among international processes, states, nongovernmental organizations, and actors.

Rethinking Civil Society in the Age of NAFTA: The Case of Mexico

Jon Shefner, University of Tennessee

Background

This article offers an analysis and critique of the concept of civil society and its relationship to neoliberalism as an economic and political project.
- It explains why analysts have so embraced the idea of civil society.

- It discusses the variety of usages to which it has been put, especially in regard to popular action in Latin America.
- It suggests that its analytic utility has been damaged by its overuse and describes a case that argues for a more careful application of the concept.
- It argues that specific analysis of social sectors will prove both more rigorous and revealing for useful theorizing and empirical application.

Civil Society   Civil society has been used to designate social movements of every kind, any respondents to a survey, and a multiplicity of political organizations not directed or dependent on governments.

- There has been little effort to standardize the use of the concept.
- Strengthening civil society became synonymous with reducing the role of the state.
- Civil society poses varying responses to neoliberalism, depending on the analysts' political perspective. Many see civil society as providing important sources of resistance to neoliberal policies.
- A strong civil society directly supports democracy by widening participation in several ways, including educating and mobilizing citizens generally to exercise their right to participate.
- Civil society can also alter the balance of power between state and society in favor of the latter.

Class   The de-emphasizing of class in most studies of civil society is a mistake for many reasons.

- Different social sectors have varied relationships to neoliberalism: social assistance groups, for example, facilitate neoliberalism by providing, minimally, for the welfare of vulnerable populations.
- Some of these civil society groups are held in favor by the state, as their work facilitates state thinning, on one hand, and provides rationale for the commercialization or marketization of social welfare, on the other.
- The reality is that neoliberalism has exacerbated class divisions in Latin America.

The PRI in Mexico   In the 1920s in Mexico, the Partido Revolucionario Institucional (PRI) created an organization that united disparate groups ranging from urban middle-class professionals to squatter communities.

- By channeling participation into mass organizations, the party created structures to address popular needs and maintain legitimacy.
- During the postwar period, the PRI pursued economic modernization by implementing import substitution industrialization (ISI) policies.
- Politically, ISI reinforced corporatism and clientelism by producing significant economic growth and rewarding Mexico's working and middle classes, generating both the skills to manufacture new goods and the economic wherewithal to consume them.

Democratization   As Mexico's economy worsened in the 1970s, PRI legitimacy waned.

- As the economy contracted and more state resources were devoted to debt service, economic inclusion through favorable labor policy and neighborhood patronage became untenable.

Q
R
S

- The imperatives of neoliberal globalization prioritized debt payment, privatization, and dismantling protectionist industrial policy.
- The results of such policies impoverished the PRI's social base.
- Neoliberal policies left Mexicans with lower wages, limited access to social welfare benefits, lower physical quality of life, fewer jobs, and increasing levels of inequality.
- Protest against electoral fraud joined middle-class and poor activists. Middle-class NGOs continue to seek issues and venues on which they can work with the organized poor.
- No single sector in Mexico could have achieved democratization; it had to be a product of struggle by multiple groups.
- The government was extremely effective in keeping challengers at bay through strategies that weakened the opposition by creating small parties that favored the PRI, or by buying off individual leaders.
- The strategy of democratization will not resolve economic grievances as fully as political grievances—democratization is about distribution of political power, but if political power mirrors economic power to a large extent, little genuine change may occur.

Conclusion   The conclusion summarizes the shortcomings of the concept of civil society.
- First, many researchers forget that civil society must be understood as equally stratified as other ways of conceptualizing society.
- Second, recognizing the strata of civil society may help us understand the dynamics and outcome of strategic efforts at unified struggle.
- Third, recognizing the strata of civil society suggests that we carefully examine coalition strategies.
  - Recognizing the strata of civil society forces us to understand that the successful accomplishment of a coalesced strategy will still yield differential impacts on the members of civil society.

SECTION THREE: REGIONALIZATION AND THE FORAY ON PRIMARY GOODS

The Globalization of Capital Flows: Who Benefits?

Barbara Stallings, Brown University

Background   Global change has brought multiple issues into high profile, including sharper economic and geographic polarization, heightened levels of inequality within developed and developing nations, and new patterns of regionalization.
- Globalization and liberalization have led to greater mobility of capital—not all regions, countries, or firms have been recipients in equal measure.
- If the benefits of globalization are to be preserved, the complex problems

Why Liberalize?

created or exacerbated by globalization must be substantially mitigated. Most governments liberalize because they think they will benefit by greater access to capital, which can help increase growth through higher investment rates, better technology, and entrée to foreign markets.

- Equally important, however, globalization involves the spread of norms and institutions.
  - In the financial area, better regulation and supervision have been promoted as have more independent central banks.
  - More generally, improved corporate governance of both financial and non-financial firms brings benefits to shareholders and the general public alike.
- Set against these potential benefits are costs that can also be large.
  - One cost is increasing inequality across and within nations.
  - Increased inequality, in turn, not only leads to wasted resources but also is likely to increase instability.
  - Volatility makes it difficult to manage an economy, and in the worst of cases, it can result in extremely damaging crises.

NOTE: These two problems—inequality and volatility—can potentially undermine globalization itself if they are not dealt with adequately.

Access to Foreign Capital

Who is getting access to foreign capital and of what kind?
- The largest recipient by dollar amount is Eastern Europe, but Sub-Saharan Africa obtains nearly twice as much as a share of GDP.
- Foreign direct investment (FDI) flows are highly concentrated—eight countries alone get more than two-thirds of all FDI.
- Eight countries receive about half of all remittances.
- In an assessment of capital flows, it is important to consider production units, where size is a crucial determinant of access to finance.
  - Large firms have easy access to foreign capital, both through FDI and the international capital markets.
  - Medium-sized firms may be able to tap local financial markets, depending on how individual countries' markets are structured, what kinds of norms regulate the allocation of capital, and the existing resources available to mobilize investments.
  - Small and micro firms are limited to finance from banks and other local lenders, in addition to retained earnings.

Volatility of Capital Flows

Volatility is a second aspect of capital flows that has been heavily criticized by those who question the benefits of globalization.
- Funds can move in and out of countries with great rapidity, making it difficult for the authorities to manage macroeconomic policy.
- This is a problem in developing countries since their economic size tends to be small compared to the large flows of international finance.
- In the worst of cases, this volatility can contribute to financial crises that can be devastating for developing economies.

Policy

The policy question in this article is how to spread benefits in ways that are more equitable and more productive than those existing at present—public officials and policy makers can do things to make their countries more attractive.
- Political stability is a top item on the list.

Problems

- More transparency in financial transactions is another priority.

The skewed distribution of foreign finance among regions and countries embodies two different sets of problems.

- For those countries with ready access to private flows, debt buildup as well as volatility are serious concerns.
- While grants have been increasing, public-sector loans have been falling and, as noted above, are now negative in net terms.

Conclusion

This article contends that it is not enough to worry about which countries gain access but also about the kinds of firms that have access to capital. This is a question of both social justice and employment and economic growth.

- New theories of banking decry the continued existence of public-sector banks, suggesting that the way to get finance to the people who really need it is to rely exclusively on private institutions.
- All of the issues—the productivity of foreign capital in terms of increasing growth, the problem of volatility, and the question of who has access to capital—are in urgent need of solution.
- If positive responses cannot be found, globalization benefits, not just financial globalization, may be called into question.

NOTE: It is important for developing country governments to work together with their counterparts in developed countries and with international organizations to look for creative solutions.

Trading Impressions:
Evidence from Costa Rica

Frederick Wherry, University of Michigan

Background

The impressions that global buyers have about different countries have important implications for international tourism and local cultural industries.

- This article demonstrates that culture cannot be used as a tool by all countries in the same way.
- International buyers have to believe that the roles local tourism and cultural industries play are suitable for the players and their stage.
- This problem of belief in the part that local cultural agents play explains, in part, the difficulties encountered by indigenous artisans in Costa Rica trying to succeed in the global markets for handicrafts and international tourism.

NOTE: Although Costa Rica leads Central America in the revenues generated from international tourism, indigenous Costa Rican artisans find themselves in receipt of few tourist dollars and little government support because most tourists do not know that these artisans exist.

Public
Narratives

The nation-state's public narratives affect its own social identity compared with the social identities of other nation-states and shapes commercial opportunities for handicrafts and other local products in such countries as

Ecuador, Mexico, and Costa Rica.
- The public narratives condition the likelihood that a country's capitalists will pursue the global handicraft market and that international actors will validate those pursuits with purchases.
- Not only are the former agricultural workers being pushed out of farm, factory, and protected government employment, but both the workers and the capitalists "see" the production of some types of cultural commodities as a means to protect cultural traditions and to validate a favorable public identity narrative for themselves.

Q R S

Costa Rica   To climb out of the periphery of the world system, the Costa Rican state obscured indigenous contributions to the national identity and thereby disabled handicraft artisans and others who might have benefited from the market for ethnic commodities.
- Costa Rica lacks neither the indigenous peoples nor their crafts, but rather their recognition by international operators.
- The Costa Rican state pursued economic strategies framed by its public narratives of social democracy, its cultural similarities to Western European norms and practices, and its obligations to and affinities with the international financial institutions.
- In the rush to leave the reputation of backwardness behind, Costa Rica did what it could to become a fully industrialized country in both a material and ideational sense.
- As the economy failed in 1981, Costa Rica asked the IMF for help.
  - The conditions of the loan exceeded the expectations of the Costa Rican electorate, and the president refused the loans.
  - In 1982, Luis Alberto Monge took control, imposing the orthodox economic stabilization measures required by the IMF.
- The country's import substitution strategy had exhausted its possibilities, and the nation turned to export-oriented industrialization.

Knowledge   Instead of relying on low-cost labor (with which Costa Rica could not
Economy   compete), the national economy turned to the lucrative knowledge economy.
- When Intel entered Costa Rica, the country's position in the global economy fundamentally changed.

International In addition to becoming a knowledge economy, Costa Rica had already
Tourism   transformed itself into a tourist economy. With the few resources the state had at its disposal, it could promote tourism by simply offering tax breaks to tour operators within the country.

Conclusion   This article has explored the historical construction of the impressions that Western buyers as well as Costa Rican citizens have about their country's cultural character.
- These definitions of the situation orient the course of the country's economic development and reinforce the other sources of state power.
- In Costa Rica, the government's fear of being associated with a stigmatized identity has sometimes diverted economic development energies away from those stocks of symbolic capital associated with indigenous

Q
R
S

peoples that might have been easily appropriated.
- Therefore, to understand the success of artisans in global markets, it is not enough to think about the individual qualities of the artisans or of the particular cultural contributions of their group to world culture; one must also think about the public culture that makes the promotion of particular cultural sectors of the economy thinkable.
- How a nation's identity is framed affects the likelihood that capital, labor, and knowledge will be mobilized in the service of particular cultural and noncultural productions.

Globalizing Restricted and Segmented Markets: Challenges to Theory and Values in Economic Sociology

Donald W. Light, University of Medicine
and Dentistry of New Jersey

Background

Efforts by the world's most powerful corporations to develop global markets have spawned literature on how transnational markets form, what stages characterize market development, and what rules of exchange are most effective.
- Studies of globalization and immigration will benefit by taking into account the relationship between goals, means, and outcomes.
- Vital public goods and services should be made distinct from technical public goods so that the dangers of pernicious competition in markets that benefit dominant suppliers or buyers can be identified and the concept of a moral economy can be developed.

Unintended
Consequences

Blindness to unanticipated consequences can result from strongly held convictions and unexamined beliefs, for example, that the globalization of markets is inherently good and benefits all parties.
- The growing integration of markets on a world scale and the parallel implementation of neoliberal economic policies have had uneven effects.
- It appears the number of people living in extreme poverty has increased recently, and world income distribution has become more unequal.

NOTE: Wade (2004) showed how the World Bank changed measures and calculations to "prove" that its convictions about competition and benefits resulting from globalization were accurate. The World Bank case shows that consequences can not only be unanticipated but also denied or buried.

Globalization
Research

Merton (1936) identified several factors that merit consideration in research on a topic such as globalization.
- One should not assume that actions are clearly purposive; often the aims are "nebulous and hazy."
- Post facto rationalizations that crop up after unanticipated consequences occur in order to make them appear intended.
- One should not assume that consequences are clear, for they are affected by the interplay of the action, the objective situation, and the conditions of action.

Policies   Policies may have latent functions in producing results other than what
                actors intended or they may serve alternative and covert purposes.
                • There is the latent function of purposive action in ordering the world to
                  serve the interests of dominant political and economic groups.
                • Portes (2000) observed that the resulting outcome of a given purposive
                  action may emerge from revisions, concessions, and improvisations of
                  means and thus be different from the initial goal.

                NOTE: For example, contrary to its explicit mandate, NAFTA did not open
                labor markets; instead, it segmented them, with surprising and sometimes
                deleterious effects such as eliminating jobs, increasing unemployment,
                fomenting inequality, stirring crime, and weakening the capacity of small
                businesses to participate in international markets.

Competition   The term *competition* embodies the radical proposition that if all parties pur-
                sue their own best interests, the results will benefit everyone.
                • As used by many economic sociologists and economists, market competi-
                  tion tacitly assumes that it is beneficial.
                • Competition, however, can only benefit society under strict conditions
                  designed to limit the clever, untrustworthy actions of opportunistic indi-
                  viduals and channel them to the benefit of others.
                • There must be many buyers and sellers whose relations are independent
                  from one another so that market transactions cannot be influenced by one
                  or more parties to the detriment of others.
                • Information on everything buyers need to know to buy smart and drive
                  the value chain must be complete and free.
                • Transactions must clear quickly. Easy entry of new competitors and
                  prompt exit of unsuccessful competitors are essential.

                NOTE: Even if all these conditions are met (and they usually are not), caveat
                emptor rules the market, and competitive actions require constant monitoring.

Corporate   Examples of market segmentation and control by multinational corporation
Control   are the expanded terms for patents in the Central American Free Trade
                Agreement (CAFTA), especially as they apply to seeds, agricultural pesticides
                and fertilizers, and prescription drugs.
                • A hidden goal of large corporations and conservatives behind globalization—
                  even a requirement under World Trade Organization rules and governance—
                  is to privatize public services and thus to open up huge new markets in
                  privatized public services.

Research   Sociology can make a valuable contribution by doing research to show how
                most public goods and services are not inherently so but are rather socially
                and culturally constructed realities adhering to norms and conventions
                shared, often informally, by the collectivity.
                • Research can identify how different societies have defined and organized
                  the same goods to have more or less of the technical attributes that econ-
                  omists claim are characteristic of public goods.
                • Societies make subtle distinctions between goods shared by the many to
                  promote efficiency and those that benefit only a few—research on such
                  distinctions should be complemented with studies of what goods and ser-
                  vices are vital to a fair and just society.

Q
R
S

Renegotiating Transnational Alliances in the Production of Asian Timber: From Managed to Free(r) Markets

Paul K. Gellert, University of Tennessee, Knoxville

Background

The Asian crisis of 1997 to 1998 and structural adjustments imposed by the International Monetary Fund (IMF) radically transformed Indonesian producers' options, diminishing their capacity to compete, even as China emerged as a major producer of wood-related products.

- The Indonesian case illustrates processes of market remarginalization resulting from the implementation of neoliberal policies.
- During the crisis, the Indonesian government signed onto an IMF structural adjustment package consisting of $43 billion.
  - This Washington Consensus approach included a tightened monetary policy and the liberalization of trade and investment aimed at economic recovery.
- Investment and growth have not been sufficient to overcome the serious debt and unemployment problems plaguing Indonesia.

Globalization

Globalization currently entails not only the opening of markets but also a reconfiguration of production patterns joining disparate areas of the world.

- Neoliberalism and changes in the scale of governance affecting commodity trade and markets continue to be of the utmost significance.
- Nuanced studies have begun to recognize the limits, resistances, and frictions that prevent the full extension of neoliberal ideas and practices.
- Illiberal forms of governance are coming to dominate countries such as Indonesia even as economic liberalization takes place.
- This article explores the impact of liberalization on a politically organized and regimented commodity chain.
  - The disquieting conclusion of this article is that the end of the plywood era in Indonesia will likely lead to expanded forest conversion and more intense processes of "accumulation by dispossession."

Patterns of Governance

Analyses of commodity chain governance should pay closer attention to institutional and structural environments of uneven development.

- Recent governance experts focus on three factors: complexity of transactions, codifiability of information, and the capabilities of suppliers "regardless of the institutional context in which they are situated."
- This revised theoretical approach offers a more nuanced understanding of value chain governance in which there are complex dependencies between buyers and sellers to market transactions where the costs of switching partners are lowered.

Regional Governance

Although this momentous change has consequences for economic development, the role of the state and interstate agreements on trade liberalization have garnered scant notice.

- The changing governance structure needs to be seen also in the context of broader shifts in regional governance.

- In addition to the benefits of market access and the risks of exclusion, there are risks of access and even benefits of exclusion.
- Bilateral and multilateral free trade agreements are reconfiguring access to raw materials in Asia.

Realignment of Power

The financial crisis of the late 1990s created a window of opportunity for international development organizations like the IMF to realign the balance of power among Asian nations and reconfigure access to natural resources.

- The neoliberal process has greatly eroded the capacity of Indonesia to compete at the regional level.
- Paradoxically, the opening of markets has given an advantage to China, a country that now emerges as the dominant power in Asia, not solely because of its large territory and population but also because of its willingness to adopt the ruthless logic of the market.
- Indonesia's capacity to compete had depended on managed structures of governance over timber production; China's influence is predicated upon the sheer exploitation of natural resources.

Conclusion

It is worth emphasizing that neoliberalism both in Asia and Latin America has entailed the reconfiguration of access to agricultural and mining resources.

- Indonesia is now poised to illustrate what David Harvey calls "accumulation by dispossession."
- Regrettably, the dispossession is local while the accumulation occurs abroad.

NOTE: The effects of this process upon the natural resources that once made Indonesia the envy of the region may be unimaginable. Then again the benefits for those controlling the neoliberal agenda are immeasurable.

Q
R
S